KEELE
the first fifty years

A Portrait of the University
1950–2000

J. M. KOLBERT

MELANDRIUM BOOKS

Published by
Melandrium Books
11 Highway Lane
Keele
Staffs ST5 5AN

© 2000 John M. Kolbert

First published 2000

British Library Cataloguing-in-Publication Data
A catalogue record for this book is available from the
British Library

ISBN: 1 85856 238 4 (paperback)

Designed and typeset by Trentham Print Design Ltd., Chester
and printed in Great Britain by Cromwell Press Ltd., Wiltshire.

John Kolbert

was born and brought up in East Barnet, Hertfordshire. He was educated at Queen Elizabeth's School, Barnet, and Magdalene College, Cambridge, where he read history. He also qualified as a Chartered Secretary and a Company Accountant. Before coming to Keele, he worked for the Metal Box Company in Hackney, East London, and for Government Communications Headquarters, Cheltenham. He joined the Registry of the University in January 1965. His booklets on *The Sneyds and Keele Hall, The Sneyds Squires of Keele*, and *Keele Hall: a Victorian Country House* have sold over 25,000 copies, and may be obtained from the University. He took early retirement in 1990 for private reasons.

He is a Fellow of the University, a magistrate, the chairman of the Board of Visitors of Stoke Heath prison, and an Associate Member of the North Staffordshire Combined Healthcare NHS Trust.

The University has specifically requested me to publish the following statement:

This book is the work of the author alone and the University, having provided access to its records and confirmation of certain matters of fact, has no association with its publication, or the conclusions and interpretations contained within it.

Contents

FOREWORD

The University of Keele has a unique history. As the first of the new universities established after the Second World War it has a particular place in university history, reflecting and pioneering in practice the then fashionable and far-sighted thinking on university curricula which saw higher education as one of the forges on which social structures and attitudes were hammered out for future generations. The continuing significance of that network of ideas at a time when accountability and cost efficiency have become the new watchwords in higher education should not be understated. But Keele is of importance too because it is the living embodiment of the life's work of a small but significant group of educators and politicians who, as a result of the extensive work done by Oxford University tutors in North Staffordshire during the early Twentieth Century, working through the WEA, found themselves with a common cause, which was to leave some permanent legacy from the North Staffordshire adult education movement. Whether local politicians, or key figures in the local community such as Thomas Horwood, vicar of Etruria, or Oxford men such as A. D. Lindsay or R. H. Tawney who had worked to develop the local adult education movement or ex-students who had themselves achieved positions of power and influence – whatever their background – they constituted a powerful lobby with a shared aspiration. This was the nucleus of the group responsible for the setting up of a university in North Staffordshire.

In this book John Kolbert paints a vivid picture of them at work, identifying key moments in the foundation and early years of the university and exploring the tensions involved in the long struggle since then to keep sight of 'the Keele ideal'. He traces the period of unrest in the late-1960s and the difficult years of the government cuts in the 1980s, giving a useful analysis of the problems which confronted Keele (and other universities). Overall, this is a story of how Keele not only survived but thrived in the face of adversity. This careful work of reconstruction is surely the fullest and most meticulous account yet available to us of the birth pains and subsequent development of this institution which occupies an important place in university history. As a Keele graduate from the pioneering years who has also had the opportunity, at an earlier point in my career to write on some of the issues dealt with here it is a delight to have to hand a text which stimulates at once reminiscence and critical reconsideration. It will be of interest both to university historians and to those seeking insights into the contemporary debate on what constitutes a university education. I commend this book to its readers and am delighted to have the chance to pen this brief foreword.

Roy Lowe, *Professor of Education, University of Wales, Swansea*

ACKNOWLEDGEMENTS

I wish to acknowledge with thanks the generous assistance I have received in my research from the following. The Hon. Lady Drusilla Scott and Sir Ian Scott, Dr. H. M. Taylor (Principal and Vice-Chancellor, 1960-1967), and Mrs. Judith Taylor, Professor W. A. C. Stewart (Vice-Chancellor, 1967-1979), and Sir David Harrison (Vice-Chancellor, 1979-1984). I was fortunate enough to have the guidance of the following who were at Keele for its foundation: Miss Marion Bailey, Mr. S. O. Stewart, Professor F. W. Cope, Mrs. Ann Finer, Professor W. B. Gallie, Professor J. J. Lawlor, Professor I. N. Sneddon and Mrs. Sneddon, Mrs. Jean Springall, Sir Arthur Vick and Sir Bruce Williams. It has been a privilege to know founding members of the University, and to enjoy their hospitality.

Other people in Keele during the early years who have been generous with their assistance and comments include: Mr. W. Bedson in Keele Village, Mrs. Mairwen Evans, Mr. E. J. Killham, Professor P. H. Plesch and Mr. B. Wardell. Members of staff with whom I have discussed these matters at the time and/or since include Dr. Helga Frankland, Professor E. M. Hugh-Jones, Professor D. J. E. Ingram and Professor D. M. MacKay; and more recently I discussed different items with Professor J. Cox, Professor E. F. Evans, Professor W. Fuller, Dr. C. J. Harrison, Professor A. Linklater, Professor J. A. Sloboda, Professor H. S. Torrens, Mr. A. A. Treherne and Mrs. Treherne, Professor G. Wilks, Dr. J. P. Wilson, Dr. Ann Worrall and Dr. G. Wright. Staff who have retired and who have been generous with their assistance include Mr. A. F. Booth, Mrs. Ann Cornes, Mr. M. J. Dent, Dr. C. S. Exley, Dr. F. Field and Mrs. Field, Dr. I. H. C. Fraser, Dr. F. J. Glendenning, Professor A. H. Gomme, Dr. K. M. Goodway, Mr. A. H. Iliffe, Dr. R. C. Maddison, Dr. J. Naylon, Miss Audrey Newsome, Mr. M. K. Paffard, Mr. J. M. Pargeter and Mrs. Sheila Walton.

Staff at other universities with a particular appreciation of Keele who have been of great assistance include Professor D. Jary and Dr. Julia Jary (Staffordshire University), Professor R. Lowe (University of Wales), Professor G. M. Pratt (University of Huddersfield) and Professor T. Roberts (University of Wales).

Amongst Keele graduates, special mention must be made of Dr. M. Clarke, Mr. G. Jones, Mrs. Morag Jones, Mrs. Jo-Ann Rogers, Mr. L. B. Stokes, Mr. and Mrs. J. Thomas, and Mr. W. Wright.

I am grateful for the assistance I have received from the *Sentinel*; for the permission of Routledge and Kegan Paul to quote from *Keele: An Historical Critique* by Sir James Mountford; for permission from the Master and Fellows of Magdalene College, Cambridge, to quote from the *Pepys* MSS.; for permission from Josef Škvorecký to quote from *Emöke*; and for permission to quote from Mr. Michael Mansfield, QC. I am grateful to Professor A. N. Porter, Rhodes Professor of History at the University of London, for permission to quote from his report.

For day-to-day assistance I am indebted to Mr. S. N. Clifford in the University Secretary's Office, Mr. D. J. Myatt in the Finance Office, Mr. M. J. Phillips, Miss Helen Burton and the porters in the Library, and to Mr. R. I. Marr and Mr. S. N. Mair for help with my computer. I am grateful to Mr. S. Morris, the University Secretary and Registrar, for his part in resolving a number of difficulties in the year before publication.

For their generous advice, guidance and encouragement for the whole of the period since I came to Keele in January 1965 I am especially indebted to Mr. A. F. Tough and above all to Dr. and Mrs. J. F. N. Hodgkinson.

INTRODUCTION

When I came to Keele to work in the Registry in 1965 the memories of the early years were undimmed. Nine of the professors who were here, and the Librarian and Miss Bailey, had been in a photograph taken in the courtyard of Keele Hall in February 1950. I have spoken to all of the founding Heads of Departments except one, and I have been fortunate to have direct first-hand experience or contact with those closely involved with the College and University for the whole of the fifty years since it was granted its Charter.

Before putting pen to paper I read the minutes of the appropriate committees, and in particular the University's Court, Council and Senate minutes. I was on the staff for over twenty-five years. What I have written rests on the official record, my own experiences, discussions with countless staff and students since 1965, press comment, and interviews since 1990. The *Sentinel* has been an invaluable companion on this journey; and *The Yew Tree*, sponsored by Keele Parish Council, has maintained a lively interest in relations between the University and Keele village in the years since 1991. Some chapters are deliberately short. They provide the setting in which the ensuing chapters unfold. I have not included detailed footnotes and references: they are mostly to be found in University committee papers, and would be of little interest to most readers. I have therefore followed the practice of Macaulay, Trevelyan and Churchill, and some other University histories in this regard.

I have been asked from time to time what is my theme. I have not sought a theme. Rather I have aimed to give a true reflection of each period by showing what it was like at the time – 'to understand an age in its own terms', as Professor Elton wrote in *The Practice of History*, in the hope that readers who were here will recognise the Keele they knew. To this end I checked each section with people who were involved at the time, and I am most grateful to those who were so helpful to me. Nonetheless it is a personal view. The importance of Lord Lindsay's achievement in the history of British universities can hardly be overstated. Overall, Keele then proved adaptable throughout fifty years in meeting the challenges and new opportunities in higher education. It is a story of which Keele can be proud.

Nearly half-way through those fifty years Sir James Mountford wrote *Keele, an historical critique* for Keele's 21st anniversary celebrations. He had been a Professor of Latin for over twenty years and was Vice-Chancellor of the University of Liverpool from 1945 to 1963. At the end of the final chapter of his book he made the following observation:

'In the world of universities there are many mansions. There is no conceivable curriculum which is universally valid: one may be preferable to others for some purposes, in some circumstances, and for some students. But there is no mistaking the fact that Keele, a pioneer, has carved out for itself a distinctive and enduring niche. Whatever expansion there may be in the university population as a whole, whatever may be the pressures for what is currently called cost effectiveness, whatever devices may be evolved for bringing the various sectors of tertiary education into closer relationship with one another, there must surely be a place for at least one institution where the kind of outlook and the pattern of existence which Keele has exemplified, are fostered and maintained. Keele is more than a page in a textbook of educational history. It is a living thing and its duty now to itself and to university education as a whole is to do all it can to ensure that its own distinctive quality is not lost amid a tide of uniformity.'

It remains true, though it is sometimes forgotten, that only if we will understand our history will we understand the present. The past is not really far away.

I wish to thank all those without whose friendship and encouragement this book would not have been written. I am indebted to friends and colleagues whose comments over many years, whether unguarded, encouraging or provocative, have given me ideas. Any prejudices which may be observed, however, are my own.

This book is dedicated to the memory of Dr. Mary Campion and to the students of Keele.

SYNOPSIS

Chapters 1-9 (up to 1950)

The developments which culminated in the founding of the University College of North Staffordshire in 1949 broke the existing mould of university education in this country. The first students were admitted in 1950. 'The Master' is Lord Lindsay of Birker, a towering figure who was Master of Balliol College, Oxford, for twenty-five years. 'The Vicar' is the Reverend Thomas Horwood, Vicar of Etruria who, in close partnership with Lindsay, played a pivotal role. The College owed a special debt to the Workers' Educational Association (chapter 2) and to the three Local Authorities – Stoke-on-Trent, Staffordshire, and Burton upon Trent. The acquisition of Keele Hall (chapter 7) is why the University is now at Keele.

Chapters 10-13 (1950-1962)

The founding of the College and the arrival of the first students was soon followed by the first tragic blow, the sudden death of Lord Lindsay.

The next two Principals, Sir John Lennard-Jones and Sir George Barnes, established Keele's place in Britain's educational system, joining that small group of nineteen universities in the United Kingdom. The early deaths of these two Principals were more heavy blows to the new College.

The short chapters each aim to give an overview of the succeeding few chapters. The title 'The Period' is an allusion to chapter 1 of *A Tale of Two Cities*.

Chapters 14-18 (1962-1972)

Under Dr. H. M. Taylor the College achieved university status. Which way the University might develop was limited by financial constraints, partly the result of Keele's four-year courses and almost total residence, and partly the result of the growing cost of higher education as the number of universities increased.

Chapters 19-20 (1972-1979)

Professor Stewart was the longest-serving Vice-Chancellor (1967-79), and had been the founding Professor of Education (1950-67). Frustrations with the old order found expression in the 'student troubles' of the late-60s and early-70s. This was followed by a period of financial attrition as a result of international and national economic problems. By the time Professor Stewart retired, Keele could be numbered in thousands rather than the original hundreds.

Chapters 21-24 (1979-1985)

Financial problems culminated in the hammer-blow of cuts in July 1981. It fell to Dr. David Harrison to preside over an unprecedented crisis and possibly the question of the University's survival.

Chapters 25-28 (1985-1995)

Universities had to adapt to a different world with new management goals and methods and more transparent accountability. Professor Fender rebuilt the University in response to these pressures with a policy of expansion and more vigorous research programmes, giving a clear direction for Keele's future.

Chapters 29-30 (1995-2000)

Financial pressures remain. A key feature of Keele has been lost; but Professor Finch has identified opportunities which will take a University more than ten times larger than its founders envisaged into its second fifty years.

Principals and Vice-Chancellors

Rt. Hon. Lord Lindsay of Birker, CBE	1949-52
Sir John Lennard-Jones, KBE, FRS	1953-54
Sir George Barnes	1956-60
Dr. H. M. Taylor, CBE, TD	1961-67
Professor W. A. C. Stewart, DL	1967-79
Dr. D. Harrison	1979-84
Professor B. E. F. Fender, CMG	1985-95
Professor J. Finch, CBE, DL	1995-

'A story happens and fades and no one tells it. And yet
somewhere, someone lives on, afternoons are hot and
idle and Christmases come, that person dies and there
is a new slab with a name on it in the graveyard.
Two or three people, a husband, a brother, a mother,
still bear the light, the legend, in their heads for a few
more years and then they die too.
For the children it remains only like an old film,
the out-of-focus aura of a vague face.
The grandchildren know nothing.
And older people forget.
Neither a name nor a memory
nor even an empty space is left.
Nothing.'
(Škvorecký. *Emöke*)

Keele Hall, 17th April 1951

Lord Lindsay (right) with Mr. J.R. Piggott, looking at plans of Keele Hall

Chapter 1

THE MASTER AND THE VICAR

Certainly, neither could have done it without the other. And without the Master and the Vicar the others could not have done it either. On the other hand, without the others the Master and the Vicar could not have done it on their own, and none of this would have happened. There were a lot of godparents for this new infant, and they were determined to see something different. As in the Baptism Service, they wanted to see 'the old Adam... so buried, that the new man may be raised up...' The Foundation Year at Keele was to become 'the outward visible sign' of the Keele Idea.

In the prevailing spirit of the time, however, experts in education said it was not wanted and not needed: they were wrong. Historically, most experts have probably been wrong. The opposition to it seems out of all proportion to the magnitude of the proposal. Why were they so opposed to it? When all is said and done, was it that important? A small college of *how* many hundred?! That hardly explains its significance. What was it, then?

Keele was not one of several new foundations as in the 1960s: it was one on its own in the late-1940s when the accepted way of founding new universities was via a long apprenticeship as a college of the University of London. Such colleges taught London courses and their students were awarded London degrees. Keele dared to be different. Keele was founded on an Idea. Its founders were adamant that there needed to be a different kind of university education and a different kind of course. The curriculum – the four-year course including the Foundation Year, and the cross-disciplinary requirement – was the Idea in practise: but it was not so much the curriculum as the underlying philosophy which made Keele special. The syllabus would not fit into the London pattern. In the 1940s that was almost unthinkable.

The happy confluence of two men, each with a powerful will, produced the driving force. These were A. D. Lindsay, the Master of Balliol College, Oxford since 1924 (and later Lord Lindsay of Birker), and Alderman the Reverend Thomas Horwood, Vicar of Etruria since 1914. These two were known as the Master and the Vicar. Who was the father? Looking back, most people would say the Master. He is properly described as the founder, but the father was really the Vicar, and the impetus for the conception came from another.

The Keele Idea was *different. It broke the mould.* Lindsay was steeped in the ideas of Socrates, and he posed the same question as Socrates in Plato's *Republic*: 'What do you mean?' In doing so he posed an awkward question for the others, for once asked, that question never goes away. It should be written on the walls of University Senate Rooms as a constant reminder. It can be brushed aside, side-stepped, and ignored; but ultimately, over and over again it demands that we question what we are doing and that we give some sort of answer. Lindsay was once asked by a super-cilious Oxford colleague if he really thought Keele would make any difference to universities in this country, and is said to have replied: 'Not to you it won't. But to unprejudiced men it will have to.'

History will not go away. It is the arbiter of truth and the worthwhileness of achieve-ment, just as the mills of God 'grind slowly, yet they grind exceeding small'. The founding of Keele is a story of burning commitment and dedication, against the odds and over a long period, by people whose enthusiasm could not be dampened or discouraged by difficulties or setbacks. Their achievement is the yardstick against which Keele's first fifty years must be measured.

Chapter 2

LINDSAY, HORWOOD, TAWNEY
AND THE W.E.A.

'It is my experience, and I am sure it is yours, that at the back of all real achievements in education or learning one finds a few individuals whose enthusiasm and direction and inspiration are the real source of life.' (A. D. Lindsay. Presidential Address to the Library Association, 1928.)

Whichever way one puts together all the interlocking pieces of the jigsaw of the founding of Keele, the towering figure is A. D. Lindsay. He was a big man, tall and broad-shouldered, with a large head and a high forehead; florid and farmer-like in appearance, with blue-grey eyes. Above all he had an assured moral conviction which underpinned his ideas, and it was his stamp of authority which made Keele possible. He was an inspiration.

If ever a man was moulded by his lifetime's experiences, Lindsay was, and one can see many of the traits of the Keele Lindsay in his upbringing and in the young don. He was born in Glasgow in 1879 into an academic family. He was guided by a good presbyterian upbringing and he grew up in the tradition of public service. His father, Professor T. M. Lindsay (1843-1914), had gone first to Glasgow and then to Edinburgh University where he held the Shaw Philosophical Fellowship and the Ferguson Scholarship. He abandoned an academic career in order to study for the ministry, but then in 1872 he was appointed to the chair of Church History at the College of the Free Church, Glasgow, where he became the Principal in 1902. He had a zeal for social work and academic work, and he published theological, historical and philosophical works, including *A History of the Reformation in Europe* and contributions to the *Cambridge Modern History* and *Encyclopaedia Britannica*. A. D. Lindsay's mother (née Anna Dunlop) was the daughter of a Member of Parliament. She was a dominating personality with a strong social awareness and a concern for good causes, especially women's education and religious evangelism. An uncle, W. M. Lindsay (1858-1937), was a distinguished classical scholar who had gone to Glasgow University when he was 16, and then to Balliol College, Oxford, as Snell Exhibitioner. He was appointed a Fellow of Jesus College, Oxford, and in 1899 was appointed Professor of Humanity at St. Andrews, where he remained until he died.

A. D. Lindsay also went to Glasgow University where he graduated in 1899. What he admired and never forgot about Glasgow was the wide syllabus and the way the ordinary classes were taken by the professors. At the end of his life he wrote in Glasgow's *The College Courant* that the experiment at Keele had in some way been inspired by his memories of the Glasgow MA at the turn of the century. From Glasgow he followed in his uncle's steps to Oxford: he failed to win a scholarship to Balliol, however, and went as an undergraduate to University College where he gained first class honours in classical moderations and *literae humaniores*. He was also President of the Oxford Union Society. After Oxford he went back to Glasgow as Clark Philosophy Fellow, and then followed his father's steps to Edinburgh as the Shaw Philosophy Fellow. He was also assistant to the Professor of Philosophy at Manchester, but in 1906 he returned to Oxford where he was elected Fellow and classical tutor at Balliol. He was to stay at Oxford for most of the next forty years. In 1907 he translated Plato's *Republic* which was published in the *Everyman's Library* series in 1935. In 1911 he was appointed the Jowett Lecturer in Philosophy, and published *The Philosophy of Bergson.*

One of the things he liked at Balliol was the easy relationship between tutors and undergraduates. As he wrote to his brother, 'They do an enormous lot for their men. What is most extraordinary to me there is the relations between dons and undergraduates – no kind of formality at all. The result is rather attractive... but it must have its disadvantages and be hard on the shy man.' Balliol provides a link with so many men and events in later years, and even in the 1980s and early-1990s Lindsay's name has often been cited as an inspiration. Soon after his appointment he married Erica Storr, a lady of strong convictions who shared many of his interests and who gave him enormous support for the rest of his life. She was never one for a fuss, and still wished to be called 'Mrs. Lindsay' after her husband's elevation to the peerage in 1945. (Keele students, however, always referred to her as 'Lady Lindsay'.) It was not long before Lindsay took his first step on his journey to North Staffordshire. In 1910 he wrote: 'They are going to put me on the University delegacy for extension teaching... in connection with the new tutorial class movement. I am very anxious to do all I can for that, and I think that I shall be able to get on with the Trade Union officials who are on the committee and the university people.'

During the First World War he served in the army in France, where he became deputy controller of labour with the rank of Lieutenant-Colonel. He was mentioned in despatches twice and was awarded the MBE in 1918 and the CBE in 1919. Here was a man who showed he could get things done. After the war he was noticeably active in academic reform at Oxford, and when the Board of the Faculty of Arts proposed an honours school in modern humanities (better known as PPE – Philosophy, Politics and Economics), Lindsay was one of the signatories. An earlier recommendation to combine modern philosophy with the sciences had not been successful. He also helped to draft proposals to the Royal Commission on Oxford and Cambridge Universities, and these included extending the range of work for adult education courses. In 1920 he became the secretary of 'The Club' for University Reform, which discussed the wider issues of how the university was governed, research degrees, entrance examinations, and so on. Lindsay's voice was also becoming heard on a wide variety of national and international issues. Then, in 1922, he left Oxford to return to Glasgow where he succeeded Sir Henry Jones as Professor of Moral

Philosophy (and so for a while both he and his uncle were professors in Scotland, as earlier his father and his uncle had both been professors). But in 1924 Oxford called him again and he returned to Balliol as Master. As the *Oxford Magazine* wrote, 'He was always a college man', and thereafter he was widely known simply as 'The Master'.

Twenty-five years before Keele was founded, we can see in Lindsay the college man with a care for undergraduates, the philosopher, the university reformer, a wider concern for extension teaching and adult education, and above all a man who believed in getting things done.

Alderman the Reverend Thomas Horwood was in many ways a complete contrast to Lindsay. He was older than Lindsay and was appointed Vicar of Etruria in 1914. He was a small man, impish, sallow looking and cherubic; but combative too, and determined. He was a canny fighter and he welcomed a challenge. Professor Gallie described him as a man of toil, passion, politics and prayer; a man with a solitariness about him; a man of irrepressible courage and unflagging energy (*A New University: A. D. Lindsay and the Keele Experiment*, 1960). His parents were poor. His father was a carpenter, and had an active interest in local affairs. He was the middle boy of a family of thirteen, and when he was 11 he went to work on a farm. At 14 he joined his father in the building trade, and within a few years he was running his own business. Then, when he was 27 he went to Cambridge to study for the Anglican ministry. After some years as a curate in London he came to the Potteries – and found it so unlike any other place he had known that he seriously considered whether even to stay. He not only stayed but he became a key figure in local affairs as leader of the Labour group on the City Council. His hallmark was that when opportunity arose to do something in the local community he would seize it: and moreover, he was especially prepared to seek out such opportunities. 'Simplicity and steadiness of aim are all that we can achieve in the short span allotted to us', he said in a BBC talk. He knew well the advice: 'Put your trust in God... and keep your powder dry'. His deep faith in the workings of Providence was supported by a firm grip on the facts and a formidable idealistic fervour; and when he saw the hand of Providence it was often hand-in-hand with his own. Lindsay called him 'The Vicar': in Stoke Town Hall he was known as 'The Bishop'.

The rise of the Workers' Educational Association at the beginning of the twentieth century provides the setting for the unfolding of the story of the founding of Keele. There was already fertiie ground in North Staffordshire. Plans for a university had been put forward in 1814. The suggestion was revived towards the end of the century by F. E. Kitchener, the first chairman of the Staffordshire Education Committee, but these proposals came to nought. The key needed for success was going to be a great groundswell of support. In 1873 the University Extension Movement was started, and Cambridge University pioneered university extension courses in the Potteries. By the end of the century it was Oxford which was running courses. Another proposal for a University College was prepared in 1899, and at a meeting held in the Mayor's Parlour in Hanley, a committee was appointed to make recommendations. 'Scientific instruction in subjects bearing on the chief industries of the district' was the key recommendation, but there was a broad base of 'commercial subjects including the study of foreign languages... instruction in the literature and classics such as would supply culture to the general public and help to meet the needs of teachers'. In aiming to promote a University College, the committee meant a local college working in connection with, or affiliated to one of the great universities, in order to meet the needs of the district and supply teaching of university standard. The following year a Council was formed for the Extension of Higher Education in North Staffordshire, and Alfred Bolton of Oakamoor gave a site for a college near Stoke Station. These efforts, too, came to nought and the Council was dissolved in 1906. Nevertheless, there were some important consequences. Alfred Bolton's site was used for the Central College of Science and Technology (later to become the North Staffordshire Polytechnic and then Staffordshire University). It was opened in 1914 as a result of joint action by Stoke-on-Trent and Staffordshire – a collaboration which was to prove important later. In addition, several centres were established for Oxford's university extension courses. Aspirations for a university college had been strengthened with the growing awareness that such a thing might be possible.

Something more was needed, though, – a greater thrust and sharper focus. In 1903 Albert Mansbridge formed an Association to Promote the Higher Education of Working Men. He had attended extension classes at King's College, London, and felt the extension movement had become too much a middle-class activity. He wanted to bring university education within everyone's reach, with the initiative, the demand for courses and the organisation all resting with the participants rather than being provided for them. He saw the universities as the 'providing body' to satisfy those demands, and the local authorities as the 'supplying body' to provide the means. There would therefore be a tight connection between demand, supply and the means, and it would be demand-led. The title of the Association was soon changed to the Workers' Educational Association – the WEA. Mansbridge was the Secretary and William Temple became the President. Temple was the son of the Archbishop of Canterbury, and had been an exhibitioner at Balliol and President of the Oxford Union; and he later himself became Archbishop of Canterbury. He brought R. H. Tawney into the movement as the first Tutor. Tawney had been a classical scholar at Balliol and was soon to become a powerful authority on economic and social history. Teaching was by tutorial classes, and members committed themselves to attend regularly and to participate in courses lasting for three years. Financial support from the Local Authorities meant that the classes were open to all. These were major achievements which were now strengthened by closer connections with Oxford.

In 1907 a joint committee of the WEA and members appointed by the Vice-Chancellor of Oxford produced a report on *Oxford and Working Class Education*, which was written by Tawney. A standing joint committee of the University Extension Delegacy was set up: one of the members was A. L. Smith, a Fellow of Balliol, and Master from 1916 to 1924. He was a strong supporter of the movement and took an important part in the summer schools which were held at Balliol from 1910 onwards. Lindsay was also a member, and this is when he wrote: 'I am very anxious to do all I can for that.' In the fullness of time Lindsay succeeded A. L. Smith as Master of Balliol.

Other developments were afoot, too. Oxford had been planning a tutorial class at Rochdale. In 1907 the class at Longton heard about it and asked Oxford for a similar class, and for Tawney as their tutor. Tawney was an assistant in political economy at Glasgow at the time. Consequently, in January 1908, with the encouragement and support of the Local Education Authorities, one of the first two WEA tutorial classes in the country was formed at Longton (building on a University Extension Guild formed a few years earlier). Tawney was appointed to a pioneer post of teacher for tutorial classes under Oxford University. For his weekends, he travelled from Glasgow to Longton for a class on Friday night, went to Rochdale for a class on Saturday afternoon, and returned to Glasgow on Sunday night.

The Longton class has become legendary. Forty members had enrolled, and the class continued for twenty-seven years. Tawney's first course was on Industrial and Economic History. His first major book, *The Agrarian Problem in the Sixteenth Century* was published in 1912 and was dedicated to Albert Mansbridge and William Temple. Tawney also acknowledged a debt to the students of his tutorial classes. The members were fired with missionary zeal. They themselves went out to give lectures and preparatory classes which they led by taking groups in turn. The Longton class Secretary was E. S. Cartwright, a brilliant organiser later described by Charles Morris (a Fellow of Balliol and later Vice-Chancellor of Leeds University) as the master craftsman of the movement. Under Tawney's direction and with the help of other Oxford tutors – F. W. Kolthammer at Stoke and Henry Clay at Tunstall, the North Staffordshire Miners' Higher Education Movement was set up to promote adult education in the mining villages. (Kolthammer changed his name to Cuthbertson during the First World War. Sir Henry Clay was later to represent Oxford University on the Council of the new University College at Keele.) In 1912 A. L. Smith persuaded Cartwright to become the Organising Secretary of the Joint [with Oxford] Tutorial Classes Committee; and Lindsay became the University Secretary of the Committee. Cartwright then set up a Joint Advisory Committee of four representatives from Oxford (one of whom was Lindsay) and five each from the Stoke-on-Trent and Staffordshire Education Committees, to supervise the work of adult education in the area. (In 1944 the Committee was enlarged to include representatives of Burton Education Authority and the WEA.)

Underpinning the special strength of the movement in North Staffordshire was the large body of active participants. In his Jubilee Lecture in Stoke Town Hall in 1972, C. A. Scrimgeour made the point that 'what Tawney and Cartwright, philosopher-kings as they were in their own right, have taught us is that, in a voluntary movement like ours, *where every individual carries responsibility for the whole*, the contribution of the outstanding person has special value only in so far as it encourages the solidarity of effort given by all active members, and engages itself with that solidarity.'

Two developments after the First World War added to the impetus to found a College. The first came from the Longton tutorial class which suggested that a University College would be a fitting war memorial, to provide 'the constant development of an enlightened and instructed citizenship in the face of the growing complexity of modern life' – an expression resonant with Lindsay's own ideas. A letter in the *Sentinel* in January 1919 in effect gave notice that a movement had begun which would not be halted: the tutorial class students called for the establishment of a university college to 'forward the industrial and commercial progress of the area and develop an enlightened and instructed citizenship'. The second was the request by the Miners' Higher Education Movement, that fervent child of the Longton class, to the Oxford University Tutorial Classes Committee for a resident tutor in North Staffordshire – and preferably R. H. Tawney. Lindsay was the Chairman of the Oxford Committee, and he persuaded Stoke-on-Trent and Staffordshire Education Committees to finance Tawney's appointment. The Miners' Movement became the North Staffordshire District of the WEA. Tawney was an inspiration. He remained a member of the WEA for forty-two years and was its President from 1928 to 1944. It was Tawney who had written the conference report *Oxford and Working Class Education* in 1908, Tawney for whom education was at the heart of social policy, Tawney who launched extramural university tutorial classes as a going concern, and Tawney who was the presiding spirit of the WEA in North Staffordshire.

Mansbridge had seen the need and found the solution. Cartwright was the organising genius. Mansbridge wrote to Cartwright that the movement in North Staffordshire 'really means the beginning of a Potteries College'. Oxford, and especially Balliol, provided enormous encouragement and support. And Tawney gave the inspiration which launched the university tutorial classes. Then there was Lindsay. The strong impulse to understand the problems of society over and above the desire for know-ledge, and the aspirations for 'an enlightened and instructed citizenship', found a ready resonance, and the tutorial class movement fascinated him. Many years later he wrote unequivocally that the tutorial class at the outset reached a standard comparable to that of honours work in a university. His life-long love affair with the WEA and its tutorial classes was not confined to North Staffordshire, but the response he found here created a bond which was never broken. He suggested to a General Meeting of the North Staffordshire WEA in 1925 that they should 'start something new – a real people's university'.

Lindsay could not have foreseen Keele, nor his own close and personal involvement with it. We can, though, already see many of what were to become the dominant threads in the founding of Keele: Tawney, the WEA, local enthusiasm and high standards, Oxford, Balliol, the support and co-operation of the local authorities, and Lindsay himself. Horwood was in the wings. It was a striking confluence of men, ideas and place.

Chapter 3

THE MASTER OF BALLIOL

In 1924 Lindsay returned to Balliol as Master. He was 45. His election was controversial: older Fellows who were senior to him in the College were passed over in his favour. Although he had been a Fellow since 1906 he had not been an undergraduate at Balliol (and so in that sense did not truly belong), and he had well-known left-wing views. As Master of Balliol he could assume a bigger mantle and find a ready platform if he cared to use it. He did care to use it. He always commanded considerable respect. He continued to take an active part in teaching and he preached once a term in the chapel. He was later described in *The Spectator* as a brilliant lecturer and a brilliant preacher. He was a non-dogmatic, non-doctrinaire thinker, and was open to fresh ideas. Yet as a lecturer he could be hesitant, apparently thinking aloud, not giving a polished performance, but showing a brilliant mind at work. He could inspire and he could convert others, though his Socratic method of questioning could be off-putting and was not always recognised as an invitation to press a case more strongly. 'Pooh-pooh! What do you want that for?' He could be abrupt: 'Dear blank, The answer is no. Yours sincerely', yet to those who knew him as Sandie there was always a twinkle in his eye.

He 'became a national figure, more by virtue of his moral fervour and wide-ranging interests than by his contributions to scholarship' (Christopher Hill, *Dictionary of National Biography*), but it was his philosophical analysis of society which underpinned his moral fervour and was the mainspring of his thought and action, and on which was built his reputation as the foremost exponent of the philosophy of social democracy. His position added weight to what he did when he took a public stance – in his support for Bishop Temple in attempting reconciliation during the General Strike, in seeking to do something for the unemployed, and in opposing Nazism. 'Something has got to be done!', he used to say. He was quick and resourceful, tolerant and frank, loyal, with apparently inexhaustible patience. First impressions, though, could sometimes be disappointing and he could appear remote. He was also untidy, the despair of secretaries – but a most resourceful administrator.

Lindsay's views on democracy were publishd in his book *The Modern Democratic State* in 1943. In turn, his theories on education were closely linked to his theories on democracy because they sprang from the same analysis of what was wrong with society. He was preoccupied with the consequences of the convergence of two major developments: the technological revolution and the democratic revolution. They had reacted on each other. The technological revolution meant that industry was depending more and more on the technical skills of the experts. However, industrialisation had divided society, broadly, into a minority who make decisions and accept responsibility, and the majority who accept the decisions and take no responsibility for them, so long as they meet their material interests. Hence the division of labour had brought with it a division of interests and a denial of democracy, with a majority taking little or no part in the direction of their own affairs. Yet the democratic revolution, meantime, had opened up participation in political and social affairs to all, and with it the need to understand society and the need for an enlightened leadership. As he wrote in *The Modern Democratic State*, 'Since a democratic community depends on mutual understanding, there can be no effective democracy without an educated people.' Lindsay repudiated the notion that power should be confined to a small and privileged class: democracy demanded that the specialist experts and leaders should have a concern for, and an understanding of, the values on which society depended. 'A modern democratic state is only possible if it can combine appreciation of skill, knowledge, and expertness with a reverence for the common humanity of everyday people.' Enlightened leadership presupposed and depended on such an understanding of society. Industry, having been confronted with increasing reliance on specialist knowledge, had turned to the universities to find the specialists. Universities had provided the curriculum to produce them: they were fulfilling the requirements of the technological revolution. But in so doing they were ignoring the consequences of the democratic revolution and the universities themselves, at a time of increasing need for enlightened leadership, were now therefore failing in their greater educational purpose. That, in Lindsay's view, was the crisis in the universities.

An important influence on Lindsay's analysis was the Spanish philosopher Professor José Ortega Y Gasset (1883-1955). In *The Rebellion of the Masses* in 1930 he foreshadowed the Spanish Civil War and warned of the danger of democracy leading to tyranny, whether of the left or right. It was therefore the duty of the intellectual leaders of society to fight such a threat, i.e. to safeguard democracy. Another theme of Ortega Y Gasset was that Europe had lost its *cultural* unity, by which he meant that vital acceptance of those ideas which historically had been common throughout Europe and which had given much of Europe a common heritage. In *The Mission of the University* (1930) he wrote of the need to reassess what the current vital governing ideas were, and the necessity, therefore, of reorganising university education to bring about the recovery of that unity of western culture. This meant not turning the clock back, but rather examining what ideas of the present time constituted the 'vital system', in order to recover a common culture. He believed that students were becoming specialists instead of being educated, and feared that universities were developing training and research at the expense of the culture which had formerly bound Europe together: they were producing new barbarians – professional but uncultural, specialists in one thing and ignorant of everything else. To counterbalance these threats he advocated a 'Faculty of Culture' at the centre of the university – including physics, biology, sociology, history and philosophy, and with an emphasis on teaching, to give an understanding of modern empirical science and of the common heritage of Europe.

Nor was Ortega Y Gasset's a lone voice. The same or similar ideas were widely echoed, if anyone cared to listen. The notion that undergraduates should share in a common awareness of the importance of ideals and objectives in a common understanding of the heritage of their generation; and of the need to acquire some understanding of what was common to all fields of learning and the ways in which their aims and methods differ, could have been taken from Lindsay, or from Ortega Y Gasset, or from Government reports or from a number of universities. In fact, this succinct summary – the notion that undergraduates should share a common awareness – comes from a Harvard University Report on *General Education in a Free Society* in 1945. Lindsay had already made his views known, that the universities had taken a wrong direction: the origin of the universities had been to educate men for the learned professions. That had meant mixing with members of other professions. In so doing universities had provided them with learning, and also a mutual understanding of one another, a common background, and a certain leisure for reflection. The drive towards specialisation in the wake of the technological revolution, however, had destroyed that very common understanding which was vital for enlightened leadership and on which the democratic revolution depended. And it was in the very institutions, which had earlier been the repository of that common understanding, that specialisation was now producing Ortega Y Gasset's 'new barbarians'. Characteristically, Lindsay went on to make constructive suggestions to overcome the problem – namely that education should include something of our heritage, something of what we owe to science, and something about the problems of modern industrialized society.

Lindsay abhorred isolation of thought however it manifested itself. 'The only chance for the future', he wrote of the social problems in the Rhonda in 1927, 'is to break down the isolation of thought in which they live'. He addressed the problem time and again: in 1930 when he visited India as chairman of a commission enquiring into Christian higher education; in 1940 when he gave six broadcasts on the BBC Empire Service with the title *I Believe in Democracy*; and yet again in 1945 when he gave the Founders' Memorial Lecture at Girton College, Cambridge. His political and philosophical thinking was the foundation of his educational ideas, and he thought of university education in terms of service to a democratic community. He summed up his views on university education in an article in *Nature* in 1950 when he said that universities did not exist solely to hand down learning, but that it was increasingly important to instil into students a spirit of scientific research, a way of handling problems, and the principles of investigation. At the same time, he said, we must also overcome the comparative isolation in which the specialist finds himself by virtue of his specialisation, because the democratic revolution repudiated the notion that power should be confined to a small, specialist and privileged class. Arising from this, he deplored in particular the separation between scientists and students of the humanities: specialisation had produced students who were no longer speaking the same language, and who no longer had a common background nor a common body of knowledge. He believed the concept of a university-trained man whose only function was technical had momentous and evil consequences. Again, during the War, in 'A Plan for Education' in *Picture Post* he wrote of departmentalism and specialisation, and also of the growing interrelationship between different branches of knowledge. 'The man who only knows more and more about less and less is becoming a public danger', he said, and went on that we must get 'the right balance between specialisation and expert knowledge on the one hand and a wide outlook and general understanding on the other'. That is a phrase which will jump to the eye of generations of Keele students who took the Foundation Year. Towards the end of his life he spoke to the Wolverhampton Chamber of Commerce in 1951 about Keele and his ideas, and he put his views of many years succinctly as follows: 'If we are going to try to keep a democratic country and maintain understanding of one another, we have to send out people from our universities who can do the technical stuff and who at the same time have an understanding of political and social problems and of the values that lie behind them.' He regarded specialisation by itself as 'the curse of modern education', and he feared that knowledge was being acquired at the expense of understanding and that true education was being replaced by training.

For the three years 1935 to 1938 he was Vice-Chancellor of Oxford University. His ability, fairness, energy and courtesy made him very effective, and the *Oxford Magazine* wrote that no-one spoke more highly of him as Vice-Chancellor than those who were university officers at the time. His major contributions during his period of office were the realisation of the need to develop science at Oxford, and the integration of Lord Nuffield's great benefactions into the university. Shortly after the end of his term of office came the Oxford City by-election. This was the first by-election to test public opinion after Chamberlain had returned from Munich bringing 'peace with honour'. The conservative candidate was Quintin Hogg, a Fellow of All Souls, the son of a cabinet minister and former Lord Chancellor, the first Viscount Hailsham. Lindsay was persuaded to stand as an Independent Progressive candidate on an anti-Munich, anti-Government ticket, and the Labour, Liberal and Communist candidates all stood down for him. Lindsay's views were that a nation could not have an effective foreign policy unless it made up its mind what it was prepared to defend in the last resort. He considered that the Government had evaded that issue. He was adopted as a candidate only ten days before the election, and he had no proper party machine to support him. Nevertheless, he succeeded in cutting the conservative majority from 6,645 to 3,434, and his campaign was given the support of three later conservative prime ministers – Churchill, Macmillan and Heath.

After the War Lindsay entered the House of Lords as one of seven new Labour peers (receiving amongst his letters of congratulation one beginning 'Dear Lord and Master'). His major speech in the House of Lords on education is referred to in chapter 6. Another opportunity for him to make his views known came in a Foreign Office report on *University Reform in Germany*, which was published in 1949. He had been the chairman of a commission appointed by the Military Governor of the British zone of Germany. The other members were all German, apart from a Swiss professor. In the event little came of it, but the philosophy behind the report was clearly Lindsay's, and it enhanced his reputation amongst German academics. What he had been preaching for so long had been heightened by the catastrophe which had befallen Germany. Key phrases in the report will by now be familiar – that a genuine 'education' should be fostered and that the unity of culture should be emphasized; the dangers of training the specialist intellect and not the whole man; and the need for men and women to learn to fulfil their duty within the social body in order to avoid a new political catastrophe. The report described the three-fold revolutionary developments which had taken place – technical, political and social – and the dangers of concealed domination by a few technical and political specialists. It proclaimed that no institution deserved the name of university unless teaching and research formed a whole, but it recommended a shift to a greater emphasis on teaching; it maintained that a university was not just a collection of professional schools and urged the need to strengthen unity. It considered it was vital to widen the scope of technical universities by incorporating a faculty of humanistic and social sciences, which would include philosophy, history, sociology, economics and related subjects. It is the section on the 'Studium Generale' which will, most of all, give Keele graduates a sense of *déjà vu*. Lindsay's philosophy was re-iterated again – the dangers of specialisation in a democratic society, the need for general education to understand society, and the need to be socially conscious; the basic principles of philosophy, sociology, history, economics and psychology were no longer a luxury. The report recommended that the teaching staffs should work out a comprehensive programme of general education and basic sciences for all students.

Most of the ideas which would shape Keele were already in place.

Chapter 4

COMMITTEES AND REPORTS

Even before the end of the Second World War it was clear that post-war Britain was going to need a large and rapid increase in the number of university graduates. Official reports laid down guidelines for the future, and Lindsay's views were echoed time and again. The same principles are repeated so often that one wonders why they were not accepted, or if accepted why they were not acted upon. Shortage of money is the main reason; plus an unwillingness to invest in the country's own future, compounded by long periods of short-term expediency. But there was also an unwillingness on the part of some whose support and encouragement might otherwise have changed the climate of opinion. There had been a conference at Leeds in 1921 with representatives from the universities of Birmingham, Durham, Leeds, Liverpool, Manchester and Sheffield, and this conference considered the question of the proposed establishment of new universities. The University College of the South West at Exeter under its new Principal, Professor H. J. W. Hetherington, wished to attain university status. (Hetherington had studied classics, philosophy and economics at Glasgow, and been a lecturer in philosophy first at Glasgow and then at Sheffield. He was appointed Professor of Logic and Philosophy at University College Cardiff from 1915 to 1920, and then Principal and Professor of Philosophy at Exeter. In 1924 he succeeded Lindsay in the chair of moral philosophy at Glasgow before becoming Vice-Chancellor of Liverpool and then Principal of Glasgow.) Hetherington was proposing a small board of academic advisers to exercise a special though unobtrusive supervision of standards. He hoped that Oxford would nominate this board. Oxford was favourably inclined, and the chairman of the UGC was well-disposed. However, the civic universities were strongly opposed to the plan. Their conference noted that 'people need to be reminded that a University is a living thing whose growth must be tended by the reverent hands of men inspired by a disinterested love of knowledge, and not an establishment to be organized and governed like a mere market for the distribution of negotiable learning', and used the phrase 'patronal relationship' disparagingly. Hetherington was not seeking 'patrons', but in the face of opposition his scheme was ill-starred. This is a long way from the 1940s, but it explains a lot of the difficulties which Lindsay was to face later.

The Ministry of Education acknowledged in a *Report on Higher Technological Education* at the end of the war that there was a strong feeling in industry that more attention needed to be paid to a liberal outlook on life, and also that institutions needed to plan their own syllabuses and adapt their examinations to their teaching. The *Report* further suggested that undergraduate courses were too short and too specialised, and that university life was too little residential.

Another report in 1946 seemed to prepare the way for Keele. This was the Barlow *Report on Scientific Manpower*. The scientific assessor was Dr. C. P. Snow, whose Rede Lecture in 1959 on *The Two Cultures and the Scientific Revolution* was to give prominence to the 'two cultures': 'Between the two a gulf of mutual incomprehension – sometimes (particularly among the young) hostility and dislike, but most of all lack of understanding. They have a curious distorted image of each other.' Arthur Koestler, in the same year, wrote 'a state of cold war is maintained between the Sciences and the Humanities' (*The Sleepwalkers*). It is, perhaps, not surprising that the *Report* attached great importance to an association of men and women which took all knowledge as its province and in which all branches of learning flourished in harmony. It stressed the importance of halls of residence and corporate life, and even pointed to using country houses or vacated military camps. It suggested that there were several large centres of population where new university colleges could be established, and particularly recommended that early consideration should be given to founding at least one new university to give the present generation the opportunity of leaving to posterity a monument of its culture. 'We also believe that such a proposal would receive warm support from informed opinion and the general body of the public.'

'All branches of learning', 'halls of residence and corporate life', 'large centres of population', 'a monument of its culture', and 'warm support from informed opinion': surely this could all find resonance in North Staffordshire. The Parliamentary and Scientific Committee, too, expressed full agreement with the general tenor of the *Report*, welcomed a recommendation on increased numbers, spoke of adequate financial support as essential, and encouraged even more energetic steps than Barlow had recommended. But, and it was a big but, 'the foundation of a new university is inexpedient'. There were two major hurdles in the way of founding a new university. The first was shortage of money. The costs of rebuilding Britain after the Second World War were enormous. Houses and factories were desperately needed, and urgently. In addition, the post-war government's programme of social reform, and especially the National Health Service, was costing much more than had been planned. Put against these pressing priorities, universities could wait. The second major hurdle was the very 'informed opinion' which the Barlow *Report* had believed would give warm support: it refused to do so.

A *Report on University Development* had been published by the Association of University Teachers at the end of 1943. Here was informed opinion most closely connected with the running of universities. Their *Report* welcomed the opportunity of extending universities' contributions to social advances, recognised the vital importance of academic freedom of enquiry, and acknowledged that a university education should be open to all who could profit from it. It agreed that on completion of their courses, students' views were often 'narrow and confined', and suggested that experiments should link the specialist with other spheres of studies and with students of other subjects. This was backed by specific proposals: that all students should pursue courses in a group of correlated subjects for one or two years; that the General degree course should introduce students to new subjects and new approaches; an emphasis on the structure and evolution of society, the social significance of various subjects and the main problems of philosophy; and the need for more contact between student and teacher. The possibility of a new university was hinted at, but no more. 'We do not wish to preclude the foundation of a new university, but consider that only special circumstances would justify this.'

What the Parliamentary and Scientific Committee meant when it said that the foundation of a new university was 'inexpedient' was that, attractive as it might be, a new university could not help appreciably in the provision of the intermediate expansion required, and might well interfere by diverting limited supplies of manpower and building facilities. It would therefore be preferable to build on the existing universities and colleges instead. Hugh Dalton, the Chancellor of the Exchequer, made it clear that he was prepared to find the money for university development, and he shared the Committee's views on the inadvisability of founding a new university at this stage.

Other informed opinion took a similar view. The Committee of Vice-Chancellors and Principals in *A Note on University Policy and Finance in the Decennium 1947-56* to the University Grants Committee recognised that the aftermath of war presented a field in which the old methods, the methods of gradual, piece-meal and laboured developments were not enough; but then the Note pointed out the daily difficulties of translating a policy into practice, of balance, of upholding quality and improving resources. In paragraph 13 the Vice-Chancellors wished to comment specifically on the proposition in the Barlow *Report* that early consideration should be given to the founding of at least one new university. The measured tones hardly heralded a ringing endorsement. The Vice-Chancellors 'would say' that if there were enough money, materials, equipment and manpower to spare for making a new university, then in the national interest those had better be spent in expanding the existing institutions. After the decade, if... if..., etc., they conceded that founding a new university outside some suitable city or town would become reasonable. A new university would then receive the warm support from informed opinion which, the Vice-Chancellors 'venture to say' would not support it earlier.

But no-one has a monopoly of informed opinion, and there were other bodies preparing to submit proposals to the University Grants Committee. North Staffordshire had also given thought to post-war needs. In November 1944 Alderman Kemp made the following proposal in a speech following his election as Lord Mayor of Stoke-on-Trent: 'At the end of the last war memorials were erected all over the country, including Stoke-on-Trent. Would not the finest expression of our gratitude to those who have served us be the firm resolve to found a university – not in the dim and distant future, but now, when the need is greatest?' This was firmer stuff. He was the leader of the Independent group in the City Council, and he had lost his son in the war. A year later, the Labour party gained control of the Council under the leadership of Alderman the Reverend Thomas Horwood, and Horwood subsequently became the chairman of all the major policy committees.

On 10th May, 1946, a committee met in the Town Hall, Stoke-on-Trent with a clear mission. This followed a resolution of the City Council that the provision of a university college for North Staffordshire be approved in principle and that a special committee be set up to investigate the whole matter and report to the General Purposes Committee. This was not a body of men and women who would simply 'wish to comment' or 'venture to say'. This special committee, the 'Exploratory Committee', immediately resolved to co-opt two members from Staffordshire County Council, one from Burton upon Trent Borough Council, one from Newcastle-under-Lyme Borough Council, two from the WEA, and one member from Oxford University, together with a local person with wide interest in education. This was Miss Farmer, a founder member of the Longton class. Lord Lindsay, the Master of Balliol was the Oxford representative (though he had wanted A. H. Smith, the Warden of New College, to serve). The WEA sent T. L. Hodgkin and Miss G. Malbon. T. L. Hodgkin was a Fellow of Balliol; his father had been Provost of Queen's College, and his mother was the daughter of A. L. Smith, Lindsay's predecessor as Master of Balliol. He had been a staff tutor in North Staffordshire for the Oxford University Delegacy for Extra-Mural Studies. Miss Gladys Malbon was another staff tutor, and she had taken over much of the secretarial work of the local WEA during the war. But she was much more than that. Her drive and energy were unstoppable. Harry Taylor, the Town Clerk of Stoke-on-Trent, said that she was the mainspring of the Exploratory Committee, and that without her the College would not have started. He wrote that Lindsay would have given up the fight on one occasion had it not been for her enthusiasm, which was fuelled by her knowledge of the WEA and Oxford, her personal contacts, her local knowledge, her ability and drive, and above all her belief in the need for a university in North Staffordshire. Alderman Barnett Stross, MP, wrote in 1952: 'If you told the truth you would say that Alderman Horwood led the way, inspired and stimulated by Alderman B. Stross, MP, who was inspired and stimulated by Miss Gladys Malbon who was inspired and stimulated by Professor Tawney.' Miss Malbon added that E. S. Cartwright should be placed between Tawney and herself. In July Alderman Kemp joined the Committee.

With the setting up of the Exploratory Committee which met on 10th May, 1946, the ideas of Lindsay and the driving force of Horwood converged. They were to prove the Committee of Vice-Chancellors and Principals wrong, and to demonstrate that no-one had a monopoly of 'informed opinion'. These were to be 'the reverent hands of men inspired by a disinterested love of knowledge'. Their resolve to provide a course of a character and quality such as was provided by no other university or college, would break the existing mould of university education in this country.

Chapter 5
THE EXPLORATORY COMMITTEE

T here had been earlier proposals for a university in the area, but they had come to nought. Horwood realised that what was needed was money. There was no obvious large-scale benefactor. However, when it was suggested that it might be financed in a similar way to Edinburgh University in the 16th century, namely by floating a fund from municipal sources, it fell to Horwood as chairman of the Finance Committee to see what could be done. 'If I have learnt one lesson', he said towards the end of his life, 'it is that there is a time to act, and if that time is once missed all may be in danger.' When the City Council approved the intention of raising a loan of £250,000, it may, in his view, have been the hand of Providence – but it was hand in hand with his own.

The impetus behind setting up the Exploratory Committee had been the right people in the right place at the same time. Tawney was now a member of the UGC. Letters from Tawney to Alderman Hollins, the Secretary of the Pottery Workers' Society and President of the North Staffordshire WEA, and to Cartwright, can be seen as the impetus. Cartwright and Lindsay, Secretary and Chairman of the North Stafford-shire Committee for Adult Education, linked together the Local Education Authorities, the Directors of Education, Oxford and the WEA. Miss Malbon at the helm of the local WEA, was prompted by Tawney's letter to write to Sir Walter Moberly, the Chairman of the UGC. Tawney saw Dr. Barnett Stross, the MP for Hanley, who arranged for him to see Horwood. Stross spoke to Hugh Dalton, the Chancellor of the Exchequer, and informed Lindsay, Horwood, Hughes (the Director of Education for Staffordshire) and Carr (the Director of Education for Stoke-on-Trent) that money was available for university development. 'Then we got busy', Carr later wrote to Professor Gallie. There was also support from Colonel George Wigg, MP for Dudley. He lived in Stoke-on-Trent, and had been the WEA District Secretary for North Staffordshire before the war. Miss Malbon had acted for him throughout the war, and had succeeded him as District Secretary when he entered Parliament.

On 13th March 1946 Lindsay had written to Moberly about the possibility of setting up a university college 'on new lines'. That was the crucial point, and this was the opening shot in the campaign. He wanted to abandon the established procedure of a new college taking University of London degrees. 'It might be possible to get this University [i.e. Oxford] to take a special interest, help to conduct examinations, and get rid of the London external degree.' Lindsay had known Moberly for forty years.

(Moberly had also been a Professor of Philosophy, at Birmingham from 1921 to 1924. He then succeeded Hetherington as Principal at Exeter, and was Vice-Chancellor of Manchester from 1926 to 1934. He was Chairman of the UGC from 1935 to 1949, and in that year published his book *The Crisis in the University.*) We can already see the orchestration of Gladys Malbon. It was she who had earlier written to the UGC asking for a meeting, and Lindsay's letter of 13th March had started: 'I think you have had a letter from Miss Malbon.' She had sent some notes to Tawney with a copy to Moberly, and had spoken to Lindsay. The groundwork was thoroughly prepared for a meeting on 27th March when an unofficial deputation from the Potteries met representatives from the UGC: Ellis Smith (MP for Stoke-on-Trent), Dr. Barnett Stross (MP for Hanley), Miss Malbon and J. F. Carr met Sir Walter Moberly, H. de Montmorency (Secretary of the UGC), and Professor R. H. Tawney. It was that meeting – at which neither Lindsay nor Horwood was present – which cast a stone into a very large pool. They were well received. The discussion was about the broad principles. The Stoke delegation made the point that they were opposed to the idea of 'examination cramming' for London external degrees. This was not for its own sake, but because Lindsay wanted to do something *different,* and the London external degree would not permit the kind of experiment he wanted. There was specific mention of *local* interests – ceramics, and those aspects of history, economics and sociology which had been of particular interest in the adult classes. A medical school was also mentioned. They stressed the importance of residence, and that it was hoped to maintain and foster the connection with Oxford. Carr said that Stoke-on-Trent would produce £300,000, and the UGC in turn stressed that their answer would depend on there being local financial support. That was where Horwood would come in. Moberly urged them to press on rapidly and prepare proposals, because the grant system was more favourable than it had been; and to lose no time in canvassing local support. Tawney then wrote to Lindsay and also urged acting quickly while the going was good. Carr placed the gist of the discussions before the General Purposes Committee of the City Council, and on 2nd May 1946 the City Council resolved that the proposal be approved in principle and that the special committee be set up: that was the University Exploratory Committee which held its first meeting in the Town Hall, Stoke-on-Trent on 10th May: ten members of the City Council with the power to add to the membership, but to retain a majority of the whole.

Meanwhile, on 5th April 1946 Lindsay had written to the Vice-Chancellor of Oxford, asking him if there was any way the Stoke proposals could be connected to Oxford rather than to London, and added that Moberly had told him of earlier proposals for 'patron' universities for new university colleges. But the Vice-Chancellor, Sir Richard Livingstone, was sceptical. And John Murray, the Principal at Exeter since 1926, wrote to say that Hetherington's plan for hitching the College to Oxford never seemed to him to be sound but rather a confession of inadequacy. The reaction at Exeter to Lindsay's applying that idea to the Potteries 'would be adverse', he wrote. 'I doubt if the reaction in other University Colleges would be friendly.' In fact, the next post brought Lindsay a letter of encouragement from the Principal of University College, Hull. Moberly's advice to press on was heeded, and by the time of the next meeting with the UGC on 25th July 1946 a great deal had happened.

During the next four years the suggestions for courses and even the nature of the proposed College were going to change radically. The alterations were partly in order to win support, partly a compromise between the ideal and the practicable, partly simply better and different ideas, and partly a response to national changes. It is not that expediency took precedence over principle: that would be to misread what was underpinning Lindsay's concept. A paper in the *Proceedings of the Aristotelian Society for 1911-1912* by Sorley, Lindsay and Bosanquet describes the process: 'If we ask an artist his purpose, he can only tell us it when the work is completed, and the purpose itself grows and develops with its execution... because in the process of execution new suggestions and possibilities occur to us which we are not able to work out... The reality... is one in which process and result cannot be separated, where, though the whole process seems to be guided by the end in view, that end is only known in vague anticipations, and dim presages, until it is developed and worked out in realisation; and the material in which the purpose is effected, whether it be human relations or marble, is not mere formless matter, but gives content and shape to the purposes executed in it.' Nevertheless, there were two driving forces from which Lindsay never wavered. The first is Lindsay's 'Keele Idea'. It is difficult to give a full and satisfactory account of what it was, because Lindsay himself never really defined it: like a smoke ring, it is easy to see it from a number of different viewpoints, but it is difficult to grasp. (The 'Keele Idea' will be dealt with later – see chapter 9.) The other was the freedom to do something different in order to achieve what he wanted. That was so important to Lindsay that he saw the founding of the College delayed and even jeopardised rather than compromise. Looking back fifty years it is difficult to understand why it was such a problem then, yet it is almost impossible to overestimate Lindsay's achievement. More than twenty-five years ago, at Keele, Lord Fulton said: 'The battle for Keele was no push-over. It had to be fought all the way. And in fighting with success that battle Keele smoothed the path for all the new foundations which have come after it.'

Lindsay, as Chairman of the Exploratory Committee, endowed it with his authority and experience. Harry Taylor, the Town Clerk, had written to the UGC to confirm that North Staffordshire was 'extremely keen to go forward with the project'. There was a paper, probably written by G. D. H. Cole, on the type of academic courses to be included. (Cole was the Chichele professor of social and political theory at Oxford, and had been an undergraduate at Balliol. He was the chairman of the Fabian Society, and had a strong attachment to the WEA.) The Exploratory Committee met on 23rd July and put together some firm proposals: 'It is imperative that the new College should retain a real freedom of development. The recognition and conferring of Degrees should therefore be a matter for discussion with the UGC.' The Committee also proposed appointing a Principal for September 1947, ready to open in September 1948 with 70-100 students, rising to 1,000 in ten or fifteen years' time; and it was envisaged that the College should be mainly residential.

In the first instance, the syllabus was for a single BA degree in the social sciences, plus teaching in the natural sciences, with history to follow later with training courses in teaching and social work. The suggested content of the degree course was unashamedly PPE. There was only one hint at this stage that there might be a four-year course – for those training in teaching or social work – though the training would be intermingled throughout the whole undergraduate course. Plans for a full science department would follow once staff and equipment were available. Another proposal was that a foreign language should be made compulsory. A system of sponsorship was suggested, to approve teaching appointments and external examiners, and to receive annual reports. This, of course, was based on Hetherington's scheme for Exeter in the 1920s, which Hetherington passed to Lindsay.

The idea of only one degree course had little appeal to the UGC. What this proposal reflects is Lindsay's experience at Oxford in persuading heads of departments to forgo specialised requirements in order to provide a broad and integrated course covering different disciplines. That is why he wanted to start with an integrated course in the first instance: then he could expand the range of honours courses and the 'lessons of hard disciplined thought' after students had been taught the technique of 'seeing things together'. The proposals were to change completely – but not the underlying philosophy.

It looks as though there is evidence of some haste to be ready for the meeting with the UGC on 25th July. There was an accompanying paper of notes which mentioned a degree course related directly to local industry, but to 'include suitable elements of the Arts course (perhaps on lines similar to those of the old general degree course in the Scottish Universities) to prevent the growth of a distorted specialisation'. This sentence clearly has the ring of Lindsay about it and is almost pivotal in the development of the whole Keele curriculum – harking back to the old Scottish system he admired, the avoidance of distorted specialisation and the obligatory mix of non-science with a science course. Gladys Malbon had again sent notes to Tawney and had been down to Balliol. Tawney picked up some discrepancies in the papers, and then raised the specific point of whether it would not be better to start with the London degree in the first instance. He was certain that it was urgent to get started. But because it was vital to the Stoke delegation for the College to be able to grant its own degrees in order to proceed with its programme, Tawney's urging was not heeded. The next milestone was a meeting with the full UGC in November 1946.

For that meeting the Stoke proposals were in a printed form and included appendices giving details of courses as illustrations, the accommodation at Meaford Hall, and a rough budget. The aim was quite clear: 'the establishment of a full university'; the Report reiterated the importance of the freedom to experiment and stressed that the courses should not be determined by the examination system of another university.

On this point, Staffordshire County Council was opposed to the creation of another university college taking London external degrees. The Report now suggested *two* honours degree courses, in Physical Chemistry and in Social Studies. This was in order to concentrate on two areas in which the new college might excel, and to avoid the high costs of establishing a full range of science departments. The proposed courses were not in fact as restricted as it might appear: subsidiary courses were mentioned and, more important, there was to be a cross-disciplinary requirement. 'It is also thought desirable that the student of the Physical Sciences and of the Social Studies should be brought into a close and working relationship with one another. To this end it is suggested that all students of science should be *required* to take at least one section of their intermediate examination from those prescribed for Social Studies...' and vice versa. Likely criticisms were met head on: the Report acknowledged that 'attempts to secure a broad understanding may... encourage a shallow dilettantism. While... a broad study is emphasized and made compulsory, weight is also attached to specialisation in a limited field in order to ensure exact and rigorous habits of thought such as marked the best academic education in the past.' This was Lindsay's 'seeing things together' followed by the 'lessons of hard disciplined thought'. The proposals were put forward 'to contribute to the educational life of the country through a new and fruitful experiment in university education', to provide 'a course of a character and quality such as is provided by no other university or college'. The initial costs were to be met partly by a loan of £250,000, shared between Stoke-on-Trent, Staffordshire County Council and Burton upon Trent.

The question of the college granting its own degrees was the main item of discussion at the meeting. It was too big a leap: the UGC would not agree to that without a period of apprenticeship – but it was not rejected, and Moberly discussed the idea of a 'patron' university. The delegation felt that they had been received sympathetically, but clearly the UGC would have to consider the whole question more widely than just for North Staffordshire. The proposed curriculum was felt to be too narrow to qualify for university status, but nevertheless, the UGC replied to the Town Clerk on 6th December that it 'would consider sympathetically an application for financial assistance in respect of a new University College in North Staffordshire provided that the basis of studies in Science and Arts be adequately broadened. If the scheme is to include the conferment of degrees by the College, the Committee will wish to be satisfied that adequate arrangements have been made for sponsorship by a university or universities and that the proposal can be brought into line with university policy for the country as a whole.' It looks as though there were several different views on the UGC, but at least the answer was not 'no'. It was encouraging that the Ministry of Education was agreeable to the proposals for teacher-training. When Lindsay was interviewed about the UGC's reply, he said he thought it would have taken much longer to get so good a reply, and was satisfied that the alterations required did not amount to anything and did not change the essential features of the scheme.

Lindsay had brought John Fulton, the Jowett Fellow at Balliol, to the meeting of the Exploratory Committee at the end of July. At the meeting in December the Committee (now calling itself the 'University Committee') asked Fulton to prepare a broader basis of studies, to consider the whole scheme and to draft the constitution. The Committee also decided to ask the Universities of Oxford, Birmingham and Manchester to sponsor 'the Stoke-on-Trent scheme', and Lindsay and Fulton to prepare a report.

The framework for a new college on new lines had now been laid down, and sponsorship would be the key to establishing a new curriculum. The plans would have to fit in with 'university policy for the country as a whole', however, and there was some resistance to be overcome. Locally, 'Observer' in the *Sentinel* had asked in April 1946 if it must be assumed that the college would be run by socialists for socialists and propagating chiefly socialist education. The Vicar was not inclined to turn the other cheek: '(You) demonstrate most clearly the vast difference between you and your class point of view and the socialist outlook... the Socialist wants... the child of the worker to have the same opportunities as the children of your class.' In November there were more jibes, this time at social studies: 'It will be a School for Socialists and will be of potential benefit to socialist aspirants for municipal or Parliamentary honours. Truly, this is a 'period of intense social change'. There is no mention of a Faculty of Conservatism, just to balance things politically.' The Vicar responded robustly that nobody before had bothered to get down to business: now at last something was being done. He added that the best thanks of the corporation were due to Lindsay, Professor Fulton and Miss Malbon for all they were doing. When the leading article in the *Sentinel* then suggested that a parochial kind of committee dominated by Stoke-on-Trent socialists was not the organisation to found a university, the writer had clearly underestimated the Vicar and failed to appreciate why he was known as 'the Bishop' in Stoke Town Hall. Horwood's contribution to the founding of Keele was in making things possible and getting them done – making the opportunity and seizing the moment. Lindsay himself said in October 1950 that it was his indomitable courage, perseverance and keenness which brought the university into being, and later that but for Horwood's enthusiasm and incredible courage the university would not exist. He was a man of unflagging energy, and that was the phrase used to describe him when he was presented at Manchester University for the honorary degree of Master of Arts on 3rd July 1953 – 'the Father of the University College of North Staffordshire, by whose exertion the idea of the college was translated into actuality.' When the Parliamentary and Scientific Committee Report in December 1946 said that the foundation of a new university 'is inexpedient', the *Sentinel* assumed that the Stoke scheme had 'gone with the wind', describing it as impracticable, impractical, useless to the needs of the area, and politically-minded. However, when the UGC's more positive reply was made known shortly afterwards, the *Sentinel* gave its support: 'the project is following the course we have urged and outlined'.

There was more serious resistance to the Stoke proposals from the Committee of Vice-Chancellors and Principals. Moberly properly asked the Committee for its view – *not* on this particular proposal, but on the general implications. The Vice-Chancellors had already made their views known when they had commented on the *Barlow Report*, and they had repeated those views in a memorandum to the Chancellor of the Exchequer. They believed that the existing universities and colleges could more than cope, that any new institutions might impair the university system, that there was nothing to justify diverting resources, and that the Stoke proposal in particular was not likely to contribute to the well-being and harmonious development of the university system. They conceded that the 'external' degree system had drawbacks, but it had not been an unsatisfactory procedure. They spoke of the integrity of the university system as a whole, and raised the spectre of academic and administrative confusion. Clearly, the CVCP was not expecting to be a fairy godmother! (One is forced to reflect on whether the size of the bogey man was not out of all proportion to the proposals in front of them.)

Stoke was not put off: there was too much to be done! Miss Malbon saw the Vice-Chancellor of Manchester and discussed the wish not to take London external degrees, and the possibility of Manchester's sponsorship. A 'Stoke delegation' consisting of Horwood, Hutson, Malbon, Carr and Taylor, went to see Moberly in January 1947 to discuss appointing a Principal. Fulton was their first choice, and he was currently working on the details of the proposals. At the end of March the University Committee resolved 'to recommend to the Governing body of the new University the appointment of Mr. J. S. Fulton as Principal'. He was in his mid-forties, and had been a Fellow of Balliol since 1928. He declined the offer on 2nd May, for at the same time the University College of Swansea also wanted Fulton as Principal, and he decided that he had more to offer an existing college than in helping to start a new one. A second name had been discussed with Moberly, but who that might be was not minuted. However, on a handwritten sheet of questions to raise with Moberly there is written in a different hand the names of Fulton (46) and C. Morris (49). Morris had also been a Fellow of Balliol from 1921 to 1942, was a philosopher, and was the author of *British Democracy* and, with Fulton, of *In Defence of Democracy*. He was the Head Master of King Edward's School, Birmingham, and in 1948 was appointed Vice-Chancellor of Leeds University. (His younger brother, Philip Morris had been appointed Vice-Chancellor of Bristol University in 1946.)

What followed was crucial, though exactly how it happened is not clear. Different people had clear but conflicting memories. Horwood's version was published in Gallie's book in 1960. He said that he went by train to Oxford alone to see Lindsay, without consulting any of the committee, to tell him of Fulton's refusal. It could easily mean the end of the whole thing. 'Master, you come to us instead. It was you we always really wanted.' 'Well, you know, Alderman, what the doctors say: that I have about three years to live.' 'Then come to us for those three years', cried Horwood. He laughed heartily and said: 'All right, Horwood, I'll come.'

A different version emerges from Gladys Malbon's diary and her later correspondence with Lady Scott, Lindsay's daughter. According to that, she spoke to Fulton, who said that he had had a talk with Horwood 'about the Master'. She then went to see the Vicar, and they agreed to see the Master. She kept the rough draft of a letter to Lindsay, which says that she wanted to talk to him about the post of Principal, and whether he might help himself when he left Balliol. On 22nd May, Miss Malbon, Horwood, Taylor and the Lord Mayor (Alderman Leason) went to Oxford in the Lord Mayor's car to see Lindsay. Miss Malbon said that they spoke first to Fulton and then to Lindsay, and that Horwood told him he wanted to talk to him about the next step. Harry Taylor also had a clear recollection of what happened, and he gave his account to Sir James Mountford later: 'Alderman Horwood's solo dash to Oxford simply did not take place, but I can quite believe Horwood relating the story to Gallie for dramatic effect.' Taylor said that Horwood, Miss Malbon and Taylor had talked it over and decided to go and see Lindsay. They travelled down with the Lord Mayor, and Horwood asked Lindsay to become the Principal. Taylor said that Lindsay replied that he did not wish to take it: he was retiring from Balliol and wanted to go to his cottage in Cumberland and do some writing. Starting the college would be a strenuous job and it needed a younger man with drive, who believed in his ideas. Horwood pressed Lindsay, who eventually said he would think about it and discuss it with Mrs. Lindsay. Mountford therefore concluded in his book (*Keele: an historical critique*, 1972) that if there had been a separate intervention by Horwood it must have been between 22nd May and 3rd July, when Lindsay remarked in a letter that he would give the Stoke experiment a start for a year or so; but that after the discussion with Lindsay on 22nd May there was no need for high drama anyway; and that no-one involved at the time found the Horwood story more than remotely credible.

Leaving aside the fact that good stories change with time, it could be that instead of two versions of the same event, there were two different events: then both versions would fit. Horwood's details do not fit the others' details: 'without consulting any of the committee' *versus* 'she went to see the Vicar and they agreed to see the Master', and again, 'Horwood, Miss Malbon and Taylor talked it over and decided to go to see Lindsay'. 'He went by train alone' *versus* four of them 'went to Oxford in the Lord Mayor's car'. Lindsay 'laughed heartily and said: 'All right, Horwood, I'll come', *versus* 'he would think about it and discuss it with Mrs. Lindsay'.

Professor Sneddon, the founding Professor of Mathematics told me that he heard the Horwood version from both Horwood and Lindsay himself. Professor Sneddon and Professor Gallie told me that they were surprised, if anything, that Horwood had not fixed it all on the telephone, for he was frequently on the phone to Lindsay. It may be that he recognised how much was at stake and thought a personal meeting was the best way to avert disaster. Professor Lawlor, the founding Professor of English Language and Literature also knew Horwood well, and his account to me makes both versions fit: that it would have been in Horwood's character to want to know the answer before asking the question formally, and that he probably went down to

Oxford on his own and obtained Lindsay's consent *before* the official deputation went on 22nd May.

The important thing was that, whichever way it happened, Lindsay said 'yes'. That gave a great impetus to the scheme: not only was there no loss of momentum, but Lindsay was totally involved. His name and reputation added *gravitas* and experience, and he had the faith to make it work. He also reinforced Horwood's commitment: they worked well in harness together, and Horwood was always prepared to drop everything to go to the aid of his college. In those few words Lindsay added enormously to the chances for success. If Lindsay had not come following Fulton's refusal the question can be asked: 'Would Keele even have started?' At the same time Lindsay stood to risk his entire reputation as a philosopher, scholar, Master of Balliol and Vice-Chancellor of Oxford, and would have risked pouring scorn on his theories of social democracy and his campaign against specialisation. But it was, as *The Times* wrote later, 'no surprise to those who knew his pioneering spirit when he accepted the invitation to become Principal of the University College of North Staffordshire', and the *Oxford Mail* later wrote: 'Perhaps the most courageous act of his life was... to go and start a new University College.'

Formally, Fulton's refusal was reported to the University Committee on 23rd July, 1947; Lindsay was invited to take the post for a period of three years on 23rd September, and the invitation was approved by the General Purposes Committee on 19th November.

Chapter 6

LINDSAY'S ACHIEVEMENT

From now on, Lindsay was virtually synonymous with the University College. He had been made a peer in 1945 and had taken his seat in the House of Lords as Baron Lindsay of Birker of Low Ground in the County of Cumberland. He had made his maiden speech in 1945 and since then he had spoken in particular on foreign affairs and on China. (His son, later the second Lord Lindsay, had gone to Peking to work at an American missionary institution, and in the war between China and Japan he had aided the Chinese communists and come to know most of the communist party's top leaders.) On 14th May 1947 – his 68th birthday – he initiated a debate 'to call attention to university education in this country'. He pointed to the need for changes following the great educational reforms of Butler's Education Act of 1944, and asked whether there was room for new institutions; and if so whether they might be experimental rather than being obliged to work for London degrees. He then spoke of the Stoke proposals, and suggested that there should be a close relation to the characteristics of the local area. During the debate, Viscount Jowett, the Lord Chancellor, confirmed 'that universities should have complete independence and freedom'. Jowett also spoke of the difficulty confronting the Government, especially of providing buildings, and explained that but for the building difficulty, the claims of new universities would have a very high priority. He then gave details of the new terms of reference of the UGC: 'To assist... the preparation and execution of such plans for the development of the universities... to ensure that they are fully adequate to national needs.' Of the Stoke proposals in particular he said the words which Lindsay must have been hoping to hear: 'Might not that be an experiment which is well worth making?'

It was still necessary to solve the recalcitrant problems of sponsorship. In December 1946 Lindsay had written to Moberly to say that favourable replies had been received from Birmingham and Manchester. That view may have been the result of Lindsay's enthusiasm and his assumption that he was talking to the converted when he was not. Whatever had prompted this conclusion there was nothing formal – nor in the event was there agreement! Indeed, a few months later the opposite looked likely. The three Vice-Chancellors met the University Committee on 10th June 1947. A great deal hinged on that meeting. Lindsay gave a long explanation about sponsorship, and about broadening the basis of studies. A proposal that 'the responsibility for organising and integrating the course would naturally fall primarily upon the department of Philosophy' was not approved. Might that have developed into Ortega

Y Gasset's Faculty of Culture? Nevertheless, Lindsay was pleased with the way the meeting went, and the Committee added another function which they hoped the sponsors would undertake, namely to make representation to the Governing Body about the general progress and development of the College. This, the Committee hoped, would provide an effective guarantee of academic standards. Lindsay wrote to Moberly: 'I think they were very much impressed by our new proposals, though a good deal impeded by the Vice-Chancellors' report... [namely the CVCP *Note on University Policy and Finance in the Decennium 1947-56* which is referred to in chapter 4]. They are all prepared to suggest sponsoring to their governing bodies if the UGC agrees – I do not think it is unfair to say that at the end of the meeting these three were personally convinced.' That would seem to be a major achievement on Lindsay's part, especially as the UGC had already said it would approve if the sponsoring universities did. But then Sir John Stopford, the Vice-Chancellor of Manchester, wrote to Moberly to say it was 'very naughty' of Lindsay to say they were all prepared to recommend sponsoring. That was June 1947. They were not yet as converted as Lindsay thought they were. It was encouraging that Sir Raymond Priestley, the Vice-Chancellor of Birmingham, wrote to say he would endeavour to get his Senate to agree to sponsorship, but since the UGC had not taken a lead on the question of university policy there might still be serious opposition: 'This *is* a revolutionary proposal and its effect upon the existing University Colleges cannot be ignored.' Oxford agreed in October that it would sponsor if Manchester and Birmingham did so too. (Strictly, Oxford's formal constitutional agreement was not given until May 1949.) Then, in December 1947, Manchester said it was deeply concerned that existing University Colleges should not be overlooked and that the proposals raised problems of a serious and far-reaching nature. It would therefore defer a decision until a satisfactory assurance had been given that the Stoke proposals were in accordance with University policy for the country as a whole.

The problem was far from solved. 'I do not think all is lost, but I think things are pretty serious', Lindsay wrote to Oxspring (the Chief Education Officer for Staffordshire). Bearing in mind what Lord Jowett had said about the difficulties of buildings, 'it is clear that it will matter a great deal whether we can say we have got Keele Hall'. Then, in January 1948 Birmingham, too, felt 'unable to give advice' until national needs had been determined. This was the low point. 'It is most disappointing', Lindsay wrote to Taylor. 'It is a heavy blow. I do not think the game is up, but I feel less hopeful than I have ever done before.' He hoped he might persuade Oxford to take responsibility alone on the understanding that Manchester and Birmingham were also being approached. But there were to be no short cuts. Furthermore, the Government now felt it could not start any new institutions anyway. That risk was averted by Stross speaking to, and Lindsay writing to Sir Stafford Cripps (the Chancellor of the Exchequer), and Moberly saying that the Stoke proposals had been favourably considered before the Government came to that conclusion. 'I hope we shall have your support', Lindsay wrote to Cripps.

Tawney had been right when he had warned that there was no time to lose. This was probably the time, about which Harry Taylor later wrote, when Lindsay would have given up the fight but for Miss Malbon's enthusiasm.

Meanwhile, following the discussions with Oxford, Birmingham and Manchester in June 1947, a revised curriculum was drawn up. The Committee felt there had been misunderstandings about the earlier proposals, and so was more explicit about its aims: firstly, to include a corrective to the prevailing departmentalism of university teaching, and secondly, to choose subjects particularly suited to the region for more concentrated teaching. It was not to be taken, as it might have seemed, that in the sciences only Physical Chemistry would be taught at honours level, nor that there would not be honours courses in the liberal arts. In the revised plan there were the following subjects, and three parts to the course.

A. Social Studies

1 *Sociology
2 *Economic Theory and Institutions
3 *Political Theory and Institutions
4 Psychology
5 History and Theory of Morals

B. Arts

1 *History
2 *English Language and Literature
3 Modern Languages and Literature – French, German, Russian
4 *Philosophy (Methodology)
5 Mathematics

C. Physical Sciences

1 *Chemistry
2 *Physics
3 *Biology
4 Geology

*subjects in which it was hoped to appoint a Professor.

The three parts to the course were: *(a)* A general or intermediate course for the first year in which all undergraduates would include one subject from each of the Social Studies, the Arts and the Physical Sciences, 'designed to give every undergraduate an insight into the methods and an acquaintance with the main concepts of the chief fields of academic study.' It was also noted that such a course should be felt to be the responsibility of the senior teaching staff. *(b)* Courses for a Pass Degree lasting two years and requiring two or three subjects, for which a choice of different groups would be encouraged. *(c)* Honours courses, to add 'the hard discipline of intensive work to the achievement of the general course'. In the first instance honours courses would be available in Chemistry, Physics, History, English Language and Literature, Economic Theory and Institutions, and Political Theory and Institutions. The honours degree would take four years.

This was certainly different from the earlier proposals. There is a marked decline of any specifically local aspects in the syllabus (of which Lindsay had spoken in the House of Lords in May). The Committee said they rested their claim on the importance for general university policy on this attack on departmentalism; and that if they started with that as their chief aim and made their first appointments with that in mind, they might succeed where other attempts had failed. Some of the fundamental ideas of Keele have now been stated: the four-year course, the cross disciplinary spread, and above all, the importance of giving 'every undergraduate an insight into the methods and an acquaintance with the main concepts of the chief fields of academic study'. It is interesting to note which subjects were proposed compared with what happened: Sociology, Psychology and Russian were delayed; Classics and Geography were yet to appear. Mathematics started in the Arts. The two departments of Philosophy – one in the Arts and one in the Social Sciences – stem from this outline.

An article by Horwood in *Universities' Quarterly* in November 1947 detailed most of these proposals. It straddled the question of a strong local connection on the one hand, and breaking down departmentalism and specialisation on the other. The two aims were probably incompatible in practice. Horwood explained that the foundations of the proposals were local industry, the wide range of social problems, and flourishing local adult education, and he identified the following three important needs: the provision of first-class teachers for the new type of secondary modern schools; a wider background for those working in public and social administration; and a larger proportion of places than was usual for extramural scholars and mature students.

Another approach was made to the UGC in January 1948 for, as Lindsay had established in the debate in the House of Lords, it was the UGC which was the body to make the decision about the Stoke proposals. These now included 'both Science and Arts and break down the departmentalism which we think is so harmful in much modern university teaching'. Lindsay put his case with determined, forceful, reasonable and skilful advocacy. He feared a refusal: but the meeting went well, and Lindsay was greatly assisted by a positive contribution from Professor P. Noble, the Regius Professor of Humanity at Aberdeen, who said he thought they should give the proposal a chance. The vote was 12:1 in favour. In February 1948 Cripps wrote to say that the UGC had passed a resolution of which he entirely approved in favour of establishing a new University College in North Staffordshire with the power of granting a BA degree under conditions of effective external sponsorship. Subject to sponsorship and to obtaining a Royal Charter, the UGC would be prepared to recommend financial assistance. That, at least, was 'as satisfactory as we could possibly hope' (Lindsay to Horwood).

So far, so good, but as Horwood said later, he well remembered the advice from Cripps that if we did not start in October 1950 it might be too late. Moreover, Manchester or Birmingham could still stall the whole project. Gladys Malbon wrote to Lindsay that it was a pity that all the eggs had managed to get into one basket. She wrote to Horwood to say: 'There will be plenty of *work* now', and added 'I hope, Vicar, we can find some way of showing our gratitude to Tawney and Cartwright. I don't forget that it was they, and particularly Tawney, who first started us on this road and I do think we should show we recognise this...'

It was indeed a great pity that all the eggs had got into one basket and that everything depended on sponsorship, for a year after Lindsay had thought that the three Vice-Chancellors were supporting the idea, a letter from the Registrar of the University of Birmingham threatened to put all the plans into reverse. Representatives of the three universities had met, and 'on the basis of the documents before the Committee it would not be possible for the members to make a clear recommendation to their respective universities either for or against Sponsorship'. The letter suggested a joint meeting in the second half of September 1948 – and it was in fact postponed to mid-February 1949. Lindsay therefore asked the chairman and the deputy chairman of the UGC, privately, about taking London external degrees should negotiations about sponsorship not be concluded successfully by 1950. Moberly was encouraging in that he said this would not prejudice the attitude of the UGC, and he went so far as to agree that the University Committee should proceed with the acquisition of Keele Hall (see chapter 7). The meeting with Oxford, Birmingham and Manchester was to discuss 'questions arising on the draft Charter, the curriculum and sponsorship'. That included most things. The Stoke representatives were Lindsay, Miss Malbon, and Dr. W. A. Jenkins, the newly appointed Registrar. Professor Roy Pascal, Professor of German at Birmingham since 1939, was in the chair. In the measured tones of the minutes of the meeting, 'considerable discussion took place on the academic syllabus and the curriculum; the North Staffordshire memorandum of 20th June 1947; and the memorandum of Professor Pascal'. The Pascal memorandum was of pivotal importance. He suggested that in the first year students should choose between different integrated *courses* rather than subjects; he wished to broaden the range of subjects under Social Studies to include such subjects as Human Biology, Human or Economic Geography, and Modern History. He proposed that there should be a 'General Degree Course' rather than a pass degree, which he thought might be regarded as academically inferior, and he wanted further thought given to which departments there should be and how they should be grouped together. He suggested that History and Geography were needed in both Arts and Social Studies, and that Mathematics needed to be in the Sciences; Arts and Social Studies might be grouped together and he wished to see cross-disciplinary study encouraged or required. He also urged the creation of a Board of Studies representative of all departments. Lindsay said that they accepted the memorandum in principle: the syllabus had not yet been settled, and they would welcome the help of the sponsoring universities. A long discussion on sponsorship followed, and at the end, Pascal said the three universities would meet again to consider their position.

In June 1949, Oxford, Birmingham and Manchester accepted responsibility for sponsorship. It had taken a long time, but it was a major achievement by Lindsay. It made possible what had earlier been almost unthinkable. The functions of the sponsoring universities were to be *(a)* to approve all higher appointments to teaching posts; *(b)* to approve external examiners for the degree examinations; *(c)* to receive an annual report on the standard of examinations and to forward this report, with comments, to the College's Governing Body; and *(d)* to make representations from time to time to the Governing Body about the general progress and development of the College. This point was regarded as of special significance. In the event, by virtue of having these powers, the sponsoring universities hardly needed in fact to exercise them.

Miss Malbon was quite clear that Pascal played what might have been the decisive role over sponsorship. He had not only given a lot of attention to the detailed syllabus, but he had also devoted a lot of time and effort on behalf of the Stoke pro-posals in creating an atmosphere of good-will – and especially in talking to Professor Charlton of Manchester about the whole thing.

Much else had happened by the time sponsorship was finally agreed. Keele Hall had been acquired, the Local Authorities had agreed on their financial participation, the Charter was already prepared, the Registrar had been appointed and a secretary seconded from the Town Clerk's office, and there were offices in Aqueduct Street, Stoke-on-Trent. Lindsay had agreed to become Principal on 19th February 1948. Balliol had asked him to continue for another year, so he would not be able to give the post his full attention until 1950 (and then in January 1949 he was admitted to hospital with appendicitis). An Estimates Subcommittee was appointed. Houses had to be built, and playing fields prepared. A Librarian needed to be appointed as a matter of urgency. It was all urgent.

Chapter 7

KEELE HALL

The post-war years were hardly the time to build a new university! Nearly everything was in short supply. It was a time of austerity, controls and rationing. The priorities of rebuilding Britain made enormous demands, and building materials in particular were in desperately short supply. There was never any likelihood that Stoke-on-Trent's college would be built on a green-field site. Instead, something would have to be found. Meaford Hall with 73 acres, situated between Stoke-on-Trent and Stafford, looked like the answer. The hall could provide fifty single study-bedrooms, teaching rooms and common rooms, and temporary buildings could be put in the grounds. Sketch plans and estimates were prepared by Mr. J. R. Piggott, the Chief Architect of Stoke-on-Trent Corporation. However, those plans fell through in April 1946, as did the possibility of a site at Hanchurch. The next hope was Trentham Park, and the University College Committee approved Trentham as the temporary site for the college. The *Sentinel* thought it an improvement on starting in the shadow of the Meaford power station, though considered the idea of a university housed in army huts was hardly in the tradition of the age-mellowed buildings of the ancient universities. A. L. Rowse, reviewing Pevsner's *Staffordshire* (published in 1974), wrote that Trentham 'would have made a more suitable *locale* for a university than Keele, with its nondescript campus', and added that Lindsay 'was no aesthete but a Scotch moralist'. That had nothing to do with it. The chance of Trentham fell through because it was appropriated by the National Coal Board. The need for more coal was paramount: accommodation was needed for nearly 2,000 miners, and Trentham could take over half of them. Stross had been in touch with the Ministry of Works and wrote to tell Horwood that Trentham had been lost; but he had also been in touch with the War Office and had been promised news about Keele Hall. That was the position at the end of August 1947.

At the beginning of the war Keele Hall and much of the immediate estate had been taken over by the military. As the Keele Estate agent explained to the District Valuer: 'Troops occupied Keele Hall on 3rd October 1939, and as it was a case of a telephone message and in walked the troops, no ingoing Record of Condition was prepared.' Now the Lord Mayor, Alderman Leason, told Horwood that according to the *Sentinel* Keele Hall was soon going to be vacated. 'I asked him why not try to see if the hall is suitable for a university?' However, it was not on the market, and the owner, Colonel Ralph Sneyd, did not wish to sell it: even though he did not live there anymore, he explained that his tax position was such that he would derive no financial benefit from a sale. Nevertheless, it looked worth following up, and in August 1947 Piggott, the architect, approached Goodwin, the agent. On 5th September the Lord Mayor and Horwood went to see Keele Hall, and that was probably enough to make up Horwood's mind. He was not the man to let such an opportunity slip, and a proposal to acquire Keele Hall and nearly 150 acres was put to Colonel Sneyd. Sneyd arranged to come up to Keele to discuss it with his agent on 13th September, and, in case Sneyd was agreeable to opening discussions, the Lord Mayor and Horwood, with Taylor (the Town Clerk) and Piggott in attendance, arranged to meet Sneyd and Goodwin at 3 o'clock at the agent's house. Harry Taylor described to Lady Scott what happened:

'At 3.25 p.m. Colonel Sneyd was closing the interview with a negative decision; Alderman Horwood said we would not take 'no' for an answer, and Colonel Sneyd asked for the talks to be adjourned while he listened on the radio in an adjoining room to a horse race in which he had a financial stake. The horse won and by 4.30p.m. the negotiations for the purchase of Keele Hall and grounds by the Stoke-on-Trent Corporation were completed. The deputation had no authority to conclude this deal and we far exceeded our legal functions in doing so... but speed was then the essence of the scheme and it was of vital importance that we could take possession of a property without delay.' This was another instance when speed and decisive action were essential, and the Vicar was on hand to see that the opportunity was seized, not lost. His position as Chairman of the local Labour Party was strengthened by his position as Chairman of the Finance Committee; and then as Chairman of the Works Department he was able to pour the resources of the City Public Works Department into Keele.

The following Wednesday the *Sentinel* reported that Colonel Sneyd was keenly interested in the proposal and had agreed to the opening of negotiations. The Stoke-on-Trent General Purposes Committee also unanimously approved the commencement of negotiations, and the proposal would go to the University Committee on 23rd September. That was the meeting which invited Lindsay to become Principal, and the Town Clerk reported that Stoke-on-Trent *had given instructions* for negotiations to acquire the site (author's emphasis: it was not until the following June that Moberly told Lindsay that the University Committee should proceed with the acquisition of Keele Hall). The District Valuer was instructed to open negotiations, and a subcommittee was set up to continue negotiations for the University College Committee. This was an encouraging development – a Hall and its estate, full of temporary buildings – and it was especially welcome news coming at the time when proposals for academic sponsorship were running into difficulties. A picture in the *Sentinel* showed Lindsay and Piggott looking at the plans of Keele Hall, but did not divulge that Lindsay said he never understood plans!

In fact, one needed to look at the Keele estate proposals with rose-tinted spectacles in order to maintain enthusiasm. The Keele Hall Subcommittee visited Keele on 13th November 1947.Without the help of the City Architects and Public Works

Department, and the Staffordshire County Council Parks Department, it would not have been possible to open the College in October 1950. Keele Hall was dirty and tatty, and the corrugated iron roof on part of it did nothing to enhance its style. The wear and tear and neglect inside required the greatest skill to restore it to its earlier condition. In addition, a new main entrance and porch was put in and staircases were replaced. The effects of military occupation had to be made good. The panelling and the main staircase had to be repaired; the former drawing room needed attention after a (?)chip pan fire and damage to the carvings in some of the panels; the floors needed cleaning – leading to the discovery of the decorative inlay surround. Outside it was a wilderness: a jungle had grown up round derelict huts, and there were the hazards of latrines and slit trenches. The site for houses 'was a blasted heath of brambles, tree stumps, old tin hats and petrol cans' (Mrs. Springall); 'conditions were frightful: it was shocking looking back' (Professor Cope); and later, 'the description of gumboots puts jollity on what was depressing' (Professor Lawlor). And yet there was also a lasting impression of a view seen through rose-tinted spectacles with a warm glow of nostalgia. Keele Hall had left the same impression on American servicemen stationed here in 1944. Lady Lindsay found the setting quite enchanting at first sight, even in the rain and drizzle of a grey day. Professor Gallie first saw it in September 1949 and liked what he saw. Keele Hall looked cold and derelict, and yet, he said: 'In fact, I liked it better that first day than I ever did again.'

But before that, there were problems of requisition. The troops had walked in on 3rd October 1939 and a 'Scheme of Dilapidations' had been prepared a few days later; but some of the Hall – the billiard room, offices and cellars – were let to Staffordshire County Council for the A.R.P. and were taken over by the War Department later. Moreover, some of the land which was wanted for the College had not been requisitioned, and some of the land which had was not required. Valuation was not easy either. It was to be valued at its pre-requisition state but on the values of January 1947, and on a restricted basis, disregarding any value other than that for the uses existing immediately before requisition: and this left Keele Hall to be valued for residential purposes only, or for demolition. Fire damage in 1940 would have little effect on the demolition value, but it meant that the District Valuer was looking for the value of Keele Hall before it was requisitioned but after the fire damage (for which there was an insurance claim). Compensation by the War Department for damage would also have to be negotiated. Four estate lodges were soon included in the negotiations, but the Clock House (the former stables, which had been converted into living accommodation for Colonel Sneyd in the 1930s) was not included; then part of the Clock House (which had been requisitioned in May 1940) was added to the negotiations in December 1947. Negotiations were not made simpler by having to deal not only with the agent, but with Colonel Sneyd in Wiltshire, trustees for the estate, the solicitors (Knight and Sons), the valuer called in by the estate (Louis Taylor) and the District Valuer; and the whole set against a background of post-war controls such as the Rent Restriction Act. Not surprisingly, the valuation was a difficult and vexed matter, and the gap between the figures put forward by each side was considerable.

There was, of course, much more to the business of running a large estate than could easily be disentangled in order to sell what could be regarded as the hub of it: the gas supply, for example. The gas main had been fractured by heavy army traffic, and the main had been cut off and sealed (on the Keele Hall side of Holly Lodge). The water supplies from the estate to the nearby farms would also need sorting out. And there were time-consuming, irritating details, such as the sale at auction of some panelling and doors (bought by the College), which had been removed in 1928 and 1939, and so were not included when Keele Hall was valued, and were not included in the sale. A visit to Keele Hall and the Clock House by the University College Committee in March 1948 prompted the agent to ask if they would be interested in the clock tower in the Clock House courtyard: 'I had a feeling that it would be nice to hear people saying 'Ah, there goes the University clock'.' In the past it had been wound up via the Head Gardener's house, so a separate access would have to be made to it to wind it up.

In April 1948 the many-sided correspondence took on aspects of a game of poker. There was a flurry of letters and telegrams, agent to solicitor, Sneyd and trustee to agent, trustee to agent, agent to trustee, District Valuer to Louis Taylor, Louis Taylor to agent, and agent to solicitor again. The Vicar, however, was not beset with doubts: he informed the Subcommittee that the District Valuer's valuation was expected soon and that the General Purposes Committee of Stoke-on-Trent Corporation would probably agree to purchase the Hall, and would desire the support of the County Council and Burton upon Trent Council. (The three authorities met at Stafford on 20th April and agreed on a 45% : 45% : 10% split.) For the squire of Keele, times had changed. As the agent wrote: 'What must be realised by Colonel Sneyd is that the 'Good old days' when one could say 'No' have gone – yes, they have been reversed – he now does what these people say must be done.' In July 1948 the gap between the parties was closed and the contract was agreed. Colonel Ralph Sneyd sold to the Lord Mayor, Aldermen and Citizens of the City of Stoke-on-Trent, Keele Hall, 154 acres, buildings, four lodges, drives, parkland, woodlands, fishponds, sewage water site, new reservoir and booster site, the Clock House, the old estate reservoir and the Whitmore Drive, all for £31,000, subject to the approval of the Ministries of Health and Education. (The four lodges were the 'Police Lodge' at the Newcastle entrance, occupied by the Staffordshire Constabulary; Holly Lodge and Drive Lodge on the drive to the village; and Keele Lodge at the village entrance.) After that there were still a lot of details to sort out about chattels and fixtures, both before and after contracts were exchanged – was there special apparatus for cleaning the chimneys? were certain items chattels and not fixtures? In addition there were still complications arising from the wartime occupation of the estate: the army was making claims for some installations and improvements on the estate, while Stoke-on-Trent was making counter-claims for the deterioration of the Hall. By now, time was pressing, and just as further negotiations might have got bogged down, Dr. Stross performed a valuable service to both the Secretary of State for War and the University College Committee: he was called to give urgent medical attention to Mr.

Shinwell at the War Office. After treating him, Stross raised the question of rival claims over Keele Hall, and suggested that the College would forgo any claims for dilapidation if the army did not claim payment for the huts; and that that would suffice for his professional fee! It was also a great help that the Clerk of Works at Keele was Mr. W. S. Perkins who, before joining the City Architects' Department, had been the Military Clerk of Works who supervised the erection of the camp and the military installations.

The purchase of Keele Hall and the estate was only a small proportion of the expenditure immediately necessary. Piggott estimated in April 1948 that it would cost £120,000 to renovate and adapt the Hall and other property on the estate to provide for 200 students and staff straight away, and that the total figure for the purchase and improvements necessary for 600 students would be £250,000.

Contracts were exchanged in April 1949 and derequisitioning was expected on 18th July. Lindsay took up the post of Principal on 1st July and moved into Keele Lodge while waiting for the Clock House to be made ready for him. The University College did not have legal existence yet, until the Charter was sealed. In May 1948 it was agreed that Lindsay and the clerks of the Local Authorities should consider a draft. Later, Harry Taylor described what happened: the clerks left it to Stoke-on-Trent; Parliament had risen, so the parliamentary agents could not help; so he and Miss Malbon did it. The petition for the grant of a charter was signed by Aldermen Horwood, Davies and Hutson on behalf of the three Authorities. (Horwood had been at the first meeting of the Exploratory Committee on 2nd May 1946, and Davies and Hutson had joined the Committee at its next meeting on 23rd July 1946.) The Charter was granted on 11th August 1949, and an 'Enabling Statute' gave the Principal authority to do what was necessary for up to three months after the opening of the first academic year.

Harry Taylor, still as Town Clerk of Stoke-on-Trent until he became the College's Honorary Legal Consultant, was already asking if the Keele Estate was interested in any further sales of land, and especially the remainder of the Clock House which was being used as the estate office and a gardener's cottage. The estate agent and solicitor regarded the college's appetite as insatiable, and thought the college's attitude was disturbing and disrupting to tenants; they deplored the loss of good agricultural land, especially as they felt that the offer for it would not be tempting enough. They made sharp comments to one another, but the reply was couched in more formal language: 'careful consideration... would be inadvisable to sell... urgent needs concerning agriculture... a policy which is wrong and out of touch with the realities of the present day... I much regret', etc. When this was reported to the Keele Hall subcommittee the Town Clerk was requested to arrange a conference with the Keele Estate Company 'in connection with this matter'.

The Keele estate was about to have major problems of its own, for on Christmas Day 1949 Colonel Sneyd died. Taylor suggested re-opening negotiations and went so far as to suggest that if any proposed purchases interfered with complete farms, then the college would be prepared to buy the whole of the farm affected, and to leave the land for agricultural use until it was required. The area envisaged for the college and its future development was 350 acres, leaving an agricultural belt to maintain the amenities and surroundings. Before the new owner, Major Howard could commit himself, he too died. His death, less than a year after Colonel Sneyd, dealt another body blow to the estate. Such plans as there had been to keep it going after Colonel Sneyd died could not survive double death duties. Parts of the estate had long since been sold; now nearly all the estate was broken up to pay death duties. Feelings were sensitive, and when two valuers acting on behalf of the college mistakenly called at a house which was not going to be sold, it required an apology from Lindsay: 'The Registrar is away. I am sorry the Valuer was so hamfisted', and then, added in hand-writing, 'I'll see it doesn't happen again.'

In April 1950 it was reported to the College Council that the Treasury had paid the College £32,055, and that arrangements were being made to transfer the property from Stoke-on-Trent City Council to the College. That was not the end of the problem, of course, but rather the beginning of more difficulties. As the Public Works Manager had written to Horwood in September 1949, 'The main trouble I foresee is in obtaining sufficient qualified craftsmen as and when required, and I think it will have to be faced that some 250-300 men may be required on the site.' Moreover, his timescale was short – completion of structural work, alterations and decoration by June 1950.

It is difficult to overestimate the importance of the part played by Harry Taylor. His whole-hearted support and his authority were crucial. He was a man with *gravitas*, good sense and practical ability. He encouraged the City Council to take respon-sibility even when the whole project looked in doubt. Keele Hall would not have been acquired without the City Council. He saw to the Charter. But it was the little things too – he looked after Lindsay and Horwood, sending a car for them, giving lunches, arranging hotels, and so on – and all done quietly and without fuss. Without Stoke-on-Trent there would be no Keele. And Harry Taylor serves to epitomise the backing and commitment which Stoke gave: the assistance from the architects, and the speed, quality and economy of the work undertaken by the Corporation Works Department actually made it all possible and let it all happen. This is not to diminish, nor to fail to recognise and acknowledge the role and participation of Staffordshire County Council and Burton upon Trent Borough Council. A *North Staffordshire* project, showing that wider commitment and support, must have carried more weight; and when financial considerations were of such importance, a burden shared was more easily borne. It is true that the 'pioneers' at Keele were the first staff and students, but they owed an enormous debt to the long list of people whose work was done before they came, and without whom there would have been nothing to pioneer.

Chapter 8

THE IMPROBABLE A REALITY

The grant of the Charter in August 1949 meant that Keele was in business – that is to say, as the University College of North Staffordshire. It is an interesting reflection of the times that the Charter specifically says: 'Female students shall be admissible to attend any of the courses of instruction established in the College, and women shall be eligible to sit on the Governing Body and on the Council of the College...'

As it said in the first *Prospectus*: 'The College has been granted the privilege of awarding its own degrees', a privilege shared in England with the ancient universities of Oxford and Cambridge, with Durham and London from the 1830s, Manchester (1851), Birmingham, Liverpool, Leeds, Sheffield and Bristol (1900 to 1909), Reading (1926), and Nottingham (1948). Southampton, Hull, Exeter and Leicester were to achieve full university status in the 1950s. The *Prospectus* went on to explain: 'This allows its authorities to regulate the course of studies in accordance with its objectives of giving to each student a broad education based upon an understanding of the heritage of civilisation, of present-day life, movements and conditions, and of the nature, methods and influence of the experimental sciences. To justify such a privilege, three Universities, called Sponsoring Universities, have agreed to appoint representatives to a specially constituted body called the Academic Council...' That was the all-important innovation, and it was a new feature in the control of a University institution. On that depended the College's freedom to initiate new courses and grant its own degrees – and hence the College's very existence. Nor was this a mere formality: the time it took to reach agreement with the three Sponsoring Universities – Oxford, Manchester and Birmingham – showed how important they regarded the issues involved. The Sponsoring Universities had an in-built majority on the Academic Council: it consisted of two members from Oxford (Sir Henry Clay, Warden of Nuffield College, and Miss L. S. Sutherland, Principal of Lady Margaret Hall), two from Manchester (Professor H. B. Charlton and Professor H. Graham Cannon), and two from Birmingham (Emeritus Professor J. G. Smith and Professor L. J. Russell); the Principal; three members of the Senate; and one more member of the teaching staff who was not a professor or a head of department. The Academic Council was going to be the guarantee of Keele's credibility in the university world, and so its powers and duties were far-reaching: 'to approve and initiate proposals for the whole curriculum and courses for the BA degree and other studies and to make representation with regard to new posts and new departments'. In addition, it had to approve nominations for the appointment of the Principal, Professors, Readers, Senior Lecturers, the Registrar and the Librarian, and the external examiners; it had powers to initiate discussions and to approve proposals on academic administration, to receive and consider annual reports from external examiners and to forward them with their observations to the College Council; and to consider the Principal's Annual Report and to forward it with their comments to the College Council *and* to the Sponsoring Universities. In addition, the Academic Council also appointed three representatives of the Sponsoring Universities on the College Council (see below). It is a sign of great goodwill and co-operation that the Academic Council and the College worked well together in such harmony. It was very supportive, though at times some thought it was intrusive on detail. It was doubtless salutary for the members of a young and inexperienced Senate to know that their decisions were being closely scrutinised. However, there was no provision for changing this arrangement until a new charter was granted – and yet at the same time, Keele's own staff were acting as external examiners elsewhere. This system continued until Keele achieved full university status in 1962.

Otherwise, the constitutional structure of the College followed the pattern generally found elsewhere:

> *The Senate* consisted of academic staff (including the Librarian), with the Principal as chairman. The powers of the Senate related primarily to academic matters, though it could always (and often did) 'discuss and declare an opinion on any matter whatsoever relating to the College'. For the first few years the Senate had about 22 members.

> *The Council* was composed largely of lay members. They were the President, three Vice-Presidents, and the Treasurer; plus representatives appointed by the Court of Governors (see below), the City of Stoke-on-Trent, Staffordshire County Council and Burton upon Trent County Borough; one member each appointed by the WEA, the Oxford Delegacy for Extra-Mural Studies, and the Universities of Oxford, Manchester, and Birmingham. The academic staff were represented by the Principal, five representatives of the Senate and one other member of the teaching staff – seven out of a total of 33 members. The Council was the executive body of the College, especially responsible for its financial affairs – and that gave it a wide interest in College matters. The office of President was largely honorary, and the first President was the Earl of Harrowby. The three Vice-Presidents were Aldermen Horwood, Davies and Hutson, and Horwood was elected chairman of Council.

> *The Court of Governors* was a large body of ex officio and representative members. It generally met once a year to receive reports and accounts, and to make certain appointments. The Chairman of Council would normally preside.

Newcastle-under-Lyme has played hardly any part even though Keele is actually in the Borough: but that reflected the hierarchy of local government, Newcastle being a municipal and not a county borough.

It may seem puzzling to readers who are not familiar with universities' constitutional arrangements that such bodies should put the executive running of their own affairs into the hands of lay people who have no vested interest in or contractual obligation to the institution concerned, and that remains the case. This is usual, outside Oxford and Cambridge, and generally the assistance, co-operation and goodwill generated by this device has been a great asset.

On 23rd June 1949 the University College Committee resolved that Horwood, the Registrar, the three Directors of Education and one from each of the three Local Authorities should proceed to make certain academic appointments as soon as the charter was approved; but it was then realised that the statutes made different provision and that the appointment of Professors and Heads of Departments was a matter for Lindsay on the recommendation of committees consisting of himself, three representatives of the University College Committee and two representatives from each of the sponsoring universities (so giving the sponsoring universities a majority vote). This was rectified at the meeting of the University College Committee on 22nd July, which also added members from the Local Authorities. In addition, the approval of the Academic Council was also necessary – though the Academic Council could not be instituted until the Senate had been created and had nominated its members; nor, until the Charter was granted, could Lindsay derive authority from the 'enabling statute'. But some academic matters needed urgent decisions. Some appointments had already been made, of course: Lindsay had accepted the University College Committee's offer to become Principal; Dr. W. A. Jenkins, the first Registrar, was appointed by the Committee from 1st January 1949, and Miss Marion Bailey, who was already typing for Keele, was seconded from the Town Clerk's office from 1st January 1949, to become the senior secretary in the university until she retired in December 1986. The appointment of Mr. S. O. Stewart as Librarian from 1st October 1949 was made by a subcommittee consisting of Lindsay, the Registrar, Aldermen Horwood, Davies and Hutson, and the Directors of Education. On 23rd July 1949, a Saturday, Lindsay called an informal meeting of the representatives of the Sponsoring Universities, the Directors of Education, Horwood and Jenkins: they agreed on entrance qualifications (broadly those generally accepted by other universities), and then discussed the academic courses. They agreed that the first year should consist of a common course of lectures supplemented by tutorial work, and that a further three years study 'was very desirable'. It was clearly essential to appoint professors and heads of departments straight away to prepare the courses, and it was also resolved that professors should be required to reside in houses on the estate (though it is not clear that the informal meeting had the authority to do so). It was agreed to advertise appointments in the following subjects:

English Language and Literature	Public Administration and Local Government
Modern Languages –	Geography
French or German	Mathematics
History	Physics
Economics	Chemistry
Political and Moral Philosophy	Biology
Philosophy	

Appointments in Social Science, Psychology and Education, and the choice of a third foreign language were to be discussed later (in some cases much later). Compared with the earlier scheme, Geology has disappeared, and there is no mention of Classics; but Geography has been included. There were not many details about the academic programme to send to applicants – since those appointed would be responsible for putting the courses together. All they were told was the following:

> 'One of the main objectives which it is hoped to achieve is to give to every graduate as wide an understanding as possible of the factors which have been operative in building up our present civilisation and of the forces that are current in the world today. Particular attention will be given to this in the first year. It is intended that the foundation studies taken before specialisation should be so presented as to give a comprehensible and integrated conception of the basic facts and principles of the main subjects to those who will not later specialise in such studies, while at the same time being a sound foundation for such specialisation. The relationship of particular studies to knowledge as a whole, the effect that the historical development of a subject had upon past civilisations and the part that it plays in present human activities, will be stressed in addition to the elucidation of its fundamental principles.

> 'It is desired to break down as far as possible any clear cut divisions between different branches of study and to ensure that each student has a sympathetic understanding of the functions and importance of all the main human activities. The Professors and Heads of Departments will have the responsibility of integrating their courses of studies on these lines...

> After a first year devoted to general studies, students will select a limited range of subjects in which they require more specialised knowledge, but it is hoped that the treatment will throughout avoid subject isolation and bring out the vital contacts of the subject with current life and thought.'

The philosophy is clear, even if the details of the courses had to be drawn up as they went along.

Next, students had to be selected and admitted, and by the time they arrived in October 1950 there needed to be in place teaching staff, academic courses, secretarial, technical and domestic staff, and above all, a library. Keele's library started with absolutely nothing! No books from Keele Hall or any benefactor, no shelves even to put them on. Insofar as the College existed, it consisted of offices over a public house in Aqueduct Street, by the side of the Town Hall in Stoke. A fair-size room with two desks in it and a cubby-hole off was the hub of it. When the new

Librarian, Stanley Stewart, arrived he was told by Jenkins: 'We'll have to get you a desk and a chair, but there is not much room. Whatever you do, don't bring any books in.' As Stewart commented to me later: 'By way of compensation there were no readers' – yet!

To create a University Library from nothing was an exciting, if daunting prospect – and a rare opportunity. Stewart had read Horwood's article in *Universities' Quarterly*. He was a Glasgow graduate and he fully supported the general philosophy. A report by the UGC over twenty-five years earlier had said that 'the character and efficiency of a university may be gauged by its treatment of its... library.' In Stewart it made an excellent start. He was a book man through and through. At a time of post-war shortages and quotas he was charged with obtaining such books *as could be obtained* in order to enable students to carry on their work from the opening of the College. (At least he was not required as the Librarian at Magdalene College, Cambridge, had been, centuries earlier, to assist the priest when celebrating mass in Chapel, and to serve the fellows at table in Hall.) The courses which students would be studying in their first year included 'the factors which have been operative in building up our present civilisation and of the forces that are current in the world today.' Beyond that he had little to go on, as the staff who would devise and teach those courses had still to be appointed.

He set about his task by travelling the country, going to second-hand bookshops, and combing the basements of public libraries and universities, searching for unwanted duplicate copies. He perused obituary notices, seeking out deceased academics whose books, and especially collections of periodicals, might be for disposal. The UGC doubted whether he could spend the money he had requested so quickly, and he was proud that they had underestimated his ability to spend other people's money. His greatest *coup* came a few years later when he acquired the library of the late Professor Charles Sarolea, the Professor of French at Edinburgh and Belgian Consul. Sarolea had become a bibliomaniac. G. K. Chesterton described his library as 'one of the wonders of the world, not to say monstrosities of the world'. It was scattered over two large houses in Edinburgh, with a huge number of duplicate copies, sets broken, and books stacked three and four deep on shelves, in cupboards and on the stairs. It included vast numbers of pamphlets. Estimates of its size varied from 150,000 to 300,000. A number of librarians and academics had already had their pick before the Librarian at Edinburgh University suggested to Stewart that he might like to see it. It was too big for most libraries to cope with it. Stewart went to view it with Dr. J. H. Broome (later Professor of French). They spent three days selecting enough books to fill a railway container with about five tons of books. This only whetted Stewart's appetite, at a time when other would-be purchasers were put off by the time and space required. He made an offer to the trustees, showing great entrepreneurial skill in acquiring the library under conditions which required delicate diplomacy and speed. Removing the books from Edinburgh without delay was part of the agreement. The railway was not ideal. Pickfords did not have enough vans, and anyway it would not be safe to fill removal vans with books. British Road Services found it difficult to envisage just how many books he was talking about, and they fixed a price per ton, sending a 12 ton lorry a day for a fortnight to shift just over 100 tons. The books were stored in an empty Methodist church school in Newcastle, waiting to be sorted, and then, from 1957, at Madeley in a disused brick-works. Until long after he retired in 1981 Stewart was still sorting those books and, by a judicious sale of the duplicates he not only in effect acquired about 125,000 volumes for the library for nothing but produced a further £100,000 for the library as well. But that was still to come. 'My Goodness, he did an excellent job!' Professor Cope told me; and Professor Lawlor said that he could not imagine someone who had done more and suffered more.

On 11th November 1949 the first meeting of the Court of Governors was held in the Council Chamber of Stoke-on-Trent. That the meeting was held there and that Hor-wood was chairman indicates how big a part the city had played in the founding of the College. Indeed, until the granting of the Charter the City Council had met all the expenses incurred. This close interest continued with the appointment of Mr. A. P. Walker, the City Treasurer, as the College's Honorary Treasurer and the appoint-ment of Mr. H. Taylor as the Honorary Legal Consultant. Horwood and Walker were to be the only recipients of honorary BA's from the University College, and Walker and Taylor later received honorary MA's from the University.

This meeting of the Court of Governors provided an opportunity to give an account of what was happening to a fairly wide local audience. It was gratifying to report a generous endowment of £3,000 from Mrs. E. W. Montford of Market Drayton, to celebrate a visit by H.R.H. Princess Elizabeth to Stoke-on-Trent. As a consequence of her gift, Mrs. Montford was made the first life member of the Court after Colonel Ralph Sneyd. An embarrassing item was the report that application forms and papers had been lost 'relevant to the Chairs in Modern Languages, etc'. Twelve chairs had been advertised for replies by mid-October (not yet including a chair of Education). How much had been lost? Mountford's book in 1972 said: 'All the applications for the first group of Chairs vanished and a further advertisement had to be issued', and this was compounded in Professor Flew's review of the book when he referred to the Registrar as 'ever warm in memory for that greatest triumph of losing all the applications for all the first Chairs to be advertised'. But they were not all lost, nor was it ever established who lost them. The re-advertisement said: 'A bundle of papers containing all the applications for the following Professorships in the College have been lost: 1. Modern Languages. 2. Biology. 3. Public Administra-tion and Local Government. 4. Geography.' There were suggestions that they might have blown out of Lindsay's car, or been left somewhere by mistake, or buried in the mountain of paper in a small, very busy and overcrowded office. They certainly never came to light when the office moved. Was it the Registrar or was it the Prin-cipal? Each was certain it was the other.

The report on Keele Hall and the other buildings on the estate will have been familiar enough to early generations of students but it must come as a surprise fifty years later. Keele Hall was described as well suited for administrative offices, teaching rooms, and living accommodation for domestic staff, guests, and some unmarried members of the teaching staff. There were living rooms on the top floor, twenty fairly large rooms on the third floor, administrative and staff rooms on the principal floor, together with the Library, a Reading room, the Senate room, a general lecture hall and concert room, and the Senior Common Room. Registry staff found themselves working in the conservatory. The ground floor/basement provided room for an accounts office, a general office, telephone exchange, a book shop, a dark room, store rooms and cloak rooms. Books were spreading wherever they could be found room.

In the grounds there were over a hundred temporary buildings left behind by the army. About eighty of them were going to be used, and they had an estimated life of about ten years. Sixty huts, which had concrete foundations, wooden walls and asbestos compound roofs, were to be used as students' residences. They measured about 60 feet x 20 feet, and would each provide five bed-sitting rooms. By October 1950 it was planned to have one group of sixteen huts ready for women students, and another group of fourteen huts ready for men students. The remaining huts would be ready for the following year, and after that there would have to be some new buildings. Nineteen bungalows were to be adapted for staff accommodation. Two large, triple Nissen huts were to be used, one for the Students' Union, refectory and chapel, and the other as a garage and gymnasium. Two concrete buildings outside Keele Hall (on what had been an Italian garden) were used for offices (and then for the Geology Department, and later still for the Architects' and the Estates and Buildings offices). It was, of course, an enormous help that the military had installed all the utility services. Work which had to be done, therefore, included the repair and adaptations to Keele Hall, including central heating and electricity; the adaptation of the huts and bungalows; and the erection of a refectory, new kitchen, and science laboratories. In addition, permanent houses were needed for the teaching staff. It was still a time of shortages, and licences to build houses were required from the Local Authorities, so preference being 'meted out to strangers', as a letter in the *Sentinel* put it, was not altogether popular: 'let them get in line like the rest of us.'

The report given to the Court of Governors on the estate and grounds said: 'Work on clearing up the estate is proceeding. It is expected that the playing fields will be ready by the opening of the session, and, while it may take some considerable time to restore the whole of the estate to good order and condition, the general clearing up will have reached such a stage that normal College activities can be carried on. There is a great deal of repair, adaptation and new construction of buildings to be done, but we expect the essential buildings to be ready by the end of September 1950. Some of the work will be done by direct labour provided by the Stoke-on-Trent City Council, but the greater part of it will be placed out on contract.'

It required optimism when looking at the immediate future, but it rested on the outstanding achievement of the University College Committee, summed up as follows at the meeting in November 1949: 'By its untiring efforts and its refusal to be disheartened by objections and difficulties, success was finally achieved. Its activities have been a lesson in co-operation and an example of how loyalty to a common objective can unite people of differing views in a successful effort to make the improbable a reality.'

UNIVERSITY COLLEGE OF NORTH STAFFORDSHIRE

PROSPECTUS

for

Session 1950-51

All enquiries to be addressed to :
   The Registrar,
      University College of North Staffordshire,
         Keele Hall,
            Keele,
               Stoke-on-Trent.

Chapter 9

LINDSAY'S KEELE

The University College of North Staffordshire was truly Lindsay's Keele. Just as the spirit was his, so now just as surely he shaped the outward and visible form. The selection of staff, the creation of courses, the admission of the first students and, above all, the 'Keele Idea' all bore his mark.

The Court of Governors had met in November 1949. The Senate would first meet in February 1950, and the Council in March 1950. In the meantime Lindsay asked the University College Committee to continue meeting (and particularly the Keele Hall Subcommittee) and it did so up to January 1950.

The Academic Council got down to business without delay. Whilst waiting for the Senate to come into existence and to appoint members, Lindsay invited the three Directors of Education of the Local Authorities to attend. The informal meeting in July (already mentioned) had made a start. It was this body, comprising Lindsay, the representatives of the Sponsoring Universities, Jenkins and the three Directors of Education, which laid down the framework for Keele's courses. It agreed the structure of the degree course and the way subjects were grouped in the Arts, the Social Sciences and the Sciences. At first, some subjects were included in two groups: History, and Political and Moral Philosophy were in both the Arts and the Social Sciences; and Geography and Mathematics were in both the Social Sciences and the Sciences. There was a tentative decision that the two principal subjects which students were to read after the first-year course should be taken from different groups. The final scheme was drafted by Lindsay and Jenkins, and was agreed in January 1950. It has stood the test of time extraordinarily well. In addition, the *four*-year degree course was confirmed in January. The UGC and the Ministry of Education had no objections, and the LEAs were prepared to make scholarships and grants tenable for four years, so there was no objection on financial grounds. Arising from this came the *concurrent* teacher training course, and consequently the decision to appoint a Professor of Education to work out the details. It was also agreed to appoint heads of departments of Classics and Geology, but not at professorial level. The subjects students could take were as follows:

A (*Arts*)	B (*Social Sciences*)	C (*Sciences*)
Latin, Greek	Economics	Mathematics
French	Political Institutions	Physics
German	Geography	Chemistry
English Language and Literature	Social Studies	Biology
History	Political and Moral Philosophy	Geology
Philosophy	Psychology	

After the first-year course, any subject could be taken as a *principal* subject (for three years) or as a *subsidiary* subject (for one year); but Psychology was available only at subsidiary level, Latin and Greek could not be taken together as principal subjects in the first instance, and Philosophy and Political and Moral Philosophy counted as a single principal subject. The concurrent course in Education was counted as a subsidiary subject in the Social Sciences. Students were to take *five* subjects: at least two at principal level and at least two at subsidiary level, and must include at least one subject from each of the three groups of subjects. Within a few years the number of subjects students took was reduced to *four*, to include at least one from the Arts and Social Sciences combined, and at least one from the Sciences. That is the structure which has been known to most Keele students.

The Academic Council also considered the question of research degrees because Dr. Vick from Manchester, one of the applicants for the chair of Physics, had sought re-assurances before submitting his application. The Registrar had replied that 'teaching and research should go hand in hand and while we are in the first place concentrating upon the general foundation work for University students we should regard it as a calamity if the fullest facilities were not given for research and the Professors were not keenly interested in that side of the University's activities.' The Academic Council suggested that, in due course, graduates might pursue research work in the College for a research degree which would be awarded by one of the Sponsoring Universities (as indeed happened), and the Academic Council reassured candidates for chairs that the matter was under consideration. It was also suggested that pending the setting up of research laboratories at Keele, it might be possible for professors to make arrangements to continue their research with their present universities. That suggestion probably seriously underestimated the amount of time the new professors would have to devote to Keele.

The new professors were appointed in February 1950, and are listed at the end of this chapter. They would take up their appointments full-time in October. In the meantime they were to give a lot of their time and effort to Keele. 'I want to try and get all the newly-elected Professors to come for discussions about our plans, etc.', Lindsay wrote, and they all came to Stoke for the weekend of 11th-12th February. Lindsay asked Stewart, the Librarian, to go to Stoke station to meet them, and gave him thumb-nail sketches of them. (Unfortunately, neither Lindsay nor Stewart committed these descriptions to paper.) What were they like? At their first meeting together, they must have fitted C. P. Snow's title *Strangers and Brothers*. They came over to Keele, and had their photograph taken in the courtyard by the *Sentinel* photographer.

There were thirteen of them. They were young: eleven of them were in their thirties. Sneddon (30), Williams (31) and Lawlor (32) were the youngest; Beaver (43) and Teale (49) were the oldest. They were all married. Several of them already knew one another. There were four from Manchester (Gemmell, Springall, Teale and Vick), two from Oxford (Finer and Lawlor); and two from Queen's, Belfast (Blake and Williams). The others came from the London School of Economics, Leeds, Swansea, Glasgow and Cardiff. Not surprisingly, the mosaics of academic career paths had crossed from time to time. Springall and Stewart (invariably known as Campbell Stewart) had both been to Colfe's Grammar School, London; Beaver and Blake had been to Kilburn Grammar School, where Blake was Beaver's fag; Finer, Gallie and Teale had spent time at Balliol, and so knew Lindsay already; and Chambers, Gemmell and Sneddon had all been to Glasgow. But at Keele there was no 'core' of Oxford, Manchester or Scots: they were all 'Keele' from the start, young, keen and with total commitment. None of them had held chairs before. Beaver was the most senior academically, as the Sir Ernest Cassel Reader in Geography at the London School of Economics. Sneddon, the youngest, already had a DSc from Glasgow. (Cope, too, had a DSc, from Manchester). Five of them were, or had been Senior Lecturers. Several had seen active war service (Chambers was awarded the MBE, and Gallie the Croix de Guerre); others had been engaged in war work, and Vick had been awarded the OBE. Many of them had therefore held positions of responsibility at a comparatively early age, but the War had cut across their academic careers and, apart from Beaver, they were largely unknown on the wider academic stage. Lindsay said that he deliberately did not want to appoint big names who might be set in their ways: a new concept was at the heart of what he wanted and he hoped to mould them to his ideas. 'I haven't always got the men I really wanted, but I think we have got a very good team' was Lindsay's summary. That team included the two secretaries who appear in the photograph – Mrs. Morton, the Principal's secretary, and Miss Bailey, the Registrar's secretary, then age 21. Already a year since she had been taking dictation from Lord Lindsay at Keele and then typing it in her office in the Town Hall until Mrs. Morton joined the staff. 'They did a stupendous job' is how Professor Cope described them to me many years later.

Lindsay was something of a father figure, and he called his new professors 'my children': at 69 he was, after all, nearly forty years older than some of them. Jenkins was ten years younger than Lindsay. He was a scientist by training with a DSc from Sheffield. He had spent most of his life in the Indian Education Service and was Director of Organisation and Methods and Secretary to the Government of Bengal. 'The recent Dominion Universities' Conference at Oxford... made me realise afresh the urgency of defining the functions of a University in the light of present day conditions and needs, and of forming policy accordingly', and having heard about the proposals for Keele, he had written to Lindsay. He was enthusiastic about the aims of the College. When he arrived at the office of the 'University College of North Staffordshire – Proposed' in 1949 there was an enormous amount to be done, and no precedents for guidance. He was very gentlemanly and kindly, most forgiving, and he inspired affection. He had to deal with almost everything: the Local Authorities, the Sponsoring Universities, the Ministry of Education, the Ministry of Health, the Regional Petroleum Officer, building licences, builders, the appointment of new staff, and buying furniture. He had to sort out which professor had which office, which department had which hut, and which staff had which bungalow. He drafted the course outline, interviewed students for admission, chased up book lists and ordered equipment. (Under the heading 'Equipment for Tutorials' it is interesting to note the state of art and the price of the technology in 1950: Professor Sneddon requested 'a small inexpensive calculating machine capable of performing the operations of addition, subtraction, multiplication and division. An elaborate electric machine is not necessary... The cost should not be more than about £70.') Furthermore, Jenkins had to move the office from Stoke to Keele, and to cope when Lindsay was ill with a cerebral thrombosis in August and September 1950, just weeks before the first term started. Building delays, government regulations and the bad weather were beyond his control. Not surprisingly there was a great deal of hassle. Jenkins became the focus of uncertainty, exasperation and blame. He had not previously worked in an English university, except as a research student at the Cavendish Laboratory in Cambridge. In the event, he was not a good match as a Registrar working with Lindsay as Principal. In 1953 Jenkins resigned. The University of Dacca had sent him a pressing and urgent invitation to return as their Vice-Chancellor, a position he had held twenty years earlier.

A lot of administrative details were taken on by Professor Vick. He was elected to be the first Vice-Principal. He was exceptionally efficient, and he was a key figure in settling small, irritating details. He also quickly took an important part in major administrative questions – quinquennial estimates and negotiations with the UGC. Lindsay said quite simply: 'I don't know what I should have done without him.'

To start with, the Heads of Departments not only had to put together their courses on their own: they also had to teach them on their own. They therefore had to have unusually wide interest in their subjects. Beaver, for example, said that Geography was 'about the whole world, about all aspects of the environment, both natural and man-made, and about people.' He was at the forefront of environmental conservation forty years before it became fashionable. Chambers had degrees from France and Germany. Gemmell had degrees in botany and zoology. Sneddon spanned pure and applied mathematics and was later elected a Fellow of the Royal Society, as was his successor at Keele, Douglas Jones. Springall could lecture at any undergraduate level in virtually any area of organic or physical chemistry. All had their ambitions for their own departments, and also had to put together the first-year courses as a matter of urgency, to be followed immediately by the principal and subsidiary courses. They would all have to participate in the committees necessary for running the College, and there were also pressing problems of housing. For the time being, they all had their present full-time jobs to do elsewhere; fortunately, they shared an infectious enthusiasm, described by Finer in the following words: 'To be associated from the start with so novel, almost revolutionary a venture in education – to have such scope for energy and creating at any age, is something which I am sure hardly occurs once in a lifetime, and I cannot conceal my delight that such an opportunity should be granted me.' Next they had to create their departments, and their enthusiasm spread. Finer's department of Political Institutions was, perhaps, the most remarkable. Eight of the staff he appointed went on to chairs – Bealey, Berrington, Blondel, Coles, Haywood, Hennock, Richardson and Rolo. Another member of his department was the anglophile John Eros, who had earlier been the Minister in the Hungarian Legation in London. Beaver built up what was to grow into one of the largest Geography Departments in the country; and, with Mrs. Elsie Beaver as Map Curator, created one of the most important map collections (much of which was dispersed and disposed of in 1998). From Mathematics, Macbeath, Noble, Fröhlich, Wallace and Russell went to chairs, and from Economics Lees, Hunter and Mills. Campbell Stewart was building up a new style of Education Department, and his team included Frank Halliwell, 'one of the four or five most influential chemical educators in the world' (*The Independent*), and William Walsh who within a few years was Professor of Education and then Professor of Commonwealth Literature at Leeds. Because all undergraduates at Keele took a four-year course, teacher training was integrated into the last three years of the course with teaching practice arranged during university vacations. This meant that the Diploma (or later, the Certificate course) did not take an extra year, and so had more appeal to students; and also, because the course was integrated into students' other studies, it ensured that at Keele the Education Department could not be marginalised.

If, as Campbell Stewart once said to me, Keele was like being in a new second form in a big school, what of Lindsay? He was a father-figure and was central to everything. Some wanted a different sort of leadership from him. He liked discussion. He was good at throwing out ideas and he enjoyed watching argument; and that could sometimes be interpreted as 'making mischief', or what Gallie described as 'acrimonious discussions'. Sneddon, on the other hand, thought it demonstrated they were a group of people passionately interested in the problems of creating a new university, and the fact that discussions were lively suggested instead that they wanted to play an active part in the process and not merely play the game of 'follow my leader'. As Jenkins described Lindsay to one of the newly-appointed professors: 'He is as you have already probably discovered, rather fond of pulling people's legs and you will very quickly get used to his remarks and comments. His main objective is to break down completely, if possible, the definite lines between the different subjects and to try and ensure that there are the closest bonds governing the different approaches to knowledge as a whole.'

Sometimes, as when he had been seeking the support of the Sponsoring Universities, Lindsay was liable to assume that he was speaking to people who already shared his ideas, and he did not set out to convert others to what he thought was self-evident. He could be autocratic. He could be off-putting. He was very good at asking fundamental and awkward questions – which could be both disconcerting and also very useful in the early Senate discussions as a means of moulding views together. He was a man with a vision still, and it was a great strength of his leadership that having made imaginative suggestions, he encouraged others to work on his ideas. He was sociable and would join staff for coffee in the Senior Common Room; and he put considerable effort into being part of Keele village life, which was much appreciated. Nothing was too much trouble for him – he wrote about Keele and his ideas, he entertained visitors, attended speech days, distributed prizes, joined local committees and addressed meetings: it was all part of his preaching about Keele.

What was the 'Keele Idea' which is so closely associated with Lindsay? Its starting point is Lindsay's philosophy which I have tried to describe earlier. The principles are clear, but then it becomes difficult to describe. When I discussed it with some of the founding professors I suggested that it seems like a smoke ring – easy to see but difficult to grasp – and they did not disagree. There are different ways the ideas could be put into practice – and putting the ideas into practice was what the courses at Keele aimed to do – and so later there developed different interpretations of what the 'Keele Idea' should be. Moreover, once the basic principles are accepted, then the way they are put into effect can evolve to meet changing conditions. Social democracy, Lindsay believed, rested on the need to understand society and society's values. To do that he thought it was necessary to rediscover society's 'common culture' – *rediscover* because he considered that the common culture which should bind society together had been lost. From the examination of that common culture there should then emerge a common awareness. That is what Lindsay regarded as vital, as a corrective to the specialisation which had destroyed the common understanding on which enlightened leadership rested. An appreciation of that common culture is therefore at the nub of the whole 'Idea': there needs to be a self-understanding society. The problem was just how to do that; and *how* to do it changes. It was a theme which Professor Frankenberg re-examined in his Inaugural Lecture as Professor of Sociology in 1970. By 1950 Lindsay was inveighing strongly against specialisation and departmentalism – 'the curse of modern universities' with 'momentous and most evil consequences'. He wrote in a paper for the International Conference of University Professors of English in August 1950: 'My mind at present is bound to be full of the educational experiment in which I am busily engaged in North Staffordshire in trying to overcome the specialisation of our modern university teaching. We are trying to ensure that all our students shall have a common background of knowledge and understanding before they embark on their more specialised studies. We have arranged a General Course which is to occupy their first year, and which would include a course common to all on 'The History of

Western Civilisation', 'Modern Institutions' and 'The Empirical Sciences'... We must somehow devise a university education which both gives students understanding of spiritual and social values and allows them to pursue their own particular expertness.' It was the same theme as in his earlier *A Plan for Education*: 'We must give our minds to getting the right balance between specialisation and expert knowledge on the one hand and a wide outlook and general understanding on the other', and explains the importance he set on 'seeing things together'. This is at the heart of the Keele Idea. This was the end for which the university became the means, and so strong were Lindsay's convictions that the labour of founding the College was much greater than it might have been had simply founding another college been the prime aim. Professor Teale and Professor Gallie probably understood and sympathised with Lindsay's ideas more than most. In 1958 Professor Teale wrote a Memorandum on the Aims of the Founders of the College in which he said:

> 'It should, however, now be clear, firstly, that there could have been a University College of North Staffordshire of the conventional type due to open its doors in October 1948 had not Lindsay insisted, against the wishes of Tawney and Moberly, on the power of granting its own degrees in order to experiment in a new form of university education. Secondly, that if the experiment had consisted simply in the sponsoring by Birmingham, Manchester and Oxford of a curriculum providing for a common Foundation Year course plus a double honours course in which science at least at subsidiary level was required, there might have been an important addition to similar courses available at other universities, but there would not have been that 'new and fruitful experiment in university education' on which Lindsay had set his heart. What he had in mind was not another variation on the theme of general studies then being canvassed in other universities, but *a new conception of the function of a university in a modern democratic industrialised society* [author's italics]. Other universities would continue to produce the specialists whose technical language and professional interests tend to place them apart from the rest of the community. But this College would aim at producing graduates who by pursuing 'an integrated course of study in which specialisation along one line of enquiry [is] backed by more general studies' might be expected to glimpse the interconnectedness of all branches of human enquiry, and experience the sense of belonging to a *community* of scholars privileged to exercise their various talents, but obliged to serve the needs of the wider community by acquiring the knowledge and skill required 'to close the gap between the natural leader and the expert and the specialist'. In general, the College was to serve as a means of reuniting a society divided as much by lack of a common medium of communication as by industrial strife, political and religious differences.'

In 1963 Teale also drew attention to the explicit claim made by Lindsay and re-affirmed by each of his successors up till then, that the College existed *primarily* [author's emphasis] to offer 'each student a broad education based upon an understanding of the heritage of Western Civilisation, the development of modern society, and the nature, methods and influences of the experimental sciences'.

Lindsay's ideas have often received approval in principle, even if not support in practice. Following a Government Green Paper in 1985 on *The Development of Higher Education* into the 1990s, the universities' collective response said: 'The nation must have graduates who will staff the professions like medicine and law; can understand and manage the social and economic challenges of the technological revolution; who have a knowledge of foreign languages and cultures; who can sustain the traditions, heritage and values of British society and Western culture; have the skills to teach the young and to provide continuing education; and more generally who have benefited from a rigorous training of the mind.' In short, it was a ringing endorsement of what had earlier seemed to be a voice crying in the wilderness.

The mechanism of putting the 'Keele Idea' into practice was the problem facing the new professors in February 1950. They had until October to come up with a solution in the form of a detailed curriculum and lecture course. Gallie believed that Lindsay had a perfectly clear idea of what he wanted, and that his plans were thwarted by those brilliant but irresponsible professors. But if so, the perfectly clear idea was not published. Sneddon's view was different, that the detail was vague in Lindsay's mind. He wrote to Lady Scott: 'He certainly gave me that impression at the time I was interviewed for the Chair of Mathematics in November 1949... It always seemed to me that Lord Lindsay knew what he wanted the end-product to be and built up the mechanism for obtaining it by having a long series of lively discussions.'

Another matter on which there has been dispute about Lindsay is his attitude to research and this, too, has bearing on Keele. It has been said by those who knew him at Keele that he did not understand about research. On the face of it that would be extraordinary, especially in the light of his record as Vice-Chancellor of Oxford. In the *Dictionary of National Biography* Christopher Hill, the eminent historian who was a Fellow and Tutor at Balliol in Lindsay's time and was Master 1965-78, says that Lindsay sometimes expressed his hatred of narrow specialisation as dislike of research which he regarded as a form of self-indulgence tolerable only if subordinated to the requirements of teaching. Gallie wrote that Lindsay was almost a fanatic about the need, virtue and *primary* duty of *teaching* [author's emphasis] in university life. Lindsay regarded that as self-evident. Gallie cites a science professor at Keele who said to Lindsay that he had virtually no time to give to his own research: 'What do you want to do research for?' asked Lindsay. A similar point was made in an article at the time of Keele's twenty-first anniversary by Springall and Rolo. When Christopher Hill reviewed Gallie's book in The *Oxford Magazine* he seems to take a stronger line than in the DNB and wrote of Lindsay's 'hatred of research *as an end in itself* [author's emphasis]; but Hill's words are carefully chosen. Gemmell wrote to Sir James Mountford that Lindsay did not appreciate the science professors' need for research, and in a lecture in 1968 Campbell Stewart, then Vice-Chancellor, said: 'He did not see the University College as a place for research – original work that arose out of teaching, yes, but research as a separate enterprise of importance to the intellectual health and reputation of both the dons and the College he did not see. Science colleagues in particular found this difficult to understand and hard to bear, except that there was not much time to undertake research anyway. The point I am making here is that Keele was primarily a teaching College and research was added by determined dons.'

Even so, other founding professors did not share these views about Lindsay. At the time, of course, the hard facts of life meant that there *had* to be an emphasis on teaching, and Williams (Economics) was clear that Lindsay did not want *teaching* to suffer if there was a clash between teaching and research. Vick (Physics) had specifically sought an assurance about research before he submitted his application form, and he quickly built up his research team when he was here. He told me that Lindsay was not against research but rather was opposed to narrow, pedestrian research in both the arts and the sciences and was certainly against narrow research being dominant. This, of course, was another manifestation of Lindsay's views on narrowness of thought leading to isolation and to the faults he perceived in society. Lindsay preferred to think in terms of scholarship.

Two factors have contributed to these different views about Lindsay. Firstly, he did not emphasize what he took to be self-evident. Teale wrote in 1963 that research was the life-blood of the science departments, and though the arts and social sciences were less dependent on postgraduate research, they too could maintain a high level of teaching only if it was backed by concurrent research, and that this Lindsay took for granted. Years earlier, in the *Report of the Commission on Christian Higher Education in India* (1931) Lindsay had stressed the importance of teachers undertaking 'original work' and 'scholarly research'. Secondly, his sometimes brusque questioning of a proposition could easily lead to a misunderstanding. The Librarian's view (and he got to know Lindsay well in the year before the College started) was that the purpose of Lindsay's 'pooh-pooh' was not to discourage but to elicit more information in order to strengthen a case. Cope shared this view (though added that he thought Lindsay's heart was not in research) and Vick, too, supported the Librarian's interpretation. Lady Scott, Lindsay's daughter and biographer, said to me that she had no doubt that her father understood about research and recognised the importance for teaching that teachers should pursue research: but that he certainly had no time for what seemed to him to be 'pseudo-research'. That probably sums up the case.

Some of the differences of view about Lindsay by the founding professors reflect their own rather than Lindsay's views. Gallie made a very interesting observation about his colleagues, drawing a distinction between those who were more or less already converted to Lindsay's ideas, and those whom Gallie regarded as more or less unconvertible. He conceded that it was not always the fault of the unconverted if they sometimes regarded Lindsay as hopelessly vague and starry-eyed – Lindsay did not tell them plainly enough or ardently enough or often enough of the main motive which impelled him, and he did not realise that his vague and sketchy remarks could be interpreted to mean different things.

Gallie also drew another distinction – between 'loyalists' and 'dissidents'. These were not the same groupings as 'converts' and 'non-converts', but he did not name names. Nor was there unanimity amongst those involved as to who was in which grouping. One view was that these were misnomers. In any case, different issues divided colleagues differently. It made for interesting gossip, but one cannot finally pigeon-hole all of the founding professors. It must be regarded as an 'individual view'.

These, then, were the new 'strangers and brothers' who met together in February 1950 for what was later described as a strenuous weekend – the thirteen professors, the Librarian and the Registrar, with Lindsay in the chair. Lindsay explained the constitutional position: this was just a 'Conference of Professors'. They discussed housing, finances, staff and syllabus, followed by an informal meeting about the syllabus that evening. On Sunday they met as the 'Senate'. Professor Stewart was able to report that they had reached general agreement on the first-year syllabus, to cover the Heritage of Western Civilisation, the Experimental Sciences, and Modern Democratic Institutions. There would be ten lectures a week on two parallel courses, and each week students would take one tutorial in one subject from each of the three groups of subjects (i.e. three tutorials a week) per term, to give a total of three subjects from each group during the year. It was a remarkable achievement to reach agreement in just a few hours. (Those who have been engaged in seemingly never-ending discussions about subsequent revisions of the Foundation Year can only marvel that general agreement was reached within a few hours.) They also agreed that the admission of students in October 1950 should be left to Lindsay and Jenkins, and the results proved very satisfactory. They met again two weeks later, and they continued to meet every four or five weeks until the beginning of July. Five more early appointments joined the early Senate meetings. Readers were appointed in Classics (Mr. Charlton) and Geology (Dr. Cope) as heads of departments. Two Wardens were appointed – Robert Rayne, a classics scholar and soccer blue to be Warden of the men's hostel ('rather a pompous description of a collection of huts', Lindsay said), and Mary Wilson, who had been the Chief Education Officer for Teacher Training in North Rhine Westphalia with the High Commission for Germany, as Warden of the women's hostel. Rayne and Wilson helped with interviewing applicants for admission. And R. B. Henderson was appointed to fill the gap of the part Christianity had played in the history of Western Europe. He was about Lindsay's age, and had been a mathematics scholar, a Lieutenant-Colonel, a headmaster, and then Reader in Religious Education at Oxford. Further academic appointments would be made from January 1951.

Of the founding staff, two had a particular knowledge of North Staffordshire. Beaver had made a survey of derelict land in Staffordshire for the Ministry of Town and Country Planning, and Cope had made the geological survey of the North Staffordshire coalfields for the Geological Survey of Great Britain. Cope's advice was therefore available when Vick and Cope met the National Coal Board to discuss the

Coal Board's plans for mining under the estate. Buildings needed to be planned in the knowledge of the dangers of subsidence. Keele Hall, which had virtually been rebuilt in the mid-19th century on the proceeds from mining royalties, was no longer protected by an earlier obligation to leave a pillar under it, but the Coal Board accepted responsibility for damage to buildings erected before 1918. Years later, Cope's advice about the siting of Barnes Hall was not heeded, and one block of residences subsequently had to be demolished.

Although most members of the Senate were occupied with their own full-time jobs elsewhere, they nevertheless took full advantage of their right to 'discuss and declare an opinion on any matter whatsoever relating to the College'. This included the site for the refectory, houses, tennis courts, the allocation of bungalows, the appointment of a chaplain, a nursery school for children, lecture hours, secretaries for heads of departments, the 'daily routine' once students came, of breakfast, lunch and dinner (but students to make their own arrangements for tea), and domestic help at home (@ 1s 9d per hour, with the usual cup of tea and insurance contributions). At the end of April wives were invited to Keele to discuss plans for houses with the architect.

Although there were a lot of army huts and bungalows for immediate use, there still needed to be some academic buildings for teaching. However much could be squeezed into Keele Hall and the temporary buildings in October 1950, there was the prospect of doubling the number of students in October 1951. A start was made with 'Orlit' huts as laboratories for Chemistry and Physics. Orlit huts were 70 feet x 32 feet, with steel stanchions at 8 feet intervals, and with walls of concrete slabs made out of cement and blast furnace slag. Unfortunately, before even the first students were admitted, finances were being squeezed: the chairman of the UGC visited the College in July 1950 and brought with him not gifts for the infant college but demands for economies. It was not going to be possible to build a separate lecture hall for first-year students, and accommodation could not be provided for more than an annual intake of 150 students. Consequently the planned size of the College was reduced from 800 to 600, and the proposed 3-unit Orlit huts for Chemistry and Physics were reduced to 2-unit huts. When Lindsay and Springall went to see the UGC they were asked about priorities, which suggested a further financial squeeze. At least Chemistry and Physics had the prospect of a building each: Geology, Biology and Geography had to manage with rooms in Keele Hall for the first year. Then an Orlit block could be built for Biology, and the two concrete buildings on the south side of Keele Hall which were being used as offices could be given to Geology. These two concrete buildings were on the site of what had been a formal garden. After Keele Hall, the Clock House and the four lodges, they were probably the most useful buildings acquired. Yet they were 'a most blatant offence to amenity that unfortunately contained usable accommodation and so were retained' (Beaver, in a lecture on *The Keele Campus and its Environment*, 1980. Some years later the Italian garden and the fountain on the south side of Keele Hall were restored.) It was difficult to get licences for building work, but 'most of the trouble we are in comes from the fact that the UGC has had this year to save a million pounds in capital expenditure. That is the real difficulty, though licences are part of the trouble' (Lindsay to Vick, September 1950). Britain's defence and re-armament programme commanded priority in the nation's budget. Tawney's fore-bodings about the timing of starting Keele had been right: it really was 'the nearest run thing'.

Technical, secretarial and administrative staff were needed too: technicians played a vital part in setting up laboratories. The Workshop made things which could not be bought, and was often asked to make things which could not be drawn! Vick spoke for all the science departments when he said of Fred Rowerth and Harry Wardell, the Chief Technicians in Physics and the Workshop: 'I don't think I could have had a better pair on the technical side'.

The professors had reached general agreement on the first year syllabus in February: to produce the details threw them together in a spirit of urgent co-operation. Lawlor, Chambers and Blake, for example, met in Oxford to devise an inter-linking set of lectures, but progress was slow. On 1st July it was agreed that Lindsay himself should prepare a detailed lecture course from the suggestions submitted: he circulated a broad scheme. His note to Charlton, for example, said: 'You will see that after the introduction on Judaism and Christianity there are 10 lectures on Roman Civilisation and 10 lectures on Greek Civilisation. This is your problem to do with as you think fit, though no doubt it will help you to know what the other people are going to say, and perhaps you will let me make suggestions.' After a discussion with Lawlor, Charlton prepared his lectures – but he also wanted to consult Henderson, Gallie and Blake. He also wanted more lectures. Meanwhile, the Registrar was pressing them for their booklists. 'I think most of these syllabuses are too full and try to do too much in the time', Lindsay said, and at the end of August a new frame-work was suggested – with students only a matter of weeks away. Williams was on the campus fairly early, and it was probably his master plan incorporating a number of other suggestions. The first term would deal with 'Man and his Environment', the second with 'Development of Modern Civilisation', and the third with 'Industrial Revolution'. At the Senate meeting on 27th September the first two terms' lectures were swapped over. Williams also put together the timetable. With such a wide range of teaching programmes there was the danger that students' time would be too fragmented to leave uninterrupted time for study and the library, and the timetable sought to cure that problem. He also created a staffing formula to give a ranking order for eligibility for new staff: this gave an agreed basis for claims for staff (though could later act as a dead hand on new developments).

'The design of this course of Foundation Lectures is to inculcate a sense of the unity of Knowledge... the emphasis during the concluding lectures would be upon the crisis of contemporary civilisation and the factors which appear to provide or deny stability to society.' That statement certainly has the ring of Lindsay about it, and a key factor in putting the lecture course together was Lindsay's active involvement, giving direction above any departmental interest.

Tutorial work was intended to follow up topics dealt with in the lectures. The overarching philosophy was to achieve a balance between thoroughness and width of study by working from the individual student's initial interests to less familiar spheres. This was to be achieved by the system which became known as Terminals and Sessionals. Generally speaking, students would take one subject each term with which they were already familiar (Terminals), and two subjects for the whole session which were new to them (Sessionals). The Terminals would also serve to keep them in touch with subjects they might be taking at Principal level the following year – especially important in the sciences and languages where existing skills needed to be kept in trim.

An appreciation of the unity of knowledge and an understanding of contemporary society were paramount. Tutorial work was there to support the lecture course, which occupied a central position. This was in line with Lindsay's 'seeing things together' and the 'lessons of hard disciplined thought'. The actual detail of the content was secondary to the philosophy underlying it.

It was not long before the whole panoply of committees was set up, so that everything should have an appropriate channel: Academic Planning, Building and Estates, Staffing and Salaries, Student Welfare, Domestic, Staff Housing, Calendar, Library, Diploma of Education, Diploma of Social Studies, Chapel, Adult Education, and the Technical College Committee. There were Senate representatives on the Academic Council and the Council. Overall, this meant that most heads of departments could expect to be members of four, five or six committees. Council, too, had its committees, and Horwood was elected chairman of the Finance and Estates Committee.

The first Annual Meeting of the Court of Governors was held on 30th June 1950. As Lindsay wrote in his *Report*: 'We knew that in deciding to start in October of this year we were taking a risk... it was always extremely unlikely that all our plans would mature without delay or modification... Students have been admitted, staff engaged, and the College will open this Autumn.' Then, at the end of August Lindsay was taken ill with a cerebral thrombosis, and told to do as little as possible: but he was nevertheless in the chair for the Senate meeting on 27th September. When Sneddon suggested to him that he ought not to carry the burden of these meetings himself, his riposte was: 'Do you want to take away my one remaining pleasure?'

Professor Stewart told the following story. 'Two of us came up to Keele from Stoke before a meeting to have a look at the estate – December 1949 – in a drizzle... scrub... about 60 Nissen huts. Part of the inside of Keele Hall was gutted by the contractors so that the staircase we now use every day could be built. One or other of the military groups who had used the Hall during the War had managed to set fire to part of the top floor and half the roof was covered with galvanised iron; the courtyard was piled with debris and building materials. A man asked the two of us, as we stood there glumly, what we wanted and we said we were looking around because we had applied for a job, and wasn't it all a bit of a shambles. 'Yes, but you must see it with the eye of imagination', said the man, with rain dripping off the undulating brim of a very old hat – he was lucky, he had gum boots on and we were in our interview suits.'

That was Lord Lindsay. He had the imagination to match his vision. Not only did he transform the improbable into reality in the 1950s, but for the future he once and for all transformed the impossible into the obvious. It was the founding of new universities later which set the seal on Lindsay's greatness.

HEADS OF DEPARTMENTS, OCTOBER 1950

A: Board of Humanities

Classics	Mr. J. M. T. Charlton
English	Professor J. J. Lawlor
History	Professor J. W. Blake
Modern Languages	Professor W. W. Chambers
Philosophy	Professor W. B. Gallie

B: Board of Social Sciences

Economics	Professor B. R. Williams
Education	Professor W. A. C. Stewart
Geography	Professor S. H. Beaver
Political Institutions	Professor S. E. Finer
Political and Moral Philosophy	Professor A. E. Teale

C: Board of Natural Sciences

Biology	Professor A. R. Gemmell
Chemistry	Professor H. D. Springall
Geology	Dr. F. W. Cope
Mathematics	Professor I. N. Sneddon
Physics	Professor F. A. Vick

The Professors of the University College outside the Great Hall, 11th February 1950:

W.A.C. Stewart   F.A. Vick   J.W. Blake   A.R. Gemmell   S.H. Beaver
(Education)   (Physics)   (History)   (Biology)   (Geography)

S.E. Finer   B.R. Williams   A.E. Teale   H.D. Springall   Mr. S.O. Stewart
(Political   (Economics)   (Moral and Political   (Chemistry)   (Librarian)
Institutions)   Philosophy)

J.J. Lawlor   W.W. Chambers   W.B. Gallie
(English Language and   (Modern Languages)   (Philosophy)
Literature)

Miss M.H. Bailey   I.N. Sneddon   Dr. W.A. Jenkins   Lord Lindsay   Professor   Mrs. J.M. Morton   Mrs. H. Graham
(Registrar's   (Mathematics)   (Registrar)   (Principal)   H. Graham   (Principal's   Cannon
Secretary)   Cannon   Secretary)
                                                                   (University of
                                                                   Manchester:
                                                                   Academic Council)

Chapter 10

THE MASTER AS PRINCIPAL

The 16th October 1950 – a Monday – the first day – the first students – proof of the existence of the College, far more than the charter, the appointment of staff, or even the buildings – the students being the sole purpose of the College's being. It was the culmination of years of planning, difficulties, setbacks and frustration. Up till then, since March 1946, it had been proposals, meetings, discussions, more plans, drafts, hopes, and at last, interviews and admissions. It was going to be a new sort of university education, whose roots went back to Lindsay's philosophical analysis of social democracy. The College, too, was in many ways the child of Stoke-on-Trent. It was full of hope, full of promise, with an awareness of something new and exciting.

What did the new students know of the College, and in particular, what did they know of the academic course, the cause of such a long and determined struggle? Not a lot! Many must have been attracted to Keele by faith rather than by good works. The first details to be issued – a single, typed sheet – had said that arrangements were being made for the first year's work to begin in October. The first-year course was described simply as 'lectures designed to give an understanding of the factors affecting the evolution of our present civilisation and of the forces operating in society today. These lectures will be supplemented by tutorial work suitable to the requirements of individual students.' The subjects for which provision was being made were listed, and 'the three-year course following the first year common General Course will consist of more detailed study of [those] certain individual subjects... together with additional subjects including probably Classical languages, Education, Psychology, Geology, additional Modern Languages and Social Science. The subjects chosen will probably have to include studies from the Arts subjects, the Social Sciences and Science, as well as a modern language'. It was hoped to be able to incorporate concurrent special studies and practical training for those wishing to pursue teaching, youth training and social service. There would be residential accommodation in the first year for 80 women students and 70 men students. No Prospectus was likely to be ready until the Spring of 1950.

All the students came on 16th October (except one who arrived on 17th). That was a remarkable achievement, for some of those on the waiting list knew they had been accepted only the previous week. Lindsay was agreeably surprised that most of them came from the local area or because of their interest in what he called 'our experiment'. Now they assembled for the inauguration of the College. Lindsay was on the platform – the Principal. A famous old man, big in every way and often called 'Master'. Some of the staff noticed that he had aged a lot in the last six months. At his side on the platform was an old clergyman, a socialist alderman, 'the Vicar': these two, and it was their achievement. Lindsay told the students that it was Horwood's indomitable courage, perseverance and keenness which had brought the university into being. 'For me', he said, 'it has been an exciting job, and for you, I am sure, it will be great fun.' When Lindsay asked Horwood to speak he stood silent for a moment and then said: 'It didn't come down from Heaven, you know. And *now* we've really got to work to keep it... It must not be left to a few'. He continued: 'Each one must accept individual responsibility and feel on their honour to see that the university is on such lines that no future history can in any sense of the word deprive it of its honour and privilege.'

And there, too, were the other academic staff – fewer than twenty-five altogether. It was they who had the task of turning Lindsay's ideas into practical teaching, not in an ivory tower but in the mud and clay of North Staffordshire, in an old mansion house and in ex-army huts. They had a curriculum to devise, lectures to give, departments to build, committees to run; they were living in a new and small community, thrown together, surrounded by one another, making new friends, likes and dislikes, and new homes for their families, with all the problems of transport, shopping and schools, and post-war austerity. Work and home were inextricably mixed. There was a shortage of money, shortage of materials, and infuriating delays. The building programme would not catch up with teaching requirements, it was said in March 1951, for at least another year. But a lot had been achieved: lectures started on Thursday, the library was functioning and there were 20,000 books on the shelves. Lady Lindsay had formally placed the first book on a shelf in August.

How much of this could the first students have guessed? Of the 159 admitted, 149 were in residence. They knew they were in at the start of a new idea – largely the brainchild of the famous old man in front of them. It was going to be different from elsewhere, and it was to be a place where students would actually know their professors. There was a sense of excitement. Lord Lindsay said he hoped they would not mind very much the unfinished state of the College – it was hoped to get it right sometime during the term. The refectory was not ready and was further delayed by bad weather. He was sorry that work on the women's huts had not been completed – 'that through building delays you are cramped in your living quarters, that your huts are so far without heat, and that you cannot yet do your washing – but it is fun to be in at the start of a show like this'. But it was much more than that.

The Scotsman wrote approvingly of Keele's reverting to the academic practice of the old Scottish universities, and said of Lindsay: 'As a distinguished philosopher he brings to his new task the spiritual and mental qualities and the wide and humane view, that such studies seem to develop to the full.' It was heartening that 'informed opinion', which the CVCP had earlier ventured to say would not support a new university for a decade, was warm in its support. *The Times Educational Supple-*

ment, for example, enthused whole-heartedly: 'a striking experiment in the strongly conservative field of English university education... wholly residential, and is here firmly set in a tradition which was deserted only at the sacrifice of fellowship and education', and again, 'a great new academic institution... Such a cosmic curriculum will inevitably tax the imagination and industry of pupil and tutor alike in a way that the narrow and well-worn paths of knowledge in the older universities can never do.' It was, as the Hon. Josiah Wedgwood wrote to the College, 'one of the best things that have happened to North Staffordshire in my generation'.

All the day-to-day details and organisation had to be sorted out. The names of the Halls of Residence were agreed – Lindsay Hall for women, and Horwood Hall for men. A constitution was needed for the Students' Union so that students could take over control of the Union in the Spring Term. From the start students' allegiance within the College was to the Union; later to their Hall. Student life flourished despite, or because of cramped conditions. Twenty-five different societies soon vied for space and time for their meetings. 'It is sometimes extremely difficult to find a time for an additional function... There is... no doubt that the residential character of the College has been invaluable in enabling students and staff to take part in the great variety of activities in the campus. The Senate is convinced that every effort should continue to be made to keep the College fully residential' (*Report of the Principal* by Professor Vick, 1952).

Lecture hours were laid down (originally 9.15 – 10.05 and 10.15 – 11.05); gowns were to be worn for academic occasions – for lectures and tutorials, dinner in Hall, and when paying official visits to members of staff. The form of Grace for dinner devised by Henderson was approved: 'May Grace be given us to thank God for all'. College colours were agreed – red and gold; and even this was unwittingly not uncontroversial. 'What are the Labour party colours in North Staffordshire?' asked the *Sentinel*. Horwood was ready with his answer: we had promised Colonel Sneyd we would do all we could to maintain the family traditions at Keele and scarlet and gold were the colours of the Sneyd family, he said. The hours rule was promulgated: visits of men and women students to each other's huts were restricted to the hours of 1.0 p.m. – 7.30 p.m., and all students should be in their rooms by 11.0 p.m. This was later modified to allow students to stay out until midnight on Saturday nights. (Fifty years later it seems to be another world. Many of the students in post-war Britain had fought in the war; yet hours rules were commonly accepted – albeit with some protest and some breach. It was not until the late-1960s that a major change in attitude prevailed. The age of majority was still 21, so universities acted in *loco parentis* for students under 21. In January 1952 the Senate considered a proposal that a student should marry, and 'agreed to raise no objections'.) For staff, too, small details needed decisions: no charge was to be made on the College bus for conveying children to school, or for wives for shopping once a week on Fridays. (This was still almost the age before the motor car.)

What was the address of the place? The Head Postmaster of Stoke-on-Trent said it should be 'U.C.N.S., Keele, Newcastle, Staffs.' The Senate wanted to omit the word 'Newcastle'; the Head Postmaster thought that if any part were to be omitted, it should be Keele. That would have given us a college at a place few people had heard of, and which was not even mentioned in its address. What should be the name of the College in Latin? It was agreed that in a congratulatory address to the University of Glasgow, 500 years older than UCNS, the College should be referred to as 'Universitatis inter Staffordienses Collegium', but then the Public Orator at Oxford suggested instead 'Collegium Universitatis in Staffordia Boreali Collocatum' and that was approved. (One can see the attraction of 'Keele' as a name.)

The classification of degrees had not been agreed yet: it would be some years before anyone would be affected. At first the idea was to have three classes of honours with no subdivision of the IInd class, plus provision for a pass degree. Then, at the suggestion of the Academic Council, it was agreed to split the IInd class honours into upper and lower divisions, but a decision on whether there should be a IIIrd class honours was postponed. A Part I in the sciences was almost introduced in 1953. Tidying up the first-year course was more pressing, and a statement of intent proposed by Sneddon was approved for publication in the next *Prospectus*: 'The object of the first year's studies is to develop in the student, at the outset, some appreciation of the nature and inter-connection of the main branches of University studies... The outcome of the First Year's studies should be to familiarise the student with aspects of knowledge which may well influence his choice of principal subjects for the degree course. The title 'Foundation Studies' serves to emphasize that the first year course is designed as a necessary preliminary to later and more specialised studies.'

Music recitals were soon to be heard at Keele, with Beethoven piano sonatas in the elegant old drawing room. At Christmas there was not only a Christmas Ball on Friday night – probably the first time the students saw the staff let their hair down (and it was followed by a sparsely attended lecture on the Saturday morning) – but the students gave a party for the children. Baby-sitting for staff children had quickly become well-organised.

The Library was soon expanding, its ranks of books marching into the basements and corridors, the galleries and the vaults. As early as February 1951 the Senate concluded that provision for future library requirements should be met by a new library building rather than by extending within Keele Hall. There were 30,000 books by October 1951 and it was looking forward to 100,000 within a few years (and then to 500,000). It was hoped, therefore, that phase I of a new Library would be in the College's plans for 1953-54, but until then every space was being squeezed. A room for the Librarian's secretary was created under the main staircase, by using a large bookcase as one wall, the bookcase and the partitions being erected in such a way that the room could be easily dismantled one day, to restore some light and elegance to the main floor at the foot of the stairs. (That time is still in the future.) Before a new Library was built, the Senate was deprived of the Senate Room, and the Principal was twice dislodged from his office, with books occupying 24 rooms, corridors and cupboards (as well, by then, as the bulk of the Sarolea Collection in store in Madeley).

A certain suspicion about any political bias of the College was probably inevitable at the time. The Labour Party's victory at the General Election in 1945 had come as a surprise and a shock, and political views were perhaps more sharply defined in the immediate post-war years than later. Locally, Horwood could be described as a combative socialist; Lindsay was well-known for his socialist views and had stood for Parliament (though it must be said that he had stood as an Independent Progressive candidate). The suspicions voiced in the local press have already been noted, and these were strengthened, just a little, every time a bus conductor called out 'Kremlin on the Hill'; and so it was only a short step from that to voicing suspicions that up on the Keele estate, behind the wall, something was going on, and that it was a hot-bed of socialism, inspired and orchestrated by Lindsay. Such a suggestion was, of course, totally groundless; but Lindsay was upset by it and felt obliged to address the problem. Speaking to the WEA in Newcastle in September 1951 he said: 'The slander is that this University College is politically minded in a way no university ought to be. There is a sort of whispering campaign which has come out to the open lately. I had a letter from this district the other day, from one to say that he had given up the idea of his firm subscribing to the University College because he had heard on good evidence that we had such a political bias. Needless to say it was bias to the Left he referred to. People don't object to bias to the Right, but bias to the Left is always looked upon with suspicion. I think any political bias out of place in a university altogether.' He went on to explain how the professors had been appointed. 'It might be supposed', he added, 'because I had something to do with the starting of this College – and because my politics are notorious in certain quarters – that I chose the professors. I think it is highly important that people in this district should know how our professors were appointed', namely by electors, two each nominated by the Vice-Chancellors of Oxford, Manchester and Birmingham.

Optimism, hope and zest flourished in the face of a catalogue of difficulties. They hadn't sounded too bad in Lindsay's address to the first students, but the reality – unremitting delays on all fronts – really was daunting. The students already knew their accommodation was nothing like ready, and the central heating was not finished. Even by putting ten to a hut instead of five, it was still not possible to get all the students into College until Christmas, and it was almost the end of the second term before single rooms were available for all. The Common Rooms were not ready until December and January, and the refectory not until Easter. Work on Keele Hall took longer than expected because dry rot was more prevalent than expected. In addition, plans for permanent residences were already being cut back by the UGC in the face of a national shortage of materials and labour and the necessity for economy. (Yet in the feudal economy of the 15th century the Benedictines, who placed a high priority on university studies, were prepared to spend lavishly to provide appropriate accommodation for monk-scholars.) Consequently, instead of two 2-storey buildings for fifty women students, there could be only one 3-storey building for forty (Sneyd House). However, by including larger double rooms and smaller single rooms, the design was modified to provide 68 places: but it would not be ready for the beginning of the next academic year in October 1951, so the same difficulties would be inherited by the next generation of students. The new laboratories were delayed as negotiations with the UGC were prolonged and estimated costs were exceeded. Houses for staff fell a year behind requirements: licences had to be obtained from the Local Authorities, then sanction for the designs from the Ministry of Local Government and Planning before the normal procedures of estimates and tenders. Every delay had a knock-on effect and put greater strain on the temporary buildings, which in any case were needed for students. And everywhere there was mud, red squelchy mud. There were several heavy snowfalls in the first winter, and in November 1951 there was a record seven inches (180mm) of rain. Mud left an indelible mark on all who were here that first year. Shopkeepers in Newcastle could identify College people by the mud on their shoes. The almost continuous rain of the Autumn, Winter and early-Spring made getting around the campus very trying, and the problem was exacerbated by the heavy lorries bringing building materials, making it impossible to build proper roads and paths.

Nevertheless, Keele had been founded and started. There was a happy feeling about the place, and years later a word commonly used was 'fun'. The next thing was to get the College officially opened. The announcement that H.M. The Queen would formally open the College on 17th April 1951 broadcast Keele's achievement to the world and put the College amongst its peers. It also acted as spur to get a lot of jobs finished, notably the refectory and tarmac paths laid to the huts. The huts, which could never be described as attractive from the outside, had become comfortable and agreeable social units. *The Daily Dispatch* wrote that each student had a luxurious 'bed-sit', and the *News Chronicle* suggested that Keele's plumbing, with its baths, showers and constant hot water, must be the envy of every undergraduate at Oxford and Cambridge.

A beautiful day certainly showed off the grounds to advantage. Lord Harrowby, the College's President, was unable to attend on medical advice, so Horwood took his place and was the first person to be presented to the Queen by Lord Lindsay in the courtyard of Keele Hall. That was the second time for him that day: at a civic luncheon in Stoke Town Hall Horwood had already been presented to the Queen, and in proposing a toast to Her Majesty the Lord Mayor had said of the College: 'So far as this city is concerned, I should like to mention to Your Majesty the work of one member of the City Council – Alderman T. Horwood, a Freeman of the City and Chairman of the Finance Committee, whose enthusiasm has been such that he has succeeded in opening the Corporation purse and getting over many major difficulties.' In the courtyard at Keele there were then presented the other Vice-President, Alderman Davies (and Mrs. Davies), and the Mayor of Burton upon

Trent. (Alderman Hutson of Burton upon Trent, the third Vice-President, had died some months earlier.) In Keele Hall the Vice-Chancellors of Oxford and Manchester and the Vice-Principal of Birmingham, the Chairman of the UGC and members of the Academic Council were presented, followed by the Hon. Treasurer and Mrs. Walker, and the Hon. Architect and Mrs. Piggott. Next came the Acting President of the Staffordshire Society and then Mrs. Montford, whose bequest has already been mentioned. The first member of the academic staff to be presented was the Vice-Principal Professor Vick, and Mrs. Vick, and then Dr. and Mrs. Jenkins. In the Library reading room, which had been the library in 19th century Keele Hall, were the Librarian and Mrs. Stewart. 'He's a very good Librarian', Lindsay said, 'but he doesn't like anyone touching his books.' In the Ballroom (the former drawing room, and known since as the Salvin Room) members of the Court, the Council, the Academic Council and, at the request of the Queen, twenty-five students chosen by lot, were assembled to hear Horwood welcome the Queen and pay tribute to 'our team' before asking Her Majesty formally to open the University College. In a warm address the Queen referred to the Universities of Oxford, Birmingham and Manchester as 'bodies generous in mind and rich in wisdom' and then spoke of the founding of the College as an act of courage and imagination. Lindsay had his address of thanks ready, but part way through laid it aside and spoke from the heart without it. Following this ceremony the Queen went through to the refectory where twenty-five students were presented to her. Usmanshah Afridi from Pakistan was

University College of North Staffordshire
Students' Union

Foundation Year Dinner and Ball

on Friday, April 20th, 1951

Reception 7.30 p.m.
Dinner 8 p.m.
Dancing 10 p.m.—4 a.m.
Dress Formal

Ticket 15/-

reported as saying to the Queen something which any one of them might have said: 'I am more than happy. I am making history.' Next to the chapel, where the Wardens were presented; and then, outside Keele Hall, the professors in alphabetical order (and their wives), Mr. Charlton and Mr. Henderson. An item which caught the eye of the press was when the Queen asked Mr. Henderson why his academic hood was black. He replied that according to popular theory the original recipients of the Bachelor of Divinity degree were too poor to afford any colours. The only laboratory ready was Geology, where Dr. Cope (and Mrs. Cope) were presented.

'Well, Ma'am', said Lindsay, 'tree and tea', referring to the tree the Queen was going to plant; and that concluded the Royal visit. A few days later celebrations continued with a Foundation Year Dinner and Ball, with representatives from other universities and local dignitaries. Replying on behalf of the guests, Mr. W. Rees-Mogg, President of the Oxford Union Society (and a Balliol man) – later Baron Rees-Mogg – spoke of his admiration for the way Keele had overcome the many difficulties which faced it in its first year.

News of Lindsay's new College spread perhaps even more widely than he knew. In the mid-1990s Professor Janota, a Czech Professor of Dutch in Prague, to whom I mentioned Keele in conversation said: 'Ah yes, the new University'.

The 'Aims of the College' were published in the programme for the formal opening, and it is worth repeating them here in full as a statement of how Keele said it saw itself at the time. Keele's 'Mission Statement', fifty years later, is given in the Appendix.

'The objects of the College are stated in Clause 3 of the Charter. They are: 'to advance learning and human knowledge and to provide such instruction as may enable Students to obtain the advantages of a University education and to qualify for Degrees in arts, science and other subjects and to provide such scientific technical and other instruction as may be of service in professional and commercial life.' Behind this broad statement of aims lies a courageous resolve to experiment in university education. Indeed, the foundation of the new University College of North Staffordshire was the outcome, not only of individual initiative and keen local enthusiasm, but also of the readiness of the University Grants Committee to support a new venture in higher education, provided the College authorities were prepared to break away from convention and to try out new ideas and methods.

'Prominent among the problems which today confront the universities of this country is the difficulty of reconciling the provision of general education, ranging over a broad field and involving the mastering of distinct disciplines, with the imperative need to specialise in a particular, and often somewhat narrow, branch of knowledge. Owing to the intricacies of modern advanced studies, a degree of specialisation appears to be unavoidable. Moreover, even though attempts be made to leaven specialisation by wider studies falling outside the specialised field, there can of necessity be no certainty whether this broadening process should precede, follow or coincide with specialisation. The authorities of this College are convinced that experimentation is needed in order to harmonise university education with modern requirements. Recognising that for a majority of students over-specialisation has its dangers, they hold that more importance in university curricula may with advantage be given to general education. But they believe that, if the most beneficial results are to be achieved, the broadening process of wider studies should come early in the career of the student. Their objects include, therefore, the provision at the undergraduate stage of courses of study which while they take account of the need for specialisation, at the same time offer more breadth and achieve a measure of integration as between the different departments of knowledge.

'The entire social and academic life of the new University College is being planned and developed with a view to the success of this experiment. Thus, the College is to remain wholly residential: almost the whole body of the students and nearly all the staff with their families live within the precincts. Every effort is being made to encourage the growth of a living and vital university community. For this reason, too, student numbers are limited: for the time being, the total intake of students in any one year is to be in the region of one hundred and fifty. Men and women students enjoy equal status within the College. Women form about a third of the total student body. Moreover, though the College is undenominational, once a week on Sunday mornings students and staff meet in the College Chapel to share in a collective act of worship, for this also is regarded as an essential part of the life of the new university. Staff and students likewise dine together every evening, the Principal, Vice-Principal or a senior member of the academic staff presiding at high table. As the College builds up to its full strength, as student hostels, more staff houses, a new refectory, science laboratories, more teaching blocks, a new university library, and ultimately perhaps an Institute of Education, are planned, prepared and completed, as the 23 acres of playing fields come into use, and as the College as a whole gradually surmounts the manifold difficulties of inception, it is hoped to facilitate the experiment by the retention or improvement of existing features and the introduction of others equally or more appropriate to the special aims of the University College of North Staffordshire.

'Perhaps the most interesting, certainly the most thought-provoking, feature of the academic life of the College is the Foundation Course of studies which all students must pursue in their first year. This takes the form of a common course of lectures to which all the Professors and Independent Heads of Departments contribute. In addition, more detailed work is carried out in tutorials, work bearing, for example, upon the methodologies of the different subjects studied. It will be observed that the College allows no freshman to specialise. On the contrary, he is encouraged to concentrate wholly on his Foundation studies. The lectures, which he attends throughout the session, are designed to enable him to gain an understanding of the heritage of Western civilisation, of modern society, the nature, methods and influence of the experimental sciences, and of the relationship which exists between the different branches of knowledge. His work in tutorial classes is carefully devised, not only to ease the transition from school life to university life, but also to ensure the maintenance of a balance in his studies between the arts, the sciences and the social sciences. The success of the experiment at the College will largely turn upon the effectiveness of this Foundation Course.

'Scarcely less important in the plan of the College is the rule that students are required to devote four years in all to the completion of their studies for a first degree. After the end of the Foundation year, the student proceeds to limited specialisation. During the next three years, he must study at least two, and possibly three Principal subjects: it is assumed that normally he will choose for his Principals allied subjects, such as English and History or Chemistry and Physics. At the same time, however, the principle of combining breadth and depth is preserved by the rule that he must also study Subsidiary subjects. For this purpose the branches of study have been divided into three, the Humanities, the Sciences and the Social Sciences; and no student at the end of his four years at the University College can graduate as a Bachelor of Arts without having studied either at Principal or at Subsidiary level at least one subject in each of these divisions. Moreover, the College visualises that, later on, students of marked ability will then proceed to further work of a more specialised kind. Beyond this, the College also seeks to meet the practical needs of modern society by offering a Diploma in Education and a Diploma in Social Studies. Students may take special courses leading to these awards at the same time as they are preparing themselves for the B.A. Degree.

'It will be recognised that the conduct of an experiment of this kind by a new University College is fraught with difficulties. To facilitate its progress and the maintenance of proper university standards the Universities of Oxford, Birmingham and Manchester have kindly undertaken to act as sponsors and are accordingly represented upon the Academic Council. Over the old, possibly Elizabethan, doorway on the east side of the Courtyard is the legend: 'Thanke God for all.' It is the hope of all concerned in the experiment that the new University College will, in its growth and development, give fresh emphasis to this, its motto.'

With the College launched there was no let up in the hectic pace, nor was this yet the culmination of Lindsay's ambitions for Keele. It was, Professor Stewart said, a time of intellectual energy, the clash and meshing of minds, the sheer ferment of the community, the relentless pressure of problems. (In his Annual Report in May 1951 Lindsay was already calling attention in particular to recommendations to amend the charter to enable the College to grant its own research degrees, and this had the support at that time of the Academic Council.)

There were thirteen more meetings of the Senate between the 25th April and 31st August. There were immediate problems, like where to give lectures! The refectory was not suitable yet, so they would be given in the central unit of the NAAFI block as soon as the platform had been constructed, and in the meantime would be given, as in the previous term, in the chapel. There were medium term problems – there would be twice the number of students in October 1951, and three times the present number in October 1952, plus more staff. Where and how would they be accommodated? By a mixture of generous co-operation and patient forbearance. And there were major long-term problems looming. The number of academic staff proposed had been cut owing to a sharp reduction in the licensable work permitted for 1951/52, and the UGC would not agree to the erection of permanent halls of residence yet. Major questions needed answers for the quinquennium 1952-57. By teaching from 9.15 a.m. to 7.0 p.m. and after, by holding classes in private houses and staff bedrooms, by using classrooms as library reading rooms in the evening, by postponing some practical work in the sciences to the following year, by housing some research students in Manchester during part of the year, and so on, it was possible to carry on – but not permanently.

Student residences were the first priority. 'Thus, the College is to remain wholly residential' was proclaimed in the 'Aims of the College'. The army huts had made possible total residence to start with: but their life-time was obviously limited (though in the event not as limited as was first thought), and so permanent halls of residence would need to be planned anyway. This was not necessarily the view of the UGC. Lindsay and Vick went to see them and came back with a report of a change of attitude on the residential character of the College. They had had to re-iterate and defend the College's position. The College Council was very supportive in holding to the position that residence for all students was fundamental to the agreed objectives of the College, and they expressed their determination to the Court of Governors to retain this essentially residential nature of the College. Speaking on the topic 'Residential Life in the Universities Today' at the Home Universities Conference a few years later, in 1957, Dr. Jenkins said: 'During the development of the UCNS, great pressure was brought to bear upon the university by the UGC to place students in lodgings rather than to ask for money for the development of halls of residence. Until that mentality changes, you will not solve the problem of adequate residential facilities. In the development of universities it should be a cardinal point that provision should be there for the residence of students so that provision can be made for the training of their social life, for training them as leaders of the nations; and the university authorities must learn to speak with one voice on this question and say to those who are responsible for developing the universities in the country that if they wish us to do our work, then we must have halls of residence in the same way as we have laboratories, and we must be able to train our students as leaders as well as to develop their intelligence.' We were fortunate that Lindsay's and Jenkins's views prevailed during Keele's formative years.

Keele Hall was no longer large enough to accommodate the non-science departments and the administration and the library. Buildings for Geology and Geography had been deferred from 1951/52; Biology, Chemistry and Physics were about a year behind schedule. In 1953/54 a start on the new permanent library would be pressing. A proposed Assembly Hall for a thousand was postponed, never to be built.

Keele's name was appearing locally and nationally more and more, and the Staffordshire Society launched an appeal for funds for the College. There were two Open Days in June and September. UCNS now featured in reports of university sporting fixtures; the Drama Group performed *Twelfth Night* at Churche's Mansion in Nantwich in aid of church funds; Professor Vick lectured about the atom bomb; eleven heads of departments gave a series of WEA lectures; and Dr. Plesch held an informal conference on cationic polymerisation (he was to be appointed Professor of Physical Chemistry in 1978). Professor Beaver's meteorological station was set up and contributed regular reports to the *Sentinel*. Keele made its mark on national radio in Richard Dimbleby's 'Down Your Way', and Professor Gemmell was heard on the North regional programme 'How does your garden grow?' – soon to become the BBC radio programme 'Gardeners' Question Time'. His voice and name became known to millions of listeners, and the reference each week (plus a repeat) to 'the University College of North Staffordshire' and in due course to 'the University of Keele' was probably the most widespread mention of any university or college.

Support came from far and wide, with reports about the College in South Africa, Australia and the United States – prompting a reader in Maine to send a cheque for $15, 'being in complete accord with these aims, and realising that all new educational institutions are in need of financial assistance'. (If only all those who read about Keele and who were in complete accord with its aims had also sent $15!) There was a most generous gift in the first year of sixty pictures and an Epstein bronze of Isobel Elsom from Dr. and Mrs. Barnett Stross. This gift, which included paintings by Jacob Kramer, a friend of Epstein, and the Manchester born artist Rowley Smart, became the basis of the College's collection of works of art and of the Keele Picture Loan scheme. Locally, amidst the support there was also some criticism: the *Pottery Gazette and Glass Trade Review* deplored students having to spend time studying 'general subjects' and thought they would be better occupied in commencing 'specialised studies'; and at a time of shortage of building licences an application to build twenty garages was seen as a luxury, and the number was halved. There was criticism too, and a question in the House of Commons, about a donation of 5,000 guineas from the electricity authorities.

Yet Keele was already not the place it had been in October 1950. The *Prospectus* published in January 1952 listed forty-four full-time teaching staff plus seven part-time lecturers and tutors. The 'strangers and brothers' now had departments and new staff. Many of them were young and were strong and colourful characters. Monica Cole, for example, who joined the Geography Department in 1951, was immaculately dressed in bright colours and known for her forthright manner and determination. She went on to become Professor at Bedford College, London, producing pioneering works in biogeography, geobotany, remote sensing and terrain analysis, and mineral exploration, with her research spanning Central and Southern Africa, South America, Australia, China and Finland. Some of the new staff were impatient for change. Some stayed only a few years. Many dedicated their working lives to Keele and retain a place in the memories of those whose lives they touched: for example, Ron Evans (Biology), Peter Plesch (Chemistry), Robert North and John Broome (French). Hugh Leech (History) had been a Balliol scholar, and as part-time Appointments Secretary for seven years helped guide graduates into careers. Many years later the 1996 Honorary Graduate Lecture was given by Michael Mansfield, QC, who had graduated in History and Philosophy in 1964 and been awarded an honorary Doctor of Laws in 1995. His starting point was Lindsay's *The Modern Democratic State* and he dedicated the lecture to the memory of Hugh Leech. Perhaps none evoked warmer affection than Paul Rolo (History, and previously Junior Dean and Tutor at Balliol) – a man of compassion and understanding, who was diplomatic and supportive, who could find solutions or put his telescope to his blind eye, where others saw problems; above all his warmth for the institution, its ideals and its students, meant that when Keele was discussed by those who knew it from the inside, his name was likely to be on their lips. There were others, too, such as Harold Hayley, Mary Glover and 'Henders', but the community was much more than academic staff and students. Sister McLellan ran the Health Centre – and it was not to be called 'Sick Bay' in her hearing. (Who was it who in response to her question: 'What is the matter with you?' replied: 'A mild attack of death, Sister'?) From Stoke-on-Trent Corporation came Tom Ball as Finance Officer and Eric Hughes, to run the estates side of things with Margaret Capper. 'Miss Rolfe is doing her best' was a catch-phrase in the refectory when things were not quite satisfactory, but it was said with affection. Tom Stacey, the Grounds Superintendent, nursed the playing fields into fine condition. Ron Hill displayed a blend of tolerance and skills and, with his wife Annie, virtually organised the Students' Union for twenty years.

Jim Roberts, first in the Students' Union for five years and then as caretaker in the Walter Moberly Hall for nearly twenty years, always had a sympathetic ear and some encouragement. The Whieldons and the Browns listened to generations of students, as did Mrs. Dale and Mrs. Lightfoot in the shop in the old army hut (which later became the studio for the Gulbenkian Fellows). The Woods moved the shop to its permanent premises in the Students' Union building in 1963 (where it moved again in 1976), serving the University for thirty-two years. When the University took over the running of the campus supermarket in the 1990's they continued in Keele Village Shop and Post Office. Several families came to work for Keele – the Spraggs, the Randles, the Pooles and the Laffords; and domestic and grounds staff like Molly Bailey and Jack Buckley could probably have written a history which would have surprised many.

Perhaps the most tireless of publicists for Keele was Lindsay. Nothing was too much trouble for him. He had a full programme within Keele, where he continued to chair the Senate, interview students for admission and again at the end of the year, preach in chapel and attend events organised by students – Horwood Hall committee put on a very successful dinner which both Lindsay and Horwood attended. Nor did he spare himself outside the College, speaking to the North Staffordshire Classical Association, the Stoke-on-Trent Institute of Cost and Works Accountants, opening a Wedgwood exhibition, and new buildings at Alleyne's School, distributing prizes at

Crewe, speaking at Abbotsholme School, and lecturing to the WEA. He went further afield too, to Chester, Huddersfield, Wolverhampton and Nottinghamshire. He inveighed against early specialisation at a school Speech Day in Derby.

Suddenly, Lord Lindsay was dead.

He had returned home tired but he was still at work two days later. Then he felt a chill coming on so he rested, but it was not thought anything serious was wrong. Only recently a medical certificate had given reason to hope he would continue as Principal for another two years, and that he would therefore see the first students graduate.

His death on 18th March 1952 was a sudden and grievous blow and a severe shock. Keele was bereft. There was a widespread sense of a tremendous personal loss. Horwood said that there was no man for whom he had a greater admiration. To staff and students he had been a guide, philosopher and friend. There were, of course, many tributes to him. Miss Marion Bailey, the College's first secretary, wrote that 'Lord Lindsay has always been to all of us the complete centre of this College'. Mrs. Doris Bates in Keele Village wrote: 'We have many happy memories of his friendship and hospitality, and we feel we have lost a neighbour whom we respected and admired deeply'. From the other side of the world the Principal of Canberra University College wrote: 'There is not a university in this country which does not count some members of its staff who had come under the influence of your late Principal... the loss to British education and to the UCNS in particular, is widely realised in this country'. A fitting tribute was paid by Professor Vick when he became Acting Principal: 'We hope that this College will always be a worthy memorial to him'.

A portrait of Lord Lindsay by Robin Goodwin was commissioned by the Senior Common Room and was finished posthumously. It shows him in the scarlet robes of the LLD of Glasgow. It was presented to Alderman Horwood by members of the Senior Common Room, and it now hangs in the Senior Common Room in Keele Hall. Another portrait of him, by Lawrence Gowing, which had been commissioned by Balliol College, was copied for Keele by Gowing in 1959 and now hangs in Keele Hall.

Opposite above: H.M. The Queen meeting Professors and their wives outside Keele Hall. (*left to right* Professor Stewart, Mrs. Springall, Professor Springall being presented to the Queen, Mrs. Sneddon (partly obscured), Professor Sneddon). 17th April 1951.

Opposite below: The portrait of Lord Lindsay presented to Alderman Horwood. (*left to right* Sir John Lennard-Jones, Alderman Horwood, Robin Goodwin and Professor Sneddon, Chairman of the Senior Common Room). 19th December 1952.

'We admire some for the Dignity,
others for the Popularity of their behaviour;
some for their Clearness of Judgment,
others for their Happiness of Expression;
some for the laying of Schemes,
and others for the putting of them into Execution.'
(*The Spectator.* Dedication to the
Earl of Wharton, volume 5, 1712.)

Chapter 11

THE PERIOD – I

In a sense it was still the best of times. It was the spring of hope and we had everything before us. But it was also the worst of times, and the season of darkness. In the next few years the infant College suffered one body blow after another. It was scarcely credible that within ten years of the death of Lord Lindsay, the College would have its fourth Principal; that death should rob Keele of Sir John Lennard-Jones at the age of 60, and Sir George Barnes at 54. There was talk of a curse on the Clock House.

It is, therefore, great credit to the College that it was able to celebrate its tenth anniversary with such confidence, and that the academic staff who had sat with Lindsay provided leadership. It is always a difficult task for an Acting Principal, whose department may suffer in his absence and who may be confronted with outbreaks of what one member of staff described as 'baronial strife'. He must be anxious not to commit the institution to a policy with which his successor may not agree, and he must, when his task is done, resume his status amongst his peers. An interregnum whilst finding a successor is probably inevitable from time to time even when retirement (or later, resignation) is foreseen; but death robbed the College of its Principal not once, not twice, but three times in less than nine years. None of them saw the graduation of students admitted in their time – Barnes was seriously ill and was unable to attend the degree ceremony in 1960. Keele was therefore in the hands of Acting Principals for a year after Lindsay's death when Professor Vick took over; for nearly two years between Lennard-Jones and Barnes when Professor Blake took over; and for one more year after Barnes died when Professor Stewart took over. Had he lived, Barnes might have remained as Principal until 1970; or had Fulton been appointed the first Principal instead of Lindsay, he might have continued in office almost as long.

And yet, during these ten years Keele did not simply just survive. It flourished. Horwood, who was older than Lindsay, continued to chair the College Council until October 1956. H.M. Queen Elizabeth the Queen Mother returned to Keele for the tenth anniversary celebrations, as she had promised when she opened the College, and H.R.H. Princess Margaret became the College's President in 1956 and was a regular visitor for the next thirty years. The College was still small – certainly by the standards of later decades when universities are measured in thousands, but even in 1954, UCNS had more students than the colleges at Exeter, Hull, Leicester and

Southampton had just before the Second World War. In 1960 the College was looking forward to becoming the University of Keele.

In the wider university world there was a far-distant sound which might be regarded as ominous. The Treasury had rejected a recommendation that the Comptroller and Auditor General should have the right to inspect the books and accounts of universities in respect of non-recurrent grants for capital development. It was the Treasury's view that such a development would go beyond the broad lines on which control should be exercised if academic freedom was to be unimpaired, and that such scrutiny should be left to the UGC. Nevertheless, that recommendation had been put forward, and that distant sound was to continue to reverberate until that knell was sounded again.

In the face of daunting prospects the achievements were considerable, and at the core of the College's success was the willingness of so many, especially Heads of Departments, to give their time, thought, energy and commitment unreservedly to Keele.

Chapter 12

LENNARD-JONES AND BARNES

More immediately, it took strong optimism to recognise that this was in any sense the best of times. In its *Report to the Court of Governors* in May 1952 the Council concluded: 'Behind the completion of the second year... there lies the solving of innumerable problems and the surmounting of many difficulties that do not usually face College teachers and staff... Nor does it seem that the next two years will see much lightening of this burden'. It was clearly, therefore, going to be of crucial importance who would be the next Principal. In the meantime the College was fortunate to have Professor Vick's safe hands.

There was by now a certain momentum of its own in the College. There was the settling down and the rhythm of the academic programme. There was the necessary growth as the number of students doubled and trebled. There was the annual cycle of events: *Henry IV* (Part 1) in the courtyard of Keele Hall in May 1952, *The Tempest* by the lake with real rain in 1953. The enthusiasm of Mr. Hayley, who was the Director of Physical Education for 31 years, overcame the almost complete lack of facilities and produced an impressive range of activities: instructional classes were started in swimming, fencing, tennis, ballroom dancing and golf, and opportunities were found for walking, rock-climbing, camping and folk dancing. In spite of the dark and muddy approach during the winter, the bare gym part of the Nissen hut furniture store was in constant use for club practice and training. (It must be said, though, that the statement in the *Prospectus* that 'First year students, in particular, are normally required to take part in some form of physical exercise, either through the various clubs or in classes organised by the Director of Physical Education' seemed an unnecessarily fierce provision to those more aesthetically inclined.) When, at last, the sports fields were usable, in the Spring term 1953, the first game was a hockey match between the professors, led by Professor Blake, and the women's hockey club (which the professors won 3 : 2).

Keele, because it was new, continued to attract widespread mention, whether it was for internal college items, such as the conference for heads of schools – an annual event for over thirty years – or in articles on higher education at home and abroad. The British Council, in particular, ensured that academic visitors from around the world found their way to Keele. In addition, the Lectures and Recitals Committee was bringing the outside world into Keele with internationally famous names which in turn attracted a local outside audience. Denis Matthews gave the first of the recitals he was to give from time to time over the next twenty-five years. It was the academic programme, of course, which continued to preoccupy the Senate. Already in June 1952 the Academic Planning Committee was recommending a review of the structure of the Foundation Year, and it was felt that there was a need for a full-time Director of Studies. Dr. Jenkins was appointed to the post, but he continued as Registrar until the appointment of Mr. J. F. N. Hodgkinson as Registrar in September 1953. When Jenkins left to become Vice-Chancellor of the University of Dacca at their insistent request, the post of Director was not renewed. A Special Senate in January 1953 deliberated on whether there should be a Part I for the final examinations. The division was between the scientists and the rest, but the Academic Council did not approve and the issue then lay dormant for many years.

Just before Christmas 1952 the portrait of Lindsay was presented to Horwood by members of the Senior Common Room. Also present on that occasion was Sir John Lennard-Jones, making his first visit to Keele as Lindsay's successor.

Sir John Lennard-Jones evoked great warmth. The impact he made on Keele in a short time was considerable, and one can only speculate what difference a few more years might have made. He was both a complete contrast to Lindsay and at the same time an ideal choice to follow him. He was a classicist and mathematician by training. At the age of 32 he had been appointed Professor of Theoretical Physics at Bristol and five years later he was elected to the Plummer Chair of Theoretical Chemistry at Cambridge. A year later, in 1933, he was elected an FRS in recognition of his outstanding pioneering achievements in quantum mechanics. He had early on spotted the potential of quantum theory for calculating the properties of atoms and molecules. When Cambridge developed a computing laboratory he became its first, part-time director. In the First World War he had flown with the Royal Flying Corps. In the Second World War he worked on problems of ballistics and became chief superintendent of armament research. In particular, he made a major contribution to the administrative machinery of scientific research, and after the War he reorganised the department for peacetime conditions as Director General of Scientific Research (Defence) in the Ministry of Supply. He was knighted in 1946 and returned to Cambridge to build up the school of theoretical chemistry.

His change in career in coming to Keele might therefore seem surprising, but news of the Keele experiment had aroused his enthusiasm. In 1952 he accepted the invitation to become Lindsay's successor, taking office in April 1953. In the event he was precisely what the College needed at that time. As well as his reputation as a scholar he had shown his ability as an administrator with extraordinary patience and devotion to detail. He had a natural modesty, and at the same time was an inspiring leader with an infectious cheerfulness of spirit. He was into everything and he knew what Keele's aims were; he knew how to work with academics and how to persuade them; and outside Keele he spared no effort in making the College widely known.

Even before he assumed office he wrote about Keele for *The Cambridge Review,* and he broadcast on the BBC's General Overseas Service about Lindsay's aims. 'All these specialists keep the machine of civilisation working', he said. 'But the question which many thinking men are asking today is where is the machine going?... A broad general training may yet be a better preparation for leadership than expert knowledge of a restricted field'; and he gave as one essential condition for success that the college must be fully residential.

He was installed as Principal at a ceremony held in the King's Hall, Stoke-on-Trent. That after all, as the Lord Mayor said, was where the idea of the College was conceived. It was a civic and an academic occasion, with seventeen other universities and colleges represented. Alderman the Reverend Thomas Horwood inducted him. As a Cambridge man and a scientist, following an Oxford man and a philosopher, Lennard-Jones said that a scientist always looked with envy on the achievements of the distinguished men of letters. He then traced back the roots of broadly-based education in Cambridge, pointing out that specialisation was of fairly recent origin and that as late as 1850 no candidate was allowed to sit the final examinations in Classics unless he had obtained at least a third class honours in Mathematics. He detailed the demand for specialists as necessary in the modern state and then echoed Lindsay's views on the inherent dangers. 'Ideas are still more potent than facts and wisdom is more precious than knowledge. 'The wisdom of a learned man cometh by opportunity of leisure... How can he get wisdom that holdeth the plough?", he asked, taking his text from *Ecclesiasticus*. In the Town Hall of Stoke-on-Trent he forbore to continue '[or] the potter sitting at his work'. His address was later published as *Trends in University Education*. The concluding words of the ceremony, since heard by succeeding generations of graduates at their degree congregations, were taken from a sentence used by H.M. The Queen when she opened the College in 1951: 'Let the College dismiss. Long may it prosper and be honoured in its sons and daughters.'

It was the measure of Lennard-Jones that he quickly grasped the essentials and the weaknesses which were developing in the academic, administrative and financial structures. He devoted a great deal of time to the College's finances, balancing the budget and reallocating funds and savings. At his first meeting of the Council there was discussion about the houses to be built on the 'Covert' site. Lennard-Jones thought it was the wrong place: it was a key site, better kept for academic development. It was a problem which would be known a few years later as Catch-22. Keele was *not* a virgin, green-field site; temporary buildings were needed until they were replaced. They could not be knocked down to make room for the permanent buildings which would replace them before they were replaced. New buildings therefore had to go in the gaps, and within reach of existing underground mains services. No other suitable site was available for the proposed houses, but from the point of view of longer-term planning, Lennard-Jones regarded the choice as regrettable. Within a few months he was discussing with the chairman and secretary of the UGC an overall development plan for the College. Another problem about housing was the rent : salary ratio. The interest charges on the loans required to build houses made rents high in relation to salaries, especially for junior staff, and for a time the Staff Housing Committee felt unable to recommend proceeding with any types of the accommodation proposed. Other building work was delayed by the shortages of the time – there was a national shortage of cement in June 1953 because of heavy demands for repairs to sea-walls on the south-east coast of England, and this was followed by a shortage of bricks and bricklayers throughout North Staffordshire.

On the academic running of the College Lennard-Jones made major contributions, and in consultation with senior colleagues he re-organized and simplified the committee structure; he also took an active role in co-ordinating departments in the Foundation Year and in conducting a review of the course. The Senate re-iterated that Foundation Year lectures should be given by heads of departments, and this was one of its strengths. It is easy to appreciate Lord Lindsay's aims in the Foundation Year, but it is difficult to translate those aims into a satisfactory practical syllabus. Some of the benefits accrue only with a process of assimilation and maturation, and may not be immediately self-evident: but there were weaknesses, and the Academic Planning Committee sought to redress them. In brief, these were that there was insufficient integration of the course; that it was too heavily loaded with material; that students did not take a sufficiently active part in the course; and that there appeared to be insufficient connection between the lectures and the tutorial classes. (It is interesting to surmise what Lindsay might have done.) The major innovation to counteract these problems was the introduction of Foundation Year Discussion Groups – weekly meetings of small groups of students with three staff (one from each Board of Studies), for one hour each week, bearing directly on the content of the lectures. There was also growing concern that the load after the Foundation Year was too heavy. With five subjects competing for a student's time (two principal subjects and three subsidiary subjects) the formal teaching load had become excessive, and the timetable was too fragmented to leave time for concentrated individual study. As a consequence it was felt that the course was failing to achieve the integration it had set out to emphasize. It was agreed to reduce the teaching load – possibly by recognising a distinction between 'support' and 'general' subsidiary subjects; or by requiring a pass in only two of the three courses; or by taking one of the subsidiary subjects during the Foundation Year; or by introducing a different type of course based on Foundation Year teaching. Lennard-Jones and the secretaries of the three Boards of Studies recommended a reduction in the number of compulsory subsidiary subjects from three to two.

Overall Lennard-Jones was probably more conventionally minded than Lindsay would have been, and he tried to steer Keele in a more orthodox fashion. It might be that without Lindsay himself, that was what 'Lindsay's folly' (as Blake heard it described) needed at that time.

With a new intake each October, but no students graduating until the summer of 1954, problems of accommodation and teaching space became acute. The provision for teaching and residence had fallen behind schedule owing to changes in *national* policy. The College was therefore obliged to limit its intake. The UGC could do no more than take note. They too were confronted with a financial squeeze, and the resources they had enabled them to meet only a small fraction of the bids from all universities and colleges: halls of residence were not the highest priority. Even though Keele was able to provide accommodation more cheaply than most other places, there was simply not the money. It must be said that the UGC did its best for Keele in impossible circumstances, and in this instance found an additional and very welcome £10,000. Nevertheless, the first buildings were starting to take shape. Sneyd House was the first block of permanent residences. 'The Hawthorns' was acquired in Keele Village. A new Teaching Block (to be the Tawney Building) for mathematics, economics and modern languages was being built, and the Conference Hall (to be the Walter Moberly Hall) was about to be started. It was going to be linked with the Teaching Block, with a quadrangle in the centre, but then plans and fashions changed. New laboratories were being built, and in November 1953 the Physics laboratories were opened by Sir John Cockcroft, the first Director of the Atomic Energy Research Establishment at Harwell, who had split the atom with Ernest Watson in 1932. Cockcroft endorsed Keele's aims for broader education, saying that not only should scientists understand the history, tradition and culture of their world, but that humanists, too, needed to understand the great power of science for both good and evil. (Just over a year later he returned to Stoke-on-Trent to give the Mitchell Memorial Lecture.)

The library continued to expand and was enhanced by the gift of the greater part of Lord Lindsay's library, and the library of the Institute of Sociology when the College took over the management of the journal *The Sociological Review*. In order to make more space available for books, the administration – i.e. the Registry, Estates, Finance and the Senior Tutor's offices – moved into temporary wooden buildings next to where the chapel would be built. (Temporary was to be measured in terms of decades.)

As it happened, the five-yearly Congress of Commonwealth Universities was held in Cambridge in 1953, and Lennard-Jones was one of the opening speakers. It provided an excellent platform for publicity about Keele to a large and influential audience. The Chancellor of Tasmania University echoed Lindsay's views about universities in a letter to *The Times*, namely that if 'they take no trouble to do more than teach the speciality, they must face the position that they abandon their claims to be universities'.

Lindsay's name was also being perpetuated in Stoke-on-Trent in a different way. In order to avoid the confusion of duplicate street names in the six towns, the corporation proposed renaming some of the streets in Hanley. (The Hanley Chamber of Trade, however, thought that Hanley, as the shopping centre of the city, had the first right to retain existing names, and that duplicate names elsewhere should be changed. Burslem, Tunstall and Longton, on the other hand, did not agree.) Appropriately, Lindsay Street replaced Oxford Street.

The British Association meeting in Oxford in September 1954 provided another platform for Keele. Lennard-Jones, who had earlier been awarded the Davy Medal of the Royal Society, spoke on 'New Ideas in Chemistry'. The Davy Medal was awarded for the most important chemical discovery of the year in Europe or North America, and in this case it was for Lennard-Jones's distinguished work on the applications of quantum mechanics to the theory of valency and to the analysis of the intimate structure of chemical compounds. Already an ScD from Cambridge, Oxford conferred an honorary DSc on him, praising his achievements as a powerful reminder of the essential unity of science.

In July 1954 the first students graduated. John Hodgkinson, the Registrar, saw it as an opportunity for a big occasion, with more honorary degrees to commemorate key figures in the creation of the College. But that was not Lennard-Jones's style. Perhaps he thought it would seem presumptuous at a time when the experiment was still being nurtured, reviewed and revised. On the day of the ceremony he was ill in hospital, but he sent a personal message to the students. Lord Harrowby, the President, was also absent, so Horwood presided, and Vick took the Principal's place. Horwood was also the recipient of the first degree the College awarded – an honorary Bachelor of Arts. The BA was the only degree the College could confer. (Horwood had taken his Cambridge BA nearly fifty years earlier and his MA in 1953, the same year that Manchester conferred a honorary MA on him.) Professor Blake gave the oration, reminding those present (most of whom were unaware of how much Horwood had done before the College was founded) that he had worked to make a dream come true in the face of criticism and ridicule. He had never missed a College Council meeting and the old fire which had seared its way through countless difficulties still burnt fiercely in him. On a later occasion, when Horwood celebrated his 80th birthday with a dinner given in his honour at Keele, Blake said: '... if I may say so, you do not hesitate to speak your mind. The truth is that you can be very firm, inflexible, not to say frank, candid and even obstinate. I feel sure, that were it not otherwise, we should not be sitting here tonight, all members of this University College, to express our feelings.' Also at the Degree Congregation, Lord Bagot presented a ceremonial chair to the College as a gift from the Staffordshire Society, for use by the President (later the Chancellor) at Degree Ceremonies. It was on the students who were graduating – the first graduates of UCNS – that the success of the new College would be judged. Their results were good, and they went on to a wide variety of positions in industry, education and local government.

By now, Vick wanted to relinquish the office of Vice-Principal. He had borne a heavy load since the College was founded and he wanted to devote more time to his department, so in April 1954 he said he wished to resign as Vice-Principal. He was succeeded by Blake. Other changes were also afoot: Chambers left to go to the William Jacks Chair of German at Glasgow University, to be succeeded as Professor of Modern Languages by the multilingual Kenneth Brooke; and Gallie left to go the Chair of Logic and Metaphysics at Queen's University, Belfast, and then to be

Professor of Political Science at Cambridge. He was succeeded as Professor of Philosophy by Antony Flew. Another member of the department, D. J. O'Connor, went to be Professor of Philosophy first at Liverpool and then at Exeter.

Towards the end of September, Lennard-Jones was rushed into hospital again. He was anxious that in his absence there should be an Acting Principal able to act with full authority, and he asked the Registrar (as Secretary of Council) to visit him in hospital on 21st October. He died on 1st November. In his obituary notice, Professor Blake said that a colleague had said of Sir John Lennard-Jones that he had the most highly developed conscience of any man he had ever known. Forty years later Professor Sir Bruce Williams told me that one could not know him without admiring him. Certainly he was a man who made a deep, good impression in the short time he was here. At the memorial service in Keele Church the Bishop of Lichfield said: 'This was a man of God'. The Council resolved that the College chapel, when built, should be a memorial to him, and that a plaque should be placed in it saying: 'This Chapel was built to the Glory of God and in memory of John Edward Lennard-Jones, Principal of the College from 1st April 1953 to 1st November 1954'. In 1999, as part of the 50th anniversary of the founding of the University College, laboratories in what had become the School of Chemistry and Physics were named the 'Lennard-Jones Laboratories'.

It now fell to Professor Blake to be Acting Principal after only one month as Vice-Principal. If Professor Vick had not chosen to give up the post earlier in the year, then he would once again have been Acting Principal. There were two important tasks: to find a new Principal; and, following the resignation of the Earl of Harrowby in November 1955, to find a new President – a task in which Professor Blake took an important initiative. The Earl died on 30th March 1956, age 91, three days after the death of the Countess, age 89.

Lennard-Jones had already raised with the UGC the question of a master plan for Keele's development, to try to rectify what had been done on a hand-to-mouth basis. Keele had grown like Topsy because there had been no alternative. The laboratories were built where there was flat ground near mains services, namely on the lorry parks of the army camp; and within the limits imposed by licensing restrictions, namely that bricks could not be used. Necessity had shaped the campus, and in 1950 there had not been time to wait for a development plan. Of the new buildings only Sneyd House (described as the new hostel for women students) received any approbation. *The Times Educational Supplement* thought all else was monstrous. But at least the science buildings had been built from the back, so that their Orlit blocks would, in the fullness of time, be covered by extensions frontwards.

Each autumn there were more freshers, more students than before in duffle coats. (It was an age of slacks, scarves, wind-cheaters and duffle coats, not yet the age of universal jeans.) Of course there were difficulties. There was not enough of anything, and single staff still had to use their bed-sitting rooms for teaching. The

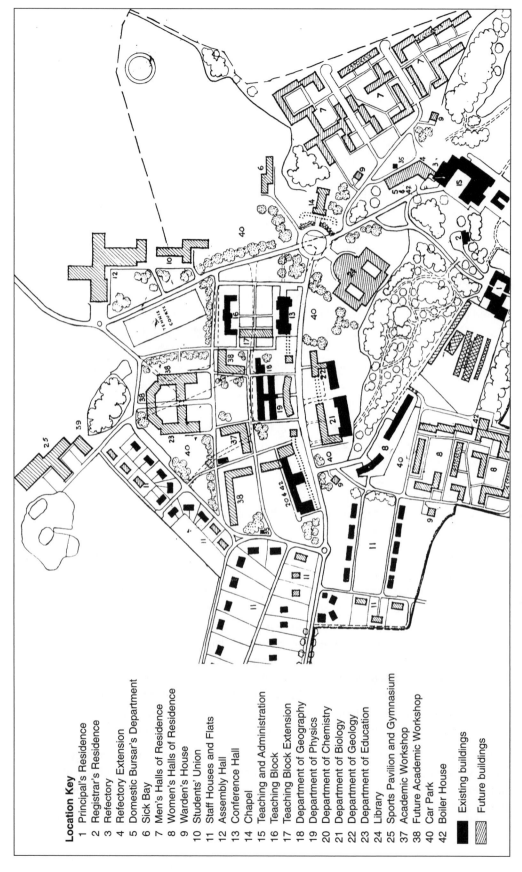

Location Key

1 Principal's Residence
2 Registrar's Residence
3 Refectory
4 Refectory Extension
5 Domestic Bursar's Department
6 Sick Bay
7 Men's Halls of Residence
8 Women's Halls of Residence
9 Warden's House
10 Students' Union
11 Staff Houses and Flats
12 Assembly Hall
13 Conference Hall
14 Chapel
15 Teaching and Administration
16 Teaching Block
17 Teaching Block Extension
18 Department of Geography
19 Department of Physics
20 Department of Chemistry
21 Department of Biology
22 Department of Geology
23 Department of Education
24 Library
25 Sports Pavilion and Gymnasium
37 Academic Workshop
38 Future Academic Workshop
40 Car Park
42 Boiler House

■ Existing buildings
▨ Future buildings

University College of North Staffordshire: Proposed Development Plan by Howard Robertson, 1957 highest priority had to be student accommodation. In June 1955, a Development Plan was drawn up by Piggott (the College's Honorary Architect) and Pickavance (who had become the College's Architect and Buildings Officer in 1952). It was based on an assumption of 1,000 students and 135 full-time teaching staff. One question it raised was whether the College should proceed with small residential blocks for 14-20 students (as some pilot blocks at the Hawthorns), or with large blocks. Opinion in the College was fairly evenly divided. The next problem was that all of the Horwood Hall huts were in the academic area, so a new hall of residence for 350-400 students needed to be built before the huts could be demolished to make room for academic development. Huts 1-12, sandwiched between the Teaching Building (Tawney) and the Conference Hall (Walter Moberly) were in urgent need of replacement (yet they were to be there for many more years). The plan also assumed that all teaching departments would move out of Keele Hall (and that, too, would not be for many years). Everything was needed at once, and a new library and the completion of the science laboratories were also high priorities. Unfortunately, the current rate of grants was such that any one project – residences, library or laboratories – would virtually exclude the other two. Added to that, there were still shortages. This time it was steel, and later bricks.

In March 1956 the University asked Sir Howard Robertson to make a report on the development of the campus. He had been President of the RIBA in 1952-54, and his distinguished career included national exhibition pavilions, interior designs for the Savoy, Claridge's and the UN headquarters in New York, as well as hostels for the Ministry of Works. His last major work had been the Shell Centre on the south bank of the Thames. It was Robertson who determined the style of residences for the future: he favoured large rather than small. He planned the academic area as a whole and wanted to counter the tendency for 'ribbon development' along Keele Drive. He commended the siting of (Sneyd) and (Harrowby) Houses – they were named in July 1956. He believed that existing faults could be mitigated: he suggested the creation of precincts to give a sensation of shelter and seclusion, and covered ways both as an amenity and to unify existing disparate buildings. He first sited the proposed Students' Union between the Conference Hall and the Teaching Building as the east wing of a quadrangle, but then moved it. There was also an Assembly Hall on his plan. Tennis courts (where there is now a car park) were to be retained as a relief from surrounding buildings. He pinpointed in particular the need for more generous standards in both building materials and space. As he said, 'underestimation remains irremediable'. (That same theme was the subject of a Reith Lecture by Sir Richard Rogers in 1995.) Robertson was also invited to be the architect for the new library.

What sort of impact was the College making on the village? When the estate was broken up the establishment of the College at least removed some of the uncertainty about what might happen to the core of the estate, and for some there was a transfer from working for the Estate to working for the College. The College employed more local people as domestic, maintenance and grounds staff than the Estate had done.

Compared with the village the growth of the College was dramatic. Within only a few years there were over a hundred children living at the College. The development of the Hawthorns actually in the village could be seen as an intrusion, and it has meant that some villagers suffer from late-night noise from students, and noise and car-parking problems from conference visitors. It is to the credit of successive Wardens and the students that feelings in the village have not been ruffled more often. Coronation Day in 1953 provided the first occasion for formal co-operation with the village, with an afternoon party at the Hawthorns The following year a garden party was organised by staff, students and villagers, and was opened by Lady Lennard-Jones. It raised £220 for the new village hall which was opened by Professor Blake in January 1955, and for which some staff were financial guarantors. As Mr. Richards of Highway Lane, the Secretary of the Management Committee, observed, as a result of the College, the name of the village would become known around the world. Another change which was imminent was a new major road which just cut across the college boundary: the M6 motorway.

Small items of interest regularly made the local news and add to the picture of the early years. The Queen gave two swans to the Students' Union. The drama society continued with its Shakespeare series – with *As You Like It*, and then *A Midsummer Night's Dream* on the lawns, with real rain and hail as Titania saw 'The seasons alter: Hoary-headed frosts fall in the fresh lap of the crimson rose'. A staff drama group produced *You can't take it with you*. Keele was even appearing disguised in fiction, in *His Father's Son* by Helga Frankland in Biology, in *Old Hall, New Hall* by Michael Innes, and in *Man's Desiring* by Menna Gallie.

The new President of the College was H.R.H. Princess Margaret, and she was formally elected by the Court of Governors in March 1956. Horwood, who had been at Lindsay's side for the inauguration of the College in October 1950, who had been the first person to be presented to the Queen by Lindsay in April 1951, who inducted Sir John Lennard-Jones in May 1953, and who had been feted at Keele on his 80th birthday, now greeted the Princess on her arrival at Keele and installed her as President of the College at a ceremony in the King's Hall, Stoke-on-Trent, on 28th June 1956. Ten years earlier a resolution of the City Council had approved in principle the provision of a University College for North Staffordshire and the Exploratory Committee had held its first meeting. Now Horwood saw this crowning achievement. Six months later he died. The Conference Hall on the campus was not quite ready in time for the installation of Princess Margaret as President, but it was anyway most fitting that this particular occasion should be held in Stoke-on-Trent. Professor Blake, as Acting Principal, expressed the College's welcome and sense of privilege. The Princess was an inspired and an inspiring choice. She gave the College and the University thirty years of dedicated service, usually coming twice a year, and bringing Keele to the attention of the world's press. On this occasion, news was certainly reported in Australia, Barbados, Bermuda, Canada, France, Hong Kong, Italy, New Zealand, South Africa, Sweden, Tanganyika and the United States.

For the ceremony in the King's Hall, which was also Degree Day for that year's graduating students, there were present representatives of twenty-seven Universities and Colleges, including twelve Vice-Chancellors. It was also a gathering of old friends and well-wishers. Lady Lindsay and Lady Lennard-Jones were there, together with quite a number whose connection went back to the days before the College was founded: W. S. Perkins, who had been clerk of works on the army camp; J. R. Piggott, who had drawn up plans for Meaford Hall to start with; C. Wainwright, who had driven the Lindsays round the estate and who was now head porter. Alderman Kemp was there, twelve years after he had advocated the founding of a College as a war memorial; Gladys Malbon, Dr. Stross and J. F. Carr, the unofficial deputation which had met the UGC in March 1946; Harry Taylor and members of the Exploratory Committee – Aldermen Davies, Harvey and Leason, Mrs Barker, and Miss Farmer, the 'person experienced in education', who had been in Tawney's class and was the first lady to become Lord Mayor of Stoke-on-Trent in 1931-32. The Sponsoring Universities were represented; and there were Professor P. S. Noble, by now the Principal of King's College, London, whose voice may have been the decisive one at a crucial moment, the Master of Balliol (Sir David Lindsay Keir), and Mrs. Montford, whose generous bequest became the foundation of a Music Department in due course. Professor Chambers and Professor O'Connor returned for the ceremony, and amongst the Keele staff were the two new professors – Professor Brooke and Professor Flew – and Professor Sneddon who was about to go to the newly-created Simson Chair of Mathematics at Glasgow.

Also present were Sir George and Lady Barnes. Sir George had been appointed Principal on 1st November 1955, to take office in September 1956. He was 51 and a man of great personal charm. He had been educated at the Royal Naval Colleges at Osborne and Dartmouth, but his poor eyesight precluded a naval career and he went on to King's College, Cambridge. He joined the BBC in 1935, becoming Director of Talks in 1941, Head of the new Third Programme in 1946, and the first Director of the Spoken Word in 1948; in 1950 he was appointed to the new post of Director of Television. The first colour television outside broadcast, transmitted on closed-circuit to the Children's Hospital, Great Ormond Street, was the Coronation in June 1953. In October 1953, on a visit to Lime Grove studios, the Queen knighted him. He was not a stranger to North Staffordshire, for in 1955 he had become the first chairman of the Wedgwood Society. Before he came to Keele, Barnes was awarded the honorary degree of Doctor of Civil Law by the University of Durham. As a consequence of his naval leanings and publications he was widely known as 'The Commander' and Betjeman wrote a poem in his memory with that title. At Keele the staff promoted him to 'The Admiral'. He immediately identified himself with the ideas behind the College and announced his intention of combating the evils of specialisation. 'My job will be mainly to tend and water this young plant, and to encourage its growth, not necessarily to plant something else', he said. Before taking up his appointment he went to the U.S.A. for six weeks, at the invitation of the Ford Foundation, to look at twelve university colleges which had a broadly-based curriculum.

Barnes would seem to have been an unlikely appointment: unlikely in that after twenty years in the BBC he had risen close to the top in a fast developing area, and that he could still expect another ten or fifteen years there. It was unlikely, too, in that Barnes had not been an academic. All of his predecessors and successors were academics, and Lindsay, Lennard-Jones, Stewart and Finch had all been professors. He was, therefore, the most different of Keele's Principals and Vice-Chancellors. He strode a different stage and he made Keele an interesting place. He could reasonably expect to remain in office for fifteen years. Had he survived, he might have been the most interesting of them all. He was very conscious of what his external role might be. He had a wide knowledge of men of affairs in the world outside universities, and he did a lot to bring distinguished visitors to Keele, especially in the field of the arts. There is, perhaps, a link between his leaving the BBC and his coming to Keele. He feared that he foresaw what he regarded as the rise and triumph of mediocrity, and he wished to defend bastions of excellence. He added to the analyses of Lindsay, Ortega y Gasset and Moberly his own reflections, namely that the mass media 'now reach and touch every individual, destroying the cement of our society by substituting for its traditional values, moral and intellectual, the easy, the smart and the trivial.'

The President, H.R.H. Princess Margaret inaugurated Sir George Barnes as Principal at a ceremony in the new Conference Hall on 20th November 1956. The Princess came the previous evening to attend a Ball given by the Students' Union. It was the first of six visits in just over two years: she attended degree days, a Senior Common Room party, a meeting of the Court of Governors, and a concert to raise funds for music in the College. (When she came in November 1957 she was greeted by a notice with letters seven feet high which said 'Welcome Home'.) Seventeen other universities and colleges were represented at the ceremony, and the proceedings were relayed to other rooms by closed-circuit television. What had been achieved so far astonished visitors, that so many buildings had been adapted or built at the same time as teaching a new degree course and that there was sense of a common purpose. Looking to the future, Barnes said: 'We must now build and plant, on a time-scale fit for a university founded in perpetuity... (and) give as much encouragement as possible to staff and students in their work. We must provide time and privacy for both to read; and we must maintain the intimacy of these precincts: the friendliness which is so quickly noticed by freshmen and by visitors... and if necessary the preservation of Lord Lindsay's idea of a single community must determine the nature and limit of our expansion.' He did not wish to limit the size of the College to some pre-ordained number and wished to encourage growth, but he was anxious that the pace of growth should not jeopardise what had been so painstakingly achieved. In 1958 he spoke of there being a college of 1200 students in the mid-1960s. He was concerned about the academic balance and any threat to Lindsay's intention that departments should be equal in importance if not in numbers.

To build, care for and preserve, and to rectify the faults which necessity had wrought were Barnes's aims and achievements. For academic development he gave great support to the library as the main teaching and research instrument of the College. For the life of the community he sought to encourage culture. 'The cultivation of taste and discrimination is not a luxury', he said at a Senior Common Room dinner. 'It is certainly not a luxury in a place of education; least of all is it a luxury in a place of education such as this which is attempting to educate the whole man.'

The Keele he was coming to was still full of builders. At the centre of the campus the Conference Hall, Geology and Geography were taking shape. The largest acquisition the College has ever made was 350 acres of Home Farm which was purchased at this time. For this the College was indebted to Harry Taylor again for his firm resolve and encouragement. He had noted the desirability of this purchase a year earlier. The UGC felt they could justify funding only 60% of it, and it seems unlikely that the Council would have agreed to go into debt by £13,000 at this time without his guidance. It has safeguarded the College's development for generations to come.

Barnes recognised the potential of the Keele estate and he seized the opportunity of restoring the grounds. Most of the beauty of the estate had been the work of the Sneyd family in the 18th and 19th centuries. Years of neglect had taken a heavy toll. The second lake for example, was like a swamp of willows. With groups of volunteers, both staff and students, Barnes led by personal example and cleared the second lake, the undergrowth around and between the lakes, and the dell between the two streams below the third lake. The dell was replanted with azaleas, and it was later dedicated as a permanent memorial to Barnes. The spectacular display of daffodils on the campus every spring is one more reminder of his untiring efforts to enhance the beauty of the campus. Various parts of the estate had been cleared before they were sold to the College (as the fifty acres of Lower Springpool Wood purchased in 1957), or by the College (a plantation to make room for the Larchwood houses, four of a group of lime trees known as the 'seven sisters' to make room for the Conference Hall, a magnificent beech tree for the extension to the Physics Department, and three old oaks and a fine Lebanon cedar for Harrowby House. A section of the cedar showing 130 years of growth rings was preserved by Professor Beaver.) There was an obligation to replant the Lower Springpool Wood: belts of beeches, oak, sycamore, poplar, larch and fir were planted, to provide an important amenity for later generations.

Before Barnes took office, Sir Howard Robertson had recommended commissioning a report from a landscape architect on tree planting on the campus. It was undertaken by Mrs. Sheila Hayward, who visited Keele in October 1956. She saw with a fresh and expert eye all the advantages of the site which it was easy to take for granted – a parkland protected to a remarkable degree from urban and industrial development – and she saw, too, the problems of the restless skyline of the teaching area, the bleakness of the playing fields (for Barnes Hall and the Sports Centre were not yet built), the ragged skyline of the Church Plantation houses, and the incoherence in the housing areas generally. She did not like the rhododendrons planted by the Sneyds. Her proposals were to reform and replant the southern ridge to dominate the views from Newcastle drive and the playing fields and to contain the ragged outline of the science blocks; to renew the belt of woodland from Keele Hall to the back of the Covert; to plant a shelter belt to the north of the playing fields; and to put loosely-grouped sycamores to the north of the Church Plantation houses. She then recommended further improvements, namely that the dignity of Keele Drive should be maintained and that there should be some specimen planting along Newcastle Drive. She suggested more trees to reduce the dominant effects of tarmac and carparking. She also made proposals for the lakes and woodland and for Clock House Drive. For the future she suggested that the undulating landscape would make a fine setting for some works of sculpture.

Barnes had a natural way of cultivating people – students, staff, neighbours and visitors from afar whom he wished to share with students and staff. He knew so many people who could 'open doors'. He instituted the 'Neighbours' Dinner' each year for farmers whose land adjoined the campus. He was president of the newly-formed North Staffordshire Romilly Association – which was concerned with problems of crime and attracted eminent speakers; Keele was the venue for the Fourth International Wedgwood Seminar (after Philadelphia, New York and Boston) for Wedgwood's bicentenary. Above all, he wanted to add an artistic dimension to the life of the College, and he did a great deal to encourage exhibitions. These included the early works of Augustus John and Graham Sutherland, and in 1960, H.M. the Queen Mother lent a picture by Paul Nash which was on display on Open Day. Barnes started the Picture Loan Scheme, lending pictures to students; and he commissioned a sculpture for Horwood Hall – the 'Seed Clock' by Jack Waldron of Burslem College. He drew on support from the Arts Council and the Gulbenkian Foundation, and in 1958 he was appointed a member of the Bridges Committee, a small committee set up by the Calouste Gulbenkian Foundation to enquire into the needs of the arts in Britain. That committee's recommendations included more help for the provinces, fellowships for artists, and help for young musicians by providing instruments – developments from which Keele was to derive benefit after Barnes's death. When he opened the Cheltenham Festival in 1957, he spoke about the College and about the BBC. He appeared on the television programme 'Brains Trust' (his first appearance on television), as later so did Professor Gemmell. And he brought a lot of musicians here – Gina Bacchauer, Nina Milkina, Britten and Pears, the Allegri Quartet and Zoltán Kodály; and also the Apollo Society – Dame Peggy Ashcroft, Albert Ferber and Cecil Day-Lewis.

Barnes's efforts evoked a response locally. The Lord Mayor of Stoke-on-Trent, the Revd. Arthur Perry, announced that the major project for his term of office in 1957 would be an appeal to endow a Directorship of Music at the College. (A few months earlier, Perry had delivered the panegyric at Horwood's memorial service.) Support included concerts in Hanley by the Hallé Orchestra with Sir John Barbirolli, and a performance of *Hiawatha* by the Ceramic City Choir and the London Symphony Orchestra with Sir Malcolm Sargent, a concert which was attended by Princess Margaret and broadcast by the BBC. There was support from local firms and amateur music societies, including a gramophone recital by Jack Oliver. In the years to follow, the initials 'J.O.' appear regularly in the *Sentinel* giving warm support to music at Keele. (Jack Oliver's bust has a place in the newly refurbished Victoria Hall in Hanley.) This fund, together with the Montford bequest earlier, was the foundation of later developments in music, and more immediately made possible the appointment of a part-time Director of Music, the first of whom was Dr. David Lumsden, and this produced a new musical life at the College. It was as an acknowledgement of its debt to the local community that the College, and then the University, for many years put on professional recitals with free admission.

Student activities redounded to their credit. Shakespeare continued with *Romeo and Juliet* in the Clock House courtyard and audiences rose to six hundred. An annual garden party raised funds for the Keele Parish Church Bells Appeal, and the first students' rag raised nearly £800 for the charities of the Lord Mayor of Stoke-on-Trent and the Mayor of Newcastle. As a direct result, the Borough of Newcastle-under-Lyme presented a silver mace to the College.

The area which frustrated Barnes was his dealings with the College Senate. His background at the BBC as a director had not prepared him for academics' enormous appetite for discussion. Moreover, the predominantly young professors had grown more confident and had enjoyed nearly two years' interregnum before Barnes came. It seemed to him that few of them were prepared to give up unfettered discussion and their privilege of expressing an opinion, and that they were all qualified to do so on most subjects. In his *Report* for 1957-58 he quoted Jefferson: 'It takes time to persuade men to do even what is for their own good.' In private he would exclaim that the Senate was a machine for generating heat rather than light. *The Times* later wrote that he never took kindly to the labyrinthine ways and anarchical habits of university committees, and that he constantly marvelled at the notorious academic inability to clothe thought with action. 'James Dundonald' wrote in his *Letters to a Vice-Chancellor* in 1962: 'It is the nature of academic persons to be peculiarly skilled in seeing all sides of a given question, and to want every side put forward in discussion, whatever the speaker's own views'. 'James Dundonald' had had twelve years' experience at Keele, for he was Professor J. J. Lawlor. In his first year, Barnes was feeling his way at Senate. By the time he was firmly in the saddle it was not long before the illness which was to strike him down was diagnosed.

What size would Keele be? The initial thought of 800 had been reduced by the UGC to 600. If Keele was going to be bigger, then how much bigger? On that would depend the physical layout, the academic programme, and even the philosophy of the College. Keele could only move within the confines laid down by the UGC. Before Barnes took office, the UGC had written to say they wished to formulate a 'shadow programme' for 1958 and 1959. Next they wished to 'crystallise' the information further. Keele responded with a 'crystallised building programme'. The first priority was to expand to 800, but the UGC felt unable to 'formulate a firm shadow programme'. Next they sought our views on expanding to 1200 by 1965, assuming that numbers would settle at that after the peak of the post-war birth-rate had passed. They also assumed that two-thirds of the increase would be science students. Keele was certainly willing, if the existing character and objects of the College were retained, and assuming that finances would be forthcoming. But they were not. The UGC also stressed the need to keep capital costs down, to prune to bare essentials and to make do with more frugal standards. When the grants for the quinquennium 1957/58 – 1961/62 were announced, it might have been a separate body from the one which had been asking about expanding student numbers. Universities were obliged to mark time for two years: the UGC was being squeezed of funds in the aftermath of the Suez crisis. When the shadow programme crystallised, the grant for the last three years of the quinquennium showed some improvement. The Local Authorities continued to give financial support, but more was needed, so the College launched an appeal. Alderman Horwood had chaired his last meeting of the College Council in October 1956, and he was succeeded as chairman by Alderman A. G. B. Owen, CBE.

Owen had the bearing of a patrician. He was tireless. He was a very successful businessman and a leading industrialist. He had left Cambridge University at 21 when his father died, in order to take over the running of Rubery Owen Co. Ltd., and had turned it into the biggest private family business in Britain. It was said that there was hardly a car, bus, van or truck which did not contain an Owen component. He supported BRM cars in British motor racing, and was one of Donald Campbell's backers in his world speed record bids. The breadth of his interests and list of appointments is scarcely credible in one man: he was involved with over eighty other companies and thirty voluntary organisations; he was very active in church work. He was chairman of the council of Dr. Barnado's Homes. He was chairman of Staffordshire County Council, and was knighted in 1961 for public service. He was very supportive of Keele, chaired the Council, preached in the chapel, and took an active part in the College's appeal, persuading others to give generously, to raise over £150,000 in three months.

One of the drawbacks of expansion, even on the small scale of the late-1950s, was the marked diminution of that intimate knowledge of students which had been a characteristic of Keele in its early days. Discussion centred on whether the halls of residence should be developed as three colleges – three miniature Keeles side by side. If so, with how much autonomy and with what sort of government? That was the question in the late-'50s and early-'60s and the word 'colleges' was common parlance until 1962, when the titles of Horwood Hall and Lindsay Hall were confirmed by the Council. (In 1963, the opening of Lindsay Refectory focused attention once more on what a 'hall' should be at Keele – not as in Oxbridge, nor as a hall of residence in Manchester or Birmingham.) There were plans to include staff as members of halls, but that was not how it developed.

The UGC had planned for the 'bulge' in student numbers, followed by a 'plateau'; but then came the 'trend' – a growing percentage of 6th-formers wanting to go on to university, so the government's target was raised to 170,000 students by 1970. Should Keele stop at 1200, or expand further? or pause for five years? The scientists saw no insuperable difficulty in expanding to 2400; others did not see how it could be avoided. Some were talking of a 'liberal arts college', and those in favour of the *status quo* tended to appear as 'loyalists'. The debates were long and wide ranging. Professor Brooke was new enough to stand aside from differences based on the past, and his analysis was clear and decisive: with expansion would come university status; the request from the UGC was also an appeal, and a minimal response could expect only minimal consideration, especially as to remain small was to remain expensive. To insist on remaining unique carried the risk of putting the College outside the university system of the country: it was not a question of loyalty, for they were all committed to Keele. The Senate accepted a figure of 2400 by the late 1970s, with provisos about funding, staff-student ratios, residence, and so on, and an immediate target of 1700 by 1968. This meant a building programme to include residences, the library, and an Arts Teaching Block (which became the Chancellor's Building), expanded laboratories, Students' Union and playing fields, a sports centre and a swimming bath, and a great sum of money for roads and mains services.

With plans for 1700 and then 2400 students, the way people thought the College should develop in the future reflected in part their perceptions and interpretations of Lindsay – and hence the notion of 'loyalists'. Twelve of the fifteen heads of departments had sat at Senate with Lindsay, but their views on Lindsay's intentions differed. There was some myth-making and iconography in the face of change. The College had grown by chance evolution as much as by conscious planning. The uneven distribution of students between departments reflected recruitment rather than policy. Professor Teale re-stated Lindsay's philosophy: that it was not specialisation as such which he had sought to correct, but the breach in universities and in society at large caused by the growth of specialised languages, leading to the lack of a common medium of communication, and so producing a breakdown of mutual understanding. Full residence and a broad curriculum were intended to combat these faults. Teale maintained that the College was now failing in its original aim if it did not ensure reasonable numbers of students in departments, for without that, students would not come into contact sufficiently with the different disciplines of different subjects. He therefore wanted the selection process to be used to correct the growing imbalance.

The Senate rejected Teale's proposals for change. Senate also, therefore, it seemed to him, rejected his statement of the aims of the founders. It could no longer be taken for granted, he felt, that the professors who had been appointed in 1950 held Lindsay's views. Had Lindsay, perhaps, appointed 'more Judases than Thomases, and more Thomases than Peters and Johns?' he asked.

Some perceived something was amiss. It was no longer the intimate College of the early-1950s. Everybody still knew everybody, near enough, but now there was talk of 1200, 1700, 2400 students. With new universities jostling in a queue for charters, Keele would no longer be the only new child. The Senate and the Principal were not always thought to be pulling in the same direction, and some staff felt frustration at delays in getting changes. Time was eroding Lindsay's ideas (though there was talk of Lindsay into the 1970s). Myth-making and iconography were being confronted by change. Perhaps it was the erosion of a sense of common purpose. Living on the campus and paying rent was losing its appeal for some staff. The College's role *in loco parentis* sometimes seemed heavy handed and left an uncomfortable feeling. The Foundation Year was not quite fulfilling its purpose. It was difficult to put one's finger on what was not quite right. It became more focused a few years later when there was a debate in the Union in 1962 'That the Keele experiment is failing'. Hugh Leech spoke strongly of a falling off from the ideals set by Lindsay, the loosening of the once close staff-student links, and an overall weakening of the Keele community spirit. Professor Stewart took a wider view and pointed to Keele's impact in the principles being embodied in the courses in the new universities. They had vindicated what Keele stood for. There was nothing to fear in change and development if Keele was to provide the challenge and the stimulus it had offered in the previous ten years. The motion was defeated by 60:136, with 31 abstentions, but perhaps the size of those figures demonstrated a falling off in the enthusiasm which had been noticeable in earlier years.

The urge to reconsider and revise the Foundation Year was triggered by poor attendance at lectures. In the proposals put forward for its improvement there was usually more mutual inconsistency than unanimity. A committee to consider its structure and content was set up in May 1955, during the interregnum before Barnes took office; it held eighteen meetings, and reported its findings in February 1957. It is difficult in retrospect to explain the quest, but everyone who had a view wished to prescribe different treatment. One proposal was for a Foundation Term in the first year, with Principal teaching starting in January; and with two terms aiming to give a synthesis of the course as the last two terms of the four-year course. To summarise the committee's findings, the lecture course was still too fragmented despite its historical framework; there were problems of 'plugging gaps'; and themes were blurred with too many topics in any one week. There remained a tendency to drift towards what Lindsay had spotted in 1950 – trying to do too much in the time. If there was too much, there was also an unwillingness to discard – or at least, no agreement on what to discard. The committee's proposals were to abandon the overriding historical framework in favour of discrete blocks of lectures. This would give heads of departments more of a free hand and relieve the Foundation Year Committee of the task of determining detailed subject matter. It would give greater flexibility, and confront the students with one thing at a time. (Later revisions of the Foundation Year also sought greater flexibility in the structure.) In order to make it easier for students without a science background to take a science subject at principal level, 'transfer' courses were introduced in Chemistry, Physics and Mathematics. Three years later, Professor Leigh from Reed College, Oregon, who was visiting Keele on a staff exchange scheme, looked closely at the Foundation Year. His conclusion was that breadth was being achieved at the cost of insufficient intensive study, and he was not convinced that the course was sufficiently co-ordinated to give a sense of continuity or a unifying theme. (Graduates have often commented, however, that synthesis becomes more apparent later.) He especially commended Discussion Groups, which also, of course, brought together staff from different departments; and Professor Leigh was impressed by the contribution the Senior Common Room made to a rich academic life by facilitating an easy intellectual exchange between staff from different departments outside formal structures.

Any doubts about the way Keele was going did not really detract much from the underlying sense of purpose, which was still strong, and perhaps taken for granted. The *Glasgow Herald* examined Keele, following some rowdy incidents at Glasgow at a Rectorial Installation. It praised the sense of common purpose, the loyalty to the philosophy, the relationships between teachers and students, and the flourishing corporate life. There was also a spirited correspondence in *The Spectator* about Keele's distinctive role, especially commending the opportunity the Foundation Year provided for students to change their minds over which principal subjects to read for their degree. Keele students readily attracted press attention, whether it was the twenty-two year old Ron Maddison's photograph of the Arend-Roland comet, discovered only a few months earlier; or Jennifer Cramp defending her Universities' diving championship; or packing eighteen students into a telephone box, which provoked correspondence from South Africa, California, Canada and New Zealand. The *Daily Express* reported: 'Students' goodnight kisses keep lecturer's daughter awake', and the reply: 'Well, one has to say goodnight somewhere' (19-year old blonde politics student). Serious news like the closure of the College by the 'flu epidemic in 1957 received less attention than the kidnapping of Miss Brighton in 1958. Drama continued to reach a high standard. *Electra* was the first production in the new Conference Hall, and then it was Shakespeare again, with *Macbeth* and *Much Ado about Nothing.*

Sir Howard Robertson's drawings for the new Library went on show at the Royal Academy Summer Exhibition, and a picture of the model of the Students' Union building appeared in the *Architectural Review*. It continued to capture professional interest. In 1974 Pevsner said it was the best building so far. In 1971 an article in *The Architects' Journal Information Library* said how the building came as a surprise, 'partly from finding so 'citified' a building in the country, and partly from the company it keeps... a chapel pretending to be a Victorian gaol, rows of Nissen huts masquerading as halls of residence and, on a neighbouring hill, a library dressed in the style of a Swiss chalet... The stairway is dramatic and imposing... [and] ends up rather surprisingly on a non-existent and fake third floor. For all the viewer knows it continues onward into heaven'. There followed more correspondence in *The Sunday Times*, and the views of a social research and market development consultant and a consultant psychologist provoked the comment in *Building Design* that 'the field would seem to be wide open for architects to move into psychiatry, town planners to take up gynaecology and interior designers to have a crack at brain surgery'. Lord Lindsay's hopes for cross-disciplinary discussion, even if not mutual understanding, were clearly being fulfilled!

In 1958 the first Lindsay Memorial Lectures were given by Professor Michael Polanyi. He was a Hungarian-born Professor of Social Studies at Manchester University where, for ten years previously, he had been Professor of Physical Chemistry. Lindsay had greatly admired Polanyi's Riddell Memorial Lectures on 'Science, Faith and Society'. At Keele he spoke on 'The Study of Man', for which he was later awarded the Lecomte de Nony award. Some of Lindsay's own lectures were published by Lady Lindsay in 1957 in a book which she dedicated to 'The Students of Keele Hall'.

News about Princess Margaret always attracted widespread press attention. The College suggested having a portrait of her painted as the new President, but the Princess chose to be sculpted instead, by Epstein. Epstein was 77. He had been at the centre of controversy for fifty years since his commission for eighteen figures carved in the stone of the British Medical Association's new building in the Strand in London, and he had also offended religious sensibilities with his figure of Christ in 1920. He had completed his Christ in Majesty for Llandaff Cathedral in 1957, and was working on his St. Michael and the Devil for Coventry Cathedral. After eight sittings it was announced that Epstein was changing his bust of Princess Margaret into a half-length sculpture. In June 1959 it was said to be completed, but two months later Epstein said he wanted to arrange further sittings. Shortly afterwards he died. He had been working on it the day before he died, and there was speculation whether it was finished. In fact he had completed a plaster cast, which was approved by the Princess. Pictures of it aroused controversy. The sculpture itself went on show at the Royal Academy Summer Exhibition in 1960, and comments ran the whole gamut: 'It does not do the Princess credit', 'a characteristic work by a great sculptor', 'a remarkable piece of Epsteinery', 'I think it is simply wonderful'. According to Lady Epstein, the Princess loved it. Another piece of Epstein, a plaster bust of Lindsay, was presented to the University in 1968 by Lady Epstein, with the condition that it be displayed within the University.

An imaginative and generous gift to the College was made by Granada Television Ltd., namely to endow a Research Chair of Communication, with the terms of reference left to the College. Donald MacKay was appointed to the chair in 1960. Ten years earlier he had formulated 'Information Theory'. He built up a team of physicists, physiologists and psychologists to study the workings and disorders of the human brain, particularly with information relayed to it by sight and sound. Another benefactor to the College was the American Embassy which endowed a lectureship in American Studies. From this there developed the Department of

American Studies in 1965, and then the David Bruce Centre, named after the distinguished American Ambassador. In 1996 the Centre received a bequest of over $600,000 from the Evangeline B. Bruce Trust. The first Head of Department and Director of the David Bruce Centre was Professor David Adams who retired in 1997, and was awarded the OBE in the diplomatic list for his work on North American studies.

It was while Barnes was Principal that the College instituted Inaugural Lectures. Anyone appointed to the Principalship or to a Professorship in future should be invited to give an inaugural lecture. The idea is very much in accord with the Keele Idea that there should be a common understanding and that the expert should be able to explain his ideas to a wider audience. Inaugural lectures in 1950-51 would have provided a very interesting insight into the founding professors' interpretation of Lindsay's ideas in practice in their own disciplines, but they already had an enormous amount to do anyway. It is regrettable that, since inaugural lectures were introduced, not all Vice-Chancellors and professors coming to Keele have availed themselves of such an opportunity. In 1959 Professor Basil Willey, the Professor of English Literature at Cambridge, gave the prestigious Hibbert lectures at Keele on Darwin's impact on the church. Keele was also the venue for the final of the *Observer* 'Mace' debating competition. At York, the inaugural address at the British Association meeting was given by Sir James Gray, the zoologist. His theme was that the sciences and humanities should seek common ground, and he specifically referred to Keele as 'the most important and courageous educational experiment in our times'. Sir Charles Snow had recently given his Rede Lecture in Cambridge on 'The Two Cultures and the Scientific Revolution'. Keele, and the ideas it stood for, were firmly on the map.

Professors Chambers, Gallie and Sneddon had gone before Barnes took office. In 1959 two more of the founding professors went elsewhere: Professor Williams to the Robert Otley Chair at Manchester (and later to be Vice-Chancellor of the University of Sydney); and Professor Vick to be Deputy Director and then Director of the Atomic Energy Research Establishment at Harwell (and later to be Vice-Chancellor of Queen's University, Belfast). The College they left was small, and they all went on to major posts. Nearly forty years later I asked Professors Gallie, Sneddon, Williams and Vick for their views on Keele from the much wider perspective of their subsequent careers. In all cases, Keele was, and continued to be very important to them. Altogether, five of the original staff appointed in 1950 became Vice-Chancellors: Dr. Jenkins (University of Dacca in 1953), Professor Blake (University of Botswana, Lesotho and Swaziland in 1964), Professor Vick (Queen's University, Belfast in 1966), Professor Williams (University of Sydney in 1967), and Professor Stewart (Keele in 1967). The first Keele graduate to be appointed to a chair was Alan Lees. He had come to Keele with 'A' levels in arts subjects; after the Foundation Year he took principal Biology and Geology, and was awarded a first-class honours degree in 1956. He was later appointed Professor of Geology at the University of Louvain.

Permanent buildings were at last starting to impose a shape on the campus, and in May 1960 the Conference Hall and the New Teaching Block were named the 'Walter Moberly Hall' and the 'R. H. Tawney Building', to mark some of the milestones in the founding of the College. Both Moberly and Tawney were still alive. In time, the Walter Moberly Hall was to be changed into teaching rooms for modern languages and lose its name, and the R. H. Tawney Building became administrative offices. Keele Hall courtyard was much improved when it was resurfaced with setts patterned with blue bricks; the inscription 'Freshers' Gate' appeared one night over the pedestrian arch, put there, as it said in committee minutes, 'by an unauthorised person'.

Above all, Barnes *liked* Keele. When he spoke to the freshers in October 1959 he said: 'We like Keele because we are building the place – a fact you will become acutely aware of because in all your four years, as in the last nine, noise by day, hazardous holes by night, and dust or mud by day and by night, will intrude into your otherwise tranquil lives. But above all we like Keele because we believe in what we are doing – that is in creating a new and fresh path to graduation.' Those were the last freshers he would live to see, for he was by then terminally ill, and he died the following September, age 56. At his memorial service at Keele, Sir William Haley, the editor of *The Times*, who as Director-General of the BBC had chosen Barnes to be controller of the Third Programme, said of him: 'Once, in his home here at Keele, he played me something on the piano and spoke of the unease I ought to feel until the music returned to its original key. It was in search of his original key that Sir George Barnes came to the University College.' In that search, Barnes brought a lot of the outside world to Keele, and by so doing made Keele more widely known to the outside world.

The College had lost three Principals in ten years, each with his own distinctive style. Once again Keele was in the throes of an interregnum. When a public appeal for a memorial to Barnes was launched a few months later, to spread education in music, the list of signatories to a letter to *The Times* says a lot about the stamp of the man: it was signed by the Archbishop of York (Michael Ramsey), Noel Annan (the Provost of King's College, Cambridge), John Betjeman, Adrian Boult, Benjamin Britten, Elizabeth Cavendish, Arthur Fforde (the Chairman of the BBC), Anthony Lewis (Professor of Music at Birmingham), Malcolm Sargent, Harold Clowes, A.G.B. Owen, and W.A.C. Stewart.

Chapter 13

COLLEGE TO UNIVERSITY

Athird interregnum in a College still only ten years old looked like an extreme case of Mr. Worthing's 'carelessness'. The new Principal, when appointed, would be required to undergo a rigorous medical examination. When the Senate met in October 1960 Professor Stewart was in the Chair. Professor Springall had been Vice-Principal for the two years 1957/58 and 1958/59, but he did not wish to continue and was succeeded as Vice-Principal in 1959/60 by Professor Stewart. The Senate was still a small body of twenty-one members, twelve of whom had sat in Senate with Lindsay – Professors Stewart, Beaver, Blake, Charlton, Cope, Finer, Gemmell, Lawlor, Springall, Teale, Mr. S. O. Stewart, and Mr. Rolo.

It therefore fell to Professor Stewart to welcome H.M. Queen Elizabeth the Queen Mother, H.R.H. Princess Margaret and her husband Mr. Antony Armstrong-Jones to Keele's 10th anniversary celebrations. The Queen Mother had promised that she would return for this celebration. It was Princess Margaret's eleventh visit to the College, and she announced at the Congregation held to celebrate the anniversary that the College was to seek university status the following year. The Queen Mother said that Keele's boldness in setting out on an uncharted course had been triumphantly vindicated. She then laid the foundation stone of the new Students' Union building – a 32 cwt stone lowered into place by a crane – and she put a half-crown in the mortar and some documents in a hollowed out cavity. The royal party then toured an exhibition in the Clock House depicting the achievements of the College, the history of Keele Hall, and aspects of Staffordshire life and culture. Items on display included a silver gilt sconce loaned by the Queen Mother (which had formerly belonged to the Sneyd family), eleven paintings by Peter de Wint, the English watercolourist who was born in Stone, archaeological finds from the digs at Holditch, meteorological records, published works, fine china, and contributions from sculptors and artists. The portrait of the Princess by Annigoni was also part of the exhibition, but on that day it was on display in London.

A slim book, *Keele After Ten Years* was published in 1961 under the auspices of the Students' Union and the Keele Society (the Association of past students). This encapsulated a view of Keele at the time and preserved some memories which might otherwise have been lost. John Barker recalled how on 'the evening after [Lindsay's] death was announced, Lady Lindsay invited some thirty students to the Clock House. She said that she and her husband had spent all their married life amongst students, and it was to students she wished to talk on the day of his death. So gathered in their sitting room, those students listened for about three hours to Lady Lindsay telling of her husband's ideals and his hopes for Keele'. There were recollections, too, of how physical education classes had been held in a Nissen hut (half of which was used as a furniture store) until part of the roof was blown away in a blizzard. Thereafter classes were held in the Economics Department's large room, having 'to be fitted into the vacant times between economics lectures and tutorials, and even then had to be conducted with as little noise as possible while a long-suffering but most co-operative Professor Bruce Williams worked and conducted tutorials in his adjacent office' (H. W. B. Hayley and Brian Stokes). Another article highlighted the 'change of mind' over Principal subjects. The obvious importance of this development at Keele never seems to have aroused the national concern it deserved. Of the first Principal year students in 1957-58, only 70 out of 159 were reading the two subjects they had originally intended; and the following year only 55 out of 156. In the five years 1956-1960, over 40% had changed one subject and 9% had changed both. This was hard evidence of the impact of the Foundation Year giving the opportunity for students to make an informed choice of what subjects to read at honours level. Such changes extrapolated on to a national basis would have staggering implications, and yet this evidence never really featured as more than just an interesting statistic about Keele. The departments which gained heavily were Political Institutions, Economics and Philosophy, and those which lost most were History, Geography and English. *Keele After Ten Years* also recalled the early development of the campus and how at one time there was only one bag of cement for three sites. Looking forward to a third college at the Hawthorns in Keele Village and then to further colleges later (the word 'college' never took root for a hall of residence), it was stressed that consideration should be given to the general aesthetics and to the importance of avoiding standardised planning and a mass barrack effect.

Another small book also evoked powerful memories of Keele's past. This was Professor Gallie's *A New University: A. D. Lindsay and the Keele Experiment*, published in 1960. From the starting point of Lindsay's philosophy and concept of democracy, Gallie traced Lindsay's hope of creating a self-understanding society with a sense of moral and political responsibility, and how he had built his Keele idea on this foundation. At a time when a number of new universities were in an advanced stage of planning, Gallie's book was widely reviewed and provoked prejudices about both Lindsay and Keele.

A link with the early years was broken with the sudden death of Mrs. Morgan the Deputy Domestic Bursar. Working with Miss Rolfe, the Domestic Bursar, she had built up a domestic staff of over a hundred and was held in high esteem by those who worked for her and those for whom she worked. She was remembered as cheerful, considerate, open to suggestions and unfailingly co-operative. The three-stemmed silver birch tree in the brick planter by the Students' Union commemorates her years at Keele.

During the summer of 1961 a group of Oxford students came to examine Keele for *Isis* magazine. They were impressed, especially with the 'extraordinary sense of involvement and participation of the students', and with the much more generous proportion of women students than at Oxford. One of the articles was written by Alan Ryan, who was at Balliol. He said that the students he had spoken to were most articulate and emphatic in their belief in Lindsay's ideal of a self-understanding society, but had expressed some apprehension that future expansion might detract from Keele's coherence and cohesion. The *Observer* made the comment about the Oxford visit that if the students at Keele would not exchange their life for that at Oxford and Cambridge, 'one imagines that the reverse is also true'. In fact, Alan Ryan joined Professor Teale's Department of Political and Moral Philosophy two years later. He subsequently became Professor of Politics at Princeton University and then Professor of Politics at Oxford and Warden of New College. Keele's philosophy students were making a very good impression on the external examiner, Professor H. H. Price, Emeritus Professor of Logic at Oxford. He found the standard they had reached was entirely comparable with any of the Arts Joint Honours Schools at Oxford, and expressed regret that at Oxford it was not possible to combine Philosophy with Mathematics or Physics or English. (Keele had, in effect, created what would have been a 'Science Greats' course at Oxford.) The following year he went so far as to say that his experience as an external examiner at Keele had greatly strengthened his opinion that philosophy was best studied at undergraduate level in combination with another subject, and that he thought the best subject for that would be physics. Within a few years, three philosophy graduates with first-class honours joined the philosophy departments: Clive Borst (Philosophy and Chemistry), John Grundy (Philosophy, Economics and Political Institutions), and Alan Treherne (Philosophy and Mathematics). While an undergraduate Alan Treherne was one of six students in the first Commonwealth Youth Exchange with Canada organised by the English Speaking Union. After graduating he went to Glasgow as a lecturer in Mathematics before returning to Keele as a lecturer in Philosophy, and later as Head of the Department of Computer Science.

In the years up to 1961 the University College produced 1,000 graduates. 4% had gained I class honours, 20% – IIi, 41.5% – IIii, 27% – III, and 7.5% pass degrees. (Twenty graduates had joined university staffs, and one hundred had gone on to postgraduate research. Another barometer of success in the eyes of the outside world was the appointment of Keele graduates to the administrative grade of the civil service in 1961, 1962 and 1963, and particularly in 1962 when Keele was the only other university to join the ranks of Oxford, Cambridge and London.) Most of them had graduated in 'traditional' combinations of principal subjects. That was not surprising, yet even *The Times Educational Supplement* seemed surprised or disappointed that out of 150 graduates one year, scarcely 20 had taken a combination of principal subjects which was out of the ordinary. It was still necessary for Dr. Taylor to explain that 'it was no part of the Keele plan that all, or even a high percentage of our students should choose 'unusual' combinations of honours subjects.

The main objects of our founders were to ensure that all students are given in their first year a conspectus of the development and achievements of Western civilisation and that thereafter every student studies at least one science and one non-science subject.' Another criticism in the press, this time in *The Sunday Telegraph,* was that Keele was producing tens of all trades, striving to be jacks. Those who were friendly to Keele said we produced well-rounded citizens on the Balliol pattern. The Registrar commented that the Keele courses 'do produce a better educated staff'. After all, staff from different departments met one another frequently as a matter of course, whether it was interviewing applicants for admission and in Foundation Year Discussion Groups, or over coffee and lunch, or in the bar, or at home where neighbours and children's friends were likely to be from different departments. Any lecturer strayed into another subject about which he knew little at some peril when confronted with undergraduates studying from a wide range of subjects. The academic pattern, the Senior Common Room and living on the campus made it easy to mix with colleagues and difficult to be an academic recluse.

Consider what the College had achieved and in what circumstances. It was entirely new and had started with nothing. Inexperienced heads of departments put together a course structure unique in universities, and it was all accomplished by a small number of people in a short time. When the College lost Lindsay, Lennard-Jones, and Barnes, yet additional responsibilities had been thrust on already busy people. In addition there were all the problems of a residential community at a time of grave shortages including food rationing in the first years. From 1953 onwards there was sure guidance and advice from John Hodgkinson, the Registrar. He had worked with four different Principals and Acting Principals, and experience made his grasp and insight invaluable in the years to come. There was probably nothing he asked his staff to do which he had not done himself. At a Degree Congregation in 1983 when he was awarded an honorary degree of Doctor of the University, Paul Rolo said that it was difficult to distinguish between his career and the making of Keele. He kept the record of almost all of the University's business, and not only worked the whole interconnecting web of committees, but also in his time, appointed staff, organised degree ceremonies, open days, and conferences (and especially weekend conferences for many years to inform schools about Keele), produced publications, organised the building programme and dealt with the UGC. He used words sparingly, 'elucidating the vagaries of academic discussion, applying genius to routine, nursing as continuity man supremo a succession of Principals, Acting Principals, Vice-Chancellors and Pro-Chancellors, pointing the road, on countless occasions, by brief memoranda and even briefer verbal interventions, to the shortest cut, usually a straight line, between a problem situation and an essential objective'. Support, too, from the distaff side must not be overlooked, especially the friendship and help given to incoming Principals' and Vice-Chancellors' wives up to the 1980s. Dorothy Hodgkinson also started a crèche at her home, Firs Hill, for the growing number of young children living on the estate. (It was developed further by Mrs. Inge Miller and became the Keele Nursery.) There was also the involvement of other people in her founding of the Keele Players, with widespread participation of staff and staff wives (or 'Keele wives' or 'Campus wives' – these terms were used in the '50s and '60s, even if not acceptable in the 1990s). The Iliffes, Irene Halliwell, Margaret Millar and Roma Williams were enthusiastic supporters, but busy term-time commitments sometimes meant that staff enthusiasm was tempered by a certain reluctance, and pressures of academic work brought about the demise of the Keele Players. Theatre trips, however, continued.

The new Principal was Dr. H. M. Taylor. He took office in 1961 and would lead the University College of North Staffordshire to its new status as the University of Keele in 1962. He was required to undergo a rigorous medical examination. He had just returned from the top of Mont Blanc, and was found fit. Some time later he fell in the darkness when the Clock House Drive was obstructed by a plank across the road. He noticed that Mr. Ramage, who treated him, seemed to know the Clock House well: well he might, for he had attended successive Principals there.

Dr. Taylor came from Cambridge where he had been Secretary General of the Faculties for eight years, and before that University Treasurer for eight years. He had therefore held two of the three main administrative offices at Cambridge. He believed that the role of the university administrator was to serve learning rather than direct it, and that the university should be the spearhead of civilisation. He was not only a past master at administration, but he was also a fine scholar. He came from New Zealand, where he had graduated in mathematics and physics. He then pursued research in mathematical physics and the quantum theory at Cambridge, where he was the Allen Scholar and Smith's Prizeman. He was appointed a university lecturer in mathematics, and during the Second World War he was invited to pursue atomic research. However, he had already joined the Territorial Army and he served in the war as a lieutenant-colonel and senior instructor in gunnery. He was the first non-regular officer to be awarded the Lefroy Medal, which is awarded biennially for furthering the science and application of artillery. After the War he was invited to become University Treasurer at Cambridge.

Taylor was also an arts man. When he came to Keele he was a Fellow of the Society of Antiquaries. (He was later Vice-President, and was also President of the Royal Archaeological Institute.) Together with his wife, Joan Taylor, he was about to publish the first two volumes of *Anglo-Saxon Architecture*, an outstanding and monumental work of scholarship based on twenty-five years of patient and meticulous research. (The third volume was published in 1978.) He was a central figure in the architectural and archaeological approach to the study of Anglo-Saxon churches, and he brought to an inchoate field the precision of description and lucidity of exposition of a scientist and an administrator.

The Times, Nature, and *New Scientist* all published profiles on him. He was said to have 'the Cambridge manner – precise, courteous, undramatic, orderly'. Those who worked with him spoke of his clarity of mind and his patience, and he was a convincing speaker. He was the Rede Lecturer in Cambridge in 1966. His other accomplishments included ski-ing and mountaineering, and cooking which, like everything he did, he took seriously. He had high standards and he expected high standards in others. It must be said that though he was kindly and sympathetic, he was not a clubbable man. He was painstakingly correct and could be stiff at times and difficult to warm to, though the *Sentinel* wrote of him as the 'Vice-Chancellor with the human touch'. One of his first actions at Keele was to set up a fund to help members of the University in need. He was appreciative of what other people did, and was always ready with thanks. He was diffident at joining staff for coffee in the Senior Common Room until it was pointed out to him that he would be most welcome. It was an ideal meeting place for conducting a large number of small items of business. He did not come to Keele new to the ideas of study across different disciplines, as his own scholarship proved; and at Cambridge he had written reports on future university policy which included proposals for joint arts and sciences courses. He believed in what Keele stood for, and his obituary in *The Times* in 1995 said that he was 'still regarded by some as the best Vice-Chancellor the University has had'.

With the grant of a new Charter in January 1962 there was 'constituted and founded in Our County of Stafford a University by the name and style of 'The University of Keele''. In July there was a ceremony in the King's Hall, Stoke-on-Trent to install the Princess as Chancellor and to confer on her the honorary degree of Doctor of Letters. She then admitted Dr. Taylor to the office of Vice-Chancellor. There were twenty-four representatives of British universities present, including the Vice-Chancellors of the universities which had presided over the foundation of the College, the University of Cambridge, Dr. P. S. Noble, who was Vice-Chancellor of the University of London, and some former colleagues – Professor Sneddon from Glasgow, and Professor Macbeath from St. Andrews. There were also some representatives of the new universities: Professor Briggs from Sussex (founded in 1961), and Mr. Thistlethwaite from East Anglia (founded in 1963). While Keele had been finishing its 'apprenticeship', Sussex was founded 'fully fledged' in 1961, so even on the day of the installation of the Chancellor, the presence of representatives from Sussex and East Anglia served notice that Keele was no longer the sole post-war foundation; nor indeed, strictly, was Keele the first post-war university because Sussex received its university charter before Keele did.

The new Charter provided an opportunity to examine the detailed structure of government of the University. There was no longer any need for an Academic Council. Its role of overseeing academic matters had come to an end. The composition of the Senate was reviewed. What had seemed appropriate in 1950, namely the professors and the librarian plus four other members representing the Wardens of the halls of residence and the non-professorial teaching staff, no longer satisfied the lecturing staff. They wanted more representatives. A proposal that there should be an additional body, an Assembly composed of twenty-two lecturers and three professors, which would have five places on the Senate, was not acceptable. The lecturers' point was that the original small group of teachers had expanded to about a hundred, and there was an opportunity to make use of their interest and concern. The Senate obviously had plenty to do, yet 80% of the academic staff were ineligible to help. Moreover, they suggested that in a residential community it was hardly possible to stand aside, and that their lively concern should be a source of strength. In the new arrangements, non-professorial membership was increased to make up one-third of the Senate. In 1962 this gave a body of thirty-one members, still able to function as an effective executive. Thirty years later the Senate consisted of 79 members, met less often and held shorter meetings: executive decision making effectively shifted away.

The new Charter also brought changes to the composition of the Council. At first it was proposed not to include a representative of the North Staffordshire District of the WEA. This came as a shock to the WEA, and was seen as a setback to the long and fruitful relationship, especially as it was the North Staffordshire District's predecessor, the Miners' Higher Education Movement, which had mooted and agitated for the College. It was also a serious blow to any notion of Keele being a local university. On the question of Local Authority representation on the Council, Keele proposed four members appointed by Staffordshire County Council, four by Stoke-on-Trent and two by Burton upon Trent, but the UGC wanted it reduced to 3 + 3 + 1.

So what should the University be called? In 1949 it could almost have been called 'Stoke'. 'UCNS' had a certain flow and rhythm to it, but it needed explaining to the uninitiated. The University of North Staffordshire – 'UNS' -was an obvious development, but might still need explaining. The College was generally called 'Keele' because that is where it is. Had the new University been an entirely new creation, then 'Staffordshire' might have joined the ranks of Sussex, East Anglia and Essex. To omit the county name risked losing widespread county support. It could hardly be called 'Newcastle' because Newcastle-under-Lyme was an authority under Staffordshire County Council for educational purposes and, of course, it would have been confused with Newcastle upon Tyne. The University is not actually in Stoke-on-Trent, so a title which might have migrated with it in 1950 could hardly be grafted on now. The name Stoke-on-Trent did not conjure up elsewhere the vista of open parkland and a large rural campus. Even the word 'campus' seemed slightly strange. It does not appear in the *Oxford English Dictionary* of 1933. It is an American word, used at Princeton. It was in everyday use at Keele, however, though not yet in print in the College's *Prospectus*. The first use of the word in an official publication at Keele may have been in the *Calendar* in 1962, in the regulation that students must not drive motor vehicles 'round the campus'. It has since come into widespread use with the newer universities and with some prisons. The name of the new University was Keele. It is a disadvantage that Keele does not appear on a lot of maps, but its location became better known with the building of the M6 service station. As the Vicar of Keele, the Revd. T. H. Brookes said, 'the new title is much more convenient'; and a Keele graduate wrote to the *Sentinel* to say that the benevolence and tolerance of Keele villagers had earned them a warm spot in the hearts of graduates.

More universities were inevitable in the 1960s. If Keele had simply been another University College taking the London degree course, however, as might well have been the case, what form then might the new universities have taken in the 1960s? Would they have had to argue for their independence and their freedom to introduce new courses? or needed a period of academic sponsorship? What had Keele achieved? 'A single college of 800 has now made it impossible for any new university to start without giving careful consideration to breadth as well as depth in university education' (Professor Stewart in *Keele After Ten Years*). If the new universities had been set up as duplicates of Keele, then the 'Keele Experiment' would have been seen to have been justified. But that would have stifled academic development instead of justifying it. Keele's achievement was not to be found in imitation but in stimulation, in the freedom to express new ideas. It was the end, not the means, which was all-important. What Keele had struggled to do was now accepted without demur: the same ground did not have to be fought over again. The new universities could begin from different starting places. New courses were generally expected to be more broadly based and to cross what H. J. Perkin called the 'Snow line': but it was *only* at Keele that every undergraduate was obliged to do so. Sussex, East Anglia, Essex and, to a modified extent, Warwick, chose schools of studies to bring together cognate disciplines and to give students a taste of another school. York, Kent and Lancaster had departmental structures and offered broad first-year courses followed by combinations of major and minor courses. The measure of Lindsay's achievement was that the new universities (Sussex 1961, East Anglia 1963, York 1963, Essex 1964, Lancaster 1964, Kent 1965 and Warwick 1965) were all able *as a matter of course* to grant their own degrees, determine their own syllabuses and develop their own philosophies – powers for which Keele's founders had fought sharply contested battles in the 1940s. It is inconceivable that in the 1960s, 'informed opinion' would 'venture to say' that there was no need for new universities. A broad basis of studies was not only taken for granted, it was almost *de rigueur.* What had almost been impossible was now taken as obvious. Fulton, the Vice-Chancellor at Sussex, readily acknowledged Keele's achievement and accepted the implication that Lindsay's spirit brooded over the Sussex experiment. Thistlethwaite at East Anglia recognised the way Keele had moved the frontier in education: 'We are all in its debt' (*The Sunday Telegraph*, 20th October 1963). Templeman at Kent, previously Registrar at Birmingham, wrote: 'When we come to look back on this post-war period and on the ferment of ideas as to what universities ought to do, we shall discover that Lindsay was far more influential in shaping opinion than many would now be prepared to concede' (*Nature*, 15th May 1964). Despite this newly allowed freedom, Keele's was still the boldest scheme of any. Even though the glamour went elsewhere, Keele was the pace-setter. But there was a price to pay for being the first: even the buildings and the lack of coherent architecture showed the difference in treatment which Keele had received compared with the new foundations: 'Keele is a mess', said the *Listener.* The past had been dictated by force of circumstance, but because Keele was not now treated as one of the 'new', it did not catch up. The College had not made its achievements widely enough known, and that was partly because it was too busy actually doing what had to be done. It took for granted what it should have been preaching. This applied not only to the philosophy behind the courses but how the philosophy was turned into practice. In variety, originality and mode of instruction, the Sessional courses, for example, were academically very impressive. Widespread interest came from abroad more than from home. University and British Council visitors continued to beat a path to Keele's door to learn what Keele was doing it and how it was done. A forty minute television film made in Belgium, one of a series of three programmes about 'The University of Tomorrow', highlighted Keele's special character, the reaction against specialisation, and the achievement in bridging the gap between the arts and sciences. 'We do not believe any system is perfect', it concluded, 'but it can with confidence be said that the Keele experiment has been a success.' The cost, however, was too heavy for the experiment to be repeated: Keele's commitment to total residence and the four-year course was not repeated elsewhere. It is remarkable what Lindsay had achieved, especially in the period of post-war austerity. In better times since, no other university has been that fortunate. To have repeated it would have required political will, and money. Meanwhile, at Keele, that commitment had the effect of curtailing Keele's growth for another twenty-five years.

'To lose the sense of the past as a living element in the
present means that one lives in a kind of blindness'
(Reaveley and Winnington. *Democracy and Industry*.
'Reaveley' was the pen name of Miss Mary Glover, the
Director of Social Service Training at Keele until 1965.)

Chapter 14

THE PERIOD – II

Memory has telescoped two ideas into one, namely that Keele was small, and that was because Keele wanted to be small. That is not how it happened. In 1950 the notion of a new College planning to grow to 3,000 students would have been met with incredulity. In the late-1950s, leaving aside Oxford, Cambridge and London, there were only five English universities with more than 3,000 students, and five had less than 1,500. In the 1960s, however, growth with a vengeance became the fashion for the new universities, and fashion was shaped by money. But Keele was not a newly-founded university such as the others, and was not counted amongst their number. Keele wanted more rapid expansion than the UGC would allow.

There has also developed a perception that there was at Keele sometime before the 1980s a 'golden age' on which nostalgia can dwell. Much was different, but there never was a 'golden age'. If it existed, when was it? Was it the years of austerity when Keele was started? Could it have been the time of a succession of short-lived Principals? Was it the time when the shortage of money stunted development? Or the time of 'the troubles'? An examination of what it was like at the time shows the perception to be an illusion based on a misreading of the facts.

Keele's error may have been its failure to make its message and achievements heard loud and clear. It was time for Keele to beat its drum and to keep repeating Lindsay's message, rather than beat its breast and agonise over elusive improvements to the Foundation Year. It was good and it needed saying so. It is to be regretted that the all-importance of the tabloid headline displaced serious philosophical discussion. Even counting the new universities founded in the 1960s, and since, Keele is still the only fundamental experiment in university education in Britain since the War. Its historic achievements in breaking the mould of degrees for new institutions via the London external, in liberating the structure and content of degree courses for all the universities which followed, in seeking a broader education and in breaking down rigid specialisation – in re-examining the role of universities – these achievements are now taken for granted. The things which made Keele so special – the Foundation Year and the four-year course – were not copied. Professor H. J. Perkin described the Foundation Year as 'the most original innovation in British university education in this century' (*New Universities in the United Kingdom.* OECD) – and he wrote that *not in 1950 but in 1969*. Socially, too, he said that Keele had proved a far greater success than many had feared, but at a cost, in the event, of slow growth. Sceptics had said Keele would never work, it was too expensive if it did work, and it cost more than the government was willing to invest in the country's future. Money. Mr. Gradgrind was quite clear that 'In this life, we want nothing but Facts, sir; nothing but Facts!' A university born and brought up in hard times, however, wanted money. It might be that a once-for-all massive endowment would be a more economical way of funding a university. Visitors from around the world came to Keele to ask questions about degree courses, the curriculum and the timetable; but it was not always clear if, nearer home, our paymasters had the same understanding as our visitors.

For the present, the 'hooves with a galloping sound' were far distant. Superimposed on the shortage of money and the trimming of development plans, two long-term developments were pulling at universities. The first was the increasing control by government. In the debate initiated by Lord Lindsay in the House of Lords in 1947, the Lord Chancellor had given the terms of reference of the UGC. Later, the Treasury had rejected a recommendation that the Comptroller and Auditor General should have the right to inspect the books and accounts of universities in respect of non-recurrent grants. Such scrutiny was left to the UGC. In 1967, however, Anthony Crosland, the Secretary of State for Education and Science, accepted a recommendation of the Public Accounts Committee Report on *Parliament and Control of University Expenditure* that the Comptroller and Auditor General should be given access to the books and records of the UGC and the universities. It was to be solely to comment and advise on the propriety, regularity and efficiency with which money voted by Parliament was administered, and that need not infringe the academic freedom of the universities. Some, like Mr. Charles Carter, Vice-Chancellor of the University of Lancaster, thought that universities had a good story to tell, of economical and effective trusteeship of public money – and that they would gain an advantage in their relations with parliament and government from laying their affairs open to public scrutiny. Others, like Sir Robert Aitken, Vice-Chancellor of the University of Birmingham, said that it looked as if the bounds of freedom would be set by the direction of the Comptroller and Auditor General and his officers, and that academic work was too easily damaged by direction from above and by administrative constraint. Time would show where the balance lay. Dr. Taylor at Keele warned that building grants were inadequate. When the allocation of grants for the quinquennium 1967-72 was announced, it was accompanied for the first time ever by a Memorandum of General Guidance from the UGC. Before the end of that quinquennium, decisions were taken to alter what had been fundamental principles when the College was founded: the Foundation Year was no longer an essential part of the degree course, and Keele was no longer a fully-residential University. How far Keele was to derive any benefit from closer government control is a matter for the reader to discern in the following chapters. Shortage of money and the trimming of development plans continued. The Honorary Treasurer's Report to the Annual General Meeting of the Court could almost be minuted in advance (and on at least one occasion the author did so). Those readers who know what financial disasters

Left to right: Alderman Leason (Lord Mayor), Mr. Harry Taylor (Town Clerk), Col. R. Sneyd, Mr. J.R. Piggott (City Architect), Alderman Horwood (Chairman of the Exploratory Committee)

22nd September 1947

Visit of HM The Queen, 17th April 1951

Different styles of lecturing!

Top: *Professor Sneddon*   *Professor Beaver*
Middle: *Professor Stewart*   *Professor Gemmell*
Bottom: *Professor Finer*   *Professor Lawlor*

The opening of the new Physics Department, 6th November 1953
Left to right: Alderman Horwood, Sir John Cockcroft,
Sir John Lennard-Jones (Principal 1953-54) and Professor Vick

Early 1960s

Left: Princess Margaret with Sir George Barnes (Principal 1956-60) and Ian Dunbar (President of the Students' Union), at the Students' Union Ball held in the Walter Moberly Hall, 1957.

Below: Dr. H.M. Taylor (Principal and Vice-Chancellor, 1960-67) at a reception in the Library

Above: The Library

*Right: The Students'
Union in the mid-
1960s*

*Right: The Lindsay
String Quartet and
George Pratt, 1972.
Left to right:
Peter Cropper
Ronald Birks (seated)
Roger Bigley
Bernard Gregor-Smith
George Pratt*

Above: Foundation Year lecture by Professor Ingram, mid-1960s

Left: Professor W.A.C. Stewart (Vice-Chancellor 1967-79) and Dr. D. Harrison (Vice-Chancellor 1979-84) discussing the new decorative titles by Maw & Co. on the wall of the Chancellor's Building extension.

Below: Biology Department extension, hiding the original Orlit block building, late-1960s

Above: the Chapel, arranged for the Service of Dedication, 1st December 1965. The screens are raised. The Free Church Chapel is behind the main altar on the left, and the Roman Catholic Chapel is on the right.

Right: a first edition of Euclid, printed in Venice in 1482. This is the oldest printed scientific text-book in the western world (from the Turner Collection, given to the University by Mr. C.W. Turner in 1968).

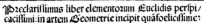
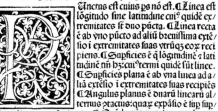

Keele Hall courtyard was resurfaced in 1959 in setts patterned with blue bricks. The inscription 'Freshers' Gate' appeared over the pedestrian arch in 1960, put there 'by an unauthorised person'.

Winners of the Granada Television University Challenge Competition.

P.BROWNSEY   P.GROVES   A.LAWRENCE   A.MACMULLEN

KEELE UNIVERSITY

were to strike Keele in 1981 may think it is premature to complain, and that the difficulties of the previous fifteen years or so were exaggerated: but they were not. It would have taken Cassandra herself to prophecy what was coming, and she would have been met with the disbelief it was her lot to bear.

The second development to disturb the equilibrium was the upsurge of student unrest. It seemed to the student generation of the late-1960s that there might be a spring of new hope. What caused this unrest? Was it discontent with the academic programme? with the examination system? with the hours rule? with paying for meals? Was it the long, hot summer? Yes and No. It was not just at Keele, or only in Britain. Was it because of the students' revolt in Paris in May 1968 – the worst street fighting there since 1944? Was it anything to do with Vietnam? or the Prague Spring? or Aldermaston? Was it the Civil Rights Movement in Kent State, U.S.A.? Possibly. Was it the new confronting the old? Was it youth culture or drug culture and magic mushrooms? It was not new and it was not rare for students to rebel against authority, to be dismissive of experts and to be cavalier in their views. That is the prerogative of the young. But why then in particular, and why so widespread? The questioning of the academic programme was not new, nor the examination system, nor discontent about the hours rule and the meals system. There had been other nationalistic uprisings in the world since 1945 and other protests. Perhaps the question should be not 'why then?' but 'why not sooner?' It is perhaps more remarkable that the students at universities in the immediate post-war years had accepted the rule book even if they broke the rules. Young men who had fought in the desert, tracked the enemy in the jungle, served in ships, flown in fighters and bombers, who had spent years as prisoners of war, had come back and accepted the system of universities making rules *in loco parentis*. On the other hand, they had been used to discipline, shortages and austerity, and were anxious to make up for the years they had lost. Perhaps it is because most of the attitudes one carries are formed – or are formed for us – whilst still at school. If the Child is the father of the Man, the students in the late-60s demonstrated the upsurge of relief and the new-found freedom released after the Second World War. This was the generation which had 'never had it so good'. It was also an exciting time, though not necessarily to everyone's liking. Those whom universities trained to question, in turn questioned authority; and for a while they wanted not simply to change the rules but to throw out the rule book.

Lord Annan observed that the militants 'shattered the spun-glass relationship between dons and students' and that 'a generation gap had opened: one side no longer wanted the other' (*Our age: portrait of a generation*). At Keele, if this applied it applied to few. Stressful as it was at times, little really changed. Then the fervour subsided: perhaps it was the employment market which brought a duller sobriety, or boredom with being revolutionaries or may be it was the wet summer terms. The longer lasting problem continued to be shortage of money.

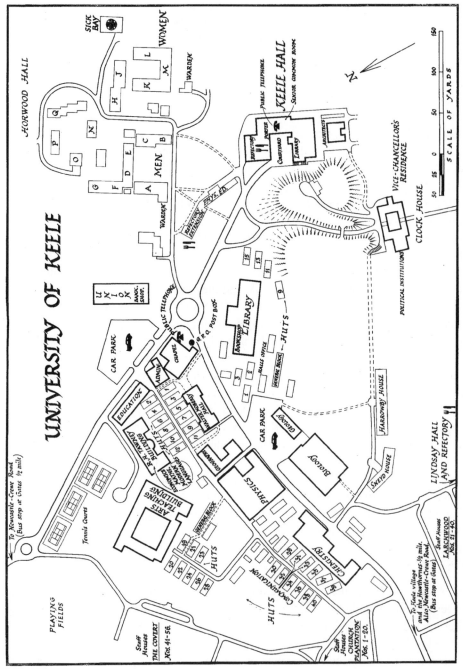

from CALENDAR 1962-63

Chapter 15

A TIME OF OPPORTUNITY

When Dr. Taylor arrived at Keele he quickly realised that the financial situation was worsening and that the Library in particular was under-funded. On the face of it, though, there were plenty of signs of confidence, with a substantial building programme about to transform the campus. As early as 1951 the College had discussed the siting and the construction of the Library with the National Coal Board, in order to avoid the dangers of subsidence. The original design was in the shape of half a cartwheel with five two-storey wings, to give a capacity of half-a-million volumes. It was, in fact, built to a different design, with a capacity for 200,000 volumes and space for 300 readers. There were plans for later expansion backwards and the possibility of expansion frontwards. A decorative feature was added – a ten foot column of Portland stone with a bronze on top of it of a hand holding an open book; but it was not long before someone painted it to look like a barber's pole, and it was removed. (In 1996 another sculpture was placed in front of the Library – 'Flame' in bronze by Diana Whelan, commissioned as a result of an anonymous benefaction.) The new Library was officially opened on 8th October 1962 by Sir Sydney Roberts, formerly Vice-Chancellor of Cambridge and President of the Library Association. It dominated the temporary buildings and focused attention on the centre of the campus.

The new Students' Union was being built nearby. It was planned first of all to link the east ends of the Conference Hall and the Teaching Block, and then to be to the east of them, and finally to face the Library. The *Daily Telegraph* later described it as having an ocean liner effect (and one must try to envisage it without the later extension) – others thought it more of a Mississippi river boat effect – tremendous scale without arrogance and freshness without naivety. Pevsner said in 1974 that it was the best building so far. It was opened by Princess Margaret in January 1963, and that summer the degree congregation was held in the ballroom.

Enough money had been raised by the early-60s to make a start on the new chapel. The development plan by Piggott and Pickavance in 1955, and by Howard Robertson in 1956 put the chapel facing the Library, near enough where the shops are now. With the change in the position of the Students' Union, the chapel was designed to go between the Conference Hall and the Teaching Block; but the final position was determined when 'Q' block in Horwood Hall was not going to be ready for October 1962. Eight huts which would have to be demolished to make room for the chapel were still required for students to live in, and the UGC wrote to say that in view of rising building costs and the consequent need to preserve huts if possible, the site for the chapel should be re-examined. The possibilities were interesting. The idea of a chapel-in-the-wood below Firs Hill had a certain appeal to it: it would be central and quiet, and not be dominating; but it would have needed redesigning to suit that site. To put it the other side of Newcastle Drive from the Tawney Building would mix it up with the car parks, though its visual impact would be impressive if no other buildings interrupted the view. The site finally chosen, for which the huts used by the Students' Union and the original chapel would be demolished, was somewhat hard close on the Walter Moberly Hall, whose entrance had to be rebuilt, but it meant that for present convenience the building of it could be phased with the new Students' Union and would cause no disruption to residences. Again, in 1964, the reason why priority was given to a new building for the Department of Communication was in order to release for students' use the huts occupied by the department.

Other buildings going up in the early-60s included stage III of Chemistry and Physics. In 1961 Professor Vick returned to open the extension to Physics, and he recalled that it had been hoped that these extensions would be started as early as 1954. Biology was even more delayed. A start would soon be made on the new Arts Teaching Block (later called the Chancellor's Building). At Horwood Hall (where 'Q' block was behindhand) 'O' block was given a sixth floor to give it a position of dominance. Rising building costs can be traced by the economies made in the internal finish of later blocks. There were still a lot of huts, and a bet by the students of Hut 6 showed that they had an enormous capacity: despite a regulation that not more than ten people should be accommodated in a study-bedroom measuring 12 feet x 9 feet, 132 students crowded into a room for coffee. Fortunately, the UGC did not extrapolate from this that the entire student body could be fitted into five or six rooms!

In the summer of 1962 the Observatory dome, long a familiar landmark in Oxford, came to Keele. John Hodgson in the Physics Department had learnt that a large refracting telescope in the Oxford University Observatory might become available. Ron Maddison (also in the Physics Department) with the immediate support of Professor Ingram, Vick's successor, secured the purchase. With the expertise of Harry Wardell and the University Workshop, it was dismantled, removed, transported, sited and re-assembled without mishap. It was lowered into the dome by a 60-foot crane. It is clear from Oxford's records that many of the great names in astronomy, such as Eddington, Einstein, Hertzsprung, Hubble, Jeans and Ryle, would have seen or worked with this telescope. (The second dome made its appearance in 1974.) At last, *The Sunday Telegraph* said, the University was beginning to look as if it was meant to be here.

The new universities founded in the early-60s were already set for a period of rapid growth. Which way was Keele to go? The quinquennium 1962/67 could have been the springboard from which, after steady growth, Keele might flourish with a more rapid increase in size. Student numbers rose from 813 undergraduates plus 38 research students in October 1962 to 1,276 plus 120 four years later. This slow growth (especially when compared with the seven new universities) was *despite* the University's wish for greater expansion. All universities were facing difficulties. In January 1962 a deputation from the UGC went to see the Chief Secretary to the Treasury, Henry Brooke, and 'heavyweight' members such as Sir James Mountford, Vice-Chancellor of Liverpool, and Sir Douglas Logan, Principal of the University of London, stressed that finances were desperate because they could see no hope of keeping to the building programme needed for the projected increases, and that in diplomatic language the increase in money was completely unrealistic. The Chief Secretary, for his part, spoke of the achievements the universities had made so far in a 32% increase in numbers since 1955, and said he was disturbed at the sort of feeling of despair they had expressed. He explained that the strain on sterling in the summer of 1961 and possible decisions the government might have to take about the Common Market and so forth made for a difficult economic situation. Meanwhile the Robbins Committee was sitting, and so presumably decisions could be postponed for the present: but not for long. The Robbins *Report of the Committee on Higher Education* (1963) signalled unprecedented expansion.

At a meeting with the UGC in February 1964, Dr. Taylor explained the strong wish of the University to expand in order to arrive as quickly as possible to an overall size which would be more satisfactory from the point of view of smaller departments. A development plan for 3,000 was already being discussed, and there was no lack of applicants or of employment prospects for graduates. But Keele could grow only slowly because of the need for residences (if it wanted to maintain a policy of total residence); and Keele was expensive because of the four-year course. In 1961 Keele had agreed to expand to 1,200 by 1967, and thereafter to 1,700; and in the light of the Robbins Report and a letter from the UGC emphasising the need for more students, Keele proposed reaching 1,700 by 1967: but the UGC reduced this figure to 1,470, expressing doubts over what they thought might mean over-rapid expansion. (For whom?) As the Vice-Chancellor reported to the Court, he had hoped that newly-founded universities such as Keele would have received special consideration: but Keele was not a newly-founded university such as the others. Even so, it seemed likely from the Robbins Report that capital grants, at least, would be forthcoming on a regular basis to enable universities to make every effort to secure the rapid expansion which the government was urging. In 1964 Keele received £1.2M; and for the 15 month period to March 1966, £700,000. Then capital funding virtually stopped: in 1966-67 there was £100,000 and the following year there was nothing, so making planning almost impossible. On this occasion, UGC money was needed for the newer universities and for converting the Colleges of Advanced Technology into the new wave of universities in 1966 and 1967. So, successively, Keele's growth was held back by lack of money at a time when, under Taylor's guidance, with such financial and administrative skills at his command, more rapid growth might have been undertaken with care, orderliness and expertise.

For the quinquennium 1962-67 there was a squeeze on recurrent grants too, producing an immediate deficit of £17,500 for 1962/63. Fifteen new posts which the Senate hoped for in 1965-66 were reduced to five posts, and were delayed until 1966-67. In the event, the proposed chair in Historical Theology, and hence its development into a Principal subject, was lost for good. Universities were told in September 1964 that they could look forward to a period of comparative stability and consolidation, and that the scale of expansion required between 1967 and 1974 would be manageable within the limits of a 'steady and natural rate of growth'. Then, in August 1965, as a result of a government squeeze on all public spending, the UGC deferred the starting date for buildings for six months – but added that this was not to be interpreted as excluding the recruitment of staff to provide for increasing student numbers. As a consequence, plans for a fourth hall of residence (i.e. Barnes Hall) were postponed. For residences, meantime, costing according to 'study bedroom units' was replaced by 'residence costing units', making it likely, it seemed, that there would be a reduction in building standards.

Taylor urged the UGC to give universities a *rolling* quinquennial programme, valid for five years ahead. 'Without such assurance', he said to the Home Universities Conference in 1964, 'many of us look askance at phrases such as we saw shortly after the Robbins Report, when we were asked to undertake an emergency expansion and at the same time to accept a 'temporary' lowering of standards... We see a bleak prospect of living with the lowered standards for a long time ahead.' His proposal would have led to great improvements in universities' planning, for large building projects and major academic developments need that sort of timescale if they are to be carried out smoothly and efficiently; but the trend was for governments to adopt shorter and shorter timescales. At the same time there was growing stricter financial control – an inescapable consequence of the rapid increase in public expenditure on higher education. 'More sophisticated' cost accounting, it was thought, would improve 'efficiency'.

As the UGC was itself being squeezed and having to impose unreasonable planning conditions on universities, so it sought 'to develop techniques of comparative analysis of University costs'. What might the UGC do with such details? Give some universities more? and most less? Universities were requested to apportion the time of each member of the academic staff to *(a)* undergraduate teaching; *(b)* postgraduate teaching; and *(c)* research. This would enable costs in different faculties to be compared. That would seem to give comparative costs; but John Hodgkinson, the Registrar, exposed it in a letter to *The Times* (16 December 1965) as both dangerous and useless. Useless because it was impossible to gain accurate answers in which totals would hide extremes; and dangerous because it would concentrate official approbation on the cheapest and be an argument for reducing any higher staff-student ratios. The requirement directly attacked the freedom of academic thought. 'The fierce competition for limited funds within each university is a most efficient method of cost control', he said; 'let us stop trying to count what cannot be counted'. There seemed little point in producing league tables which were likely to be both misleading and meaningless. Be that as it may, the trend was towards a policy which was more dirigiste; towards a policy of the UGC being not so much a buffer between the universities and the government, as asserting its function to interpret the government to the universities and the universities to the government. With this came responsibility for something like a general strategy towards what was called firmer planning and attention to cost effectiveness. Lord Radcliffe, on his installation as Chancellor of Warwick University in 1967, spoke of his fear of the benevolent application of principles 'appropriate enough to the organisation of a factory, inculcated by men who do not understand that in the pursuit of knowledge, the cultivation of intellect, the art of teaching, the only certainly false doctrine is a belief in certainty'. But who would listen? The UGC's 'Preliminary Memorandum of General Guidance on Quinquennial Planning 1972/77' said that the recurrent grant would contain strong pressures to reduce unit costs, and guidance was given on what the average size of departments should be.

Financial support from the Local Authorities was important in providing some sort of financial cushion, and their contribution amounted to about 10% of Keele's recurrent budget. At a time when it was impossible to make adequate provision for renewals and reserves (1962), followed by a year of strict economy to restrict the deficit to £8,500 (1963), their support was very important. Worse times were to follow: the government's prices and incomes standstill was followed by rampant inflation. Mr. Walker, who had been Honorary Treasurer from the start of the College, wrote in his final report in 1967: 'There have been many disappointments and frustrations and constantly restricted finances but there has always been the prospect of better times ahead. Without being unduly pessimistic, I believe that we have now arrived at one of the most difficult periods in the financial history of Keele.' The importance, too, of income from conferences can be appreciated. Miss Rolfe, with a minimum of resources, her courtesy and excellent standards known and noted, was quietly and efficiently attracting more and more income from vacation conferences. The 32 conferences in 1960-61 contributed £12,600 to the halls of residence account: seven years later 116 conferences contributed £57,500 – over 16% of the halls income. More than a thousand people attended a National Evangelical Conference in 1967. It was not only one of the first very large conferences at Keele, but it was also acclaimed as a milestone in the development of the evangelical movement. Miss Rolfe also, personally, took a full share with the Registrar and his staff in showing parties of visitors around the campus on summer evenings. Such public relations exercises, together with Dr. Taylor's regular monthly column in the *Sentinel*, his visits to schools and his attendance at meetings and functions, all contributed to the groundwork necessary for launching an Appeal Fund in 1963, in which Sir Alfred Owen, the Pro-Chancellor, took such an active part.

Yet it must be said that to a visitor unaware of the financial difficulties, delays and frustrations, the campus seemed to be a thriving place. As Taylor wrote in the *Sentinel* in January 1963, it was astonishing how much had been achieved in the fifteen months since his arrival, particularly in the centre where the Library and the Students' Union provided for the first time some indication of the general scheme of development which had been settled about six years earlier. By the summer of 1964, Lindsay Hall was being built (the refectory there had already been in use for a year), taking advantage of the sloping site, with the majority of rooms facing south and seen from the motorway. The Arts Building was nearing completion and its first extension was being planned; the Sports Centre was a forest of steel girders, and the chapel foundations were being laid; Biology was being completed, and Geography and Physics were expanding. In the village, the Hawthorns was being developed as the third Hall of Residence.

A plan for the general development of the University, first to 1,700 students and then to 2,400 or 3,000, was drawn up by Peter Shepheard of Bridgwater Shepheard and Epstein in April 1964. By and large, this plan laid out Keele's development for the next twenty-five years. Peter Shepheard was an architect, town planner and landscape architect of distinction. He had been involved in the master plan for Stevenage New Town and the landscaping of part of the Festival of Britain South Bank Exhibition. He was responsible for the master plan and building at Lancaster University. He was Visiting Professor of Architecture at the University of Pennsylvania and was President of the Institute of Landscape Architects in 1965-66. He became President of the RIBA in 1969-71 and was knighted in 1980.

The main principles of the plan were as follows. First, 'to preserve what remains of the beauty of the site by avoiding the destruction of woodland and isolated trees where possible, and arranging new buildings to form new groups and quadrangles with existing ones'. Some of the existing buildings, and in particular the science departments along Keele Drive, were to be transformed in appearance by their extension (as intended in the early-1950s). Secondly, 'to solve the problem of vehicular traffic which at present penetrates the whole site by arranging a road skirting the edge of the academic area from which access can be gained by cul-de-sacs or loops to any parts of the area which need it, while leaving the whole area free of through traffic'. This was to be the ring road – obvious afterwards, but by no means so obvious at the time. Thirdly, and as a consequence of having a ring road, 'to emphasize the central Forum which has been started by the siting of the Chapel, Library and Union at one point. The abolition of the roundabout enables more communal buildings – shops, future assembly hall, common rooms, extension of Library, etc. – to be grouped here, and the addition of covered ways and paved areas will help this to become a gathering place.' The idea of a 'forum' – 'piazza' was another description – suggests something warmer and less windswept than the paved area proves to be for much of the year; that, and the small amount of covered ways – apparent especially when it is raining – has made it more of a crossing place than a gathering place. Fourthly, halls of residence were to be sited outside the ring road. Horwood was to be extended south-eastwards, and halls 4 and 5 were marked along the ring road (opposite the Students' Union and the Chancellor's Building, where later the 'Science Park' buildings were built). A further hall, for the expansion to 3,000 was to be sited at the Newcastle entrance (this was to be Barnes Hall), or to the west of Larchwood. It was thought that staff would continue to be mostly residential, in which case a lot more houses would be needed; and they would be built much more densely than hitherto. A number of sites were earmarked, including the north side of Keele Drive, the east side of Newcastle Drive, and at the back of Horwood; more flats were planned too, including twelve flats at each end of the Larchwood (fortunately never built there).

Peter Shepheard was conscious of the beauty of the landscape and the need for a comprehensive plan of tree planting, including trees associated with each new building project. He did not favour evergreens, however, which would have served as windbreaks and hidden expanses of tarmac all the year. The need for car parks was recognised, but not yet on the scale required for the 1990s.

Major developments which in the event did *not* happen include an Assembly Hall and an Administration Building close to the centre; and buildings between the Walter Moberly Hall and the Tawney Building to provide a quadrangle. The major development was to be the ring road.

The Foundation Year continued to tax the ingenuity of those who had invented it and their successors. Once someone pulled at a thread it was difficult not to unravel the garment, and the weaknesses were recounted almost with dismay: it afforded neither a coherent pattern of instruction nor a systematic discipline in learning, it was said. There was no mechanism to link the discussion groups to the lecture course. Sessionals and Terminals had nothing to connect them with the lecture course or the discussion groups. There was no adequate training in academic discipline. Students attempted too much – or too little. It lacked intelligible purpose. What was needed, the critics said, was for the Foundation Year to be considered as and fashioned into a recognisable whole; and it should demand the active participation of students. Detailed proposals to cure these ills followed. But one of the founding professors dissented: his view was that the premises of the Foundation Year were firstly that there was a unity about all knowledge, and secondly to break down specialisation and departmentalism. This was to be achieved by showing inter-relationships and differences in techniques, and by stimulating interest in areas which fall between conventional boundaries, by providing a coherent and integrated view of knowledge as a whole as far as was practicable. The new proposals, he thought, were ill-considered, showed little evidence of having been argued systematically, and focused too insistently on the lesser aspects of the course. 'We need a full-scale analysis of the aims and methods of the Foundation Year as a whole', he concluded. If there had ever been a Director of the Foundation Year (Dr. Jenkins had that title briefly) it becomes clear that he would never have satisfied everybody; and at times he would have pleased nobody. In 1964 the suggestion was that there should be an 'overseer'.

The upshot in June 1963 was, briefly, that there should be three levels of work involved: the lecture course, now made up of thirty blocks of lectures; fifteen essays to be assessed by the staff members of the discussion groups; and three examinations on a total of nine themes. (Sessional courses would continue to be examined as hitherto.) That was not the end of the committee's work, however: it was to consider the introduction of interdepartmental themes in the lecture course and examinations, and to undertake a complete review of the lecture course. There was certainly no sign of any waning of interest in and commitment to the Foundation Year.

Years earlier, Professor Beaver's eye had caught the Western Region railway engine 'Keele Hall', and he had asked British Railways if he could be told when the engine was scrapped. To the credit of their filing system he was notified in 1964, and the nameplate was bought to hang in the Geography Department. Another acquisition by Beaver, at the instigation of Alan Walton, a lecturer in the Department, was 40,000 boxes of air-photos taken between November 1939 and May 1945. Five-and-a-half million prints cover German-occupied Europe and the north shore of the Mediterranean. They remain the property of the Ministry of Defence and the Public Record Office, and are on permanent loan to the University. In the 1980s the air-photo library grew with the acquisition of the John Bradford collection of over 150,000 prints from the Pitt Rivers Museum in Oxford. The library has been of great interest and assistance not only to geographers and military historians, but also to bomb disposal experts, planners, architects, civil engineers, archaeologists, authors and lawyers. In 1985 the City of Hamburg paid £300,000 for re-formatting a large part of the collection in return for the use of the originals in the search for un-exploded bombs. The University presented Hamburg with a statuette entitled 'Peace', generously donated by Royal Doulton Ltd. The collection has been described as a modern Domesday Book of Western Europe.

With the growth of the University there developed a programme of public events. There were concerts by world-famous musicians – the Amadeus Quartet, Dennis Brain, Joan Sutherland, Kodály and, within a few years, John Ogden, Janet Baker and Paul Tortelier. There were several series of lectures: the second set of Lindsay Memorial Lectures was given by Professor Butterfield on *Universities and Educational Needs of our Time*, the Earl Lectures in local history were endowed (anonymously at the time) by Mr. Jack Leighton of Newcastle, and the Bartholomew Lectures on behavioural development were endowed by Mr. J. Bartholomew of Longton. The Wolverhampton Chamber of Commerce gave an annual Foundation Year prize. There were Inaugural Lectures by Dr. Taylor on *Our Anglo-Saxon Heritage* and by newly-appointed professors – on *The Science of Communication – a bridge between Disciplines* by Professor MacKay, and what was called an 'Ingram Spectacular' on *Radiophysics – a new probe of the Universe* by Professor Ingram, the new Professor of Physics.

The University received a number of gifts, some from students' parents, including a walnut dining table, silver entrée dishes, a dinner service from the British Pottery Manufacturers' Federation, glass and silver. There were pictures from stately homes in the Great Hall of Keele Hall – 'Venetian Life' by Sir Luke Fildes on loan from Colonel Aird, and portraits from the Earl of Harrowby and the Duke of Newcastle. Some very successful developments in the arts were a legacy from the Barnes years. A grant from the Calouste Gulbenkian Foundation provided for one-year resident fellowships in the creative arts for three successive years and, in accordance with the wishes of the Foundation, they were instituted in memory of Barnes. It was hoped that the fellowships would then be established on a permanent basis by the University. They were awarded to artists from different fields, first to the playwright John Hall, who had written plays for both stage and television; then to Laurence Leeson, the painter, and to Bryan Macdonald, the sculptor. Gulbenkian generously renewed the grant for two more years, and the University provided funds for an additional year, so providing fellowships for Roger Dean, sculptor, Ian Henderson, painter, and Norman Jackson, poet. From 1968-69, however, money was too scarce, and despite good intentions the fellowship lapsed. All the Gulbenkian Fellows left their marks on Keele: John Hall in his encouragement of drama, which enjoyed some years of extraordinarily high standards. The painters, poet and sculptors left more tangible works, some of which are in the University's collection. Norman Jackson published poems under the title *Beyond the Habit of Sense*. Dr. Taylor was sculpted by Dean (the only portrait he produced during the year) and was painted by Henderson, and both works were presented to the University. Reginald Haggar, reviewing Macdonald's work, revived a notion put forward earlier by Mrs. Haywood, when he suggested that the University should utilise the special gift of the creative artist to enrich the campus. What better setting, he asked, could sculptures have than the magnificent park at Keele?

Music, too, benefited from Barnes, from the gift of his piano, and from his memorial fund. Part of the cost of the organ in the new chapel was met with balances in the Perry Musical Directorship Fund and the Barnes Memorial Fund. In 1964 the appointment of George Pratt as a full-time Director of Music not only consolidated the work of the music societies but meant that he could provide an academic subsidiary course and, later, draw up the principal course. In the first instance the University's policy was to develop the study and performance of chamber music, and the subsidiary course included a substantial proportion of performance. Largely through the efforts of George Pratt, the University was able to take the emphasis a stage further with a gift from the Leverhulme Trust and grants from the Calouste Gulbenkian Foundation for a string quartet for an initial period of three years. This would permit the quartet to develop without being dependent on performing to earn a living in the first instance. The precedent of the Alberni Quartet at Harlow with the help of the Gulbenkian Foundation, and the appointment of the Amadeus Quartet at York, suggested that Keele could make a real contribution to the development of chamber music in Britain. Funds from the Northern Arts and Sciences

Foundation, the Midlands Association for the Arts, the Leathersellers Company and Mr. J. W. F. Morton, enabled the quartet to remain at Keele for a further two years. They took the name of 'Lindsay', and proved to be one of the most successful ventures in the University's fifty years.

The real contribution of the Gulbenkian Fellows and the better provision for music was that artistic endeavour permeated the Keele community and added a dimension far greater than the individual contributions. The hut near the Library (which had previously been the shop) was the Gulbenkian Fellows' studio, and was open house to anyone who wanted to drop in to watch or ask, and the Fellows went to discussion groups to talk about their work with students and staff. The same effect could be seen again when the Lindsay String Quartet grew to impressive maturity during the five years they were on the campus.

In the local neighbourhood the University was criticised for not being 'involved' or 'integrated'. Certainly, all that some people saw was the old, high estate wall as they drove past the campus. The name of one of the bus stops – 'hole-in-the-wall' – was hardly seen as inviting. But the facts do not support the criticism. The Registrar and Professor Stewart pointed out Keele's involvement locally – with the Arts Festival, Radio Stoke, local teachers and magistrates, local councillors, a Keele graduate as MP for Newcastle, and a member of the Keele staff elected MP for Stoke-on-Trent. Concerts attracted audiences of up to 600, as did drama, which included a free matinée for old-age pensioners and handicapped children. The carnival each year raised more money per student than any other university in the country – a total of more than £2,500 in 1966 – money for the charities of the Lord Mayor of Stoke-on-Trent and the Mayor of Newcastle. Students preached in local churches; they decorated more than 200 homes for old people in the course of ten years. Teaching practice took 80-90 students a year into schools over a wide area. Monthly articles in the *Sentinel* on the weather by Professor Beaver were well established, and in 1965 Ron Maddison started his monthly articles on astronomy. The University was a major employer, purchaser and ratepayer.

There was yet more local involvement when university status was achieved. Keele's Department of Extramural Studies (soon to be renamed the Department of Adult Education) took over from Oxford responsibility for university extramural activities in the area. 'University weeks' were held in Burton upon Trent, Stafford and Leek, and courses were provided to complement BBC educational broadcasts. Keele participated in the work of the National Extension College, and this led to the publication of *A Programmed Course in Old English* by Barbara Raw in the English Department. By 1964-65 there was a flourishing range of courses with local industry and with local doctors, magistrates and police; courses for general audiences in art, literature, economics, history, biology, automation, politics, astronomy, design, and town planning. There were lectures before each local Hallé concert. Eighty students were working for London external degrees (a shock for the ghosts of the late-1940s!); and there were numerous refresher courses. There developed very successful and long-running residential summer schools, including an enthusiastic chamber music school and an international summer school on ceramics which was able to take advantage of the authority and reputation of Reginald Haggar. He was a cornerstone of art education in North Staffordshire, and as an artist, scholar, teacher and friend he was an inspiration. The Department also played a leading role in the training of detached youth workers, post-qualifying social workers and probation officers, and in the development of social gerontology; as well as developing courses in medieval Latin and architectural history.

There was not, however, despite the helpfulness of the staff, the warm relationship with the WEA which the story of Keele's foundation, and Lindsay's high regard for the movement had perhaps presupposed. Differences and misunderstandings continued: they each had different approaches and there were differences in temperament. The Department was able to measure success in student numbers, but as the *Sentinel* observed during correspondence in its columns in May 1971, 'success is not only to be measured in numbers and the close ties with the local community which the WEA have steadily built up since Tawney's days are a valuable factor in the work'.

Another development, long sought after but slow in coming, was an Institute of Education at Keele. That aspiration dates back to the first year of the College, but UCNS was small, new, and busy with other urgent priorities; and proposals for the quinquennium 1952-57 were rejected by the UGC as premature. For the next quinquennium proposals were included among the College's priorities and were accepted, but only in competition with other developments. Success was achieved in 1962-67 after long negotiations with the constituent colleges – Madeley, Alsager, and Crewe – with the universities with which they had been linked, the Ministry of Education, and the Local Education Authorities. What helped was that the future of the three colleges was more assured than earlier, and they were programmed for expansion. Keele, for its part, had space for the Institute in the new Chancellor's Building alongside the Department of Education. The Institute was inaugurated in 1964, with Professor Stewart as its first Director. It co-ordinated initial teacher training and in-service courses for teachers, and developed a Modern Languages Teachers' Workshop and the Keele Science and Technology Centre. Teacher training in the colleges was further enhanced with the development of the Bachelor of Education degree, which was awarded from 1968 onwards.

Up till 1963, the admission and examination of students had been the responsibility of a number of professors each taking the role of 'Senior Tutor' in turn. This brought in fresh views, and it worked well in a small College; but in a job which has a twelve month cycle, a lot of experience was being lost in changing the Senior Tutor each year. With increasing student numbers there was a need for a permanent appointment. The first permanent Senior Tutor was Alan Iliffe who had joined the staff in October 1951 as a lecturer in psychology. In 1962 he was appointed Nuffield Fellow, to carry out a detailed study of the Foundation Year. He was a most perceptive admissions officer, with disarming skills at interviews. The last of the old-style Senior Tutors was Professor Ingram. In his report for his year he made the same point which Professor Teale had made earlier – the need to decide an optimum size for each department rather than let selection be driven by fashions in 6th forms. Ingram was an enthusiastic proponent of the Keele Idea and was in the forefront of the conferences held in the 1960s to explain to heads of schools why it was important that all students should study some arts and some science. He preached the view that people could not really be considered properly educated unless they appreciated that some choices had to be made and some decisions taken by using careful objective analysis while other problems required a much more subjective approach to unravel complex problems of human nature: and that the Keele curriculum would lead to some understanding of the different approaches required. 'No student can be considered as properly educated today', he wrote in *The Times* in April 1972, 'unless he has some knowledge, both of the approach of the humanities and their methods of assessment, and also the meaning and reasoning of the scientific method in action.' He saw the Foundation Year as the epitome of what Keele stood for, and he regarded teaching in the Foundation Year as a major challenge for an academic to produce the best teaching to meet the widest academic audience. He left Keele in 1973 to become Principal of Chelsea College of Science and Technology. When Keele celebrated its fortieth anniversary he came back (he was then Vice-Chancellor of the University of Kent) to preach at the Service of Thanksgiving. After forty years there had been a shift in the Keele Ideology as compared with Lindsay's Idea of 1950. Lindsay's starting point had been that it was not specialisation as such but the breach created by it and the consequent decline of mutual understanding which gave rise to the underlying malaise and the weakening of society; and it was from this that he had developed the ideas of breaking down specialisation and restoring mutual understanding amongst educated people. With the experience of providing syllabuses to meet Lindsay's requirement, there had grown up more emphasis on the mechanics of doing it, and a tendency therefore for the broader education and the cross-disciplinary requirements themselves to be seen as what Keele stood for, rather than those things being the means of rectifying underlying faults. It was salutary when Ingram returned to the wider vision, to why it was important to understand the different ways of academic thinking and decision making, and to the underlying benefits which the flexibility of the Keele courses should engender. He was awarded an honorary degree in 1983.

Another change needed was the establishment of a full-time Appointments Office to help students find employment when they left Keele. Hugh Leech in the History Department had been part-time Appointments Secretary for seven years. His successor was Audrey Newsome, and her achievement (with the encouragement of Dr. Taylor) was to combine the appointments office with an educational, vocational and personal counselling service. The basic premise was to help students make considered choices and decisions in Keele's educational context. There was a parallel development when the National Association of Mental Health highlighted a need for counsellors in education, and in 1965 Keele and Reading set up the first full-time courses in this country in counselling and educational guidance. For her pioneering work in counselling, Audrey Newsome was awarded an honorary degree by the Open University in 1983.

From the start of the College Christian worship was central, and Lindsay had preached at the first service on the first Sunday of term in the Library Reading Room in Keele Hall. Within a few weeks a large army Nissen hut in the centre of the campus was prepared for chapel services, and it was Lindsay's intention that a permanent interdenominational building should be built at the heart of the campus. A College service, with a sermon, was held every Sunday, with a succession of distinguished preachers, and part-time Church of England, Roman Catholic and Free Church chaplains were appointed. There were weekday services, active societies, and a flourishing Sunday School run by Mary Glover who, with her forceful personality, deep religious commitment and wise counsel gave invaluable service to the chapel. (The restoration of the formal garden outside Keele Hall is a memorial to her contribution to Keele.) Occasional joint services were held with the village, and there was strong support for moves towards ecumenical worship.

G. G. Pace was appointed as the architect for a permanent chapel in 1958, and a chapel appeal fund was launched in 1960. Pace was working on the controversial restoration of Llandaff Cathedral after the War, and the Chapel of the Resurrection at the University of Ibadan, and was also consultant architect to a number of cathedrals. How the chapel came to have such a dominant site has already been explained. Sketch plans show a chapel faced with sandstone, but the substantial gift of bricks of the University's choice from the Berry Hill Brick Company resulted in a chapel built in a striking blue Staffordshire brick. When new, the building was stark. The design and the finish both outside with twin turrets, and inside with bare bricks, rough plastering, laminated timber trusses and structural reinforced concrete, provoked every shade of opinion from warm approbation and admiration to shock and disapproval. Whatever one's views, the chapel certainly cannot be ignored.

In the 1960s the design represented an advance in ecumenical building: it is three chapels under one roof. The layout of the main chapel followed the then current Anglican liturgical arrangement, with the congregation facing east and the altar table free-standing, but with the choir at the west end with the organ. The pews, though solid and heavy, are not fixed, so different seating arrangements are possible, such as the congregation facing north. The gallery on the south side was designed so that if empty it would be unnoticed: but this also means that visibility from the gallery is poor, except from the front row. At the east end of the main chapel is a large screen, behind which is a chapel space serving two altars – Roman Catholic and Free Church – giving the twin turrets seen from the outside. Screens can be lowered in front of each of the two altars. By raising the large screen behind the altar of the main chapel, the whole chapel space can be used as one. Overall, it is an austere building, described by Pevsner as 'a very personal statement'. It was given Grade II listed status by English Heritage in 1998.

The dedication of the chapel on 1st December 1965 was a major religious and royal occasion. H.M. Queen Elizabeth the Queen Mother accompanied Princess Margaret. First there was an honorary Degree Ceremony in the Walter Moberly Hall. In the procession of over ninety, only twenty could recall the early-1950s at Keele. Six of the fifteen founding heads of departments had left for appointments elsewhere. It was symbolic of the way Keele was not looking back, but was facing the future with confidence. The Princess as Chancellor conferred on H.M. the Queen Mother the honorary degree of Doctor of Letters. Professor E. M. Hugh-Jones, who had succeeded Williams in the chair of Economics, was the Public Orator. He gave a characteristically apt and polished oration, receiving the compliment from the Queen Mother: 'So simple and informal, such a pleasant change'. Next came the dedication of the Chapel in a service conducted by the Rt. Revd. A. S. Reeve, Bishop of Lichfield; the Rt. Revd. Monsignor Laurence Emery, Vicar-General, Protonotary Apostolic; and the Revd. B. Arthur Shaw, Chairman of the Chester and Stoke-on-Trent Methodist District, together with the three University chaplains. Professor Ingram gave the final reading from *Colossians*, concluding: 'Let your speech be alway with grace, seasoned with salt, that ye may know how ye ought to answer every man'.

Two days later the Drama Group performed T. S. Eliot's *Murder in the Cathedral* there – an ideal setting, used again for the same play in 1984 and 1994. In June 1966 Lord Fisher of Lambeth preached at a special united Service of Thanksgiving in which Anglican, Roman Catholic and Free Church clergy took part. It was an interesting measure of change that there could be a united service: for in 1960 the memorial for Sir George Barnes was a meeting which he had specifically asked for and to some extent designed, which bore little resemblance to a service, so that his many Roman Catholic friends could attend.

The concept of a chapel to serve the whole Christian community dated from the foundation of the College and Lindsay's vision; and the achievement of a permanent building was due to those who followed, and in particular Sir John Lennard-Jones. The chapel could never have been built had it not been for the strenuous efforts of the Principals and the Appeal Committee, the support of churches of all denominations (and especially the untiring efforts of the Venerable George Youell, the Archdeacon of Stoke-on-Trent and Anglican Chaplain), and the generosity of local industry and individual donors. It is dedicated to the memory of Lennard-Jones, and his family gave the pulpit in his memory. When the chapel had been a Nissen hut, the Chapel Committee had been reluctant to permit secular use (after it was no longer needed for Foundation Year lectures); but the new chapel was an ideal setting for *Murder in the Cathedral* and then for other drama productions. It is the only venue possible for organ recitals. Then other recitals and concerts were put on in the Chapel. It was a good setting for small degree congregations, mostly held in December, and from 1996 the summer degree congregations have been held there too. (The main degree congregations in the summer continued to be held in the

King's Hall, Stoke-on-Trent until 1995, with one exception when it was held at Trentham.) From the early-1980s the chapel has been used for final examinations. In the years since 1965 it must be said that nothing has softened the solid oak pews.

The two-manual organ is by Rushworth and Dreaper, built to George Pratt's specification and voiced in the style of 18th century Dutch and North German organs. The first recital was given by Dr. Francis Jackson of York Minster in May 1966. It showed that the instrument was best suited for the baroque style rather than for great romantic works. The upper work is light throughout to allow a wide range of tonal colours, so that what is happening in each part is never lost in a big sea of sound. It was shown off to great advantage at its inauguration and in the next few years by David Lumsden, Lionel Rogg, Daniel Chorzempa and Arie Keijzer (whose extemporisation on a theme of Charlotte Sneyd of early-19th century Keele Hall, which was given to him at the interval, culminated in a double fugue to provide a stunning second half of a recital).

Keele's first honorary degrees (other than the degrees already awarded to Alderman Horwood and to Mr. A. P. Walker by the College, and to Princess Margaret by the University) were conferred in the summer of 1965. The first was to Sir Walter Moberly. Professor Hugh-Jones began most appropriately with the centuries-old exhortation in places of learning from *Ecclesiasticus*: 'Let us now praise famous men, and our fathers that begat us', in recognition of the steadfast encouragement and support he had given as chairman of the UGC. Then followed Sir Alfred Owen, the University's tireless Pro-Chancellor; then Sir Barnett Stross, MP (who was knighted in 1964), a man with a fine local, national and international reputation, who had given strong support in political circles. Mr. Leslie Farrer-Brown was next, the Director of the Nuffield Foundation, whose generous assistance made it possible to equip the Nuffield Library with multiple copies of books for use in the Foundation Year. There were also honorary degrees for Mr. Harry Taylor, whose whole-hearted support, shrewdness, tenacity and loyalty enabled the College to come into existence; and for Mr. J. S. Ramage, the Senior Consultant Surgeon at the North Staffordshire Royal Infirmary, who had come to know succeeding Principals only too well. For all of them Hugh-Jones produced eloquent and erudite orations, and he continued as Public Orator until 1972. In 1968 Dr. Taylor (who had retired as Vice-Chancellor in 1967), whose career had started as a theoretical physicist and who had been awarded an honorary LLD by Cambridge, was awarded an honorary DLitt. On the same occasion Mr. A. P. Walker received, uniquely, an honorary MA to go with his honorary BA of ten years earlier. Of those who had been closely involved with Keele's foundation, Professor J. G. Smith and Mrs. Gladys Harris (Gladys Malbon of the WEA) received honorary degrees in 1966, Dame Lucy Sutherland in 1969, and Baron Fulton in 1972. Of the founding professors who had gone on to other things, there were honorary degrees for Blake in 1971, Vick in 1972 and Williams in 1973; and later there were honorary degrees, too, for other founding members of the College after they had retired – Professors Stewart and Gemmell, Mr. S. O.

Stewart and Miss Marion Bailey, all partners in the creation of Keele. Professor Cope was awarded an honorary degree in recognition of his life-long research in geology, but he died two months before the Degree Congregation when it would have been conferred on him in the year 2000.

Chapter 16

FRUSTRATION...

K eele had stuck resolutely to Lindsay's original scheme of a common Foundation Year for all students, as the first year of a four-year degree course; and, with the acquisition of the Keele estate, to a policy of total residence. For a small college of 600-800 the problems posed by having a four-year course and total residence were not insuperable. But it is a different matter when talking about a university of 2,000 or more: then those problems are on a different scale. At the end of 1964, Sir John Wolfenden, the Chairman of the UGC, felt that the extent to which growth in numbers should be matched by additional accommodation raised 'important issues of policy'. Total residence at Keele, based on an agreement made in the late-1940s, could hardly command the highest national priority when set against the needs of other universities, though the UGC did acknowledge an existing commitment to provide places for up to 1,700 (though with no guarantee when). The choice was between higher numbers with a lower percentage in residence, or remaining unique and small. A target of 2,150 students therefore meant that 450 would be non-resident. This also prompted questions about the four-year course – both the expense of a growing number of students, and the mechanism for running it. The largest lecture theatre seated about 500. For a larger intake would lectures be repeated? or shown on closed-circuit television? or would a larger lecture theatre be built? At the same time it was becoming apparent that far from the expansion in student numbers being significant in the sciences, as was expected earlier, there was instead a national decline in science students, and at Keele this was being exacerbated by the change of mind encouraged by the Foundation Year. A report by Alan Iliffe on the student intake of 1962 and 1963 showed that two-thirds of them changed their mind over one or both subjects they wished to read at Principal level, with a drift away from the sciences. The report also found that following the Foundation Year students felt confident about reading unfamiliar subjects, and that those without corresponding 'A' levels in English, history, geography and biology did as well as those with 'A' levels. (The report was later published as *The Foundation Year in the University of Keele*, The Sociological Review Monograph 12, July 1968.) Moreover, the year away from their chosen Principal subjects while taking the Foundation Year, and then having to read two Principal subjects, were seen as disadvantages in the recruitment and training of science students. This led to strong support from the science staff for the introduction of three-year degree courses (i.e. without the Foundation Year) for those wishing to read two science subjects, and for the possibility of specialising in only one Principal subject during the final year. One science professor strongly disagreed, however. That was Professor Gemmell. He did not waver from the convictions of 1950: he thought that to abandon the principles for which Lindsay had founded Keele – namely to produce graduates with an understanding of many types of problems and with a common background – in order to produce a hypothetical few physical scientists doing what other universities were doing, was absurd. Especially for scientists he regarded the Foundation Year as crucial to the aims of the founders and the ideals for which the College stood and to which they had all been committed. The Senate took no action – on this occasion.

On the wider scene, Dr. Taylor warned that building grants were becoming woefully inadequate, and that the whole concept of universities as self-governing institutions was coming into question. These two matters are, of course, closely related: a way to call the tune is to starve the piper. In 1965 volumes I and II of Dr. Taylor's monumental work on *Anglo-Saxon Architecture* were published. Mrs. Taylor had died suddenly in January, and in May he spent a month in Cambridge. He realised that without the expert help of his wife he was unlikely to be able to start and finish volume III if he stayed on as Vice-Chancellor till he was 67, and so in June he announced that he would retire in September 1967 on reaching the age of 60. In February 1966 Professor Stewart was appointed to succeed him, so on this occasion not only would there be no interregnum, but the incoming Vice-Chancellor knew from first-hand experience the background of Lindsay and the whole history of the College. He had been Acting Principal in the interregnum between Barnes and Taylor, showing himself to be determined, decisive and impressive. He had already stated in the mid-1950s what he believed were the basic assumptions underlying Lindsay's Keele, and he re-iterated them in a lecture during his first year as Vice-Chancellor. They were as follows:

> '1. University study should be related to an intelligent person's life in contemporary society, which must include, of course, a sense and knowledge of history. University and higher education in general, has too often become misdirected so that the creative possibilities of specialisation have been narrowed into a departmentalism.
>
> 2. On this assumption it is possible to outline the main areas of knowledge of which every university student should know something. These are the Humanities, the Social Sciences and the Experimental Sciences.
>
> 3. All intelligent persons will want to master some subjects in a scholarly way and opportunities for specialised study must be offered. But general education must not simply be left to the optional choice of each undergraduate. It is part of the curricular responsibility of the university to provide a basis for a general education. These courses are to be obligatory.
>
> 4. The rate of expansion of knowledge, particularly in the sciences, has produced and will increasingly produce an informational spiral for the future undergraduate. Within subjects, and certainly between subjects, the questions to ask in universities are, what are the most significant aspects of this increasing knowledge which an

undergraduate should attend to, and, more profoundly, what new combinations of knowledge and cultural synthesis are becoming apparent between subjects?

5. Those who intend to teach or to be social workers should not be trained in a post-graduate year, but should take their so-called vocational studies alongside their degree courses, each contributing to their general education.

6. The best conditions for academic life are residential, for undergraduates, dons and their families.'

Looking at the new universities of the 1960s he went on to say: 'In four things Keele is different. First, it has a Foundation Year of general education which none of the others has. Second, it has four years for everyone, which no-one else has. Some of the others wanted a four years course but the money was not available for that. But if they had had a fourth year almost certainly they would not have used it for a Foundation Year purpose. Third, Keele requires some representation of science and non-science for everyone. No-one else does that. Fourth, it is more completely residential than any other university.' He went on to rehearse some of the arguments for and against a residential university: 'On the one hand Keele is a place where facilities for work are always at hand and this is good: on the other hand it is said to be an artificial, isolated community both for dons and undergraduates. It is a community which produces more stimulus in this area than any other through extra-mural, educational, social service, religious and general cultural offerings: it is a small, self-satisfied and self-sufficient township whose dons don't mix and whose students come from a distance for two-thirds of the year. It is a liberal, tolerant community where conflicts of opinion are accepted and necessary rules are few: it is a centre for extremism in clothes, appearance, politics, rowdiness, sexual behaviour. It is a place for unique intellectual opportunities, where hard work must be done to a good level and self-discipline is at a premium: it is a pretentious campus, too well appointed for real effort which encourages laziness and the tendency to get by, where dons and undergraduates alike have an easy time at the public expense.'

Stewart was a man with inexhaustible patience. Had Taylor continued his term of office as Vice-Chancellor he would have found the attitudes of the late-60s and the early-70s alien to all that he stood for and that much more difficult to contend with; but when the frenetic unrest of the 'student troubles' gripped the place, Stewart was patient to the end – to the extent of causing exasperation amongst those who wanted and expected to see more immediate and firmer action.

As the load on the Vice-Chancellor grew heavier, he increased more formal arrangements to ensure he received academic advice not only from the chairmen of the three Boards of Studies but also from advisers elected by each Board. He also decided not to chair most of the subcommittees of the Senate himself. That was perhaps unfortunate in the cases of the Library Committee and the Foundation Year Committee where his position might have enabled him to give firmer direction to policy.

As the University was growing it was feasible to revive the aspirations of the Exploratory Committee in the 1940s for a medical school. It could be no more than a pipe dream in the 1950s, for Keele was small and a medical school would have taken a disproportionate share of resources. Moreover it would not have fitted in with Keele's particular curriculum, and the money which would have been necessary was not likely to be forthcoming from the UGC. But what about the 1960s? The impetus was a report on medical education by Dr. Nicholas Malleson of the University of London, recommending new medical schools which would pioneer liberalising changes in the curriculum. Courses which stressed the non-vocational side of medicine could have found a place in the Keele pattern and would have boosted the University's innovative advances in education. Against a background of expanding to 1,700 students by 1967, and the building of the Medical Institute at the hospital in 1964, it seemed timely to apply for a medical school: the pre-clinical courses could be at Keele and the clinical courses at the Stoke-on-Trent complex of hospitals. There was strong support from the local medical profession, from the Birmingham Hospital Board, the Local Authorities and from local Members of Parliament. Sir Barnett Stross had asked in the House of Commons as early as 1962 if Keele would not be 'ripe beyond all other places' for a new medical school. A Foundation Committee drew up proposals to establish a school of human biology within the University and a clinical medical school at the hospital. The course would be wide-ranging, to provide a foundation of studies also for those professions allied to medicine. A three-year course within the school of human biology would cover core traditional training plus psychology, genetics and statistics and some clinical courses such as epidemiology and the principles of bacteriology and pathology. *The Times, Daily Telegraph, The Guardian*, and *Financial Times* ran headlines like 'Keele to have medical school', and the *British Medical Journal* and *The Lancet* ran articles on 'Keele's Medical School'. *New Scientist* wrote of a new type of medical training which, it suggested, must be adopted sooner or later if doctors were to be fitted for the practice of modern medicine. With government support and money it might have been possible, and it would have given an enormous boost to Keele.

The Labour Government (1964-1970) had promised four more medical schools. So far there was only Nottingham. What was optimistic for Keele was that the hospital facilities already existed, and it was thought in 1964 that students might be admitted in two or three years' time. The government then set up a Royal Commission under Lord Todd, in June 1965, and meanwhile expansion was to be in the existing medical schools. Soon, fifteen universities were vying for a medical school, and in August 1967 Southampton's bid was successful. That decision was additionally prompted by the rebuilding of Southampton General Hospital. The DES emphasized that this did not preclude Keele's application, which was waiting for a decision from the Royal Commission. Their report was published in April 1968: then it had to be considered by the government, the UGC and other bodies involved. Six months later Stephen Swingler, MP for Newcastle-under-Lyme (and formerly a WEA lecturer in North Staffordshire), was told by Mrs. Shirley Williams, the Minister of State at the DES, that there was no hope of an early decision for Keele. Jack Ashley, MP for Stoke-on-Trent South, raised the matter again a year later, but the government was still considering recommendations. But it was all to no avail: what really closed the door was the recommendation in the Report that as a pre-condition, a university needed to have 4,000 students to support an annual intake of 150-200 medical students. Keele was too small. Moreover, it transpired that the 'Malleson' approach to medical education had not found favour with the UGC's medical and biological advisers. There was neither encouragement nor support: Keele ought to think of the development of a medical school in terms of decades.

The quinquennial grant for 1967-72 was the occasion for the UGC's more positive guidance to universities. The UGC suggested student numbers: not as precise targets or as directives or ceilings, but as a financial guide; and the UGC went further at a meeting in April 1968 when they said they could give no official approval to any step which would diminish the number of places for non-scientists. They referred to relative costs between different universities, though said they would not expect or seek to achieve uniformity. Further expansion at Keele in the years 1972-77 would not be unacceptable (somehow less enthusiastic than saying it would be acceptable) provided it was compatible with national policy and provided, too, it was not tied to maintaining 100% residence. Then, within a few months there were fresh cuts in government expenditure. A letter from the UGC dated 1st August wanted replies by 19th September. (The University's financial year begins on 1st August and this was now the middle of the vacation.) The completion of Barnes Hall was postponed, to leave an incomplete hall as a monument to successive cuts in the building programme. When the UGC visited Keele in November 1968 the chairman said they did not wish to change or modify substantially the ideas for which Keele stood. However, there needed to be extremely serious decisions taken on what size Keele should be; and any future residences would have to be financed by commercial loans.

Total residence had been abandoned. It must be said that Keele had received favoured treatment hitherto, and continued to enjoy a high proportion of students living on the campus: but nevertheless it was a major change to one of the ideas Keele stood for, on grounds of cost.

With the development of the Library, the Students' Union and the Chapel giving a focal point at the centre of the campus, the appropriateness of a ring road to take traffic away from the centre and to have a pedestrian area there rather than a roundabout became more obvious and more pressing. But roads are expensive to build, and the task was made more difficult by some recent building – the house just by Biology (which was still at an early stage) was one such problem: it was in the way. The ring road was to be built in four stages between 1969 and 1973: stage I, from the Covert roundabout to Horwood boiler house; stage II from the Covert roundabout to Chemistry; stage III from Chemistry to Clock House Drive (i.e. close to Sneyd and Harrowby and the back of the Library); and stage IV to provide the link from Horwood to Keele Drive. It would have to be phased to match non-recurrent grants. Stage I was the first priority. The Traffic Committee recommended stage III next, but stage II was more urgent because the Covert road was narrow, and dangerous for children and pedestrians, and a wider road would be required for servicing the Departments of Physics, Chemistry and Communication, the Workshop and the Computer Centre. Stage III would not be effective until stage IV was completed – and that meant demolishing the old R.A.F. hut and other usable buildings near Keele Hall.

It seemed an expensive undertaking at a time when academic and even administrative buildings were needed. Some thought it far from obvious why it was necessary, pointing out that it would take traffic out of the centre, which was used part of the day, part of the week, for part of the year, and concentrate the noise, smell and danger in and around residential areas which were occupied and used all the time. One idea was to build stages I, II and IV, without III, to avoid the detrimental effects on the Library, Geology, Sneyd and Harrowby, as there was no need to go round and round a ring road. And what about the trees, and especially the large oak tree at the bottom of the Covert road? The Residents' Association, and especially Mrs. Katrina Hill, with an indefatigable concern for the environment and amenities and the threats to the splendid natural setting of the campus, regretted and deplored the decision to build stage III; and the degree of consultation and full discussion was called into question.

Another contentious issue was the building of speed traps. Before the ring road was started, fifteen rows of setts across the width of the road were built on Keele Drive. But it was more comfortable to go over them quickly rather than slowly, so a different design was adopted, after examining traffic control arrangements elsewhere: ramps. Drivers did not like them; some residents wanted more of them; low-slung cars scraped on some of them. At this stage, Dr. Andrews and Dr. Wilson (in the Department of Communication and Neuroscience) examined the problem thoroughly, and visited Rolls Royce at Crewe. They looked at the effects of a ramp at different speeds in relation to discomfort to passengers, inconvenience to the driver, and damage to vehicles, and concluded that the 'speed selective effect' of these ramps lay in the wrong range of speeds. Unsatisfactory effects were actually occurring within the range of permitted and desirable speeds. They recommended a longer ramp, which would operate in a higher speed range, and an increase in height, which would give an ever-increasing penalty with higher speeds. A new type of ramp was therefore provided on the first stage of the ring road – a wave curve, 40 feet long, rising to 5 inches at the centre. However, small discrepancies in its profile meant that it was effective at 40 miles per hour instead of at 30 miles per hour. A modified ramp, 10 feet long, rising to 3 inches, near Chemistry, very effectively reduced speed, especially as it left the road surface at an angle rather than in a curve, giving a progressively more severe jolt with increasing speed. The optimal profile was going to be not the one which almost halted traffic, but one which kept drivers within the speed limit. To have to use bottom gear at a ramp would only lead to acceleration away from it, but if it could be negotiated in third gear, acceleration away from it would be less. Dr. Andrews and Dr. Wilson concluded that the ideal profile would be between the two – 20 feet long, rising to 4 inches, and with an angle at the onset. Unfortunately, work was already in hand, and the style of the ramp near Chemistry carried the day – 9 feet wide, rising to $3^1/_2$ inches at the centre. Radar detection was also tested, but it was felt that a physical deterrent was a better course to follow.

Building the ring road and Barnes Hall (and the building of the M6 and the laying of North Sea gas pipes) provided Keele's geologists with an opportunity to carry out detailed work on the area. The Apedale fault is close by and is discernible on Keele Road on the way to Newcastle. Near the boiler house and round the back of the Students' Union, at least three members of the Department looked at the excavations and agreed that there was a very severe disturbance and a smash zone present which must be linked to a fault somewhere. During the 1940s Professor Cope had determined the existence of the Home Farm fault but it was uncertain where it surfaced. In the 1970s Dr. Exley mapped it running from the escarpment overlooking the Westlands to the University playing fields, where it was established by clays and crushed coals in a drain. For a time it could be traced from a bump in the drive alongside the playing fields. Barnes Hall was to bear witness to the Home Farm fault. Three-storey buildings were planned, but the UGC wanted lower unit costs and so four-storey blocks were built. Despite the building precautions taken, to build there was, literally, flying in the face of nature. 'M' block cracked, and is no longer there. The existence of another fault was discovered from the evidence of a National Coal Board bore hole made above the Observatory. Dr. Exley extrapolated where it went, namely across the site for Barnes Hall. Consultant expert opinion, however, did not agree. Does it exist? If so, it has been designated the Horwood fault. A Lindsay fault has also been designated. Some of the University's history may yet be chronicled in a series of geological faults.

When it came to the proposed Administration Building it was a much more recent activity which gave pause for thought. As the old Keele Estate maps showed, there used to be a lake before the present first lake, but it had been filled in. Its existence was overlooked until a survey revealed a bed of silt and the need for expensive foundations. However, lack of money saved the trouble: the proposed Administration Building has not been built for lack of funds.

It is not surprising that the University policy of providing houses and flats for rent to enable staff to live on the campus could not survive growth and straitened finances. It was in many ways a luxury. It offered considerable advantages, and was a key factor in the days of a small College in adding a lot to the sense of community. It offered staff the great advantage of living within a few minutes' walk of their work, though not everyone welcomes living so close to their colleagues. There were real problems, however. Families of staff who died in service and staff retiring had to leave their homes at particularly difficult periods in their lives. House prices began to rise sharply. Aware of this, and seeking to take responsibility for their families' housing while at the same time continuing to enjoy the amenities of campus life, a small group of eight staff founded the University of Keele Staff Housing Association in July 1967. The Association bought some land from the University and in the late-1960s built twenty-two houses at 'Springpool'. There were benefits all round. Individuals secured an interest in the capital values of their houses while the University, at no cost, had additional housing available for its staff. The ability of staff at Springpool to remain after retirement, and for spouses to continue in the houses after the death of the staff member were features adopted by the University itself when, much later, it began to sell University flats and houses. Proposals to form another housing association in the mid-1970s were not successful.

Readers may be as surprised as staff were to learn that a report by the Comptroller and Auditor General in 1970 suggested that Keele was generously over-provided with buildings for almost everything – that there were academic buildings for almost 2,600 students; Library, central administration and maintenance for over 5,000; dining and catering for 4,700; and social provision for over 3,000. (This was at a time when there were just over 1,600 undergraduates at Keele.) The Vice-Chancellor therefore accepted an invitation to attend a meeting of the Public Accounts Committee to express a contrary view. Particularly pressing, or so it was thought, was an extension to the Students' Union building, which had been proposed in 1967: but then, in 1970, the UGC felt it necessary to question the need, even though work was due to start in 1970/71. At a time when they proposed Keele should grow to 2,400 they proposed also to defer the extension for a few years. The Registrar pointed out that the Students' Union had been built for a student population of 1,200; that the figure of 2,400 for 1976-77 was the UGC's suggestion and that it had not yet been discussed; and that the case for an extension had been apparent to the UGC two years earlier, when the chairman had written that the present building would be cramped and crowded by the end of the quinquennium. 'I hope this resolves your difficulty about why additional space was thought to be necessary.' But the UGC had invented 'rations' of space for various functions, which were never discussed with the University, and was concluding that the present building could take exactly double the number for which it was originally planned. 'This I deny', wrote the Registrar. It was not so much a question of the decision being unwelcome, as that it appeared to undermine the whole basis on which planning had so far been conducted. The UGC conceded that if there were a case for higher usage than elsewhere, then the Union extension might be reinstated. On the matter of student numbers the UGC was asking whether they could afford any increase beyond 2,400 on the basis of four-year courses – but they were prepared to consider a higher number if that expansion were in three-year courses. They would therefore 'pencil in' 3,000 for 1977 on that basis; and in that case, they said in January 1971, they would 'unfreeze' the Students' Union extension.

The scene was therefore set: up to 25% of students living off campus; student residences to be funded by loans, and then by 'commercial development'. More important, 20% of the target of 3,000 students would be taking three-year courses, which were introduced in 1973. The Foundation Year was no longer compulsory for all students. It could no longer be claimed to be an integral part of the Keele degree course: it became an optional extra. One of the things absolutely fundamental to Lindsay's Idea in 1950 was abandoned on grounds of cost. With the introduction of three-year courses, those courses which included two principal subjects from the social sciences led not to the degree of Bachelor of Arts but to the Bachelor of Social Science; and three-year courses which included one or two principal subjects from the natural sciences led to the degree of Bachelor of Science. In addition, for most cases where a student read two principal subjects from the natural sciences, it was possible to take just one of them in the final year to graduate with single honours.

Was this, then, the chipping away of the dream? Simon Hoggart in *The Guardian* thought it was (13 February 1971). The Vice-Chancellor admitted that it had been a heart-searching decision, but explained that it had been reached partly through seeking to extend the variety of what Keele had to offer. The vital combination of general and specialised education was to be maintained, and the changes would help keep up the number of science students. The number of three-year students was to be restricted to no more than 20% of the total, and the four-year courses remained the staple by which we stood. 'The most important and interesting problems of science and society today are cross-disciplinary: Keele's founders saw this twenty years ago... To imagine that he [Simon Hoggart] has to mourn the end of an academic experiment and the abandonment of an ideal is to misunderstand and con-fuse the nature of the proposed changes. We are in fact contemplating embarking on a new phase in the development of 'Lindsay's Keele", he replied. There had been lively debates about the shape of Keele, and there were certain demonstrable logistic and academic advantages in growing beyond 2,400; and 'the soundest basis for such growth seems to be the concept of parallel three- and four-year systems with a heavy emphasis on maintaining the four-year programmes for 80% of our students while offering the central values of a Keele education to the remaining 20% in three-year courses.' Later he said: 'Of course, the time of hard reckoning is likely to come in the quinquennium 1977-82 and after, rather than in 1972-77. Will the three-year element be treated as the thin end of a wedge?' In fact, the time for hard reckoning had already passed. In October 1976 the number of three-year students admitted was almost 30% of the intake, and three years later it exceeded 50%. The Foundation Year itself finally came to an end in 1999: it did not quite last fifty years.

Chapter 17

... AND TROUBLES

If only it were true that all publicity is good publicity, Keele would have enjoyed a few golden years.

Some discontent was surfacing when Barnes was Principal. Formal dinners became a dead letter and this was followed by agitation against the wearing of gowns and the 'permitted hours', as they were called, during which the sexes could mix within their halls of residence. The Senate had reaffirmed the regulation that gowns should be worn on certain occasions (indeed, members of staff were certainly expected to wear gowns: even in 1965, Senate resolved that members attending the Senate and staff attending special lectures should wear gowns). In June 1961 the Senate refused to extend the 'permitted hours' of 12.30 p.m. to 7.30 p.m. (and 8.30 p.m. on Sundays) to 10.0 p.m. on Sundays, and a Students' Union resolution reported at Dr. Taylor's first Senate meeting in October 1961 'deeply regrets the Senate's refusal to accept an overwhelming expression of student opinion on matters primarily of student concern and urges Senate seriously to reconsider its attitude to gowns and the hours rule'. The question was not going to lie down. The Discipline and Welfare Committee was unwilling to recommend a change, thinking that to do so would tend to reduce opportunities for private academic work, and because it thought that any extension of the permitted hours during which members of the opposite sex could be alone together would produce an undesirable increase in the strain to which such couples would be subject if they were to maintain an adequate standard of sexual behaviour. The committee did recommend, however, that the hours might be changed to 4.0 p.m. – 10.0 p.m. instead of 12.30 p.m. – 7.30 p.m., but in February 1962 the Senate regarded that as too permissive. The Residence Regulation was relaxed only a little, and now read as follows:

'(a) No woman is allowed inside a Men's Residence and no man is allowed inside a Women's Residence, without permission, except between the hours of 12.30 p.m. and 7.30 p.m. (10.0 p.m. on Saturdays and Sundays only).

(b) Undergraduates must not be outside their own hall without permission after 11.0 p.m. except on Saturdays when the time is midnight.

N.B. The breaking of the above two rules is regarded as a serious offence and may render those breaking them liable to be excluded from the University.'

Some of the popular press focused on Dr. Taylor – 'Strict new don angers courting students' (*Daily Express*).

Student representation on policy-making committees was not yet an issue – indeed, in *Keele After Ten Years* John Barker had written: 'The President of the Union has a seat on the Court of the College, a rare privilege in university life'. A few years later such a sentence could hardly have been penned, but in 1960 it was the *staff* who were wanting greater representation.

At the beginning of 1964/65 there suddenly arose the issue of the sale of contraceptives in the Union shop, which Dr. Taylor vetoed. 'As an integral part of widespread investigations into the problems of human relationships on the University campus, the Union Committee took the decision that there was no objection in principle to making these goods available', said a Students' Union statement. 'Peter Simple' in the *Daily Telegraph* wrote that he wished he had invented such a statement. 'As I sit here trying to compose statements by imaginary university students which shall combine pseudo-sociological jargon and dubious syntax with the purest blend of hypocrisy, it is intolerable to have real (or apparently real) students taking the words out of my mouth' (17th November 1964). It was only a minor row, but unfortunately it caught the news headlines.

Not long afterwards there was more unwelcome publicity. The chapel was temporarily in the Walter Moberly Hall while the new chapel was being built, and the service was being broadcast live on Sunday morning, 24th January. Suddenly a hymn was drowned by the record 'Leader of the Pack'; the lesson was also drowned, and the service went off the air for about five minutes. The irreligious nature of the incident was compounded further. The record was one which had been banned by the BBC. Sir Winston Churchill had died earlier that morning, and it was a time of something like national mourning. The previous Sunday, just after the chapel service, Mrs. Taylor had died, and her funeral service had been held in Keele church during the week. The incident may have been intended only as a prank on the BBC by one or two individuals but it was outrageous and thoroughly distasteful, and particularly sad for Dr. Taylor at such a time. Keele was getting bad publicity at the same time as the new universities were attracting laudatory articles in the national press.

It was a few years later, when Professor Stewart was Vice-Chancellor, that more widespread discontent became the fashion. Some of the issues had nothing to do with Keele, but they served to fan the excitement. Examinations, meals, the Foundation Year, hours rules, student membership of the Senate, approved lodgings, 'Action for a Free University', political activists, exasperation, secret files, sit-ins, break-ins, disciplinary procedures, Wardens' courts – all these things fit in somewhere, like a kaleidoscope. Various national and international trends were seen as liberalising by many, and degenerate by others. London had become the 'swinging capital'. There were drugs law cases, a rally in Hyde Park seeking to liberalise pot, Parliament passed the Abortion Bill and legalised homosexual acts between adult men, introduced compulsory breath tests and decimal currency. Che Guevara was shot in the Bolivian jungle, Britain announced its withdrawal east of Suez, and traffic in Sweden switched to driving on the right. There was a hunger strike and sit-in at the London School of Economics and anarchy at Hornsey College of Art; anti-Vietnam war protests in the U.S.A. spread to London; there were the shocks of the deaths of Martin Luther King and Robert Kennedy; there was the hope of the Prague Spring; *Last Exit to Brooklyn* was cleared on appeal of being obscene, mini-skirts grew shorter, and stage censorship was abolished. All in all, heady change was felt to be in the air.

The whole idea of universities acting *in loco parentis* was questioned, and the age of majority was lowered from 21 to 18 on 1st January 1970, so altering the relationship between universities and students. Academic, social and political issues all played a part. It was discontent about examinations, the content of the Foundation Year, and student membership of the Senate which started 'the troubles'. Social discontent focused on the hours rule, catering arrangements and disciplinary procedures. In a letter to the *Sentinel* on 6th June 1968, Godfrey Smart (President of the Students' Union in 1968-9) said that there was not one specific grievance but a feeling amongst students that their views were not sufficiently considered, and that they were not involved in the administration of the University in a way which reflected their involvement in the institution. There had recently been produced a detailed report by the Students' Union Academic Committee on the Foundation Year, which Senate's Foundation Year Committee was considering; but nothing had been done yet. Discontent about final examinations resulted in an 'Exam-in' – a discussion attended by about 150, including some staff and heads of departments, which lasted five hours. 'The troubles' at Keele at least started on an academic note. There were those who regarded the examination system as part of a question about the distribution of power within the University, and that led to discussion on the function and nature of education. This was the starting point for 'Action for a Free University', whose members held frequent meetings to ridicule the system. It was disciplined and non-violent. It extended to some students sitting at high table at lunch time; then there was a mass breaking of the hours rule, and about a hundred students went to the Vice-Chancellor's house singing 'We shall overcome' and 'The Internationale'. A sit-in in the Library was called off when it was time for the staff go home. This would have been the time to defuse the discontent, but the University authorities were not clear what the demands were, and felt that many students were not clear either.

Those who wanted reform wanted it instantly, and really did believe that there was an opportunity to make major changes. The nature of the residential community meant that it was easy to catch a mood at Keele and for that mood to spread very quickly. But university decision-making was not designed to react quickly, and conservative attitudes were not sympathetic to demands for change and the picketing of

Senate meetings. The expectation by some students that changes could be made more quickly than was likely was probably at the root of misunderstandings, certainly in the late-1960s. In June 1968 Malcolm Clarke, the President of the Students' Union attended the Senate meeting. That itself was a considerable achievement. He was there to press the Union's case for more student participation in University committees, for the abolition – or at least some relaxation – of the hours rule, for some changes in the requirement for off-campus lodgings to be 'approved' by the University, and for some amendments to some of the disciplinary procedures. The Senate sat long, adjourned and reconvened at 8.15 p.m. Senate would not abolish the hours rule, but it extended the 'permitted hours' to 12.30 p.m. – 12 midnight, Monday to Friday, and 10.30 a.m. – 12 midnight at weekends; Wardens' courts were to be replaced by disciplinary panels including student members. A statement was issued the following day accepting that student participation in the governmental process was desirable and pointing out how many committees already had student representation.

The statement went on to say that Senate was 'not prepared to take a hasty decision on the question [of representation on Senate itself] and has accordingly referred the question to the Exploratory Committee'. This was a new committee to consider student participation in University affairs and (though soon forgotten) staff participation in Union affairs. The Committee consisted of five staff, five students, and a chairman appointed by the Senate. This seemed entirely reasonable to the Senate – a procedure to allow full and measured consideration. Meanwhile, at Sussex University seven student members were added to their Senate.

Clarke was disappointed not to take back a better response. He knew he had not got enough to satisfy the Union General Meeting a few days later and that the meeting would demand some sort of action. Spray paint slogans appeared in twenty-one places all over the campus. On 17th June the Union General Meeting demanded student observers, the repeal of the lodgings requirement, clarification about the Exploratory Committee and, by 306 to 160, direct action to emphasize their case and 'to compel' Senate to reconsider. Clarke resigned because he did not believe that direct action would achieve further changes, and having lost the vote he felt it was better for someone else to take his place. The direct action taken was to occupy the Registry (the wooden hut next to the chapel) for forty-eight hours – almost an initiation ceremony in the rite of passage of student protest. That evening the Vice-Chancellor was holding a sherry party for the outgoing and incoming Union committees. There was debate by those protesting whether they should attend such an event, but good sense and polite behaviour won. Small talk was perhaps more interesting than usual: 'Hallo, Mr. [X]', said the Registrar to a young man now wearing a suit. 'The last time I saw you, you were on my office roof.' It was hardly drastic, but the Union policy of 'direct action' was considered an affront to the conduct of business by reasonable discussion. 'It should never have happened here', said the student paper *Cygnet*. 'All the principles of Keele should have prevented it...

Keele is not alone... perennial student dissatisfaction has metamorphosed into radical social dissent.' The Vice-Chancellor had written in *Keele After Ten Years*: 'In the next ten years... our difference, our protest, our originality must remain strong too', and students seeking reform expected it from those words. (Three years later Malcolm Clarke, by then a postgraduate student, was elected to Newcastle Borough Council, and following local government reorganisation he became the youngest Mayor of Newcastle in its 800 years' history.)

The vacation might have defused any serious agitation. A joint statement by the CVCP and the National Union of Students encouraged student participation in aspects of decision-making and discipline. Unrest at Keele over the next two years was as much a result of student power politics, and agitation elsewhere. Fewer were involved but they were more active. 'Action for a Free University' subsided as quickly as it had appeared, leaving activists to join the Revolutionary Socialist Students' Federation.

The Exploratory Committee discussed everything at great length. It seemed that the steam had gone out of the protest movement: Union General Meetings were not always quorate. The Wardens of the Halls were asked to design an experiment under which students in certain blocks would assume complete responsibility for discipline in those blocks. This was the 'Hawthorns Experiment'. With credit to the Wardens, Iolo Roberts and Eileen Lake, and to the Hall Chairmen, Julian Comer and Sheila West, the heavens did not fall in. Blocks made their own rules, such as: 'In extreme cases of anti-social behaviour, a block meeting should be called... at the wish of at least twenty-one people.' 'There are no fixed rules. Problems will be dealt with as they arise at block meetings called by two or more members of the block. Decisions will not be taken unless half of the block is represented; and a two-thirds majority will be needed in cases of disagreement.' 'No rules, but a series of guide-lines. Please don't leave piles of dirty dishes on the draining board, especially over Sunday night.' With a high degree of involvement, goodwill and enthusiasm, the hours rule as an issue faded in importance as the experiment proceeded. Comments ranged from 'more domestic, homier, friendlier, more conducive to study, and not at all distasteful', and 'a more highly developed sense of responsibility for both public and community than are to be found elsewhere in the University', to 'as useless as everyone said it would be', and 'a sop to the minority of revolutionaries here'. The more positive view prevailed, and the scheme was extended to other halls.

A twenty-four hour sit-in in the Great Hall by about sixty students in February 1969 was in sympathy with a student dispute at the London School of Economics. Other-wise much of the discontent seemed to have run its course: that is until the Explora-tory Committee presented its report to the Senate in May 1969 – thirteen pages long, the result of nineteen meetings. The nub of the matter was student membership of the Senate. Senate, though far from unanimous, decided that the weight of staff opinion was that the case for student participation in the academic decision-making bodies of the University had not yet been proved. The real sticking points were 'reserved' areas of business and the Union's insistence that their representatives on committees should be treated as delegates. Senate did, however, decide to investigate establishing a General Purposes Committee (i.e. Senate plus student members) to make recommendations on those areas of business which were not specifically reserved for the Senate; but it was a cosmetic measure which was overtaken by events.

The Exploratory Committee also produced a Minority Report, sixty-five pages long, plus appendices. This looked at problems in a different way and claimed at length that the root cause of unrest was the 'fundamental learning contradiction' between the functional need of capitalism for large numbers of 'organic' intellectuals, and the inability to tolerate this mass realising its critical potential – and then went on to detail radical new proposals. The Senate first considered whether the Minority Report could be discussed without its political content, and then rejected its main premises, purposes and conclusions (though it should be added that there was some recognition that parts of the report contained material of value for future deliberations).

The refusal to accede to student membership of the Senate provoked some reaction: 'such high-handed action by this authoritarian body constitutes an abominable and total repudiation of any pretence this University has to being a liberal institution'. The Exploratory Committee had generated its own momentum and enthusiasm, and the staff members had not warned the student members sufficiently of what the Senate's reaction was likely to be. Perhaps they had expected a more liberal attitude from their colleagues. Two days later Professor Stewart held a meeting with members of the Union Committee to review what had happened. He referred to existing student membership of the Deputy Vice-Chancellor's, Discipline and Welfare, Foundation Year and Library committees, and bodies dealing with lodgings and residence; and he outlined the events of the previous twelve months, concluding that there was a general feeling that the Union's political affairs were in a mess, and that until that was resolved, the attitude of staff in general was unlikely to change. He urged calm, patience and determination, and expressed his willingness to talk to the Students' Union. And that was the end of another academic year.

In October 1969 agitation was re-fuelled by the Parliamentary Select Committee on Student Relations, which said: 'Student representation on Council and Senate in the Universities... should be accepted'. The following day Leicester admitted students to its Senate. At Keele, *Concourse*, wrote about a 'gradually escalating programme of militant action', but that was followed by an article about student apathy. The militants proposed the election of eight students as 'senators-in-exile' and organised a picket of the Senate meeting; but the Union's policy was that disruption was unlikely to lead to increased participation, and a militant proposal was defeated. No disciplinary action was taken against a student who kept a pig in his room to use in a protest. It is not clear that at the time this constituted an offence against University regulations: members of the opposite sex were not allowed inside residences except between specified hours; bicycles and accessories were not allowed inside build-ings; and fireworks, firearms and the like were not to be brought into the University. It was only later that horses and ponies must walk or be ridden only on the roads (Vehicles Regulation) and that no pets of any description were allowed in the residences (Residence Regulation).

But then there were troubles at Warwick where a large number of students broke into the Registry and found documents on staff, students and business interests. Reports that the University held 'secret files' sparked off sit-ins and break-ins at Edinburgh, Manchester, Kent, Birmingham, Liverpool and Nottingham. At Keele, the Vice-Chancellor agreed to go to a meeting in the Students' Union, where the mood was one of heckling and jeering. About 400 students left, fairly satisfied, and about 250 stayed on. Despite the Vice-Chancellor's assurance that there were no documents in Keele like those found at Warwick, flour bombs were thrown from the balconies (action which was denounced by both the political militants and the Students' Union Committee). A Students' Union Emergency General Meeting called for unspecified direct action (by 160 votes to 80), and in the early hours some students forced a window in Keele Hall, broke into filing cabinets in the Vice-Chancellor's Assistant's office, and jostled the Head Porter in an attempt to get hold of keys. It was pointless and nihilist. While the Emergency General Meeting motion remained the official policy of the Union, a number of committees with students members suspended their meetings. Disciplinary action was taken against seven students: four of them were found guilty, two of whom appealed to the Council.

The next focus for disturbance was the biennial Open Day held on 2nd May 1970: noisy by day by the Students' Union building, and noisier by night down at Hor-wood. Requests from finalists for quiet were ignored, and peace was only restored when one of the participants carelessly trod on the record player. (There followed five more disciplinary cases.) A petrol bomb was thrown into the Senior Tutor's office in the Registry hut that night, and another into Horwood General Block. This was much more serious, and was investigated by the police as cases of arson. A few days later, a (very noisy) 'Festival of Peace' concert culminated in an outburst of spray paint graffiti. The official Students' Union line was a willingness to negotiate at formal and informal levels, but the reality was that tensions heightened to their worst. There were nightly patrols of staff and students, and staff manned their offices during the night till the end of term. Things got worse when the results of the disciplinary proceedings were announced: suspensions and fines. Any punishment was regarded as grounds for 'action': and now there was no good humour – it became ugly. In the early hours of Sunday 7th June paint bombs were thrown into the Registrar's house. There was a sense of shock and outrage at the personal nature of such an attack. On 9th a petrol bomb was thrown into the Architects' Department, on 10th a group went to the Vice-Chancellor's house and burnt an effigy, on 14th a window in the Registrar's house was forced, and on 14th and 15th large windows in Keele Hall refectory and the Library were smashed. But in that week the militants shot their bolt. An Emergency General Meeting was heated, and called for 'total disruption': but it was inquorate. Most students had had enough. A moderate motion was passed later by about 400 : 200, that wilful damage was unacceptable, condemning acts of vandalism and seeking to re-establish mutual trust.

An open letter to the President of the Union in April 1970 made an offer:

> 'During a sit-in two years ago some of your members abandoned in the Registry one black bishop. After the more recent occupation of the Senior Common Room, a black knight was found to be missing.

> 'While greatly deprecating the recent invasion, we hope that goodwill will be quickly restored in the Keele community, and accordingly propose an exchange of hostages with due ceremony.

> 'Some of us have perforce become expert in playing chess with three bishops, and we must suppose you now have players who excel with three knights. We therefore challenge the Students' Union to a five-board chess match to be played on these terms after the Easter vacation.

> Chess Players of the Senior Common Room.'

That was the end of it, really, but for one widely reported and long remembered incident.

Professor Beaver's weather columns in the *Sentinel* continued every month. In June 1970 the 'mean temperature provided a new high record and the sunshine total was much above normal... The mean temperature was 60.4°F (15.8°C) – a record, and four degrees above normal. The sunshine record was an exceptionally good one – 260 hours (normally 175)'. On 19th a number of students took their clothes off, in public, near the Students' Union. Shock!! This incident and a photograph on page one of the *News of the World* gave more publicity than anything else, and lingered on in the public's memory for years to come. This was still the age before 'page 3' took on special significance in some of the tabloid newspapers. It was one of the least significant manifestations of protest, yet, as *The Sunday Telegraph* commented, nudity was worse than larceny, and nakedness more shocking than hooliganism. It provoked Staffordshire County Council and Stoke-on-Trent City Council to announce that they were deferring their annual grants until the problem of the 'lunatic minority' was solved. 'Peter Simple' made some wry comments, and the punishment produced some humourless correspondence in the press. It had not quite been the pastoral scene which Professor Griffith of the London School of Economics supposed in his letter to *The Times*: 'Their offence was to sunbathe in the nude on the campus', but rather as Professor Lawlor corrected him, that they 'appeared naked in the area of the Students' Union'. They caused serious offence to employees and residents, and provoked a fair share of excitement and ridicule. The police were called when they tried to get served in the campus shop. The Vice-Chancellor investigated, and by 29th-30th June he had received clear evidence on which to take disciplinary action. But term was about to end with graduation day on

1st July. If a disciplinary panel were to be convened it could not have met until after the end of term, by which time any finalists involved would no longer be within the disciplinary jurisdiction of the University. To expedite the decision, and to treat all on an equal footing, he decided to exercise his own disciplinary jurisdiction. Punishment was deliberately limited to what a disciplinary panel could impose; and the students had the right and the opportunity to appeal to the University Council on 7th July. The Vice-Chancellor wrote to thirteen students, telling them they were to be fined £10. Eleven of them who were not finalists were also to be excluded from residence for the following year (i.e. excluded from living on the campus for a year, not sent down from the University). Four of them activated the grievance procedure. One appeal was allowed by the Council and one became a test case: Glynn v. University of Keele and Another. He had lodged an appeal on 3rd July, but had gone abroad before receiving notice that the appeal would be heard on 2nd September, and he had not been present for it.

When the new academic year started, the Students' Union decided to take legal action, seeking a writ of certiorari to quash the sentence, because normal disciplinary procedures had not been followed. In the meantime there was a chance that some sense of perspective and humour was gradually returning to the scene. How else could a meeting which was 'occupying' the Walter Moberly Hall move on to the Vice-Chancellor's house in order to levitate it (or at least to try to levitate it) 300 feet into the air by humming? Then some of them broke into the Registry as boredom and a sense of futility gave way to rowdyism. In December Sir John Pennycuick, the senior judge of the Chancery Division said that the Vice-Chancellor must be considered as having acted in a quasi-judicial capacity: had he, therefore, complied with the rules of natural justice? He had not. Whatever the rights of the case, the judge thought it a great pity that the Vice-Chancellor had not sent for the students concerned. Nevertheless, although the University had acted contrary to natural justice in excluding Glynn without giving him a hearing, the offence merited a severe penalty 'according to any current standards'; and he concluded that he ought to exercise his discretion by not granting an injunction. The fact that Glynn had been deprived of the opportunity to throw himself on the Vice-Chancellor's mercy was not sufficient to justify setting aside his decision.

In retrospect, what were 'the troubles' all about? At first there was some intellectual foment, some utopian ideals in the wash of a tide from Paris. The Exploratory Committee achieved some of its aims – but much was set at nought by misunderstandings and different expectations: student members were expecting success and their enthusiasm had not been sufficiently dampened. Or was it that some Senate members had failed to read the omens accurately? The Senate could have conceded more. The Students' Union Committee could have been better organised; and they were unlikely to make progress while demanding delegates rather than representatives. The upsurge in unrest again, from March to June 1970 was decidedly unpleasant; and then disproportionate attention was paid to the antics of a few. Professor Stewart used to ask the following questions: Was there even much disruption to the proper functioning of the University? Was a single hour of teaching lost? Were the examinations disrupted? Were the main committees prevented from doing their normal business? Was there any interruption in the smooth running of successive degree congregations? The answers were 'No'. Indeed, not even all the students were aware of the fuss and bother. When a group of mountaineering finalists climbed on to the Library roof after finals – a harmless prank – they were surprised to find themselves taken to the police cells for the night! They were not part of the revolution – they were not really aware of it going on around them. Real disruption happened the following December: the water supply failed as a result of power cuts at the pumping station, and the University was closed with immediate effect, three days before the end of term. But that was soon forgotten.

Afterwards, one of the students said: 'We fancied a sunbathe so we took our clothes off... We were not trying to be deliberately offensive to anyone. I don't really see what all the fuss is about.' Professor Gemmell, the first Professor of Biology in the country, said that it enabled us for the first time to distinguish males and females (perhaps originally a quip of Professor Hugh-Jones). Twenty years later the *Sentinel* wrote simply: 'As a light relief there was nude sunbathing.'

Above: the view from Lindsay Hall

and *below:* Horwood Hall in the late-1960s

Chapter 18

KEELE COMES OF AGE

ortunately there was good news too. Memories of the unrest of the late-1960s must not overshadow the successes in the period leading up to Keele's twenty-first anniversary. As *The Sunday Telegraph* had said, the University was beginning to look as if it was meant to be here. The Library, Chapel and Students' Union at the centre of the campus, the big Arts Building, Horwood Hall and Lindsay Hall, and the science departments expanding and hiding their Orlit block beginnings, meant that the huts were no longer dominant, and they were becoming fewer. Matching the physical growth of the campus was the University's academic and extra-curricular development.

The appointment of the Lindsay String Quartet was proving to be a striking success – a young quartet not long out of the Royal Academy, appointed as Leverhulme Fellows in 1967: Peter Cropper, Michael Adamson, Roger Bigley and Bernard Gregor-Smith. The worthwhileness of the idea was that they were relieved of the pressures of earning their living in an orchestra or by teaching. 'When they are ready they will give at least one recital per term at the University', George Pratt wrote in *The Times Higher Education Supplement*. And when they were ready they repaid their debt to Keele generously, giving value to the musical life here and in the locality far in excess of one recital per term. They were trained by Alexander Moskovsky, formerly a member of the famous Hungarian Quartet. A quartet, he once said, was like being wedded to three other people, none of whom you love. He imbued them with energy and idealism. His weekly commitment of four hours of tuition began at 9 a.m. and continued, if need be without a break, up to 6 p.m. Some still remember the quartet's open rehearsals in the old billiard room in Keele Hall, the walls hung with egg boxes to dampen the acoustic. Their inaugural recital was not until November 1968 – Haydn, Bartók and Beethoven – and this was followed by lecture recitals in Stoke, Burslem and Leek, organised by the Department of Adult Education. Gerald Larner wrote in *The Guardian*: 'When they have the technical security to take risks they could become an exciting string quartet', and a few months later he described them as 'one of the most interesting phenomena on the present musical scene'. From then onwards they gave regular recitals at Keele, including two attended by Princess Margaret. International success came at the Liége International String Quartet Competition in 1969 when they came third to a Russian and an East German quartet; and they made their Wigmore Hall début in February 1970. They also quickly became firm favourites at the Victoria Theatre where they were more informal, performing 'in-the-round', Peter Cropper introducing works in what Larner described as 'a disarmingly mixed up but by no means incoherent way'. Michael Adamson left towards the end of their five years here, and his place was taken by Ronald Birks. The irony is that although the venture was so evidently successful, and similar schemes were clearly viable, the venture has not been repeated. The four of them received a Keele honorary degree of Master of Music in 1986, though by that time Roger Bigley had recently left the quartet, to be replaced by Robin Ireland. After five years at Keele, they became Quartet in Residence at Sheffield University, then took a similar position at the University of Manchester in 1979.

Drama flourished at Keele from the early days of the College. In the 1960s Keele had a play in the final of the NUS Drama Festival three years out of four, winning with *The Maids* by Genet in 1962, and winning decisively with the best one-act play in 1966. This was Beckett's *Endgame*, which was then put on at St. Martin's Theatre in the West End and seen by Princess Margaret. Drama also went to the Edinburgh Festival Fringe: Frank Doherty of the English Department and Jack Emery put together, and Emery gave a solo performance of *A Remnant by Beckett*. A BBC African Theatre competition awarded first prize to Guillaume Mbia for his play *Until Further Notice,* and another play of his, *Three Suitors One Husband* was performed in Paris. Experimental drama reached the finals of the NUS Drama Competition with *Vietrock* in 1969; and *Paradise Lost* reached the finals of *The Sunday Times* Drama Competition in 1970. As well as Jack Emery, Keele could be said to have nurtured the playwrights Peter Whelan and David Pownall, director Bill Alexander, and actors Bernard Lloyd and Frank Mooney; and in television and radio, Gerry Northam. In television, too, Keith Clements at the BBC helped to launch breakfast television, and in the mid-1980s transformed Elstree film studios ready for EastEnders.

Keele also shone in debating and in general knowledge quizzes. Keith Ovenden, with Jeremy Bruford of Cambridge, formed the British University debating pair in a tour of Australia and New Zealand in 1966; a few years later Keele won the National Student Debating Tournaments for *The Observer* Mace, winning the national semi-final on home ground in the ballroom in 1971. In 1972 Ray Dutton and Tony Waters both reached the four-man final – the first time the final had included two speakers from the same university. Keele won 'University Challenge' in 1968, soundly beating Oxbridge colleges to be the first participant to provide a winner and a runner-up a few years earlier. The real challenge was the televised match between the winning team and Keele staff (Alan Iliffe (Senior Tutor), Wynn Williams (Classics), David Battye (Computer Science) and Michael Paffard (Education), with Leo Rivet as non-playing captain). The rehearsals put the staff team to shame but in the performance which mattered, on television, the staff were convincing winners. Keele enjoyed another run of success in 1971; and Aubrey Lawrence, who had captained the winning team in 1968 went on to become 'Brain of Britain' in 1972 and appeared in 'Mastermind' in 1978.

Years later some other graduates of the 1960s were known as 'The Keele Three' or the 'Keele Connection' – three Permanent Secretaries in Whitehall: Moray Stewart at the Ministry of Defence, John Vereker at the Department for International Development, and Richard Mottram at the office of Public Service and Science and then at the Department of the Environment, Transport and the Regions. Mottram was to be the star prosecution witness in the trial of Clive Ponting over the leak of documents about the Falklands War. Another graduate of the 1960s, Eric Sorensen moved from a career in the Department of the Environment to become Chief Executive of the London Docklands Development Corporation, a Civil Service Commissioner, and – until he caused a stir by stepping down from the post – the Chief Executive of the Millennium Commission. Also in the Department of the Environment, David Edmonds was an Under Secretary of State before moving into the private sector; and he was appointed Director General of Telecommunications in 1998. He became the University's Honorary Treasurer in 1997. In the Palace of Westminster, Bill Proctor became one of the Principal Clerks of the House of Commons.

The healthy body has not been neglected at Keele, and there were national successes in cycling, judo, basketball, the 100 metres and the long jump. For the less athletically inclined, there was some relief that the sentence in the University's *Prospectus* – 'First-year students in particular are normally required to take part in some form of physical education' – was at last deleted.

In a number of different and unexpected ways Keele was reaching out to the wider world. In London, *Time Out* was started almost casually by Tony Elliott in August 1968 to raise money for his year in France. In nine months it grew from a two-page broadsheet to seventy or so pages and a circulation of 13,000, and it reached 32,000 on its hundredth issue. With the subtitle 'London's living guide' it has grown into a weekly publication of about 200 pages, and the Time Out Group is an international company. On the air, 'Gardeners' Question Time' reached a thousand editions in 1972 and an audience of ten million, still with Professor Gemmell, who also appeared on 'Any Questions', 'Women's Hour' and 'A Word in Edgeways'. Professor MacKay could also be heard on 'A Word in Edgeways'. The new building for his research Department of Communication (later renamed Communication and Neuroscience) was opened in October 1966 by Lord Adrian, the eminent brain physiologist, and featured in an article in *New Scientist*. It also brought to Keele an international gathering of forty leading brain scientists from nine countries, including some from behind the Iron Curtain. Professor MacKay's own research interests regularly took him across the world: in 1969-70, for example, the Vice-Chancellor's *Report* noted that he had visited the U.S.A. three times on lecture tours, visited the U.S.S.R. as guest lecturer, had attended an international planning conference in Paris, given seminars in Freiburg and Pisa, and lectured in Tubingen, Berlin, Naples, Edinburgh and Cambridge.

Gifts to the University enhanced its reputation for research and scholarship. In 1964 a Unit of Cardiology was set up in the Biology Department by Mr. J. Max Sanderson, the thoracic surgeon who had introduced heart surgery to North Staffordshire, and it soon attracted a major benefaction from Mr. W. E. Dunn of the Goldenhill Iron and Steel Works. Research showed that brain damage, which was common following open-heart operations during the 1960s, could be greatly reduced by the use of a pump which generated blood pressure and flow waveforms similar to those generated by the natural heart. Joint research with the Birmingham Regional Hospital Board and English Electric produced a new type of pulsatile heart pump for cardiopulmonary bypass surgery – the idea of Mr. Sanderson and Dr. Gordon Wright, who had graduated from Keele in 1964. Soon after this work was published, pulsatile flow became standard practice throughout the country and brain damage was diminished. There was a lot of publicity in February 1967, reporting the first hole-in-the-heart operation on an animal in Britain, at Keele – on Kim, a young mongrel dog. Other work associated with open heart surgery produced techniques to reduce embolic organ damage; then the emphasis shifted towards non-surgical treatments and the prevention of coronary heart disease, in collaboration with the Russian Academy of Sciences, other cardiac centres and other Keele departments. One of the articles published on the Unit's work produced requests for reprints from 150 universities and institutions around the world. The Unit's high standing was confirmed in a report by Sir John McMichael, Emeritus Professor of Medicine, University of London, a distinguished cardiologist and formerly Director of the British Postgraduate Medical Federation and President of the World Congress of Cardiology. He said that the integration of research physiology with the practical needs of cardiology at the hospital had led to the development of a standard of investigative endeavour 'of a very high order', an atmosphere of joint enthusiasm and a unique degree of mutual integration. Not only in theory and in principle but also in practical achievement, an integrated bio-medical unit had been created 'which would do credit to any more formally recognised medical school establishment'. But nothing came of his report, and the Unit continued to lack the basic funding it needed for further development. Running costs have been met largely by the W. E. Dunn Charitable Trust; short-term projects have been funded nationally by the Medical Research Council, the British Heart Foundation, and the National Heart Research Fund; and locally by the West Midlands Regional Health Authority, the North Staffordshire Heart Foundation, the Market Drayton Heart Association, Round Tables, and the villages of Audlem and Hankelow.

Another generous gift to the University was a remarkable collection of books from Mr. C. W. Turner, a retired civil servant. He had spent a life-time building up a library on the history and development of mathematics, science and early technology from the 15th to the 19th century. Through his friendship with Professor Ingram he decided to present it to Keele. It comprised 1,400 books and pamphlets in first and early editions. These included the first edition of Euclid, printed in Venice in 1482, and most of the important later editions for the next four hundred years. The Isaac Newton material was outstanding and was believed to be the second largest collection of books owned by Newton after Trinity College, Cambridge. There was a complete collection of Newton's principal works in first and later contemporary editions, and Newton's annotated copy of Boyle's *Medicina hydrostatica*. The collection also included a copy of Galileo's *Il Saggiatore*, annotated by the author, and Copernicus's *De revolutionibus orbium coelstium*. The gift was to ensure that this collection should remain intact for scholars in the future, and Keele awarded Turner an honorary degree in 1969. In the different and difficult financial circumstances of the late-1990s the University sold the Turner collection (see chapter 29).

Astronomy, like Music, developed slowly into a Principal subject. It built on lectures given in the Foundation Year, widespread local support, and the setting up of the Observatory in 1962. Lectures by Professor Vick on the origin of the universe had soon become the starting point in the Foundation Year lecture course (though the first astronomy lectures had been given by Peter Plesch). The Astronomical Society was an early student society which has flourished without flagging. Professor Vick's successor, Professor Ingram, quickly achieved an impressive reputation for his inspiring introductory lectures at the beginning of the Foundation Year. A course was started in the Foundation Year and was also offered to the general public through the Extramural Department. Patrick Moore's regular visits to Keele (he was awarded an honorary degree in 1994) and Ron Maddison's dedication and enthusiasm at a time of exciting developments in space exploration – the sputnik was launched in October 1957, and Armstrong and Aldrin walked on the moon in July 1969 – all helped to give astronomy a large following both inside and outside the University. The project to build a research grade instrument was initiated by members of the extramural class. Mr. Harry Thornton of Merseyside provided the stimulus with a gift of £2,000 to purchase a 24-inch diameter mirror, and William Boulton Ltd. of Burslem built the observatory as a generous gesture of goodwill. The new telescope and observatory were opened by Princess Margaret in 1975. An academic subsidiary course was very popular, providing a science discipline which could be taught using varying levels of mathematics without losing the appreciation of the physical principles involved. The external examiner was impressed: Maddison's 'genius for building and adapting observatory equipment has probably strengthened further this reputation (the Oxford refractor, the home-built reflector, the radio bowls as interferometers, the mounting of the huge naval binoculars, the Schmidt camera, the mounting of the eclipse camera, the plate-measuring engine, constitute an assemblage probably unique outside the large professional observatories)... The whole situation seems to me an achievement in fostering astronomy as a cultural topic at university level, which ought to be more widely known than it yet is.' A major academic step was the appointment of Aneurin Evans to the Physics Department in 1971. His research and reputation in the field of interstellar material led to the growth of a productive research team, and eventually, in 1994, this long gestation produced a Principal course in Astrophysics with Aneurin Evans as its Professor.

As the number of undergraduates grew, the list of subjects available could also increase. Especially in joint honours courses, the addition of even one subject considerably enriched the academic offering. The first additional principal subject was American Studies, available from 1961, then Psychology from 1963, Law and Sociology from 1965, Russian Studies from 1966, and Education (in combination only with Chemistry, Mathematics or Physics) from 1968. This meant that the number of possible combinations of principal subjects which could be taken at Keele had risen from 28 to 125 (and there were also joint courses in Economics, History and Politics, and in Philosophy, Economics and Politics). That is what was possible on the timetable, not that students took all of the unusual combinations which were available – but there were some interesting possibilities. Professor Price from Oxford had already spoken highly of the combination of Philosophy and Physics. A science subject with Economics was popular with employers in industry. Law or a language could go especially well with another discipline.

There were more students coming from overseas. The Students' Union launched a South African Scholarship Fund in protest against apartheid. The Fund enabled Sam Nolutshungu to come in the mid-1960s, the first of several to come from South Africa and Rhodesia. He was to become 'one of the foremost scholars to have enriched African studies in the field of both political science and international relations' (*The Independent*, 20th August 1997). His academic career bridged England, Africa and North America, and shortly before he died he was offered the Vice-Chancellorship of the University of the Witwatersrand in Johannesburg. There was also warm support locally in the tradition of Sir Barnett Stross (who had started the 'Lidice shall Live' movement during the Second World War) for three students helped by the North Staffordshire Appeal for Czechoslovak students who came to Keele after the Warsaw Pact invasion of 1968. Earlier, two Hungarian students had come to the University College after the Hungarian uprising in 1956. In 1965, Keele's first 'academic grandchild' was noted in the press: John Moulton came up in 1965, eleven years after his father had graduated.

A familiar figure around the place to generations of students from 1960 onwards was Neil Baldwin – a rotund, jovial figure, totally unselfconscious, on hand to welcome new students. He has not been a student here, yet Keele has been one of the loves of his life – the others being football, the church, circuses, the Boat Race, and being with famous people. In 1995 there was a Thanksgiving Service in the Chapel for his thirty-five years of work for the church at Keele, and students organised a 'This is Your Life, Neil Baldwin'; and there was another Thanksgiving Service in 2000.

From the first year of the College, music recitals were given at Keele. During Sir George Barnes's time, the arts were especially encouraged, and concerts were free. Some musicians, such as Pears and Britten, David Martin, Denis Matthews and Gervase de Peyer came several times; 'Opera for All' came, and the BBC broadcast 'Music to Remember' from Keele. Some great names were heard in the 1960s –

Joan Sutherland, Janet Baker, John Ogden, Julian Bream, Paul Tortelier, and the Amadeus and Smetana String Quartets. The Music Society played an important part, too, and provided a platform for, amongst others, Christian Blackshaw and John Lill. There were occasional professional orchestral concerts in Hanley, but otherwise those who wanted to hear orchestral and chamber music concerts generally had to go to Manchester. As 'J.O.' had written in the *Sentinel* in October 1965: 'Chamber music is not adequately represented here... occasional string quartets or piano trios are no substitute for a regular series of chamber music concerts. If Haydn's string quartets are scarcely heard here, what prospects are there for those of Bartók?' Little did he know that within eight years, all six of them would be performed to large audiences in the Walter Moberly Hall. It all changed in the late-1960s and early-70s, and it started with a students' festival of folk music held in July 1965. Within two years this had become a closely-packed interlocking programme of talks, workshops, demonstrations and concerts, giving Keele an important place in the folk revival and the annual National Folk Festivals. Students next planned a Potteries Arts Festival for a week in May 1968, with classical and folk music, poetry, exhibitions, drama and films. After a chamber music concert the *Sentinel* commented: 'Goodness knows when we last heard two Beethoven string quartets at one performance in Hanley.' The Festival, with Jim Lagden, a student, as its director, was successful and it was repeated. In 1972/73, it developed into the Stoke and Newcastle Festival of orchestral concerts and piano recitals, with performances spread throughout much of the year. In the late-1960s an annual festival was also started at nearby Penkhull, centred on the church of the Revd. Arthur Perry; and at Abbotsholme School an Arts and Film Society started, with world-class performers, under the guiding spirit of Gordon Clarke, who had earlier been a part-time Director of Music at Keele. The tradition of concerts in the Potteries goes back to 1887 when George Meakin of Messrs. J. and G. Meakin gave £200 to Hanley Corporation to provide high-class concerts, which attracted audiences of 3,000.

At Keele, meanwhile, rising costs and dwindling money for concerts meant that free concerts were becoming fewer. The argument for free concerts was still strong, especially from Professor Brooke: 'the University has a continuing and outstanding debt to the surrounding area for its foundation and financial support. In some measure at least, and at relatively small cost, the University can do something to redress the balance.' But there was also another proposal that recitals should be supported by payment for seats – 'the resulting saving would come near to paying for an additional academic appointment.' This led George Pratt, the Director of Music, and the author (who was then working in the Registry) to propose that music, the neighbourhood and the University would be better served if a dwindling number of recitals were replaced by a self-supporting subscription series of concerts. Encouraged by the University, the first series of twelve concerts was given in 1971/72. Season tickets encouraged regular concert going, and ticket sales averaged 400 per concert for the next five years. Fortunately, the first year of 'Keele Concerts' coincided with the final year in residence of the Lindsay String Quartet. They had already given eight recitals since 1968. They now gave two recitals as a quartet, and two more, one with George Malcolm (harpsichord and piano) and one with Janet Hilton (clarinet), to conclude the first series with a packed house and fifty people turned away. Well-known musicians continued to come: Campoli, Moura Lympany, Gerald Moore, Fou Ts'ong, Ricci, André Tchaikowsky and the Bartók Quartet. These concerts also introduced some lesser-known outstanding musicians, in particular the Japanese pianist Reiko Matsuzaki who was immediately re-booked for the following year. Lecture recitals included Eric Fenby ('Delius' Amanuensis'), James Blades ('Fifty Years of Percussing') and Litz Pisk ('Movement and Form'). In fact, the lesser known artists actually subsidised some of the great names. The first President of Keele Concerts was Lady Barbirolli. Sir John Barbirolli had received an honorary degree from the University in December 1969, a few months before he died: his support for music at Keele went back to the 1950s, when the proceeds of a Hallé concert in Hanley were donated to the Perry Fund. It was the Perry Fund, together with money raised in memory of Sir George Barnes, which led to the appointment of George Pratt as Director of Music, and it was George Pratt who secured the Leverhulme grant which led to the appointment of the Lindsay String Quartet, who in turn for some years were the mainstay of the new Keele Concerts. As Professor Dickinson, the Professor of Music from 1974 to 1984, wrote in 1977, 'no series at Keele would have seemed complete without a recital from the Lindsays'. Twenty-five years later the Quartet returned, as President of the concert series, to give a special anniversary concert: Keele Concerts had become a long-term success story. In the early days of recitals, before the ring road was built, it seemed that the chiming of the Library clock and the change of gear of a bus always managed to find a quiet passage to disturb.

Keele celebrated twenty-one years of College and University in 1971-72. There was a Thanksgiving Service, and it was primarily an academic celebration. There were, too, the trappings of festivities – including a band concert and fireworks – and there were gifts to celebrate the coming-of-age: these included twenty-eight pieces of modern silver from the Goldsmiths' Company; Royal Doulton crystal ware; a silver serving tray with two pairs of decanters from Newcastle Rural District Council; and the sculpture 'Square Forms (Two Sequences)' from Dame Barbara Hepworth, which used to be on display in the courtyard of the Chancellor's Building. At the end of the year the Lindsay String Quartet gave their farewell concert in the Chapel, attended by the Princess. In the autumn, the Staffordshire Society planted trees on the campus to conclude the celebrations, and three of the Gulbenkian Fellows (Leeson, Macdonald and Henderson) presented the University with works of art. The anniversary was an occasion to affirm the University's achievements. Early in the year the biennial Earl Lecture was given by Sir Nikolaus Pevsner on 'Some Aspects of Staffordshire Architecture'. He fell down some steps just before he delivered his lecture, but that did nothing to diminish his distinctive sharpness and clarity. He had stayed at Keele from time to time while doing his research on Staffordshire and was ever ready to give his views over dinner on high table. His volume on *Staffordshire* was published in 1974, the last in his monumental series *The Buildings of England.*

The highlight of the year was the visit of H.M. the Queen Mother with Princess Margaret. They met over six hundred people connected with Keele; there was a Royal Ball in Stoke-on-Trent, at which the Lord Mayor and the Vice-Chancellor were joint hosts; and an honorary degree congregation in the Walter Moberly Hall. This was the last occasion on which Professor E. M. Hugh-Jones was the Public Orator, and he burnished both the phrases and the wit to elegance. The first of the honorary degrees was conferred on Sir James Mountford. He was a classical scholar (and had revised Kennedy's *Latin Primer*, known to generations who had learnt Latin), and was Vice-Chancellor of Liverpool for eighteen years. His book, *Keele, an historical critique*, was commissioned by the University for its anniversary, and in it he devoted special attention to the principles underlying the curriculum and developments since 1950. 'The author's assessment rejects the lore of nice-calculated less or more and certainly does not tax the UGC with vain expense', said the Orator. Mountford gives a balanced view that up till then, at least, 'it could fairly be argued that, in comparison with institutions of similar size and range of activities Keele has had few, if any, legitimate grounds for serious complaint, and that in the matter of student resident places up to the limit now approved by the UGC and in the provision of loans for staff residences it has indeed enjoyed privileged treat-ment'. There followed honorary doctorates for Professor Gilbert Ryle, the Waynflete Professor of Metaphysical Philosophy at Oxford – 'the Copernicus of modern philosophy', a warm supporter of Keele's philosophy courses and the joint honours system; and Sir Leslie Scarman, a High Court Judge and the first Chairman of the Law Commission for England and Wales, whose Lindsay Memorial Lectures in 1967 had dealt with proposals for law reform. There were two more honorary doctorates for Vice-Chancellors closely connected with the early years: Professor Vick, who was then President and Vice-Chancellor of Queen's University, Belfast; and Lord Fulton, Vice-Chancellor of Sussex who, as a Fellow of Balliol had been brought into the early negotiations about the founding of the College and who might have been the first Principal. (Sir Nikolaus Pevsner was awarded an honorary doctorate the following year.) Honorary masters' degrees were awarded to Reginald Haggar, best known, perhaps for his paintings of the Potteries, but also a designer for leading manufacturers and an authoritative scholar and lecturer on pottery and ceramics; and on Guy Pearce, a man in that fine tradition of local businessmen who sit on the University Council and give much of their time and patience to university and students' affairs. Lord Fulton replied on behalf of the honorary graduates, and this was the public occasion on which he said: 'The battle for Keele was no push-over. It had to be fought all the way. And, in fighting with success that battle, Keele smoothed the path for all the new foundations which have come after it.' He went on to say: 'I can perhaps speak with some little authority – certainly with continuing gratitude – on behalf of the group of new universities which followed a decade after Keele. The ground fought over and won by this university was turned into friendly, peaceful territory for your successors.' He referred to Mountford's book and also to Drusilla Scott's biography of her father, *A. D. Lindsay,* which had recently been published.

The press also reviewed Keele so far. *The Times* wrote of an 'experiment that succeeded', saying 'there can be few places where the spirit of a founding father is so keenly felt as at Keele: Lord Lindsay's name is constantly mentioned in conversations', and by now, of course, there were students at Keele who had been born after Lindsay had died. 'Keele was the first to do much that is now generally taken for granted – the first to start American Studies, to create a unified biology department, the first to run concurrent education and training courses. Keele's passionate belief in broad education which underlies the Foundation Year... had become the axiom of university planning.' *The Times Educational Supplement* was more critical, commenting that the Senate had 'given way' to UGC pressure to start three-year courses; that the Foundation Year itself was 'now under serious scrutiny' (as it always was); and that Keele had paid dear for remaining so small for so long. 'And yet in some respects for all the criticism, Keele still leads the way.' *The Guardian* asked whether the acceptance of three-year students was too big a price to pay for expansion to 3,000 students. Granada television made a programme, 'The Dream on the Hill', provoking a comment in the *Listener* that a university is a place in which a student's mistakes ought to be left behind, not immortalised.

Mountford had given a lecture on 'The Context of Keele' a few days before the honorary degree ceremony and his starting point was the influence of Tawney. He took the opportunity to expand on what he had already written in his book about the role of the UGC and its support for Lindsay during the early negotiations; Moberly had been succeeded as chairman by Sir Arthur Trueman, 'a grimmer, more rugged and less flexible personality, who had little understanding of Lindsay and even less sympathy with his educational doctrines'. By the time the College opened, he went on, six of the sixteen members of the UGC who had participated in the negotiations had retired from the committee, and of those who remained several had been amongst the waverers. At least two of the six newcomers had no use for the Keele concept at all. There was a period of little encouragement until Keith Murray (who was knighted in 1955) became chairman in 1953. Mountford re-iterated his view that Keele had not been *un*fairly treated, '*provided* one has regard to the measure of expansion which the UGC has from time to time thought appropriate', and the point of the proviso is that Keele got no 'expansion' money. Then the UGC, with Sir John Wolfenden as its chairman from 1963 to 1968, exerted a restraining and at times a cramping influence on development. Mountford foresaw that the pressures on Keele to adjust to the standards and norms of other universities would be exerted more strongly. Nevertheless, he was in no doubt that the main principles on which the Keele curriculum was founded had justified the faith of the founders, and he concluded with an endorsement and a warning: 'Yet about one thing there can be no mistake. Keele was launched as an experiment in university education and all the evidence... shows that the main principles on which the Keele curriculum was founded have justified the faith of the founders. It is those principles of a wide range of interests and knowledge, combined with such study in depth as a career today demands, which have made Keele distinctive and which, though it is not always acknowledged, have influenced the pattern of university studies in newer and older institutions alike. Keele now faces an insidious and continuing challenge, which if not wisely combated would erode and ultimately destroy the very principles on which the College and University were based. Such an outcome would be damaging not only for Keele but to freedom in university education as a whole in this country. But let none of us be despondent, even if we cannot brush aside our apprehensions; for I hold fast to the belief that the challenge can be successfully met if the present generation at Keele shows the same inspiration and the same resolution as that which was shown by the small band who came to this campus twenty-one years ago.'

The Vice-Chancellor also gave an anniversary lecture, with the title 'Recollections and Anticipations'. It was a wide-ranging lecture, and he concluded: "Lindsay's Keele' is therefore both right and wrong as a slogan for the seventies. Right because the principles on which we have built are sound and the architecture is mainly Lindsay's although the general plan and the working drawing and the construction rightly belong to his colleagues and their successors. 'Lindsay's Keele' is the wrong slogan if we begin to treat inspirational memory as the tablets of Sinai.' Nevertheless, and he quoted from Drusilla Scott's *A. D. Lindsay*: 'the sorts of questions Lindsay asked are still relevant – how can the divisions of specialisation be bridged, how can some unity in culture be discovered, how can communities be kept human as they grow larger? New answers are always having to be found and Keele may look back at the mortally ill, tired old man who began it as one who had the youthful spirit to keep looking for them.'

'Though prudence, intrepidity, and perseverance united, are not exempted from the blows of adverse fortune; yet in a long series of transactions, they usually rise superior to its power, and in the end rarely fail of proving successful.'
(From *A Voyage round the World* by George Anson, Esq. 1761.)

Chapter 19

THE PERIOD – III

Sir James Mountford's book, *Keele, an historical critique*, was published in 1972. Three-year courses were planned to begin in October 1973, with the possibility of single honours in the final year in some science subjects. In the final chapter of his book he commented as follows: 'The proposed introduction of a three-year course poses fundamental questions. If Keele stands for anything it is the concept of breadth of study throughout the whole course: the Foundation Year, the two-subject Final and the insistence on some science and some non-science have been basic to the unified Keele programme... The worst and least acceptable course of action would be to abandon for three-year students *both* the Foundation Year *and* the two-subject Final. That would mean that for such students Keele would be indistinguishable, apart from residence and size, from any one of two or three dozen other universities... The crux of the matter would seem to lie in the Foundation Year itself. This, above all else, has been Keele's distinctive hallmark. It is, admittedly, not the only possible avenue to a broad conspectus of knowledge; but it is a programme which has been refined and elaborated with enormous care over the years; and the great preponderance of the evidence shows that it has been a successful venture and one which it is worth a great deal of effort to preserve in some form for all students... A separate kind of Foundation Year designed for different groups of students... rejects the concept that there should be a core of knowledge common to *all* students... The essential problem for Keele is how it shall remain faithful to its doctrine of breadth.'

There follow years of endurance in the face of growing uncertainty, overshadowed by deep economic gloom. In 1971 the £ went decimal, and in June 1972 the government floated it having spent, it was said, £1,000 million in an effort to stop the slide in its value. Six months later the Chancellor of the Exchequer spoke of 'the gravest situation by far since the end of the War'. OPEC raised oil prices and industry faced paralysing disputes. Already, early in 1972, power cuts were expected, with a high risk on Wednesdays and Saturdays, medium risk on Fridays, and low risk on other days. The felling of dead trees, including victims of Dutch Elm disease, eked out coal supplies in the boiler houses. In 1973-74 there was the three-day week, and the Fuel and Electricity Control Act stipulated a maximum temperature of 63° Fahrenheit in all offices, laboratories, etc. Soaring inflation in 1974 raised the cost of living by 26%, and the price of a gallon of petrol rose from 42p to 72p. In April 1975 pay rises for the previous twelve months had averaged 32% (but not for academic staff).

In September 1976 the government applied to the International Monetary Fund to borrow £2.3 billion to prop up the £, which had fallen to $1.63. There were General Elections, with all the uncertainties they bring to continuity in national policy, in March 1974, October 1974 and May 1979. It is against this background that universities had to struggle, to pursue their ends without the means. Keele, moreover, had to face the consequences of its adverse publicity earlier, and watch applications for entry drop for the first half of the 1970s.

Clearly, the UGC was faced with containing universities' costs. In March 1973, the *THES* wrote of 'the harshest quinquennial budget in their history' and of the cuts made in 'student unit costs' – the harshest being at Brunel (13%) and Keele (12%). From now on there is publicity given to ranking orders in different lists, the existence of some of which rested, perhaps, only on rumour. Articles purported to examine the quality of degrees, research orientation, ratios and costs, inequality in research income – drawing conclusions from imponderables and adumbrating self-fulfilling prophecies. In 1979 came the rumour that Keele might be axed: the Stafford and Stone Labour Party Chairman had been told 'authoritatively', he said, that Keele was on a list of five earmarked for possible closure. The rumour was denied by Dr. Rhodes Boyson at the Department of Education and Science: but might there be a list somewhere?

Whether faring well or badly in these lotteries, one was reminded of Kipling's reference to those two impostors, Triumph and Disaster.

Stewart announced in October 1977 that he would retire in September 1979, so giving the University ample time to find his successor. He had chosen to retire early – he would then be 63 – because he thought it valuable to make room for younger people now that expansion had slowed down, and expecting – or at least hoping – that there would be a more settled economic climate by then, with our targets for growth in the 1980s more firmly established. The timing was also calculated to fit in best with the cycle of university affairs.

Instead, at the end of 1978-79, no funds could be made available to the Senate for new developments in 1979-80. In June 1979 the government cut £55M from the budget for education and science, and the UGC urged universities 'to examine very carefully all recurrent expenditure to which you are not irretrievably committed'. We did not even know the final grant for the year just ending to meet costs already incurred, still less the grant for the year beginning 1st August 1979. The CVCP spoke of 'damaging and lasting consequences... out of all proportion to the savings made'. Stewart's final year, he wrote, 'ended in a worse state than could ever have been imagined' (*Report of the Vice-Chancellor to the Council*).

Chapter 20

YEARS OF ENDURANCE

The UGC was 'a little concerned' about Keele because 'clearly a four-year course was more expensive'. That is what the Chairman of the UGC, Sir Fred Dainton, told the Vice-Chancellor and the Registrar in October 1973. He was edging towards a ratio of 70 : 30 for four-year : three-year courses. Nevertheless, when the UGC came to Keele in 1976 he indicated their warm approval for the Foundation Year. (Is it possible that after twenty-five years the Foundation Year was still not fully accepted and taken for granted when discussing Keele courses with Keele staff at Keele?) He added that the UGC was delighted by the outlook of the groups they had met – the University knew where it was going, was holding fast to the Foundation Year and showed that it appreciated the meaning and purpose of that course, and could provide ample justification for it. Although the introduction of three-year courses 'could seem to some to have been an abandonment of the original Keele concept', clearly it had led to the recruitment of able students. He urged that Keele was not by any means to feel that the UGC was opposed to the Foundation Year, and that any decision as between four-year and three-year courses must be regarded as a matter for Keele and not for the UGC.

The gradual breakdown of the quinquennial system of financing universities is documented in successive annual reports of the Honorary Treasurer and the Vice-Chancellor. In January 1973 the quinquennial settlement provided for an increase of 40% in resources, to meet a 65% increase in student numbers. The atmosphere at the committee meeting which considered claims for new academic posts in May 1974 was described as more like a funeral parlour than the Moroccan souk of previous years; but in the expectation that things would get better, the Senate approved an arts centre as an objective for a future appeal. Peter Shepheard produced a sketch, showing it between the Walter Moberly Hall and the Tawney Building, where it would displace the temporary buildings housing the Registry and Finance Offices, and huts 1-12. Then the immediate outlook for 1974-75 took a sudden dramatic turn for the worse when, inflation having reached unprecedented proportions, the government's compensation went barely half-way towards meeting the spiralling cost increases. It was impossible to borrow money at rates we could afford to pay for soaring building costs. At this stage, half-way through a five year period, the quinquennial financial planning structure, on which much of the independence and confidence of universities was founded, was in ruins. The University was advised that it would be wise to avoid any substantial deficits at the end of 1974-75, because revised grants for

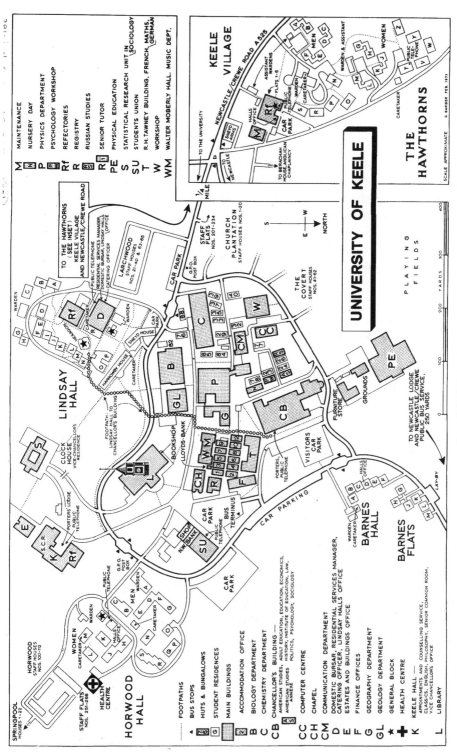

from CALENDAR 1975-76

1975-76 and 1976-77 were unlikely to make them good. Indeed that was the case; and it was not until three months into the financial year 1976-77 that the final grant for that year was known. 'Keele faces financial blizzard' (*Sentinel*, 11 November 1976), and was told to prepare for a 4% drop in funding in 1977-78 and to expect at least as hard a time in 1978-79. Quinquennial planning was replaced by announcements made at short notice and in a piecemeal fashion. Can it be that that was the policy which the government had been creeping towards, anyway, in order to get away from a longer-term financial commitment? Certainly that view was expressed.

It was not surprising that the UGC had said when they came in 1976 that it was difficult to advise any university to enter into commitments without a 'general horizon' agreed. They were committed to the reintroduction of long-term planning on the needs of individual universities, they said, as calculated by the UGC; but it was not possible for them (or at least, they were unwilling) to define the criteria used to determine need. For Keele, the four-year course was a factor which increased the cost of producing a graduate.

Struggling with economic restraints and uncertainties the UGC adopted a policy of 'cash limits', i.e. making the universities bear the brunt of inflationary uncertainty. The problem for the universities was that they had virtually no possibility of spreading or passing on the risk. Hence the importance of additional income from a rapid expansion in the conference trade by offering university facilities for large-scale conferences and meetings in term time as well as vacations, students and academic staff notwithstanding. A few years later some of the rooms in Keele Hall were taken away from their use as the Senior Common Room, to be used instead for board meetings and wedding receptions. When, in July 1978, the government announced grants up to 1981-82 it effectively imposed a constraint on student intake: any excess beyond what the government estimated numbers should be would result in a cut in the grant. But what that number was meant to be was difficult to plan for. Keele had suggested 3,100 for 1980-81 – a realistic build-up bearing in mind the development of new departments. The UGC proposed 3,000, and then 3,200 was agreed in February 1978 and, by implication, was confirmed in May. Yet in July the UGC said that the grant was based on 2,900: 'The Committee would wish me to stress the importance both of adhering to this target and of not allowing the pattern of admission in the intervening years to produce a high growth rate of numbers at the end of the period.' A change of government then brought a review of public expenditure, and with it 'the financial position has become intolerably obscure' (*Report of the Honorary Treasurer 1978-79*). In such uncertain and difficult times, the suggestion by the Students' Union that they should purchase a race horse (rejected in the Union by 76 to 49) would at least have been more exciting and would have produced a not much more uncertain financial outlook.

Was there an underlying urging towards overall uniformity? Already in 1965 the trend towards a more dirigiste policy has been noted, and staff time had been apportioned to undergraduate teaching, postgraduate teaching, and research for costs to be compared (see chapter 15). Then in 1969-70 the CVCP conducted an enquiry into the use of academic staff time, asking staff to record in extraordinary detail how they spent their time over three separate weeks. In its report in 1972 (*Report of an Enquiry into the Use of Academic Staff Time*) the CVCP said that the main purpose of the enquiry had been to secure results in a form designed to meet the needs of the UGC: so much so that the introduction said: 'We were therefore glad that the UGC, in return for a promise that we would conduct a sample enquiry of the present kind every five years, agreed to withdraw its own enquiry'. From 8.0 a.m. till 11.30 p.m, seven days a week ('it is known that some members of staff do work unusual hours') staff were requested to specify the 'major uses of time' of each half hour under the headings A: Undergraduate Time; B: Graduate Course Work Time; C: Graduate Research Time; D: Personal Research Time; E: Unallocable Internal Time; F: External Professional Time; and, failing all else, 'Private and Free Time'. For anyone who wondered quite what 'Unallocable Internal Time' might be, it was defined as 'time spent on reading, study, discussion and conferences which, while possibly contributing both to teaching and research is not allocable to one or the other... and work related to the building up of a library, unless the books concerned are ordered for particular student groups (A or B) or a particular piece of research (C or D)'. Such was the attention to detail required that there were notes to explain 'How to Complete the Diary': 'Please mark by a cross (X) for *each* half-hour of *each* day, that *one* use of time which best represents how you used that half-hour.' For people who might work in smaller allocable units of time the advice was: 'If you spend exactly 15 minutes on one use and exactly 15 minutes on another,' [exactly?] '*choose one of the two at random*' [so it didn't really matter after all]. Even 'Private and Free Time' was defined as covering 'eating, recreation, sleeping, family contacts: work for the community not related to your professional status (e.g. being a churchwarden): non-productive travel time to and from your normal place of work' [productive travel time must presumably be included somewhere else] '(but travelling on official business should be included under the category to which the business belongs): marking school examination papers, writing novels as a spare-time occupation, and other such activities which, while 'work', neither derive from your university post nor contribute to your professional status in that post.' But what about eating *and* thinking? And suppose a great new idea occurs to one over dinner? or on top of a bus? Presumably it would not count – unless it took exactly 15 minutes (in which case it might or might not be chosen at random) or more than 15 minutes. Would Archimedes's great discovery have featured in his diary as 'Unallocable Internal Time', 'External Professional Time' or as 'Private and Free Time', – or even 'A', 'B', 'C', or 'D'? or was it too short a time to record? and which activity was Newton engaged in sitting under an apple tree? Some regarded the exercise as an unreasonable intrusion, or as bizarre and futile. When the report was published, phrases such as 'a fuller understanding of the relative costs', 'divergence from national averages', and 'to use their resources better', did not inspire confidence in those who were inclined to be cynical of the purpose and the worthwhileness of the exercise. It was a voice from outside the system, Professor Beloff, the Principal of the new, independent University College at Buckingham, who warned in the *THES* that the UGC had developed into a large and bureaucratic machine which had developed an equalising formula for the expenditure of money. 'This makes universities more comparable, means that they are run on similar lines and are subject to more direction, for example, over fields of expansion', and this at a time, he suggested, when they needed differentiation and variety, independence from pressures from government, foresight and orderly planning. (Interestingly, Professor Finer had succeeded Professor Beloff in the Gladstone Chair of Government and Public Administration at Oxford.)

Another UGC Working Party reported on Capital Provision for University Libraries and proposed that libraries should become 'self-renewing', i.e. that 'new acquisitions will be offset to a considerable extent by withdrawals'; and it sought to establish 'norms' for size, with 'adjustments for special circumstances'. The Library Committee at Keele concluded that the report challenged and put at risk the nature of the university as a teaching and research establishment and a repository of 'the learning and culture of the present and the past'; and the Students' Union observed that the word 'scholarship' appeared not once throughout the report. With hindsight, at least 'self renewing' would have been preferable to the long freeze on new acquisitions which did so much damage in the 1980s and 1990s.

A major achievement during these years was a large-scale revision of the Foundation Year. Yet it is difficult to explain afterwards how the changes, when finally agreed, could have taken so long. After all, what was now thought to be necessary to amend had, only a few years earlier, been deemed to be satisfactory and an improvement on what had gone before. Is it that people in groups agree to action which, as individuals, they know are futile? (the 'Abilene Paradox'). No. Certainly in the 1970s the Foundation Year provoked full and frank discussion. Is it that some shared the view of Dickens's Mr. Dombey and were 'far from being friendly to what is called by persons of levelling sentiments general education'? No. Rather they shared the opinion of Thomas Arnold that no-one should criticise a university who has not 'known it well and loved it well'; and they were well qualified on that count to criticise. Perhaps someone had ignored the injunction: 'When the chief men meet in council, no-one present should twirl a spindle; for if such a thing were to happen, the discussion, like the spindle, would move in a circle and never be wound up. (Frazer. *The Golden Bough*). Or was it an example of 'Lollipop Theory', that the same people who come to one decision will make a different decision when wearing different hats (*The Accountants Review*, 1970).

I will deal only briefly with the two sets of recommendations following a review which started early in 1972. The Foundation Year Committee considered over a hundred memoranda from staff and students, and it was only too aware that not only would its recommendations fail to find unanimous approval, but that some conflicting views could not be reconciled by compromise. The main proposals were to replace the two year-long Sessional courses in the Foundation Year and the two year-long Subsidiary courses in the following year by a single broadening course: students would take four such courses, three in the Foundation Year and one the following year. The three one-term courses (Terminals) would be replaced by two 12-week tutorial courses. There would be a revised lecture course on which students would write six essays, and Discussion Groups would continue. Of the three Boards of Studies, one or other rejected the proposed new year-long courses, the revised Terminals, the revised lecture course, the Discussion Groups, and the end of year examinations. The Board of Social Sciences, in particular, regretted that the committee had failed to state a coherent view of the Foundation Year, wanted a discussion paper on its philosophy, and urged the committee to re-think the underlying philosophy of the lecture programme. In 1950, when time had been short, necessity had wrought agreement. Seven of the original heads of departments were still on the Senate – Stewart, Beaver, Charlton, Cope, Gemmell, Lawlor and Springall. This time, however, there was not the same pressing urgency, and Senate took no decision. Policy, Staffing and Development Committee, with the assistance of the chairman and deputy chairman of the Foundation Year Committee, was asked to advise Senate on the advice it should give to the Foundation Year Committee. Consequently, the existing course carried on for the present; but clearly some changes were necessary, and it is probably because that was generally accepted that a later set of proposals got a fair wind. The review of the Foundation Year therefore continued.

An indictment of the course was the 'post-box' system of essays (whereby students posted their essays in a box) and the lack of contact between writer and marker. The Board of Humanities had proposed 'that in support of the common lecture course, each department should offer a number of essay topics and arrange supervision periods to prepare students for these topics and discuss the marked essays with them'. This was the starting point around which the whole revision was to revolve. It resulted in a structure which lasted longer than any other pattern of Foundation Year teaching. It may be that the effort of this revision – certainly the mountains laboured greatly – finally inhibited the desire to re-examine the structure again. As secretary of the Committee I attended seventy-five meetings in the further two years it took – many with the chairman (Professor Fuller, Professor of Physics) and the deputy chairman (Professor Hunter, Professor of Psychology), with the Vice-Chancellor and his advisers, the chairmen of the Boards of Studies, the Librarian, the Students' Union Academic Committee, some departmental meetings, the Foundation Year Committee and subcommittees, Policy, Staffing and Development Committee, the Senate, and some Open Meetings. Two hundred students attended the final Open Meeting to discuss the proposals – even though not one of those present would be affected personally by the changes.

When the proposals finally reached the Senate they provoked impassioned opposition from Professor Broome, who produced and waved in the air a 'Topic' chocolate bar in reference to the proposed Topics. These were four-week programmes of tutorials in groups of 8-10, in which students handed in written work in the third week and had it returned in the fourth week. An alternative pattern was to meet for one hour in the first week, two hours in the second week, and one hour in the fourth week; and some tutors preferred to hand back written work individually rather than spend an hour all together in the fourth week. From this there developed interdepartmental double topics and departmental double topics. Topics replaced the former essays, but they were going to be much more expensive in staff time. In order to find the necessary time, Discussion Groups were discontinued. In many cases it was felt they no longer fulfilled the aims for which they had originally been introduced; but the loss of Discussion Groups was the most controversial change, and twenty years later some staff still shook their head sadly at me at their demise. There were also introduced more, specialist lectures as preparation for specific Topics. The requirement was to take nine Topics, in various combinations. They offered departments a wide flexibility and provided new opportunities for students to have tutorial contact with more departments and disciplines. It was, above all, the flexibility of the structure which made it adaptable to changing needs. On the first day of the new Foundation Year in October 1977, when staff were still coming to grips with the new nomenclature and the new pattern, it was clear that the new students as they emerged into the foyer of the Chancellor's Building after their first lecture were thoroughly conversant with the whole system of Topics, Double Topics and the tutorial structure.

There was, once again, a proposal that there should be a Director of the Foundation Year. The argument was put forward strongly by Dr. C. J. Harrison, a lecturer in history and himself a Keele graduate. Despite the size, complexity and academic peculiarity of the Foundation Year it was run without direction, he contended, and it was that absence of effective leadership which in large measure caused the earlier difficulties. He proposed a five-year appointment, from the present teaching staff, not renewable. However, contrary views were that such an appointment might diminish the wider participation on which so much depended; moreover, the exact role was difficult to define in that a less than senior appointment seemed unlikely to fulfil the role which it was thought might exist, but the role hardly existed to sustain a senior appointment. As the Registrar asked: 'Who was he going to be able to tell what?' A heartfelt comment from a member of the Classics Department was: 'Sit still. For God's sake don't change things *again*', and with a sigh of relief, at the end of 1978 a scheduled meeting of the committee was cancelled for lack of business.

Another reorganisation in the 1970s was the structure of the government of the University. From 1950 heads of departments were usually professors, and the headship of a department was a permanent appointment. All professors were members of the Senate. Students were not members of the Senate or the Council. The Students' Union now wanted twelve students on the Senate, and Jim Moran (President 1973-74) lamented that Lord Lindsay's ideal of a community of scholars seemed to have been a casualty of the previous twenty years, and he wondered what Lindsay would have thought of an institution which denied 70% of its members a meaningful voice in its government. However, it must be said that it did not seem to have been an issue which concerned Lindsay as Master of Balliol, Vice-Chancellor of Oxford or Principal of Keele. Lindsay had left behind no detailed 'testament of faith', but he did say in the first Foundation Year lecture to the first undergraduates that they were engaged in the pursuit of truth in the company of friends. Paul Rolo (who was appointed to the Chair of History in 1972), though claiming no authoritative insight, had been an undergraduate at Balliol and then Junior Dean there, and had come to Keele in January 1951 at Lindsay's invitation and served as a Warden at his instigation. He commented at length on the phrase 'community of scholars'. It seemed to Rolo that Lindsay simply wanted to emphasize that the kind of pursuit of knowledge which he described as education was our common goal; he was defining the purpose of the University rather than making any comment on its mode of government, and while he believed passionately in education, 'University politics seemed, as far as I could gather, quite irrelevant to him... he never regarded that machinery as an exercise in democratic experience... he did not regard the organs of University government as the best forums for consultation and discussion... on the other hand he enjoyed discussion, outside formal committees, both as an intellectual game and as a means of pooling mental resources... The very idea that any undergraduate might have wanted to play an active part in the formal aspect of decision-making never seems to have occurred to him at all, indeed he felt that undergraduate time was too precious to be devoted too keenly even to the management of the Students' Union... His own way of life was Spartan, and the University's material needs, other than very basic shelter for books and people, interested him little. He did not understand why they bothered others... Egalitarian yes – but authoritarian, within the University, equally so.'

But times were changing. Membership of the Senate was a matter for the University's statutes, as 'approved by the Lords of Our Most Honourable Privy Council' (*Charter*, s.26). The University Court could make recommendations to the Privy Council by Special Resolution on the proposal of the University Council, and the Council was obliged to give the Senate an opportunity of reporting on any proposals. Moreover, the Court needed to pass its Special Resolutions by a three-quarters majority, and to confirm what it had done by another Special Resolution at a later meeting. This may all seem cumbersome, but it was quite deliberate and made precipitate action impossible.

The statutes were revised, in accordance with the government's policy that students should be members of universities' governing bodies. The President of the Students' Union, the Chairman of the Association of Postgraduate Students and two full-time students now became members of the Senate, though they were excluded from 'reserved areas of business' – matters affecting the personal affairs of individual members of staff, the admission, assessment and personal affairs of individual students, and the final decision on the content of courses. There were similar provisions for three students on the Council. Revised statutes also affected the position of professors: in future, heads of departments would be appointed for periods of five years – not necessarily a professor or the most senior member of a department – and would be members of the Senate; but professors were no longer automatically members. This meant that the Senate would not get bigger and bigger as more professors were appointed, though there was no immediate effect. In 1976-77, the last year of the old provisions, the Senate had a total of 56 members, and in 1977-78, 61, including students.

Local government reorganisation also made some amendments to statutes necessary because of Local Authorities' membership of the University Court and Council. The first proposals were withdrawn from the agenda of the Court meeting in February 1975, to allow the Borough of Newcastle-under-Lyme to make comments. Hitherto, reflecting the Local Authorities' involvement in the founding and funding of the College, the Court included eight members from Stoke-on-Trent City Council, eight from Staffordshire County Council, four from Burton upon Trent County Borough Council and, more recently, one from Cheshire County Council. There were also some *ex officio* members. On the University Council there were three from Stoke, three from Staffordshire and one from Burton; and it was Council membership which was really at issue. What was being proposed was eight from Staffordshire, four from Stoke, two from Cheshire and two from Newcastle on the Court; and 4, 2, 1 and 1 on the Council. Newcastle had not been represented on the Council before. However, Newcastle contended that in the case of the new 'second-tier authorities' which were not now Education Authorities (and Stoke was not now an Education Authority) the largest single representation ought to be given to that authority within which the University was situated, and that Newcastle should have six members on the Court and three on the Council.

At the next Court meeting in March, the University Council made no change to its earlier proposals. Newcastle's views were repeated. Burton's representatives regretted that the new East Staffordshire District Council – Burton's successor – would not be represented. Council's recommendations were passed, but by less than a three-quarter's majority, so the whole matter was referred back again. In order to allow time for any amendments to be reported back to the Senate for comment, the next meeting of the Court was not until October 1975. This time the proposal for Council membership was Staffordshire 4, Stoke 3, Newcastle 2, East Staffordshire 1 and Cheshire 1 (and corresponding changes on the Court). Newcastle was still aggrieved, and its members felt there was little point in attending the meeting since their views were well-known. The proposals were passed almost unanimously, the Burton member thanking the Court for the consideration given to the further amendments. In December 1975 the approval was confirmed. Students had attended the Council as observers from May 1976, and sat as members from October. Shortly afterwards, gowns were no longer worn by academic members.

Another conflict of opinion with the Local Authorities surfaced over the future expansion of the University. Staffordshire County Council expressed the view that some student accommodation should be within the community rather than cloistered from it. At a meeting between the University, Newcastle and Staffordshire, the County was asked what precisely this meant, and replied it was a comment rather than a reservation or objection. Newcastle asked what it proposed should be done: Newcastle was the housing authority, and could not make provision for students. It then emerged that there was disquiet about staff housing within the green belt – though no mention had been made of that point earlier. On the wider question of planning, Staffordshire accepted in principle the University's ultimate extension on to Home Farm (with the provision of tree belts). Peter Shepheard, the Development Architect, had suggested a main entrance near the north-east boundary of the University, but the Newcastle Planning and Development Officer said it was too near the Gallowstree Lane roundabout and suggested an entrance near the existing Home Farm entrance.

Keele and national politics impinged on one another from time to time. Amongst the candidates in the General Elections were graduates Ian Taylor for S.E.Coventry (who was appointed an MBE in 1974, and was later MP for Esher and Minister for Trade and Industry), Malcolm Keir for Hertfordshire East, Mike Steele for Deptford, and John Golding for Newcastle-under-Lyme; a member of staff, David Chantrey, for Stoke-on-Trent South. (Michael Whincup had stood for Sutton Coldfield in 1964 and 1966, and John Lees had stood for South Fyld in 1966.) Former members of staff elected were Bob Cant for Stoke-on-Trent Central and Brian Walden for Birmingham Ladywood. (Clare Short, who had also been a student at Keele, repre-sented Birmingham Ladywood from 1983.) In the House of Lords was Lord Melchett, who had been a postgraduate student. The White Paper *Education: A Framework for Expansion* announced in December 1972 by Mrs. Thatcher, the Secretary of State, had set out a ten-year strategy to expand student numbers by about 60%, but with a reduction in terms of grant per student and with a warning of the need for economies of scale. This was overtaken by an economic crisis in the following autumn, and just before Christmas 1973, in a written answer in the House of Commons, Mrs. Thatcher postponed building projects – and at Keele this meant the Chancellor's Building extension, the Administration Building, and student accommodation. Later, in 1977, on the day following the conservative victory in the Stechford by-election (formerly the seat of Roy Jenkins) Mrs. Thatcher, by now in opposition and leader of the Conservative Party, came to Keele – not to discuss university affairs, but to address a conservative candidates' conference. After that, in Conservative Association clubrooms in Britain there could be seen photographs of the party leader with prospective candidates taken in the Salvin Room, Keele Hall.

Other distinguished national and international figures also came to Keele. In 1976 the David Bruce Centre sponsored three lectures to mark the American bicentennial celebrations. The first was given by Lord Home, former Prime Minister and Foreign

Secretary, and was attended by David Bruce. The other two lectures were given by Roy Jenkins, the Home Secretary (who had been at Balliol when Lindsay was Master), and George Ball, who had been the U.S. Permanent Representative at the United Nations. Later, the first Bruce Memorial Lecture was given at Keele by Sir Harold Wilson in February 1979. In 1980 Dr. Kurt Waldheim, the Secretary-General of the United Nations, also gave a lecture following the conferment of an honorary degree on him. (In 1988 he was deprived of his honorary degree by the University Council.) The International Relations Forum and the Politics Department attracted Dr. Garret FitzGerald, the Taoiseach of the Republic of Ireland, General Gowon, who had been Head of the Federal Republic of Nigeria, and Enoch Powell – whose lecture on the 'nuclear fallacy' was attentively received at a time when his presence elsewhere was an excuse for rowdy behaviour. Professor de Duve, the Nobel Prize-winner for Medicine in 1974, came to lecture in 1978 and was awarded an honorary degree in 1982.

Keele was still hoping for a Medical School, even though Norman St. John Stevas at the Department of Education and Science had replied to Jack Ashley, MP, in January 1973 that there was no need for a further medical school in Britain. Two years later, following a reorganisation of the administrative arrangements of the Health Service, Dr. Hunter, the Vice-Chancellor of Birmingham, who was involved both regionally and nationally in medical administration, suggested it was time to make another application; and so a committee was set up to investigate. Earlier, in the 1960s, Keele had been judged too small, but the University had grown and was set to grow further. All specialities except one were represented by consultants in the North Staffordshire area, and there was an emphasis on joint research and post-graduate work. Keele had appointed a second Professor of Psychology in 1972, S. J. Hutt, who with Dr. Corinne Hutt (who was also appointed to the staff) had a special interest and an international reputation in child development and paediatrics. There was medically-oriented research in the Departments of Biology, Chemistry, Physics and Sociology, and the University had been receiving grants from the Medical Research Council, the Department of Education and Science, the West Midlands Regional Health Authority, Cancer Research, the British Heart Foundation and the Multiple Sclerosis Society. Professor Olive Stevenson was appointed to the Chair of Social Work in 1976 – Keele's first woman professor – and her research on specialist advisers and social services staff in relation to the physically handicapped was supported by the Department of Health and Social Security. The Department of Communication had been conducting clinical work at the hospital since 1969, and was preparing to host an international conference on hearing. The Research Unit in Biochemistry had been established in 1971, funded by the University Appeal Fund, and the W. E. Dunn Unit was being appraised by Sir John McMichael (see chapter 18). Three-day courses for doctors concerned with training General Practitioners were being provided by the Department and Institute of Education. Four Keele staff held honorary appointments with the Regional Health Authority. At the Hospital Centre postgraduate training had increased and there was some undergraduate training from other medical schools. The Medical Institute in Stoke-on-Trent had sponsored a purpose-built Medical Research Unit, and in 1974 the University and the Medical Institute had established a Centre for Postgraduate Medical Education and Research. Moreover, the Todd Committee had reported in 1967 that the Hospital Centre was outstandingly suitable to become a teaching hospital.

Within a year of being set up the committee reported. Membership comprised representatives of Keele, the Birmingham Medical School, the Regional and Area Health Authorities, and consultants from the hospital. The chairman was Professor Sir W. Melville Arnott, a distinguished Professor of Medicine at Birmingham for nearly thirty years. The Committee recommended to the Secretary of State for Health and Social Security and to the chairman of the UGC that an undergraduate medical school should be established. It proposed an intake of 35 in 1979, rising over five years to 120 a year. Above all, it could start fairly quickly as a new teaching hospital would not be required; and the capital cost was estimated at £11-12M, as against about £50M for the as yet incomplete medical school at Nottingham.

When the UGC visited Keele in 1976 they explained that the DHSS was considering the number of the intake into medical schools; but that any decision awaited the report of the Royal Commission on the National Health Service. Any link that Keele might make, said the UGC, would be seen sympathetically, and work done would not be wasted even if there should be no medical school at Keele for twenty-five years. At a meeting a year later, in May 1977, the UGC said it was a question of numbers and that the future was extremely obscure. The DHSS at another meeting said there were no plans to increase the intake, and that the choice of where any new development was to come would be for the UGC to decide. Somehow there seemed to be a circle with no way into it.

Nevertheless hope still sprang eternal. From the University's point of view, it would vitalise academic thinking, extend and strengthen work in a number of Departments, and reinforce links with the local area. As for numbers, it seemed in October 1977 at a meeting with the DHSS, that the government was committed to an increase of 850 in medical intake if it was to reach its target in the early-1980s. Locally, the establishment of the Department of Postgraduate Medicine at Keele seemed to go to the brink of founding a School of Medicine, but in June 1978 the Minister of State at the DHSS did not see 'any demand for a new medical school for some time to come'.

Space, that is to say whether the University had enough or too much of it, continued to be a problem which was difficult to resolve. In the late-1970s there was thought to be the capacity (for teaching) for 2,050 arts/social science places and 720 science places. The UGC interpreted it as 2,160 + 1,080, and started to refer to 'planning norms'. Yet when the UGC Physical Sciences Subcommittee visited Keele in April 1979 they found that the space in Physics 'could not be described as lavish' and they noted pressing needs for accommodation in Geology. As far as the huts were concerned, the Vice-Chancellor had asked the UGC when they came in 1976 whether they advised their retention or destruction. The chairman was unwilling to pronounce an impression gained from a one-day visit (though, of course, the huts had been there since 1944). He felt it was possible that when the time came the University would find it was not possible to destroy the huts, in that some of the difficulties pointed to seemed to demand an extended use if no capital was available for new buildings. That, as the Vice-Chancellor said, symbolised the changeability of the atmosphere in which the University was expected to plan. One consequence of there being few new staff appointed in 1977-78 was that with the completion of the Chancellor's Building extension fourteen huts could be demolished, the savings on heat, electricity, water, telephones and maintenance more than covering the new costs in the Chancellor's Building. In February 1978 the Students' Union proposed that the remaining huts should be retained; but, judging by the bad state of the mains services beneath the huts, their time was limited. At least they had provided good size living rooms. The size of 'UGC' rooms varied from 12.5 down to 9.8 square metres, while the loan-financed rooms had shrunk to 8.1 square metres (though the reduction was offset by better provision of handbasins and showers). Barnes Hall was still not complete ten years after its first occupation, as a result of changes in UGC funding; and subsidence was to cause one block in Barnes Hall to be demolished. Its disappearance did much to improve the general view from the drive. The reality of economies was to be found in deterioration in the quality of finish in the new blocks – leading to more expensive maintenance and cleaning. Aurelie Tees, who had succeeded Miss Rolfe as Domestic Bursar, listed over twenty points which were not satisfactory: doors not strong enough for hooks, lack of bookshelves, the need for skirting boards, for adequate cupboards, for vinyl tiles in kitchens, hooks in bathrooms, and so on. (She was awarded the MBE in 1991 for her work with the disabled and she retired in 1996. She died a year later, and Scots pines were donated by her sister and planted on the campus in her memory.)

Whatever – one could say despite – the changes, whether of our own making or forced on us, one must never lose sight of the daily business of the University, and new academic developments, the successes of the students, the daily routine of lectures, tutorials and laboratory classes, essays, the hours spent in the Library and hours spent in the Union, and the flourishing student societies. There were new departments: International Relations, building on the earlier combined honours course in Economics, History and Politics; Music, a Principal course building on the successes of the subsidiary course and the flourishing extra-curricular societies and concerts; Electronics; and Computer Science. International Relations counted as two Principal subjects; Music and Computer Science and Electronics were not only welcome additions to degree subjects, but also added to the riches of Keele's combinations of subjects – possible combinations with Music included Computer Science, Electronics, Mathematics, Physics and American Studies (bearing in mind the Music Department's emphasis on American music); and with Computer Science included Geography, Philosophy, Politics and Psychology. By the summer of 1977,

5,700 students had taken degrees in 158 different combinations of subjects or single honours in seven subjects – International Relations, Biology, Computer Science, Electronics, Geology, Mathematics and Physics.

Retirement took more of the founding fathers – Beaver in 1974, Springall in 1975, Cope in 1976 and Gemmell in 1977. Gemmell had also completed more than 1,200 broadcasts and he was later awarded the OBE. George White, a driver, completed fifty years at Keele, working first for the Sneyds and then for the College and University. Jim Roberts retired as caretaker of the Walter Moberly Hall in 1975, and died a few months later. He is commemorated by a prize for the student who contributes most to amateur music making at Keele. Jim Pickavance, the Architect and Buildings Officer who had done so much to transform the army camp into a campus, had retired in 1972 and died in 1976. Ron Hill, the Union Steward and Annie his wife were killed in an aircraft accident, and they are commemorated by the row of mountain ash trees between the Chapel and the Library.

There were successes and honours. In 1976 Rajan Soni and David Chell won the first Intervarsity Debating Competition organised by the Oxford Union and Lloyds Bank Ltd. In 1974 there were two awards for Keele graduates on the staff: Dr. E. Derbyshire, a graduate of 1954 (Reader in Geography and later Professor of Geomorphology) was awarded the Antarctic Service Medal by the U.S.A. in recognition of his contribution to the progress of science and international co-operation in Antarctica; and Dr. R. C. Maddison, a graduate of 1957 (Senior Lecturer in Physics) was awarded the Mitchell Memorial Gold Medal, which is awarded to a distinguished engineer or scientist as a memorial to Reginald Mitchell, the designer of the Spitfire. Previous recipients included Sir Geoffrey de Havilland, Sir John Cockcroft, Sir Bernard Lovell and Dr. Barnes Wallis, and later the medal was awarded to Helen Sharman, the first British woman in space in 1991. In 1977 John Hodgkinson, the Registrar, was awarded the OBE in the New Year Honours List (and in 1983 he was awarded an honorary degree by the University); and the Queen's Silver Jubilee Medal for service to the University was awarded to Stanley Stewart, the Librarian, Marion Bailey, the senior secretary since she was transferred from the Town Clerk's office in 1949, and Selwyn Hankey, the plumber, who knew every foible of Keele's departmental and domestic plumbing systems.

Part of the campus wall fell down on the A525 as a result of mining damage: it was re-aligned and rebuilt to a lower height in a combination of brick and stone. Trees were felled and planted. In 1977 the decision was taken to fell the thirty-six sycamores in Keele Drive and to replace them with silver limes. Eighteen of the trees were probably dangerous and eleven more would have needed extensive surgery. Age, army lorries and campus road building had finally taken their toll on one of the splendours of the campus which would take generations to re-emerge. Similarly, the lime trees outside the Walter Moberly Hall – the remainder of the 'seven sisters' – had to be felled. New trees were planted, including three oaks outside Biology, the gift of Mrs. Compton in memory of her husband, whose shop,

Mandley and Unett, was well-known in Newcastle High Street. There were twelve trees from Keele Parish Council and a mountain ash from the Women's Institute. Colin Lee, a graduate, made a donation for trees; six trees and eighteen creepers were given by Horwood Hall Social Committee from their bar profits, and two students from the Hawthorns gave a hornbeam. A plantation on the perimeter of the playing fields in memory of Katrina Hill (the wife of Eric Hill in Classics) perpetuates the memory of her active interest in the beauty of the campus. Princess Margaret planted a whitebeam on the lawns below the Clock House to commemorate the Queen's Silver Jubilee. The University also received a very fine herbarium from Mr. E. S. Edees in 1975 – over 10,000 items, the basis of his book *Flora of Staffordshire*. Another gift was from Mr. E. J. D. Warrillow, for many years the photographer for the *Sentinel*. His valuable collection of 1,800 photographs, mainly of the Potteries, spanned a hundred years from the 1870s to the 1970s. Honorary degrees were awarded to both Mr. Edees and Mr. Warrillow.

Awareness of the creeping loss of rural beauty and the prospect of building on the Observatory Hill provoked the formation of the Keele Environmental Group and a petition signed by 132 staff and 93 students requesting no further building there. But they were unable to save the view of the hill, with its sheep and its donkeys. Successively the open outlooks were lost, with Lindsay Hall in the 1960s, then Barnes Hall and the Sports Centre, softening the bleakness of windswept snow across the drive in winter. Then the view of the Observatory Hill was lost with the (not quite matching) 'Science Park' buildings, and then the views from Keele Drive with the Holly Cross and the Oaks residences. With more students there was another extension to the Chancellor's Building, more residences, more shops in the Students' Union extension (opened in 1976), more cars, more tarmac, and the suggestion in 1972 that there should be a charge for car parking.

During the octocentenary celebrations of Newcastle-under-Lyme in 1973, the first lecture in a series was given by Professor Charlton on Romans and Celts in the area: there had been a Celtic settlement near Maer, a Roman fort and administrative building at Chesterton, where the remains of two baker's ovens were discovered, a Roman villa and farm at Hales, including a bath house nearly thirty yards long, and a Roman street system under Wolstanton golf course.

As for university dons, what can only be described as a battering process had begun. A long-running pay settlement, or rather lack of settlement, dragged on. Already aggrieved, an agreed 'cost-of-living adjustment' of 20%, due to be implemented in October 1975, just fell foul of the curbs in the government's new incomes policy, and they received 4%. This became known as 'the anomaly'. And at the end of the 1970s, the CVCP was writing about early retirement schemes to encourage staff to leave. Nevertheless, with a show of confidence Keele pressed on to launch a new appeal to set up a Development Trust with two initial objectives: a medical sciences building and an arts centre.

Stewart was Keele's longest-serving Vice-Chancellor. What he had inherited was still Lindsay's Keele – one which he had helped to formulate. Sir Robert Aitken, the Vice-Chancellor of Birmingham University, anticipated in 1967 the Public Accounts Committee's recommendation that universities should be scrutinised and be accountable to Parliament for their spending, and recognised that such a recommendation would 'bring the universities nearer to becoming an instrument of state and of the government of the day instead of being independent sources of ideas, criticism, and long, forward views.' In 1976 Sir John Habakkuk, Vice-Chancellor of Oxford and Chairman of the CVCP wrote on the contrary that 'the ability of individual universities to exercise their autonomy has not been impaired' (CVCP *Report on the period 1972-76*), but the tightening grip from outside had certainly affected what Stewart could do inside Keele: the options within which there was autonomy and freedom of manoeuvre were seriously curtailed. Had Keele been a new university in the 1960s he might have had more scope for his ideas; but he noted in 1968 that the UGC was becoming far more of a policy-making organisation and that the old autonomy of the universities had gone. When the New University of Ulster conferred an honorary DLitt on him in 1973, their Public Orator said that there had not been 'a keener eye than his on the dangers confronting the university of today from the modern centralising tendency'. Three major currents had swept the University along regardless. The student troubles broke that warm bond with staff which had been characteristic of Keele in its early years. As Princess Margaret said at his final degree congregation, it was not much fun being a Vice-Chancellor between 1967 and 1972. 'But we were lucky because Campbell Stewart had a good Scot's sense of humour and was entirely unshockable.' Second, the academic developments were simply frustrated by the serious shortage of money, inflation, and the breakdown of the quinquennial system. If Keele was to grow it had no option but to conform, to provide three-year courses, and to abandon the Foundation Year as a requirement for all. Stewart made the best he could of it. 'The cry that three-year programmes had sealed the fate of 'Lindsay's Keele', he wrote, 'strikes me as being both touching and bunkum.' But was there scope for a more forthright response? and to nail Keele's colours more firmly to the mast? The opportunity might have been seized to restate the *whole* of Lindsay's underlying philosophy from which the Keele pattern had emerged and on which it rested, to deplore publicly the changes which were being forced on Keele, and to regret the loss of what was so clearly worthwhile. Nevertheless Keele preserved as much as was possible in the circumstances. All universities can put forward a case for special pleading, but the *additional* cost of Keele in the overall expenditure on universities, just as the *extra* savings made later in the financial cuts of 1981, was always going to be minuscule: Keele was altogether 1% or less of the total universities' budget. Third, the shortage of money also forced total residence to be abandoned (though this is not to ignore Keele's good fortune in continuing to maintain a very high proportion of students on the campus). One relic of early Keele Stewart had to retain, unwillingly, was the army huts of the 1940s. In addition, the demise of the Institute of Education by another act of government policy, must have been a personal disappointment for him.

Nevertheless, throughout his twenty-nine years at Keele, shared with devoted support by Mrs. Stewart, he was careful, courteous and kindly, a man of great equanimity. He felt and cared deeply about Keele and served it longer than any of his predecessors or successors. In particular, in a series of lectures when he was appointed, when Keele celebrated its twenty-first anniversary and in a valedictory lecture when he retired, he reconsidered and re-assessed Keele's place in university education. To his great credit his patience remained undiminished, his optimism undimmed, and his faith in what Keele was doing and what Lindsay stood for, unshaken. He died on 23rd April 1997 as the result of a tragic accident while visiting friends at Keele.

'I beg I may without offence confess my present inability to discern the cogency of the commission's conclusions.'
(Samuel Pepys. *Pepys MSS.*)

Chapter 21

NO ALTERNATIVE

The narrative for the next few years focuses much more on national developments. I have deliberately unfolded the saga in considerable detail because the consequences of what happened were so far-reaching.

In May 1979 Mrs. Thatcher won the General Election and became Prime Minister until 1990. It was to be a radical government. She had been Secretary of State for Education and Science in Mr. Heath's Cabinet, 1970-74, and Leader of the Opposition, 1975-79. She was determined to set an entirely new course for the economy and her first priority was to reduce the budget deficit. Mrs. Thatcher wrote in *The Downing Street Years* that by exerting financial pressure on the universities, the government increased administrative efficiency and provoked overdue rationalisation. She said that some critics were genuinely concerned about the future autonomy and academic integrity of universities, and she conceded that they had a stronger case than she would have liked. With the prospect of inflation worse than the government had expected, with another increase in oil prices following the overthrow of the Shah of Iran, and with the British economy in a cycle of low growth and high inflation, the government immediately determined to cut government spending. Sir Geoffrey Howe said in a budget speech that finance must determine expenditure, not the other way round. The Secretary of State for Education and Science, Mark Carlisle, warned the UGC that they must make drastic cuts. The quinquennial system of financing universities had collapsed in the crisis of 1973-74: what the universities needed for financial stability and longer-term planning was the restoration of that system. In 1981 Sir Keith Joseph became Secretary of State, with a personal commitment to university education – but above all with a commitment to the control of public spending. There was to be no alternative if the government was to sustain welfare support on a declining financial base and to make higher education more widely available.

Economic crises therefore faced all universities. Keele was small and had to withstand much fiercer cuts than almost every other university. There was less scope for the government to finance diversity such as Keele offered. The cutbacks, and in particular the uncertainties arising from the succession of short-term expediencies were a constant distraction.

Or was this all really a display of whingeing by a privileged sector as the accumulated fat of generations was taken away by a government desperate to make economies which were already being forced on to the defence and health budgets? Was it not time for the universities to adjust to the needs of the consumer society? But when and where did the government set out what it required of universities? Where was the debate reported in *Hansard*? Where was a White Paper? Was a major change in ideology to be put into practice without so much as a debate?

Was it reasonable for the UGC to do this job? Or should they have said to the government that they would have no part in so precipitately reconstructing the system without the time to accommodate the changes? and that if that was what the government wanted then the government should be seen to do it. Mrs. Shirley Williams, the former Education Secretary, said that the UGC, or at least the chairman, should have resigned rather than carry out a foolish, unwise and ill thought-out set of policies. But the UGC believed that they were better placed to 'reshape the system' and with more understanding than the Department of Education and Science would have shown, and that otherwise 'we shall cease to control our own destiny' (UGC to CVCP, 24th October 1980). And so the UGC did not resign in protest: not even one member. According to Anthony Sampson in *The Changing Anatomy of Britain* several members had considered resigning but decided they would be wrong to desert the committee when times were bad. For their part vice-chancellors all had the duty to do the best for their own institutions. Resignation or protest would have little effect, save perhaps to temper policy in the succeeding few years. So, if they did not hang together, there was the prospect that some might hang separately.

The guidance offered to universities was replaced by diktat, and long-term planning by short-term expediency. The change in attitude is perceived perhaps in the use of the word 'system' to describe the universities. The gravamen of the charge against the UGC in this book is not that they carried out government policy but that the *extra* damage which they inflicted on Keele was out of all proportion to any additional savings made. It was the UGC who decided what the rules should be: Keele, as it happened, did not fit those rules comfortably. As for the Foundation Year, they had already determined, whether actively or by default, that it should be limited in size, so what answer were they looking for when they said in July 1981 that they wished 'to have further consultations on the possible phasing out of four-year courses'? It becomes clear that the UGC of the day did not fully understand the structure of Keele's courses as published each year in the *Prospectus*.

Each successive measure can be explained away, though not always convincingly; but overall it is difficult to justify the extraordinary treatment meted out to Keele in July 1981 – a policy which the UGC was to agree was unworkable. It looks like punishment for being different. The *extra* by which Keele suffered was something like 10% of the postage budgets of all universities, and for this, careers, courses, and the most striking philosophy of university education in this century (newer universities notwithstanding) – all this was put in jeopardy.

Lord Briggs (who had been on the UGC subcommittee which planned the new universities) said: 'It is frightening to feel that the retreat has been so disorganised.' Lord Robbins, the architect of the expansion in the 1960s, and Chancellor of the University of Stirling, described the government's cuts as monstrous: 'Any self-respecting committee should have refused to impose them, and at least some of them should have resigned. What are they about?' The UGC maintained silence. In a rare press interview during a visit to Keele in May 1982 Dr. Parkes, the Chairman of the UGC, gave the answer: he was merely carrying out the instruction of the elected government in his treatment of universities.

Chapter 22

BACKGROUND TO CRISIS

D r. David Harrison succeeded Professor Campbell Stewart as Vice-Chancellor in October 1979, without a break: it was business as usual, and that was his theme. Dr. Harrison came from Selwyn College, Cambridge, where he was a Fellow and the Senior Tutor, and a University Lecturer in chemical engineering. In his Inaugural Lecture as Vice-Chancellor he gave an account of the nature of this branch of engineering and followed it by his observations on universities. He drew attention to the government's wish to exert what was called 'steerage' and expressed the hope that the helmsman's touch would be sensitive. He warned that there was such a lack of assurance of the level of long-term resources that planning was almost meaningless. An article in the *THES* when he was appointed spoke of his keeping alive the community spirit and of his being a difficult man to ruffle. One was reminded of Dr. Taylor's 'Cambridge manner'.

Despite the difficulties Keele was in good heart, its optimism based on that remarkable coherence afforded by an academic syllabus which facilitated an extraordinarily wide informal and well-informed social intercourse. Within the previous three years student numbers had risen by 21% while academic staff had increased by only 6.6%, demonstrating the sort of efficiency now demanded by the government. Applications for admission for 1981-82 were 17% up on the previous year, compared with a national increase of 4%, and applications for three-year courses were especially buoyant. New principal subjects had been introduced. The Research Unit in Biochemistry combined with the Department of Biology to become 'Biological Sciences', offering Biochemistry as well as Biology. Management Science was developed to combine specifically with science subjects. Long-term academic policy was being discussed so that proposals could be formulated as soon as finances would permit. There were new taught postgraduate courses in American Music, Education, and in Social Science Research in Education. The Department of Social Policy and Social Work attracted grants of nearly £300,000; Biological Sciences nearly £200,000; Psychology, Education and Chemistry each nearly £100,000. Research income was at its highest level since 1969-70. A new language laboratory was opened in Keele Hall. Adult Education courses flourished and increased; and, following a series of eleven national seminars at Keele on the care of the elderly, a three-year project to monitor the benefits of pre-retirement education had attracted a grant of £75,000. A remarkably successful and long-running 'War Studies' group started in 1980. 'Two tutors were unable to lead the full programme this year', said Mr. Owen Powell, 'so we decided to run a course of our own. It means we are not on the official evening classes list, but we still have a very good programme lined up, with representatives from the Russian and American embassies, Army, Navy and Royal Air Force.' The enthusiasm of this class, still going twenty years later, can be likened to the WEA classes of seventy years earlier.

The new Department of Postgraduate Medicine was formally opened in October 1980 by Mr. Patrick Jenkin, Secretary of State for Social Services. It was established at the hospital in 1978 following the success of the Medical Institute there and the decision of the University and the local consultants to become involved in medical education, and it was encouraged by the West Midlands Regional Health Authority and the Board of Graduate Studies at the University of Birmingham. In particular this development stems from the decision of the Regional Health Authority to devote so many sessions to research under the auspices of Keele. The department was now in a position to undertake responsibility for a major part of the training for the three-year post qualification period and to plan for development in General Professional and Higher Medical Training. The W. E. Dunn Unit was also working closely with the hospital. Keele's claims for an undergraduate medical school 'would be bound to stand very high', said the Secretary of State, if and when a new medical school was needed: but there was no prospect of that.

Keele graduates were being appointed to chairs in other universities: Norman Tutt (graduated 1966) to Applied Social Studies at Lancaster, and Anthony Smith (graduated 1962) to Experimental Physics at Strathclyde. There were honours for staff who had gone elsewhere – knighthoods for Roy Shaw, Secretary General of the Arts Council since 1975 and formerly Director of Adult Education; and for Professor Bruce Williams, the founding Professor of Economics, who had been Vice-Chancellor of Sydney since 1967; a CBE for Denis Lees, who had been in the Economics Department and was now Professor at Nottingham; and an OBE for Professor Robert North, the first Professor of French and now at Birmingham.

Student drama took on a new lease of life and reappeared on the Edinburgh Fringe. The Rag was revived. Once more Keele students (Will Stallard and Owen Gavin) were in the final of the *Observer* 'Mace' debating competition. The Hawthorns party for senior citizens living in Keele was repeated again. Musical concerts were reorganised. The *Sentinel* said that the greatest contribution by Keele Concerts had been to create a public for chamber music in this district; following a fall in audiences in recent years, the concerts once again looked set for a new era of success. Keele students and staff were amongst the 800 performers in the orchestras, brass bands and choirs playing Havergal Brian's 'Gothic' Symphony in the Victoria Hall in May 1978 – a performance which features in *The Guinness Book of Records*. Further afield there had been a Purcell Room recital in London by Dwight Peltzer, Cecil Lytle and William Brooks, all of whom were Fulbright-Hays Visiting Professors at Keele. Even the end of the huts was in sight, to be hastened, paradoxically, by the financial cuts.

There was, though, one area where the outlook was not at all optimistic: Russian. The number of students studying Russian at school had declined. The Atkinson Committee concluded that the number of university departments should be halved, and so the UGC recommended running down Russian at Keele (and also at eighteen other universities). At a meeting in July 1980 they said they had not yet taken a firm decision; that recommendations were not value judgements but were based on practical reasons; and that it was not being done as an economy exercise. Of course, the chairman of the UGC recognised that refusal to co-operate would be a perfectly proper attitude for universities to adopt; but in his opinion that would be an act of corporate suicide because if it was thought – and especially in Parliament – that universities were not responsive to new needs and changes, then pressure for direct intervention – hints of which had already been given, he said, – would increase and would be increasingly difficult to resist. If Keele chose to say 'no', then the UGC would ultimately withdraw the appropriate grant – but 'would not, however, be vindictive'. Why Keele had been selected was not a matter which Dr. Parkes, the chairman, felt at liberty to discuss.

The starting point for this exercise, then, was declining numbers, from a national total of about 700 reading honours Russian in 1971 to just below 500. Yet far from being part of the problem and a victim of falling 'A' level students, Keele was specially able to be part of the solution. Graduates in Russian were still needed, and the army and the government alike were unable to recruit enough. The Foundation Year not only exposed a large number of students to some Russian but also created its own demand and provided a 'transfer' course for students to go on to read principal Russian. To close the department would not mean that these students would study Russian somewhere else. Russian at Keele was alive and well, recruitment was buoyant and Keele had the eighth largest department in British universities. Several books by staff were in press. Over the years, too, distinguished Russian poets and authors visited the department and attracted large audiences: Yevgeny Yevtushenko in 1975 and 1978, and Joseph Brodsky in 1978 and 1985. (In 1987 Brodsky was awarded the Nobel Prize for literature.) Edward Limonov came in 1980, and then Zhores Medvedev who gave two seminars – one on *The molecular biology of ageing* and the second on *Politics in the Soviet Union: the future*. The problem for the Atkinson Report had been shortage of students: but that was not a problem at Keele. Whatever it was the chairman of the UGC felt unable to discuss must remain unknown. Yet in 1986 the House of Commons Foreign Affairs Committee urged the government to give greater priority to Russian language and Soviet studies, and less than ten years after the Atkinson Report an external review of the research undertaken by Mr. Pike, Mr. Andrew and Dr. Polukhina said that the University was 'to be congratulated on its foresight in supporting this vulnerable group through difficult years' (Professor Elsworth, University of Manchester). So Russian survived.

What of Keele's philosophy and those intertwined factors which had originally led Lord Lindsay to stake so much on founding a new College? Some of the advantages of the four-year degree course were highlighted and were self-evident in the crisis over Russian. But the UGC had already chipped away at the Foundation Year. Although three-year courses were soon available across the full range of dual honours combinations, to say that they also fulfilled 'the fundamental Keele requirement for cross-disciplinary study which, we believe, produces the broadly educated Keele graduate', as had been said by the University in an article in the *Sentinel* in October 1977, represented a watering down of the philosophy of earlier years. The Vice-Chancellor wrote in the *Staffordshire Magazine* in January 1980 that 'the double discipline degree programme is the end result of Lindsay's thinking whatever may have gone, and we still adhere to that'. But there had been much more to Lindsay's thinking than this particular end result, and Keele was not renewing the message of its founder: instead the dream was slipping away.

Meanwhile, the 'hooves with a galloping sound' were coming closer and would soon shake the whole financial structure of British universities. Already in August 1979, before the beginning of his first term as Vice-Chancellor, there was a letter on Dr. Harrison's desk from the chairman of the UGC saying that the student targets and the financial allocations for 1980-81 and 1981-82 already given in the UGC letters of July 1978 and as recently as May 1979, would have to be reconsidered, and that fewer students should be admitted in 1980 than in 1979 (and thereby reducing income with very little reduction in expenditure). Quinquennial planning was now but a distant memory. It was a valuable foretaste for the new Vice-Chancellor to note how suddenly the ground could shift under his feet, and how much closer direction was about to be applied to the management of affairs. In May 1979 Keele's provisional allocation for 1979-80 was £7.23M; then in October it was revised to £6.82M – with the financial year already well underway. (There had been a downward trend in the rate of inflation, but even so it was a cut in real terms of 3.3%, which was applied fairly uniformly to all universities after the start of the financial year.) This cut, together with the budget deficit and the rising cost of fuel, left a gap of about £400,000. Local Authorities were also subjected to a financial squeeze, and so Staffordshire County Council cut its grant to the University by £20,000. Of course, the Association of University Teachers was concerned that the cuts already imposed in library books and laboratory materials would undermine the ability of staff to do their jobs effectively and would inevitably lead to lower teaching standards and have an adverse effect on staff morale. But this was only the beginning.

In October 1979, as part of its consultation policy, the UGC suggested three possible future levels of grants up to 1983-84 (which might be described as moderate, standstill, and worse), and asked for preliminary replies by the end of November, and a detailed reply assuming a standstill, by the following July. The position was further complicated by the government's policy that overseas students should in future meet the full cost of their tuition fees – that they should be financed either by their own governments or by themselves. This move, coming on top of the government's refusal to exempt universities from the public spending stringency imposed on the rest of the public sector, led to what Nigel Lawson has described as 'a seething hostility towards the Thatcher Government within the universities' (*The View from No. 11*); and led to Oxford University's decisions in 1985 and 1987 not to bestow an honorary degree on Mrs. Thatcher, a customary honour for Oxford-educated Prime Ministers since 1946. The *Daily Express* thought this 'symbolises the refusal of many academics to acknowledge the realities of modern Britain' and their failure to come to grips with 'the fresh wind of realism that Thatcherism has blown through most of our sacred cow institutions'. By the time the Vice-Chancellor addressed the University Court in February 1981 the climate within which the UGC worked had become bleaker, and the shift towards central control was becoming more apparent. The decline in the unit of resource was, properly, a matter for government policy; but with it came the dirigiste view expressed by the Secretary of State that if institutions were to remain free to decide for themselves how far to heed or disregard advice on rationalisation, there would be a strong risk that the necessary contraction would bring about major distortions in provision. Or, as the chairman of the UGC wrote to the CVCP in October 1980, 'it is not adequate, as some Vice-Chancellors might wish, to say to the UGC 'give us such money as you can spare, and we will sort out our own priorities for retrenchment and innovation' [because] the sum of a set of local aspirations may not form a sensible overall picture for the system and the students who wish to enter it'. We have evidently reached the stage where, despite all the past evidence to the contrary, it is thought that someone somewhere knows best and can forecast what the national provision should be; universities' considered academic programmes were deemed to be merely 'local aspirations' within plans for national provision. Yet in a letter to the House of Commons Select Committee on Education the chairman of the UGC had said: 'It will be for each university, as is proper, to make decisions within its total resources and in the light of advice given' and that there 'will, in the event, undoubtedly be some departures from UGC recommendations'. Then, at a meeting with the UGC in February 1980 there was some glimmer of hope of amelioration and slight grounds for thinking that the future was not as gloomy as had been feared. In June 1980 it was possible to restore some of the cuts made to departments, and the grant for 1980-81 of £8.2M made it possible to re-instate the original commitments of 1979-80. It looked, perhaps, as though the screw was not being tightened any more.

In his letter to the CVCP in October 1980 already referred to, Dr. Parkes wrote of the intention to provide level funding to the system as a whole. He went on to state what was to be the role of the UGC, developing further the terms of reference which Lord Jowett had expounded in the debate in the House of Lords in 1947. Institutions might need their resolve strengthening and financial help if they had to contemplate the closure of departments and possible staff redundancies; the UGC could no longer sustain a philosophy of *laissez-faire* with regard to the development of all but the most expensive subjects (though not all would agree that that had indeed recently been their policy). Where resources were going to be taken away as well as added, steerage was necessarily going to become more overt. Then, shifting the emphasis from finances to university government, there were already too many people, Dr. Parkes thought, who believed that universities were incapable of internal reform and that the UGC, composed largely of academics, had too cosy a relationship with the universities. 'I have been told by too many people recently that the time for peer judgment is past and that the universities should either be controlled directly by the government machine... or by a UGC composed of hard-headed businessmen or trade unionists... It is also their view that diktat should replace discussion.' That universities should somehow be run more like businesses is a theme which will recur. The universities were not invited to meet those who had the chairman's ear, nor told who they were, nor told in what ways they had allegedly failed the nation. Given the recent confrontations of the government with trade unions, and some of the less spectacular achievements of business, it is not clear what advantages were to be found in the presaged composition of such a new UGC. 'The greatest threat to the UK universities today', wrote Parkes in his letter to the CVCP, 'is *not* a financial one.' So the shift in emphasis would seem to be complete.

On 30th December 1980 the UGC sent a letter headed 'The Readjustment of the University System to changing resources and demands'. The Secretary of State had announced a reduction of £30M overall in the recurrent grant for 1981-82 – a cut of 3.5%. Taking into account the possible loss of income resulting from the new policy on overseas students' fees, 'the potential reduction for the academic year 1981-82 may be of the order of 5 to 6%'. That being the case, 'the Committee's legitimate role and duty to offer guidance... now assumes a new importance', it was said. The Committee saw its role 'not as a formal planning body, but as a body most able to assist institutions, severally and together, to react in ways helpful both for their own future and as part of a national system of higher education where restricted resources must be used effectively'. Universities could look forward to the grant letters the following spring to give guidance on home student numbers and how the UGC would be 'most able to assist'. Already the level funding proposed as recently as October 1980 was out of date.

Spring turned into summer before it was known what was happening. Some thought that the announcement was deliberately deferred in order to make a concerted reply more difficult. Perhaps it was because the UGC was grappling with the unthinkable, or perhaps it was to give the universities the summer vacation in which to identify the salient issues. The way it was done, with people going to the offices of the UGC to collect their letters created a sense of the theatrical. It was certainly not comedy: it simply added a touch of farce. 'It is probably difficult', the Vice-Chancellor said later, 'if you were not actually present, to take a full sense of how things really were in the period immediately following July 1981.'

Chapter 23

THE STORM

W hen the UGC letters of 1st July 1981 were first read – probably on the way home by those who had gone to London to collect them – there must have been some sharp drawing in of breath. A table of figures gave the recurrent grants for 1981-82, for 1982-83 (tentative), and 1983-84 (tentative). In every case the amounts went down. Ignoring the decimal places there was a pattern as follows: Oxford £31M, £30M, £29M. Cambridge £30M, £29M, £28M. Birmingham £27M, £26M, £25M. Bradford £11M, £10M, £9M. Leeds £30M, £29M, £28M. Liverpool £28M, £27M, £26M. Sheffield £23M, £22M, £21M. Surrey £10M, £9M, £8M. Most of the other universities fared slightly better. The dismay can be imagined of those reading the worst results: Aston £12M, £10M, £9M; Salford £11M, £9M, £8M; and Keele £7M, £6M, £5M. This, then, was the 3.5% cut from the government and the guidance and help from the UGC.

Combined with a falling grant was an enforced overall reduction in student numbers of just under 5%. This was despite peak demand for university places from 18-year olds. Most universities, but not all, were given a reduced student number target. Those which fared worst were Surrey with a reduction of 14%, Aston 20%, Salford 30%, and Keele 17%.

Amazement, dismay, surprise, anger, incomprehension and disbelief as butchery axed 12,500 students were the first reactions in the press. The UGC 'does the dirty work for the Secretary of State for Education' wrote the *Daily Mirror*. 'The North of England has been unfairly treated, while the south has got off relatively lightly', said the Vice-Chancellor of Bradford – a statement which a member of the UGC described as 'a flimsy argument'. 'There is no way of scotching the no doubt mischievous suggestion that the sad fate of Aston, Bradford, Keele, Salford and Stirling might have something to do with the absence of any of their representatives on the UGC', suggested *The Guardian*, while the *Daily Telegraph* put it another way: 'not one member of the UGC was educated at any of the eighteen campuses most viciously hammered last week; and only one member even worked at one of those (City) which suffered 'above average' cuts in resources'.

In short, by 1983-84 there would be, overall, 2.2% fewer science students and 8.4% fewer arts students, while universities would overall have 11-15% less income (depending on imponderables in the calculations), and 5% fewer places. 'Most universities are above all puzzled', wrote *New Scientist*. 'The UGC has given no official hint about the logic behind its decisions', and the government 'has inscrutably washed its hands of any responsibility for how the cuts are made. All this has left the universities mystified.' The total recurrent grants in 1983-84 (tentative) was going to be £808M. For less than another £15M the cuts in the eleven worst affected universities need have been no worse than 18%.

According to European Community statistics, in 1983-84 the U.K. had 5.5% of its students in third level full-time education. The European Community average was 8.5%, ranging from Germany with 12.5%, to Ireland with 5.2% (*Eurostat,* 25th edition). The U.K. was lagging behind Germany, Denmark, Belgium, the Netherlands, Italy, France, Spain, Greece and Portugal.

The Sunday Times asked: 'Are we destroying the seed corn?' and suggested that 'at least three universities could close within the decade – Salford, Stirling and Keele are already small and weak and have been cut so savagely that it is doubtful whether they can ever recover.' It quoted Dr. Parkes's reply when he was asked by a House of Commons subcommittee if he was saying that some universities might go bankrupt: 'I am saying precisely that, sir.' Certainly, just a few years later the CVCP wrote in a paper on 'The Future of the Universities' in January 1986, 'a glance at the standards set by our principal competitors shows that we have been losing ground not gaining it with every indication that our relative position is about to get worse'.

So what was the rationale? What were the UGC's ground rules? What criteria were used to select universities for major cuts? Dr. Parkes told the Parliamentary select committee that the UGC had considered students and subjects before institutions, unique factors, the variety of courses offered and the importance of the research being conducted. But *Keele's* unique factors did not stand the University in good stead. It was the only British university in which *all* graduates had studied some Arts/Social Science and some Science. *No-one* had refuted the philosophy on which Keele was founded. The course structure permitted an extraordinary efficiency in the variety of combinations of subjects which could be taken at honours level. Official reports *still* preached the desirability of interdisciplinary studies, most recently the *Chilver Report*, echoed by Lord Swann in his Inaugural Lecture to the Higher Education Foundation in March 1983. Regrettably, as David Harrison sometimes said at Keele, the preachers did not always practise what they preached to others – and no collection plate for Keele went round after the sermon.

For 'the system' generally, the UGC wrote, there was a slightly greater than average cut in numbers in the arts; a substantial reduction in numbers in social studies, in order to improve staff-student ratios and to strengthen research; while in the physical sciences numbers were expected to grow slightly by making fuller use of resources. What had the UGC written to Keele? Their last full-scale visit had been in 1976. Keele's grant was cut from £8.2M in 1980-81 to £7.04M in 1981-82, £6.23M in 1982-83 and £5.64M in 1983-84. How this related to 'the system' was not made clear. Indeed, from the criteria Dr. Parkes told the Parliamentary select committee, Keele might just as easily have fared amongst the best. The University's own draft budget for 1981-82, prepared before the UGC letter was received, showed that it needed £8.125M.

Specifically, the UGC 'wished to see' Russian-based studies discontinued, and they also 'endorsed' the University's proposals for a shift of emphasis from Social Studies towards the Arts. The UGC knew full well the University's wish and reasons for retaining Russian; and as for a shift in emphasis from Social Studies towards the Arts, Keele had made no such proposal to be endorsed! The Committee 'invited' the University to consider discontinuing Electronics as a single honours subject, and eliminating single honours in Mathematics, Physics and Biological Sciences, wanting a greater concentration on combined honours in the sciences. ('Single honours' at Keele generally meant simply the option, for those who were taking two science subjects at Principal level, to study just one subject in the final year if they wished to do so. The elimination of the option of taking single honours would have saved little effort or money.) Lastly, 'the Committee would, in any event, wish to have further consultation with the University on the possible phasing out of four-year courses'. It is those four-year courses – and that is to say the Foundation Year – which were specifically Keele's unique factor. Whatever it was that the UGC now diagnosed as in some way unsatisfactory at Keele must, of course, be viewed in the light that, as the Vice-Chancellor pointed out to them in May, 'the present mix of subjects has been built up over the last thirty years with your advice and help'.

The problem was where to find such substantial savings in such a short time: the financial year started on 1st August. Salaries and wages accounted for nearly three-quarters of the total recurrent expenditure. The cuts indicated a loss of 125 academic and academic-related jobs and 140 other jobs. At a meeting with the Vice-Chancellor, Parkes re-iterated that the UGC's approach had been entirely 'subject based' and that in no sense had the Committee ventured into value judgements on institutions as a whole; and the idea that the Committee had somehow ranked universities was press misrepresentation. Moreover, the UGC had not formed a view against four-year courses in principle but had raised the question in general terms in the light of decreased resources, not on educational grounds. With the exception of Russian, the absence of any UGC recommendation to discontinue any other subject area was a considered view taken in part to assist the comprehensive joint honours programme. The Vice-Chancellor's conclusion was that the criteria for the cuts remained resolutely undisclosed.

It now became apparent that the UGC's calculations of how many students read what subjects did not agree with the actual numbers! Although it is straightforward enough – the vast majority of students read two subjects at principal level – by the time the numbers of students reading what subjects were turned into official statistics, the results became seriously misleading. (The Universities Statistical Record is a national computerised record operated on the universities' behalf by the

Universities Central Council on Admissions (UCCA), to provide statistical material for the UGC and for the universities themselves.) The problem of the USR was how they chose to classify students reading two subjects from two different Boards of Studies, because the USR statistics were derived from UCCA course codes arranged in eighteen main subject groups. For joint honours courses in different Boards of Studies – by far the largest group of students at Keele – the location of the course in one of the eighteen groups was determined arbitrarily, with wide variations from year to year. But those statistics were almost irrelevant at Keele because the University planned and operated not on the basis of combinations but on individual departmental loads. In addition, Foundation Year students' course codes were unrelated to Foundation Year teaching, and subsidiary teaching was not connected with course codes anyway, so about 40% of the teaching load was not, and could not be, represented by the USR statistics. In other words, the statistics the UGC chose to use, and in which Keele had no say, did not add up. What the UGC was cutting, however, depended specifically on what they thought Keele had, and it became clear that what they thought Keele had was not the same as what Keele did have. 'We have been told by your officers', the Vice-Chancellor wrote on 13th October, 'that an erroneous comparison has been made, and all the evidence we have suggests that this error influenced an absolutely crucial decision about the total size of this University which now threatens the livelihood of some 250 Keele staff.' The Senior Tutor, Dr. Cohen, had been given to understand by UGC officers that the basis used was USR figures and not 'load', and, as the Vice-Chancellor later explained to the University Court, the UGC admitted they had overestimated the teaching load in the Social Sciences by 30%.

At a meeting on 22nd October the chairman explained away any possibility of there having been an error: although the UGC had expressed their decisions in *numbers*, Keele was told, the whole of the working had been done on *load* figures; they had understood, and they had *not* been working on a false base. They did not disclose the details of the calculations.

The UGC wished to see a greater reduction in the Social Sciences than in the Arts. One member commented that they thought Keele had wanted to reduce Social Sciences by 30% and that this fitted their global picture. As for the Foundation Year, when asked whether the savagery of the cut indicated a judgement on it, the chairman replied with an absolute 'no'. Almost in the same breath, however, the UGC would nevertheless wish to discuss further the question of four-year courses. Then, astonishingly, in order to keep the system afloat and bearing in mind the demographic figures (i.e. there was still a growing demand for places), Keele was told it should consider whether three-year courses should not be substituted for four-year courses in order to provide more graduates from the same number of students. (Did the country really have to look to Keele to abandon its Foundation Year in order to keep 'the system' afloat?) The chairman added that the Committee had declined to define different types of institution: they treated all universities as having the same general esteem and claim for funds. It must be said it did not look like that from Keele.

Although the chairman had advanced a favourable view of Keele's joint honours to the Vice-Chancellor personally in July, there did not seem to be wholehearted support from members of the Committee in October. Keele staff who met them thought they perceived prejudice against joint honours: that the chairman of the Arts Subcommittee regarded joint honours as inferior to single honours; that the chairman of the Social Studies Subcommittee seemed to favour only those joint honours within the social sciences (i.e. not combining with an arts or science subject); and that in the sciences, joint honours were not regarded as designed for those continuing at a professional level. Yet some of the most productive areas of scientific research have been precisely in those areas at the borders of different traditional disciplines. Lord Lindsay, one imagines, would have been sadly disappointed with them.

The University's Honorary Treasurer, Mr. A. G. Hayek, told them that the timescale was completely unrealistic. If nothing else, four-year courses constituted a longer commitment and hence needed a longer period in which to effect a run-down than three-year courses. He said to them that if Keele had been treated more nearly at the average in terms of both grant and student numbers, he could have envisaged some possibility of effecting orderly cuts, but that the timescale and the severity made the situation unworkable. *The chairman of the UGC agreed with him*. He offered as an excuse only that the Committee had been labouring that point with the authorities for some months. So which authorities had taken the decisions about Keele? Mr. Hayek said to the University Court in February 1982: 'I cannot believe even now, with all the evidence to the contrary, that the government is not contemplating some relief to allow for a more businesslike solution for Keele and for the universities in general'. Those were the words of a successful businessman about the government of the day, which was urging that universities should be run in a more businesslike fashion. Indeed, at about the same time, Sir Keith Joseph (the Secretary of State for Education and Science) said in a televised debate at Aston that there had been 'some arbitrary element' in where the UGC axe fell. But in May, lest it be thought that the government might do something to rectify this arbitrary element, he wrote to the Vice-Chancellors of Aston, Bradford, City and Keele to tell them: 'The one thing universities cannot do is to assume that the Government are bound to come to the rescue: the answer lies in the universities' own hands'. The universities had already learnt that the government was not inclined to come to their rescue; broadly speaking it was not true that the answer lay in their own hands, for the answer had been dictated to them.

With a UGC visit planned in May 1982 there was an opportunity to prepare a considered response. One of the papers for the meeting said that, as Lord Robbins had pointed out, the UGC did not have the professional resources at their disposal to make detailed academic judgements on individual departments or on the universities themselves. Yet they had chosen to make those judgements in order to make selective cuts. What criteria had they used? Given the difficulties in establishing the criteria, why did they not, as Lord Robbins suggested they should have done, make a cut across the board? They had taken on themselves a responsibility for which they were not equipped, and in the process had compounded the damage done by the government. It was difficult to see how in any sense they had fulfilled their function of protecting universities in general.

When the UGC visited Keele they displayed their skills in parrying questions, discussing general principles, showing mild surprise, expressing concern at misrepresentation, saying what they would like to see, and distancing themselves from the damage they were causing. The UGC was *not* trying to create different types of institutions, they insisted, and moreover the relative situations of July 1981 should not be regarded as fixed. (Indeed, it was only a few months earlier that the chairman had said they treated all universities as having the same general esteem and claim for funds.) Yet a few years later there was discussion of a 'premier league' and an 'élitist cadre' of universities which might be given extra funding to encourage them to become international centres of excellence – at the expense of the others (*The Times*, 29th July 1996). The Foundation Year was described by the chairman of the UGC, as a fascinating experiment but, he asked, could we still afford it? (Was that being disingenuous?) He went on to indicate that the Committee had not discussed the Foundation Year in detail (though presumably enough to have questioned its very existence). He also said that in an ideal world everyone would have it, but that it was not an ideal world; and that the UGC had no criticism of the Foundation Year as such. Then it was explained that it was not just the financial cost, but that in the context of opportunity for young people, every place in the Foundation Year was at a price of a place for additional students – but that this was a matter for Keele to decide. Keele was also told how important it was that the library stock should be protected as much as possible, and that they hoped its needs would be recognised. Dr. Parkes found that morale was high and that Keele seemed to have coped very well with the cuts; and he also commented that there was a very great research impetus on the science side which had been built up over the past two years.

The conclusions we must draw from the cuts and the comments of the UGC would seem to be that they regarded Keele highly, did not altogether understand the course structure or how the student load was calculated, and that it was unfortunate that, in accordance with the rules they had themselves drawn up, Keele happened to come off so badly that the chairman agreed they had forced on the University a situation which was unworkable. When it was evident that a very few universities would fare so much worse than all the others, might not the UGC have considered whether such small additional savings were worth so much damage, and have provided a safety net? At the end of May they announced some modifications in a limited number of cases to the proposed grants or student numbers. But there was no relief for Keele.

Were the cuts, then, as applied to Keele, on educational, financial, or political grounds? As far as the educational programme was concerned the UGC wished to assist Keele's comprehensive joint honours programme, and the chairman volunteered that in an ideal world everyone would have the Foundation Year – Keele's very cornerstone. Could it have been financial? If the cuts had been no worse than 18% for the eleven universities worst affected, the difference would have been £13.5M in 1983-84, and Keele's share would have been just over £1M (out of a total of £808M). So was the sacrifice at Keele really needed to keep 'the system' afloat? – about £1M from Keele, bearing in mind that in the next few years £80M was spent on universities to pay staff to leave. Dr. Parkes had already written in October 1980, before the cuts, that the greatest threat to the universities 'is *not* a financial one'; and three years later as outgoing chairman, in a speech to Vice-Chancellors at Imperial College, he said: 'The question must then arise – do we stagger on until the end of the century with a group of half-dead universities or do we kill off some in order to restore some liveliness to others? The killing off process need not necessarily imply closing down' [what, then?] 'although it might do in some cases. Whatever decisions are taken in this area, they are more likely to be informed by political considerations than by academic or economic arguments.' Giving its advice to the government on *A Strategy for Higher Education into the 1990s* in September 1984 the UGC said: 'Any policy that diminished the role and status of the universities would damage many aspects of our educational, cultural and industrial life.'

Questions remain, therefore: was the driving force political? who wrote the agenda? and who made the decisions?

One figure puts the whole of this episode of cuts into perspective. The government's plan was to reduce recurrent expenditure on universities in Great Britain from £879.62M in 1981-82 to £808.07M in 1983-84: a difference of £71,550,000.

Chapter 24

HOW TO SURVIVE

So what did Keele do next? The timing of the announcement had not helped: anticipating the cuts the Senate had considered whether to schedule extra meetings, devolve responsibility or defer final decisions. Seeing that a 10% cut, say, in a budget of £10M, if applied to 'pay' expenditure, would mean the loss of ninety salaried posts, deferring action – at least in the absence of a forewarning by the UGC – had been the only realistic choice. When the extent of the cuts was known, of course, there was a great deal of activity during the vacation. Granted the UGC's wish to avoid any leaks, nevertheless, for those very few universities which were going to fare so much worse than the others, might it not have been reasonable for the chairman to warn privately and in confidence those vice-chancellors, so that the machinery for urgent action could have been in place without delay?

Keele immediately refuted any suggestion of proposals for a shift in emphasis from social studies to arts. A working party on the Foundation Year soon reported on the implications of the possible phasing out of four-year courses. These were, briefly, that *with* the Foundation Year Keele would remain unique and distinctive, offering a very wide range of knowledge in the first year. It clearly satisfied a need and a demand, and graduates of the four-year courses were frequently commended by employers. The Foundation Year enabled students to make well-informed choices of principal subjects, especially in non-school subjects. It enhanced academic cohesion between departments. And, as it happened, the unit cost for the Foundation Year was lower than that of the principal years. The loss of the Foundation Year, however, would provide a simple solution at a stroke to the requirement to reduce student numbers. Some at Keele believed that was the UGC's objective. It would result in much easier control of the size and intake of departments. It would result in savings in administrative time and effort, both centrally and in departments. On the other hand, some departments which recruited well from the Foundation Year might not be able to make up their shortfall. Once discontinued the decision would, in practical terms, be irreversible. The working party recommended that the Foundation Year be retained, and also the existing balance between the four-year and the three-year intake.

The underlying reality was stark. It certainly *seemed* that Keele was being invited to 'conform' to the more usual pattern of universities. It certainly *seemed* as though the extra cuts for Keele matched the extra costs of the Foundation Year. It is certain that the phasing out of four-year courses would have dealt a severe blow to Lindsay's creation.

The Vice-Chancellor wrote a succession of papers formulating a way forward, on 'Academic Policy', 'Strategy for the early-eighties', 'Supplementary Papers', and 'Future Strategy'. Drastic cuts were staring the University in the face: loss of funding: loss of jobs. The severity meant that the problems could not be shuffled off on to a few Departments: none could hope or expect to escape. To this extent there was a reluctant willingness to accept the Vice-Chancellor's strategy. To Dr. Harrison's credit there was no 'bloodshed', no compulsory redundancies: the price to pay to achieve that was in drastic and random staff losses, especially amongst senior academics. But savings had to be made before any staff left – the financial year in which there was an immediate shortfall of well over £1M had started in August: so major cuts had to be made straight away in non-pay items which represented only a quarter of our total budget. This meant in particular library books, minor works and departmental consumable items. There is a limit, though, how much and how often these cuts can be made; and if there were to be a hard winter there would be a crippling fuel bill. Heat, light and power took almost 20% of all non-pay expenditure. The heart of the solution was going to be loss of jobs: in his paper on 'Academic Policy' the Vice-Chancellor was looking for sixty-five posts during the first year, with more to follow. A significant factor was the question of security of tenure of academic and academic-related staff. Any compulsory redundancies could be very expensive. On the other hand, if the government decided that university staffs were being obdurate, legislation could sweep away what had long been regarded as a bastion of academic freedom. Sir Keith Joseph was quite clear about that in a letter to the Vice-Chancellor of Surrey, reported to Keele's Senate in May 1982: 'If the staff will not agree to go and cannot, under existing statutes be dismissed, then the only way in which universities can avoid making potentially crippling economies in order to go on paying unnecessary academic salaries is to ask for their statutes to be amended. It has always seemed to me anomalous that universities that have allowed themselves to become dependent for the great bulk of their income upon the voting of funds by Parliament should have denied themselves the capacity to respond flexibly to changes in the level of that support. Academic tenure exists to protect freedom of thought and of expression – freedom in teaching and research. These are vital freedoms. But their cause is not served by the abuse of academic tenure to protect not freedom but individual jobs irrespective of the consequences to the universities, other members of staff and the students.' Many thought that the Secretary of State was drawing a very fine line. Moreover, the university charters which underpinned academic freedom necessarily had the approval of the Privy Council. Any support for staff from the CVCP was not forthcoming, for the Vice-Chancellors agreed that redundancy or compelling reasons of financial stringency should be a reason for terminating appointments.

The Joint Campus Trade Unions produced a strategy to try to delay redundancies, by favouring more cuts in non-pay items in order to gain time, and in the vain hope that public campaigning and parliamentary lobbying might win some concessions. Dr. Harrison's point was that he was already buying time with cuts of 37.5% in library books, departmental consumables, research materials and travel; an almost total cut in minor works and staff attendance at conferences; and a 32.5% cut in vacation grants for students. He was looking for staff losses of 19 out of 84 from the Humanities (22.6%), 26 out of 115 from the Social Sciences (22.6%), and 11 out of 84 from the Natural Sciences (13.1%), losses in academic-related staff of 22%, technicians 16%, secretaries 20%, and manual and ancillary staff 20%.

The UGC remained intransigent on Russian in its unwillingness to remove the threat of further financial penalties unless its advice was followed. Senate's Policy, Staffing and Development Committee considered that no case had been made to justify closing Russian, but under threat of penal consequences was prepared to recommend no further intake of students. It is not that the University was not 'free to continue with this course', the UGC wrote, 'despite the Committee's advice... but the Committee cannot guarantee in advance that it will be able to find the resources to support the course in future years'. Outside Keele there was widespread support for Russian, and suggestions that an unprincipled surrender to the unjustified demand of the UGC was no way to save Keele. The Senate shared this more robust view and did not accept its committee's recommendation to stop Russian.

In January 1982, despite the adverse publicity relating to the cuts, student applications to Keele were up by 12.6% against a national increase of 3.6%; and research income for 1980-81 (i.e. before the cuts) as a percentage of total University income was at its highest since 1968-69. In addition, the Department of Adult Education saw its highest ever recruitment into sustained courses at Keele. It was also a very encouraging gesture that the Development Projects Committee was about to recommend building research units both at the hospital and on the campus.

For its part, the UGC offered help in 'restructuring'. The government made an extra £50M available to universities for 1982-83 to pay people to go. At the end of 1982 the UGC estimated that the total cost of compensation to academic staff would be £90-100M. In the event, various schemes to encourage resignations continued long after the present round of cuts. The Public Accounts Committee said that a greater measure of flexibility was desirable in future contracts – in other words, security of tenure now had a short future. The UGC was considering what advice they should give on the matter, presumably on the same grounds as they had administered the cuts, that universities would be safer in their hands.

Within less than a year the cuts were well underway – non-academic staff by 20%, academic-related by 20%, and academic by 5% with another 5% in train – but it was at a heavy financial cost on reserves paying for the voluntary redundancy schemes to encourage resignations. It took the government seven months to make funds available for the cuts they had imposed. Losses included eight professors and the Registrar. The Vice-Chancellor's strategy still needed another ten staff from the Humanities and fourteen from the Social Sciences. As the losses were proportionately greater than the decline in student numbers, so the teaching load for those who remained grew heavier. What started as measures 'for present planning purposes' became 'an accepted academic shape'. The haemorrhaging of the professoriate continued. In 1982 and 1983 Goldman (American Studies), Millar (Chemistry), Charlton (Classics), MacKay (Communication), Roberts (English), Broome (French), Rolo (History), Kay (Law), Hutchinson (Postgraduate Medicine), Hunter (Psychology), Lampert (Russian), and Stevenson (Social Work) all went. By January 1985 there was likely to be only one professor left in the Humanities. On the non-pay front, no British university library was on record as having suffered as severe a cut as Keele. But it was not nearly enough.

While the cuts were being put into effect, the UGC explained in February 1983 what their underlying philosophy had been: they had decided on clear targets for student numbers because they did not wish to see the quality of education available to students deteriorate too markedly; and they wanted staff to have time to sustain research and scholarship. (These views were clearly more appropriate for universities which had suffered less than Keele.) They were aware of the anomaly whereby fee income was not cash limited, and so imposed a limit on numbers: universities which took too many (i.e. more than the UGC target) were thought to be 'demonstrating a readiness to devote a greater proportion of their recurrent grant to teaching and a smaller proportion to research and scholarship than the Committee had in mind'. It was a far cry from Sir John Habukkuk's view in 1976.

Yet, where it could, Keele still flourished, and support for and interest in the University was manifest in a number of different areas. There was an anonymous gift of £10,000 and an interest-free loan of £17,500 for an electron microscope in Biological Sciences. The W. E. Dunn Unit developed a 'pulsing' pump which mimicked the operation of the heart, and this was a great advance on 'roller' pumps with which, in heart surgery, blood did not reach all parts of the body at an even rate. The Stoke-on-Trent Marathon Club made the medical projects of the Development Projects Committee a prime candidate for sponsorship funds and raised thousands of pounds – £8,300 in 1982 and £11,000 in 1983. The Computer Centre and the Observatory computerised a telescope to locate and track very faint objects – a modification which had cost many thousands of pounds in Australia but which, in the tradition of the Keele Observatory, was achieved for a very modest few hundred pounds. There were grants from the Department of the Environment to Geography to evaluate factors affecting the strength of sea floor sediments for oil drilling rig operations; and from the National Coal Board to Geology for surveys in the vicinity of the M6/M62 interchange to determine the position of a fault.

Concerts were reorganised in the face of declining audiences, assisted by sponsorship, including support from Hawthorns Hall for a 'cello recital by Tim Hugh before he had embarked on his international solo career. The Fourth Delius Festival was staged at Keele, directed by Dr. Philip Jones of the Music Department. Altogether about 10% of the student population was involved in the Festival in one way or another. The climax was the first performance in this district of *A Mass of Life* –

even though the North Staffordshire District Choral Society had taken part in its first performance in London in 1909. The like of this Festival had not been seen here before and, wrote the *Sentinel*, 'is scarcely likely to be seen again'. A few years later the unfinished score of 'American Rhapsody' was completed and edited by Philip Jones, and was performed by the Royal Philharmonic Orchestra in the Royal Festival Hall. It was later recorded on CD. In 1984 the fiftieth anniversary of the deaths of Elgar, Delius and Holst provided the inspiration for Keele Concerts Society's 'British Music Week', including also music by Havergal Brian and Vaughan Williams.

The Athletic Union won the men's Unicorn Trophy at Crystal Palace. The Drama Society revived open air Shakespeare with *Twelfth Night* in 1981 and *A Midsummer Night's Dream* in 1982. David Pownall's *Master Class* about Stalin's persecution of Soviet musicians was reviewed in *The Times* in January 1983, and opened at the Old Vic a year later. Major public lectures continued to be staged here. The second David Bruce Memorial Lecture was given by the Rt. Hon. Edward Heath in November 1982 on 'An Atlantic Approach to North-South Relations' (postponed from May because of an Emergency Debate in the House of Commons on the Falklands crisis).

There were more gifts and prizes for students: the Paul Rolo award; the Ian Harmer prize in memory of a student who died during his second Principal year; the Alan Walton Memorial Prize in Geography; and the Katy Muir Memorial Fund to help students in need. By the early 1980s, prizes donated by staff or in memory of staff comprised the Elsie Beaver Prize in Geography, the Burnaby Memorial Prize in Geology, the Sheila Carson Memorial Prize in Philosophy, the Marjorie Cruickshank Prizes in Education, the Katia Lampert Memorial Bursary, the Hugh Leech Travelling Scholarship, the Jim Roberts Memorial Prize, and the Springall Prize in Chemistry. Sadly, more of the founding staff died – Professors Springall, Charlton and Teale, and Miss Mary Glover. Graduates came back to visit: C. R. Bell as an external examiner in Sociology and Social Anthropology; Mrs. Nwanyidirim K. Asinobi, now a Federal Minister of State in Nigeria; and a group from Whitehall for a politics seminar – Bill Proctor, a Clerk in the House of Commons; and David Edmonds and Eric Sorensen, both of whom were working for Mr. Heseltine.

There were more trees on the campus. A Countryside Commission grant plus donations from staff provided trees to commemorate the Queen Mother's 80th birthday. Hawthorns Hall Council and students provided some trees at the Hawthorns. The woodland plantation on the ridge above Springpool and Horwood was named 'Stacey's Plantation' in appreciation of Tom Stacey's contribution to the campus landscape in his twenty-seven years as Grounds Superintendent. Donations from the Police Angling Club supplemented other tree planting programmes. Keele Parish Council contributed to the cost of trees at the rear of the Sports Pavilion. Professor MacKay gave the Cedars of Lebanon between the Walter Moberly Hall and the Tawney Building; the hybrid hawthorn trees along the edge of the main road in the triangle at the end of Keele Drive were planted as a memorial to Margaret Whieldon, and nearby is a fern leaved beech in memory of Dr. Ron Evans of the Biology Department. A group of Cedars of Lebanon on Keele Hall lawn beyond the fountain, replacing some older trees, commemorate Cordelia Goodway, an early graduate. Professor Rolo's retirement was marked by a Giant Redwood at the Hawthorns from the members of the International Relations Department.

There were 34% more applicants for October 1982 than there had been three years earlier, so it would seem Keele was poised to be buoyant. It also capitalised on the assets of its courses and its campus to become one of the first universities to make a video film to aid recruitment – 'Keele for Choice'. For this we called on the expertise and goodwill of a number of graduates – Ray Johnson who directed it, Bill Proctor at the House of Commons, Geoffrey Richards at Shell, David Pownall the playwright, Keith Clements at the BBC, and Sam Nolutshungu at Manchester University. However, the UGC then required a 12% drop in student intake in order to meet their targets. Thereby hangs a tale of Keele being fined by the UGC. The year 1982-83 started with serious staff losses, an alarming depletion of revenues and a further drastic cut in non-pay expenditure. In addition there was another twist of the financial screw: the government halved students' tuition fees, which were generally paid by the Local Education Authorities and were received independently of the UGC recurrent grant. They were £798 in 1980-81, £900 in 1981-82, but then only £480 in 1982-83, thereby reducing such small leeway as that independent source of income permitted. It was a measure strangely at variance with the criticism levelled against universities by Sir Keith Joseph that they 'should have denied themselves the capacity to respond flexibly to changes in the level of [financial] support'. The UGC gave universities some advice: they hoped they would bear in mind the need for sufficient support staff for social studies departments; and that forward planning would pay particular attention to those non-pay areas important for the continued health of research and teaching; and the importance of expenditure on the maintenance of premises. 'In some instances', they said, 'there is evidence that this is substantially below what is needed.' But such advice was largely irrelevant in Keele's circumstances of struggling to break even. It seemed that the UGC had combined the art of self-fulfilling prophecies with surprise at the consequences of what they had done. A helping hand to assist the forward planning about which the UGC was expressing concern was not forthcoming. It all depended on arithmetic again – how they counted our numbers.

In July 1981 Keele had been told what its numbers were to be for 1984-85. In December 1982, 'Target failures get two weeks to toe the line', as the *THES* put it. In the UGC's view Keele and a number of other universities had admitted too many students: the UGC had never said what interim numbers were expected but somehow Keele had exceeded their unstated target. Keele's mix of three-year and four-year courses made the calculations more complicated than elsewhere, but in any case the University claimed it was on course to meet the required target. Seven universities – Hull, Dundee, Heriot-Watt, Swansea, Essex, Cardiff and Keele were 'fined' a total of a quarter of a million pounds. (Salford and Bradford were threatened but then reprieved.) Keele's 'fine' was £20,000. The University told the UGC what its projections were, and asked on what grounds they did not agree, especially as no number had been given against which to measure any alleged overshoot of what the UGC called 'an evident progression' to 1984-85. On this occasion the chairman replied: 'Without wanting to get involved in detailed statistical aspects I do not think the figures you have provided for the next three years invalidate the Committee's view that admissions in 1982-83 did not represent 'an evident progression' towards the target.' The Vice-Chancellor replied that he doubted whether the Committee had a case which would stand up to numerical scrutiny. (An officer of the UGC expressed surprise at a meeting of University Finance Officers that letters from the UGC were accorded the sort of textual analysis normally reserved for the classics.) The whole episode generated ill-will out of all proportion to any saving. *The Guardian* reported that the fines were nominal, designed to make universities realise that targets would be enforced more vigorously the following year and so suggesting there would now be a policy of fines. Keele could ill afford the loss of £20,000 especially at a time when its Development Trust was seeking funds for medical research projects. As the Vice-Chancellor of Hull reminded them, the UGC had told a House of Commons Select Committee in 1981 that a university which exceeded its numbers would not be penalised unless students were suffering as a result.

Scarcely was the ink dry on the letters in June 1983 than there was an amazing volte-face in September. The reduction in the number of university students had (not surprisingly) produced an increase in applications to polytechnics, and the government decided to reduce that number. But by so doing, the total number to be admitted into higher education in October 1984 was going to be below what the DES called the 'qualified demand projection'. Would the universities therefore please resume some of the burden which was being shed by the polytechnics? – i.e. admit additional students in 1984 and 1985 only (to start with); but the government was *not* proposing to make any additional funds available except the fee income (the level of which the government had recently reduced). Moreover, the UGC said the matter was urgent.

In the summer of 1983, changes in public funding by the Chancellor of the Exchequer, plus 'revised pay assumptions' for 1984, reduced Keele's grant by £68,000. Then in March 1984 it was announced that the grant for 1984-85 would be £8.01M – i.e. £210,000 less than already announced earlier, because the government was assuming 'a measure of increased economy in expenditure'. The advice accompanying this announcement was that all universities should seek to preserve the health of both research and teaching. When the UGC sought universities' views with a questionnaire called 'Development of a Strategy for Higher Education', room for manoeuvre was limited by the policy set out by the Secretary of State in a letter of 1st September 1983 to the chairman of the UGC. Universities should be less dependent on public funds, he repeated, and he wrote of the need for fundamental changes, for greater differentiation between institutions, for a further shift towards technological, scientific and engineering courses and to other 'vocationally relevant' forms of study, and then greater selectivity in research funding. Amongst the replies was the succinct comment by St. John's College, Oxford, that the title and the claim that it invited open debate was false because the options for discussion were already limited by the stated premises.

A visit to Keele by the UGC Social Studies Subcommittee in November 1983 found that 'they had not sensed any fall in morale of the kind they had observed in some other universities'; and they were aware of the pressures on the library and hoped more resources would be made available. Above all they found the students 'delightful, articulate and extremely loyal to the University – but not slavishly loyal'. A few months later the UGC Biological Sciences Subcommittee was impressed by the changes and improvements since their previous visit in 1976, the spirit and enthusiasm of several younger staff, the initiatives of individuals and the vibrancy of research in certain areas.

The University was clear in its determination to hold fast that which is good, and re-affirmed the structure of tutorial teaching: groups of four (maximum six) for principal subjects; a maximum of six for subsidiary subjects; and eight (maximum ten) for Foundation Year sessional subjects. A paper by the Vice-Chancellor on 'Future Strategy' reviewed what had been achieved and posed questions which now needed answers. The strategy so far had been to reshape the University with reference to UGC advice and with voluntary staff reductions. Were it not for further cuts in funding Keele would have been close to break-even for 1984-85, instead of which there was still over £500,000 to find. The nettle to be grasped was the loss of at least twenty more academic posts. (Fifty or so posts had already been lost out of 282.) Otherwise the savings so far and the efforts to generate additional income would be wasted, and the remaining reserves would be quickly dissipated: hence there was the need to consider phasing out courses and merging or closing departments. It was a question of how many distinct activities the University could sustain. If the Senate was convinced they were necessary for Keele's survival, it must consider the academic balance of the University, its reputation, comparable courses elsewhere, and any special cost considerations. Prior questions were: was a radical approach required? what were the criteria for closing a course or a department? and then, which courses or departments should be considered for closure? Policy, Staffing and Development Committee accepted in May that a radical approach was required. There was still security of tenure for staff, but the Secretary of State was planning to proceed with a plan to appoint commissioners to amend university charters. In the event he did not intend to alter existing contractual rights but to limit tenure in future contracts.

The President of the Keele Association of University Teachers, Dr. David Vincent (History), challenged what he regarded as the apocalyptic tone of recent statements, claiming that the University was not on the edge of a financial precipice but just some way from the end of the wearisome journey towards stability and re-expansion. He saw the Vice-Chancellor's strategy as little more than an applied staffing formula and an attempt to sacrifice four departments in a last ditch effort to restore solvency. However, the Senate knew that the University Council had to be satisfied with their response – otherwise the Council would be likely to impose further restraints without delay. The Council was indeed determined to fulfil its constitutional role and duty. The Finance Committee had recommended to Council in June 1984 that the Senate be directed to present proposals in July to reduce recurrent academic expenditure by £600,000, including the loss of twenty posts. (The Council amended 'directed' to 'asked', but the weight of the request was much the same.) The Vice-Chancellor was able to satisfy Council in June that his strategy paper had been accepted by Policy, Staffing and Development Committee and would now go to the Senate. The timescale was pressing. In a five-hour meeting the Senate accepted the Vice-Chancellor's paper in principle but rejected his proposed economy package. The concern of the Finance Committee was that only if the academic direction of the University was made clear within the immediate future would those staff adversely affected be able to take advantage of the UGC's compensation scheme (for which time was running out). Two more papers by the Vice-Chancellor proposed ways of saving over £600,000, and included proposals for a Department of European Studies (subsuming French, German and Russian); reviewing Sociology and Social Anthropology and Social Work; reviewing the relationship between International Relations and Politics; the possibility of not admitting any more students to Classics or Applied Statistics and Operational Research; reviewing courses in Music and Philosophy; and further rationalisation of some subsidiary courses. This was intended to lead to a saving of twenty more academic posts, five more academic-related posts, and four more technicians (to give savings of over £450,000), with most of the other savings to be found from 'organisational changes' in departmental mergers and closures, and reductions in 'unit costs' in the Health Service and Wardens. Not enough had happened to satisfy the Council by the time it met in July. The Senate's response was felt to be insufficiently detailed, particularly in terms of timescale, so the Council reduced the non-pay budget provision by a further £175,000 out of £674,000. This sum would be released on the recommendation of the Finance Committee in the light of actual savings made, mostly on the pay budget.

Earlier, Dr. Harrison had announced his departure from Keele to become Vice-Chancellor of Exeter University. These proposals were his parting shot at the end of a term of office dominated and dogged by the cuts of July 1981. The news that the Vice-Chancellor was leaving came as something of a shock at Keele: never before had a Vice-Chancellor or Principal left to go elsewhere, and at this particular time staff were still reeling from the aftershocks of 1981. Yet, as Ngaio Crequer wrote in the *THES* in May 1984: 'Imagine you could start from scratch and create a university with the diversity and breadth that now seems everyone's goal. One that gives a broader education, allowing students to postpone crucial decisions on choice of subject, yet not at the expense of specialisation later on. One that creates rounded citizens, with all students having to do some arts and some science for at least a year. In fact, that university – Keele – already exists... the UGC cannot grasp its complexity... though diversity is the new god, they suffer for it.' The article went on to say that though Keele was very badly hit in 1981, it managed to make difficult decisions and plan a new future while still keeping morale high, and maintaining a collective spirit and resolve. Keele had lost 13% of its academic staff since 1980. Aston, Bradford and Salford had fared worse; Hull lost 12% and Exeter 11%. Altogether thirteen out of thirty-six institutions in England had lost staff. The *THES* concluded that the new Vice-Chancellor would find Keele in very good heart. It can be seen that the springboard for renewed growth was already in place.

The account of Dr. Harrison's real achievement is to be found in a report to the UGC in November 1985, after he had left, which said: 'it should be stressed that despite the severity of the 1981 cuts the University has virtually achieved financial equilibrium in 1984-85 and would be in equilibrium in the coming years were it not for the further, annual, erosion of the University's grant in real terms. Whilst this erosion is affecting all universities, this University's success in coping with the original severe cut should be recognised.'

David Harrison was awarded the CBE in 1990. In 1994 he returned to Cambridge as Master of Selwyn College, and in 1997 he received a knighthood for his services to education and nuclear safety.

The Conference Hall, Students' Union and the Chapel, September 1958

HM Queen Elizabeth the Queen Mother, HRH Princess Margaret and Mr. Antony Armstrong-Jones with Colin Thomas and Jocelyn Ryder-Smith (President and Vice-President of the Students' Union) on the occassion of laying the foundation stone of the Students' Union building on 2nd May 1961. (The foundation stone with its inscription has since been obscured by an addition to the building.)

The new Chapel. Note that the roundabout is there.

The Dandelion Clock by Jack Walden in Horwood Hall, 1967

Left: Keele Drive in Spring, and centre left: The Dell, which was dedicated as a permanent memorial to Sir George Barnes. Both are reminders of his untiring efforts to enhance the beauty of the campus.

Centre right: Clock House Drive.

Right: Autumn colour in Lindsay Hall.

'Action for a Free University' takes over the Registry, 1968

Doomed huts, 1977

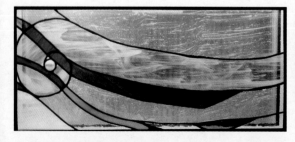

Right: Keele Winter 1981-82

Centre: Sports Centre, 1968

Bottom: The Four Elements
left to right:
Air has qualities cold and dry
Fire has qualities dry and hot
Earth has qualities hot and moist
Water has qualities moist and cold
(Stained glass panels in the
Department of Chemistry
by Miho Suganami.)

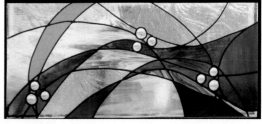

Left: Dr. Mary Campion planting beech trees to form an avenue between the Chapel and the Chancellor's Building, which she gave to the University on her retirement in 1990.

Below: The oak tree at the bottom of the Covert, 1973.

The mid-1960s,

and twenty years later.

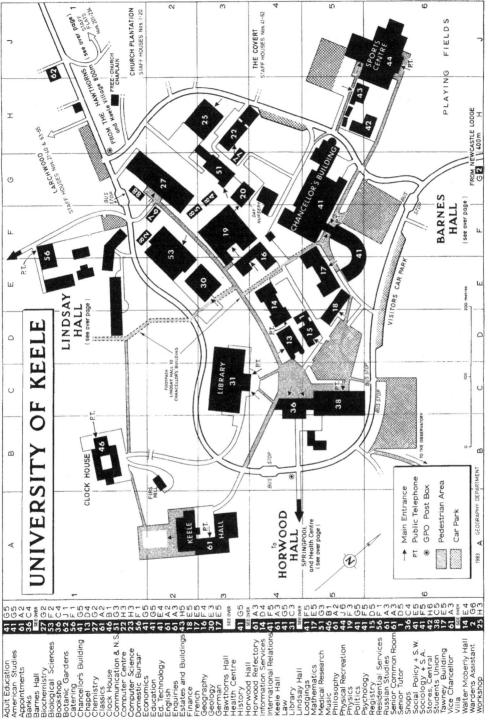

UNIVERSITY OF KEELE

from CALENDAR 1984-85

'I cannot understand how any government can fail to
make education its top priority, given what is at stake for
our children and the country.'
(Sir Claus Moser)

Chapter 25

THE AFTERMATH

Those universities which were particularly hard hit in July 1981 and onwards suffered the sort of economic recession which wiped out parts of British industry. That they continued with such determination is a mark of their flexibility and the resolve of their governing bodies. It was suggested that universities ought somehow now to be run more like commerce and industry, even though a report by the CVCP to the UGC in 1978 (on *Industrial Democracy*) had pointed out: 'While universities have management functions similar to any other employer, their main responsibility is to further higher education.' It is a measure of changing attitudes to, and perceptions of universities, that such a sentence should ever have needed to be penned, especially by the CVCP to the UGC. Comparing the ancient standing and centuries of experience of our oldest universities with the recent development and chequered progress of much of industry and commerce, some wondered whether perhaps the universities might not instead have offered advice to industry. The Midland Bank, for example, was about to make a loss of £505M in one year – the largest loss so far by a British quoted company. But attitudes and perceptions were changing, and measurement was in terms of input and output and then throughput, like industrial products. There was also a trend, already noted, by which people were being de-personalised by language. 'Universities' became the 'university system'; 'administrators' became 'administrations'; and to 'tackle the problem' expressed an intention to abolish something, or someone, inconvenient.

The aftermath of the storm was a new and detailed blueprint for the way universities were to be run. This was a *Report of the Steering Committee for Efficiency Studies in Universities*, set up by the CVCP under the chairmanship of Sir Alex Jarratt, Chancellor of the University of Birmingham. Recommendations were made on the way universities should conduct their affairs, and changes in the committee structure at Keele were quickly implemented. In this enthusiasm I heard it said: 'Let's shake up the administration and see what happens.' The spirit of the late-1980s was more abrasive than earlier, and Keele's new Vice-Chancellor, Brian Fender did not disdain to shout and bang on the table. The growing pressures of the 1990s displaced some of the common courtesies – a few words on personal matters, the sending of letters of condolence. The art of 'administration', a profession dating back to Pepys at the Admiralty, was displaced by a higher profile, more interventionist 'management'. Keele appointed Directors – of Administration, Academic Affairs, and Research Development and Business Affairs, 'to reflect', according to the Annual Report, 'a positive view in the role of university management'; and later Directors of Finance, and Personnel. (Directors were not, of course, answerable to shareholders as in companies.) Some regarded the changes in titles as signalling a change in attitudes to work and to other people.

The compelling conditions of pay settlements made these changes the accepted wisdom of a new reformation. Financial considerations still dictated savings on the pay budget – i.e. staff reductions and early retirements. Some of those who could retire early were pleased to go, in contrast to the 1960s when members of staff coming up to retirement had been reluctant to leave. The true cost of continued savings was not only that classes grew larger and individual attention became less, but that the experience of senior dons – the academic assets – was lost not only to generations of students, but to younger staff coming into the profession.

I have detailed the suffering: what had been achieved? An article on universities in *Management Today* (October 1984) said that it was as if universities had been punished for an assumed profligacy when they had, in fact, brought down the unit of resource per student by 13% over ten years; and furthermore that the DES had stated that the cuts had saved nothing! The DES put the failure down to inflation, but *Management Today* believed that lack of forethought and ignorance of educational realities were more credible explanations, and rehearsed the cost: £100M to prevent universities from going bankrupt, plus £20M to the public sector to cope with the extra numbers of students going to polytechnics. All this stemmed from the government's belief in the need to reduce public expenditure on universities. After 'rationalisation' and 'restructuring', 'efficiency' became the new byword and the guiding principle which set the tone. If government measures so far had not proved effective enough, then more direction rather than less was thought to be the answer. 'By increasing efficiency and trimming costs, universities are being encouraged to offer courses as cheaply as possible in order to attract more students' (*The Sunday Times*, 10th June 1990).

Suppose – just for a moment – that Keele had somehow had the freedom (that autonomy to which lip service was still paid) *not* to adopt all of the procrustean reforms dictated by various reports and enforced by threats of withholding money. Would Keele necessarily have finished worse off? Indeed, might not some of the difficulties acknowledged later have been averted? Did the efficiency measures of the Jarratt Report, for example, fit Keele better than its own evolved management structure – which had weathered a disastrous financial storm and almost achieved equilibrium by the time David Harrison left? Would his successor have needed to say to the Council: 'I am conscious that as the University expands it is difficult for Council (and to a lesser extent Senate) to keep a full picture of developments' (October 1992)? That these bodies, responsible for all the crucial decisions, now found it difficult to keep a full picture might have been avoided had they continued to meet monthly rather than termly, and had those monthly Senate meetings, which sometimes lasted five hours, not given way to termly meetings lasting two hours or so.

And with the diminution of widespread staff involvement in committees, staff felt unduly excluded from the decision-making process. The new Vice-Chancellor also reduced the number of meetings of the Assembly – the termly meeting at which the Vice-Chancellor addressed and could be questioned by all members of the academic staff. Add to that the virtual demise of the Senior Common Room as a meeting place and the disappearance of high table for lunch (high table dinner had already gone in the 1970s), and you have a loss of the cohesion formed by the common interest and widespread discussion which had characterised Keele for twenty-five years. There was sometimes a certain defensiveness, too, and I was once greeted with the words: 'There are some good things going on as well' (May 1993).

Perhaps these points cannot be sustained in the face of changes which were un-stoppable. Jarratt was, in a sense, the logical outcome of the 1981 cuts and was the new blueprint we had to follow. What had appeared to be – and what at times had been – a more leisured ethos of university life (and not forgetting the injunction in *Ecclesiasticus*) was swept away to become a memory of the past. We were also a long way away from the attitude of the late-60s and early-70s when a young Keele revolutionary said to me: 'This is a fun place, man.' It was not a question of what was better, but what was seen to be more cost-effective. Is it that old men forget? or is it that like Peter Pan, those who preferred the old ways were simply refusing to grow up? No university could afford the luxury of staying as it was, least of all Keele. But those who were overtaken by the rush of events are entitled to ask what had happened to the spirit of hope and to the philosophy which had flourished and sustained the founding of Keele, even in the prolonged austerity of the post-war years. It can only be a pipe dream to muse on what might have been achieved by spending the money used for running down universities on building them up instead. Well might Mr. Pickwick ruminate on the strange mutability of human affairs. 'Pro-ductivity', that touchstone for pay rises in industry, was now demanded in univer-sities too, but without the pay attached: each academic was teaching twelve students in the mid-90s, as against nine in 1980 and five in 1970.

I have taxed the reader's patience with a lot of detail in order to show how serious was the assault on Keele, and how Keele had to navigate uncharted waters. These few years since 1981 were the most significant in the University's history since Lindsay had achieved the unthinkable in the years up to 1950. The price we had to pay was a very heavy one but, even if it was not obviously apparent at the time when Brian Fender came, the tide had already turned and Keele was poised for recovery.

The Keele which Brian Fender left in 1995 must be compared with what he found in 1985; and harking back a further ten years serves to illustrate how drastic were the changes, not least in attitudes and appearances. Universities have become cor-porate enterprises with images and glossy reports, and Keele has had to become an academic business rather than an academic community. The preferred title is 'Keele University' instead of 'University of Keele', and a new logo was commissioned to coincide with the fortieth anniversary. 'We are currently developing a strategy', the

Vice-Chancellor wrote to all members of staff in 1991, 'whose implementation will do much to ensure that Keele does project an appropriate and consistent image... the crest is no longer to be used as a substitute for the University logo.' Another new logo in 1997 seemed to provoke more puzzlement then enlightenment when it was brought into use.

There was a great sense of relief when the Income and Expenditure account eventually turned into profit. It was hard pounding and the nearest run thing. It is clear that by the time Brian Fender left Keele he had infused the University with bustle and activity and set it firmly on the path to growth. 'I will be very sorry to leave Keele', he said. 'It's a university with an exciting future.' He left to become the Chief Executive of the Higher Education Funding Council for England. Just before that he had been elected chairman of the CVCP, though he did not take up the position. David Harrison, his predecessor as Vice-Chancellor, was chairman of the CVCP for 1991-93.

Chapter 26

BLUEPRINT FOR CHANGE

Following the departure of David Harrison, Professor Donald Thompson, Professor of Law since 1964, became Acting Vice-Chancellor for five months from October 1984. Council released money it was withholding, and proposals put forward by Professor Thompson muted the gloom-mongerers, repaired some of the damage, and ensured that the momentum for recovery was sustained. There was some restructuring, mostly in modern languages and in sociology and social work, and there were new appointments in modern languages, electronics, management science and biological sciences. Keele's research income in 1984 rose by a dramatic 30%, setting an important trend for the following years. The emphasis was going to be on the sciences, which are generally in a better position to seek substantial research funding than the humanities and social sciences but, as Professor Thompson warned at a degree congregation in December 1984, the wisdom and perception to know what to do with science and technology is not limited to scientists and technologists. Indeed, he was echoing Lord Lindsay's warnings before Keele was founded. And he repeated to the University Court his corrective view that it was wrong to associate the quality of the intellectual life of a university in terms of the research income it generated.

How was the government going to achieve its goals of more widespread, more efficient and more cost effective (i.e. cheaper) higher education? The blueprint for universities' future was being prepared and the chain of command was being strengthened, namely Government – Department of Education and Science (which was to change its name to Department *for* Education) – UGC (which was to be subsumed in the Higher Education Funding Council for England) – CVCP. Vice-Chancellors did not necessarily concur that they were part of the enforcing mechanism, and a flurry of papers by the CVCP in 1985 on 'The External Examiner system', 'Academic appeals procedures at postgraduate research degree level' and 'Universities' internal procedures for maintaining and monitoring academic standards' might be seen as a restatement of their independent position. In January 1986 the CVCP voiced its exasperation, saying that the government was asking for more and more and thinking it could provide less and less without adulterating the quality of what was produced.

The UGC was receiving clearer indications from Ministers, and the Chairman of the UGC was formally a Second Permanent Secretary in the Department of Education and Science. Already in August 1984 the UGC set out its policy in *A Strategy for*

Higher Education into the 1990s: 'We expect to give more advice to universities than in the past'; 'we shall discriminate in favour of universities which tackle the problem of small departments'; 'universities need to acquire what they now lack: a deliberate bias towards change'; 'we believe that every university should examine its machinery of government to ensure that its decision-making process is effective'. Overall, the UGC was 'vitally concerned to safeguard the academic freedom of universities and individuals. Indeed, the protection of university institutions from undue political intervention is the very justification for our existence as a Committee' (Chairman of the UGC to the Secretary of State, January 1985).

The *Strategy* paper was in fact a strong plea to the government for additional resources. The UGC's aim in 1981, they said, had been to minimise the damage to the system, but nevertheless great harm had been done and confidence in the government had been shaken. They now urged the government not to replace them with a representative body which, they said, would be ill-constituted to handle issues of selectivity and would be seen as a pressure group whose views would be discounted. It sounds as though the UGC's position was becoming uncomfortable. What came from the government was more of the same. Funding for universities for 1985-86 was going to be £7M less than had been previously announced. 'If anything', the UGC wrote to say, 'the universities' difficulties will increase', as they faced an average annual decline of 2% in UGC grants. For its part, the DES told the UGC that the government welcomed their commitment to the rationalisation of small departments. As for students, a policy of loans instead of grants was suggested: its implementation would just be a matter of time.

At about the same time, the UGC and the National Advisory Body for Public Sector Higher Education said they believed that the objectives of the Robbins Report of 1963 formed 'an appropriate basis for considering the present and future role of higher education in our society', and re-stated Robbins thus: 'courses of higher education should be available for all those who are able to benefit from them and who wish to do so.' Hence the government's need for cost-effective efficiency. Their joint statement added that 'Robbins's final objective – the transmission of a common culture and common standards of citizenship... is even more relevant in today's multi-cultural society than it was twenty years ago.' No university had propounded as its philosophy this objective more explicitly than Keele, and no university had broken as much new ground as Keele did in its affirmation – long before Robbins – of those beliefs.

In March 1985 the new Vice-Chancellor took over. Dr. Brian Fender, 50, came to Keele from the Institut Max von Laue – Paul Langevin (ILL) in Grenoble, a world centre for the use of neutrons in the study of a wide range of biological, chemical and physical systems, funded jointly by France, Germany and the U.K. A graduate of Imperial College, London, he had gone to Oxford in 1963 as lecturer in inorganic chemistry and Fellow of St. Catherine's College, where he was also Senior Tutor. He went to Grenoble in 1973, and was Director from 1982. He was awarded the CMG in 1985, and was appointed a member of the Science and Engineering Research Council and chairman of its Science Board. At Keele he had the title of Professor bestowed on him for the tenure of his appointment. Vigorous in leadership and engaging in conversation, one of his claims was that he was good with people. He was readily accessible, especially to heads of departments, and he took an active interest in academic appointments. He was inspirational and positive to some: to others, brusque. He was a 'shaper' of events: challenging and dynamic, thriving on pressure, and with the drive to overcome obstacles. Whereas David Harrison's roots had gone back to the past and his instinct was for consensus, Brian Fender showed impatience with what had gone before and he was a proponent for strong central leadership and change. He quickly got to know most members of staff by name, and it seemed to take him no time to settle in at Keele. That was just as well. Even before he arrived in March, the Finance Committee recommended that he be charged with producing a strategy to effect enough savings in the academic area to make substantial inroads on the estimated deficits. This strategy was wanted by October at the latest, with the savings starting in 1985-86. Time was short: action was in accordance with the Jarratt Report.

Sir Alex Jarratt had been a civil servant for twenty years, during which time he had been seconded to the Cabinet Office, been Secretary to the National Board of Prices and Incomes, and served in the Department of Employment and Productivity and the Ministry of Agriculture. He was lured away in mid-career to become Chairman of Reed International, and of Smiths Industries, a Deputy Chairman of the Midland Bank, and Chancellor of the University of Birmingham. His committee's concern with efficiency studies did 'not extend to issues of academic judgement nor... with the academic and educational policies, practices or methods of the universities'. First and foremost, the Report said, universities were corporate enterprises. It was based on a study of six universities (Edinburgh, Essex, Loughborough, Nottingham, Sheffield, and University College, London). It conceded that the quality of life and international status which the country enjoyed was in large measure a reflection of the excellence of the universities in the past. But for the present and future 'we see a need for change throughout the university system... planning for selectivity and having the means to achieve it... the search for value for money... Even if universities have a clear view of what they want to do, they will not be able to achieve their aims unless they have the necessary structure to effect adequate rates of change and the will to produce it. We see this as the greatest need for the universities in their preparation for the period up to the end of the century.' Looking at the role of the UGC, and noting that some of its recommendations made in 1981 about closures and inter-institutional collaboration had not been adopted, Jarratt recommended that the UGC should improve its effectiveness in managing the university system. Furthermore, the government should examine the role, structure and staffing of the UGC. Next, he wanted to strengthen the relationship between the secretariats of the UGC and the CVCP, and to 'increase the dialogue between the UGC and the university system': more UGC intervention could achieve greater value for money. Together, the UGC and the CVCP were recommended to develop a range of performance indicators covering inputs and outputs. The Report acknowledged that quantitative performance measures played some part in the allocation of resources in most institutions but felt that this usually merely supplemented qualitative judgements made by colleagues and views about short-term political pressures. Jarratt thought that universities apparently needed to know what they were trying to achieve and hence there needed to be far more work on measures of output. The word 'scholarship' does not appear in the Report.

As for the universities – not just the six they examined but, based on that, the whole 'system' – there were detailed recommendations on what they should do: namely, examine their structures and develop plans to meet key requirements. It went on to tell them how. University Councils should prepare strategic plans to underpin academic decisions and bring planning, resource allocation and accountability together: Councils should play a much more active role in academic and financial planning, with Planning and Resources Committees reporting to both Senate and Council. A degree of tension between Senate and Council was considered to be creative and beneficial. Senates should continue to co-ordinate and endorse detailed academic work. Universities should develop rolling academic and institutional plans, with vice-chancellors adopting a clear role as chief executives. There should be fewer committee meetings involving fewer people, with more decisions delegated to officers. Pro-Vice-Chancellors, and Deans for each faculty or school, should become part of the structure. Departments should be made more efficient by charging them for central services such as the use of lecture theatres. Cost centres were to be the new tool for measuring and enforcing efficiency. Reliable and consistent performance indicators should be developed, and staff development, appraisal and accountability should be introduced. Every university was to prepare plans to implement these recommendations within twelve months, and the UGC should take progress into account when allocating funds. In all this, it was said of university administrators: 'We have been impressed by the range of tasks undertaken... there is agreement that the administrations serve their universities well.'

There seems never to have been any doubt that this policy was right: nor, indeed, any suggestion that the universities, the very nature of whose intellectual business is the questioning of received wisdom, should even debate how their future was being shaped. There were two interesting observations made in the next few months. The first was by the UGC in May 1985: their preliminary view was that these recommendations would not lead to substantial economies. Nevertheless, the UGC was not going to forgo the cards which Jarratt had just dealt to them, and said they would pay special attention to the rationalisation of departments and to selectivity in research funding. (There was no present intention of taking into account, for funding purposes, the quality of teaching, because the UGC had no reliable way of assessing it. Those who make a study of UGC letters could therefore predict that it would only be a matter of time before it was thought that performance indicators could be developed and funding allocated accordingly.) The second interesting observation is that by October 1985 one member of the Jarratt Committee, Mr. Ian Beesley, the head of the Prime Minister's efficiency unit, was reported as showing impatience with the universities' lack of action, saying it was imperative for them to drop the complacency and inertia characteristic of their closed community, and start a proper debate on seeking greater efficiency. This was in line with the UGC's view that it fell to vice-chancellors to overcome institutional inertia, to motivate staff and to recognise the need for long-term change and to manage universities both for survival and excellence. It must not be forgotten, however, that since the publication of the report in March, universities had been engaged in teaching and examining undergraduates and postgraduates with depleted staff, preparing budgets within increasingly difficult constraints imposed by government, preparing a response to a government Green Paper and replying to a UGC questionnaire on research plans; and then pursuing research and preparing for lectures, tutorials and laboratory classes for the following year and admitting new students. Even so, at Keele in October 1985 a new committee structure was being put into place.

In September 1983 the Secretary of State had written that universities should explore what scope there was for rationalisation and co-operation, both within and between universities and other institutions. The UGC had encouraged the idea, asserting that 'the most radical way of increasing the size of departments and diminishing their number is by the merger of institutions. Mergers are at the moment a fashionable idea... [and] will have to be combined with reorganisation.' In addition, the DES was thought to be in favour of the removal of the binary line. (Since 1965 higher education had been provided mainly by universities and polytechnics and though officially held to have parity of esteem they were funded on a different basis and at different levels: universities received about 65% more money per student than the polytechnics. Clearly this could be seen as a 'problem' to be 'tackled'.) Mergers might therefore kill several birds with one stone. 'Merger' could equal 'rationalise', but there is little evidence to support the UGC's view that it was 'fashionable'. However, it was certainly an idea which appealed to the new Vice-Chancellor and to Dr. Philip Hunter, the new Chief Education Officer for Staffordshire.

Rumours of such a thing had been discounted in December 1984 by the Acting Vice-Chancellor, and again in March 1985 by the new Vice-Chancellor. There were still more drastic rumours to worry about, with Michael Fallon, MP, advocating the closure of Keele and Stirling, and the North Staffordshire Polytechnic and the North London Polytechnic. (Possibly this was a case of a new MP kite flying to his fellow alumni at the St. Andrews University London Club, or else testing the temperature for a forthcoming Green Paper on Education. He later apologised to John Golding, Keele's local MP.) Then Edwina Currie, MP, said at Keele that 'a university which is now below 3,000 students has got problems. It simply isn't big enough.' Keele was still less than 2,700. Fortunately, the steam had gone out of such rumours of closures, prompting the *THES* to publish an article on 'Nonsense of closures', almost echoing

Dr. Basilio in *The Barber of Seville* on how to start a rumour and spread calumny. The *THES* highlighted the real issue as the government's failure to take seriously its responsibility for the resourcing of university excellence.

In fact, rumours about a merger had become well-founded. In July 1985 a press release said that following an approach by the Vice-Chancellor, the North Staffordshire Polytechnic and Staffordshire County Council had agreed to take part in an exercise to establish whether the existing strengths of the University and the Polytechnic could be further enhanced through a programme of collaborative initiatives; and this included the possibility of amalgamation leading to the creation of a new regional university. This was the target, even though the Vice-Chancellor was reported in the *Sentinel* as saying that a merger was only one of the options under consideration. A working party was set up, chaired by the County Clerk and Chief Executive of the County Council. A decision in principle was to be sought at the meeting of the University Senate in February 1986, with a final decision, if approved, a year later. Not everyone was happy at what was happening, as the *THES* announced in October 1985: 'Deputy Vice-Chancellor quits over merger'. (He was not a member of the Working Party.) When he announced his resignation as Deputy Vice-Chancellor at a meeting of the Council in October, Professor Thompson did not give a reason, but was quoted in the *THES*: 'It is a reasonable inference that this is because of the discussions and to distance myself from them.'

A report of the working party went to the Senate in November 1985. At a special meeting in January 1986 the Vice-Chancellor introduced a debate on whether the *idea* of a merger had sufficient merit to justify planning the next stage. Reactions by staff were broadly positive. Keele students voted against it even before the report was published as a 'crude, cost-cutting exercise'. They were opposed to a possible dilution of Keele's ideals, and were sceptical about the retention of broadening elements in the curriculum. The Polytechnic's Students' Union feared the closure of a site (for the Polytechnic occupied sites in both Stoke and Stafford), cuts in courses, overall shrinkage, and an overall shift to science and technology at the expense of the humanities and social sciences.

Early on, there was concern over funding. That needed to have been solved at the outset. At the end of February the proposed management structure for a new 'University of Staffordshire' was set out, based on six schools each with a Dean. The Vice-Chancellor's Committee would be the senior management group, made up of the Vice-Chancellor, Pro-Vice-Chancellors, Deans, Directors of Schools, and the Directors of Administration and Academic Affairs. Three main Senate committees were proposed – Planning and Resources, Academic Standards, and Research – as promulgated by Jarratt and shortly to be implemented at Keele.

It could have been a major pioneering, educational development, with the creation of a new major regional university, and opportunity for innovation rather than just merger, with greater scope for diversification, an extended range of courses, and broader access to higher education. Many of the strengths of the University and the Polytechnic would have dovetailed together or enhanced one another. There would have been some challenging difficulties to face, especially running interdisciplinary courses spanning more than one site, and coping with the unequal provision of amenities between Keele, Stoke and Stafford. The combined student numbers were over 9,500, and the combined academic staff about 775, with 40% of the staff in science and technology. But, as the Board of Social Sciences at Keele said, it was not clear what the educational philosophy would be. Whilst the government might have thought of 'rationalisation' as a way of saving money, in fact more, not less, would be needed. There was going to be no support for a merger if there were to be staff losses; and the new, joint institution could not reasonably expect to start out with less than the combined sum it took to run them at present – rather, as a new university it could expect to be funded wholly at the 'university rate'. More widespread research would clearly cost more, and there were bound to be some start-up costs. *The Times* wrote that there were no plans for cuts or redundancies, but mention of 8,000 students was noticeably less than the existing combined totals.

Once comments were invited, reactions ranged from a guarded welcome from the AUT, more guarded from the NATFHE, cautious interest from the staff at the Polytechnic, opposition from some staff in both institutions, caution and suspicion from the students, and calls for fuller consultation. The NATFHE supported the principle of collaboration across the binary line, but was sceptical in the financial and educational climate of the time whether a merger would sustain the best traditions of each.

Would the money be forthcoming? The Vice-Chancellor said he was confident it would if the merger went ahead – but the political will had to be there. Following a meeting with civil servants at the DES the chairman of the working party said they had indicated that they hoped to be able to send a letter 'which would refer to the possibility that there might be additional funding'. Policy-watchers should have noted 'hoped', 'the possibility', and 'might' as being very cautious. The UGC said they were unable to give the proposals detailed consideration until late in the summer.

When it came to making decisions, Keele's Senate approved but the Polytechnic's Academic Board thought the proposals would destroy their distinctive qualities, and asked the Board of Governors to oppose it: 'Colleagues in the Polytechnic have every right to be proud of its past achievement and current standing as a large regional and national higher education institution. They have no interest in simply becoming a university if that means abandoning those distinct qualities that polytechnics represent.' The Polytechnic favoured further collaboration which might eventually lead to a merger, but rejected the working party's proposals. A joint academic planning group did encourage and assist further collaborative interaction, notably in the science and medical areas with research into new methods of healing fractures.

Dr. J. F. Dickenson, the Director of the Polytechnic, had described the process towards a merger as 'a short courtship to be followed by a slightly longer engagement'. It was always going to be an arranged marriage: it was never a love-match. In the event the marriage broker did not produce the money and the bride was unwilling at the altar.

Other changes were afoot too. Within a period of less than two years Keele had not only a new Vice-Chancellor, but a new Chancellor and a new Pro-Chancellor. It was announced in May 1985 that Princess Margaret would retire as Chancellor in February 1986. She presided at her last degree congregation in July 1985 and attended a Royal Ball at Trentham in aid of the swimming pool appeal. In thirty years she came to Keele fifty times, twice of them with H.M. Queen Elizabeth the Queen Mother, and she missed only three summer degree congregations. Every visit was attended by extensive press coverage. The restoration of the fountain in the formal garden outside Keele Hall commemorates her years as Chancellor. Her successor was Sir Claus Moser, on whom she had conferred an honorary degree in 1979. He had been the statistical adviser to the Committee on Higher Education when he was Professor of Social Statistics at the London School of Economics, and had made his mark in the appendices of the Robbins Report in 1963. He went on to be Head of the Government Statistical Service in the Cabinet Office for eleven years. He was Warden of Wadham College, Oxford, since 1984, and a director of N. M. Rothschild and Sons and of the Economist Newspaper. He was also Chairman of the Royal Opera House and a Governor of the Royal Shakespeare Theatre, a Fellow of the British Academy and an honorary Fellow of the Royal Academy of Music. Seven other English universities had conferred honorary doctorates on him. Following his inauguration as Chancellor there was a flypast by four planes from the Birmingham University Air Squadron – 'the first time in the history of the Royal Air Force', he commented, 'that a flypast has been given for someone with the rank of sergeant'. In 1990 he sparked the foundation of a National Commission on Education. 'Education costs money', he said, 'but then so does ignorance.' Amongst the first honorary degrees he conferred on the occasion of his installation were Doctors of Science on Professor Gemmell and Harry Law, one of the first graduates in Biology and Chemistry, so tracing a link back to the foundation of the College. The following year, honorary degrees conferred included a Master of the University for the great footballer Sir Stanley Matthews, Stoke's hero, who had become a legend in his own lifetime.

Lord Rochester, Pro-Chancellor since 1976, did not wish to continue for a third term of five years, and he was succeeded in October 1986 by the Duke of Westminster. Mention should be made of other lay support generously given to the University. Mr. A. G. Hayek, who had succeeded Mr. A. P. Walker as Honorary Treasurer in 1968, held office until 1987 – two Honorary Treasurers covering nearly forty years. Mr. G. N. Bell, the senior partner in Knight and Sons, Solicitors, was a member of the Council for over twenty-five years from 1968, and during that time was a rock of support as an adviser, and as chairman of the Finance Committee.

In January 1985 the library clock, which had stopped for most of 1984 at 2.35, started again. Perhaps it was a good omen.

In order to encourage the arts, a way was found to provide some modest financial support by selling a painting. A picture of a hunting scene by Gaspard Dughet, bought as an investment out of development appeal funds, was sold to the Iveagh Bequest for Kenwood in 1986. Drama revived and returned to the Edinburgh Festival Fringe in 1984, once again directed by Ray Johnson. Another graduate, Bill Alexander, had become an Associate Director of the Royal Shakespeare Company and was described in *The Times* as the second youngest of the six young Turks running Stratford and the Barbican under Nunn and Hands. Shakespeare continued to attract large audiences in the Clock House courtyard with *Romeo and Juliet* in 1984, *The Winter's Tale* in 1985, and *The Merchant of Venice* in 1986. Even larger audiences watched the television series *A Very Peculiar Practice* at 'Lowlands University' – not based on Keele but partly filmed at Keele. (Any impressions that some of the fictitious characters might be based on real people were possibly strengthened by seeing familiar shots of the campus and hearing familiar problems aired – students' grants, early retirement, 'research profile' and 'rationalisation'.) Concerts continued to attract world famous artists. Especially memorable was a recital by Tortelier, who played three of the Bach 'cello suites. He was presented with a Royal Doulton figure of a girl with a dove, to which he responded by giving a short address on peace. Financial sponsorship eased the pressure of rising costs, and Mr. Anthony Wood, the Managing Director of Arthur Wood and Son, who had been chairman of the society since it was reformed, handed over to Mr. Stuart Lyons, the Managing Director of Royal Doulton. Both later became members of the University Council, and Anthony Wood was appointed Deputy Pro-Chancellor in 1996.

Small sums of money gave very good value in encouraging the range, quantity and quality of the arts. There were musicals – starting with *Chicago* in 1986 and *Cabaret* in 1987. The 'Arts Umbrella' promoted cultural visits and poetry readings. The long tradition of voluntary staff organising art exhibitions continued, and in 1986 Royal Doulton Ltd. put on a major exhibition of new work by Dame Elisabeth Frink and the students of the Sir Henry Doulton School of Sculpture. That was when 'Icarus' by Michael Talbot took up his abode in the foyer of the Chancellor's Building. Keele received appreciative comments in *The Times* and *Financial Times* for its revival of Handel's *Berenice* ('First prize for sensible originality in the Handel tercentenary'), produced by Frank Doherty and conducted by George Pratt, with costumes designed by Jean Springall. George Pratt was about to leave Keele for a chair at Huddersfield Polytechnic, and was given a special Keele Concert by the Lindsay String Quartet and the Choral Society to mark his twenty-two years of service to music at Keele. In 1993 there was a rare chance to hear another work by Handel – *Theodora* – which George Pratt came back to conduct.

A more recent anniversary marked at Keele was the 40th anniversary of VE Day on 8th May. Professor Sir Harry Hinsley, Master of St. John's College and Professor of the History of International Relations at Cambridge, gave the Lindsay Memorial Lecture on 'British Intelligence in the Second World War'. Not only had he spent the war at Bletchley Park as a key figure in breaking the German wartime Enigma code and assembling the 'Ultra' intelligence but he had recently completed the five volume official *British Intelligence in the Second World War*. In a single scholarly lecture with, apparently, the whole of those five volumes at his fingertips, he detailed the achievements of intelligence, and concluded that otherwise the Allies 'would have been celebrating the fortieth anniversary of VE Day in 1988 and not, as happens to be the case, in 1985'.

The following year saw another remarkable Lindsay Memorial Lecture, by Robert Latham on 'Pepys and his Editors'. Latham, born in nearby Audley and educated at Wolstanton County Grammar School, had recently finished editing the definitive version in eleven volumes of *The Diary of Samuel Pepys* (with Professor W. Matthews), described in *The Times* as 'one of the glories of English publishing'. Once again, in a single lecture, Keele was treated to a thoroughly masterful exposition.

Another local connection of distinguished scholarship resulted from a project initiated by Dr. Richard Swigg in the English Department in 1985, to record the entire collected verse of a major contemporary poet, Professor Charles Tomlinson. He was born in Stoke-on-Trent and went to Longton High School. (Both Tomlinson and Latham had gone on to Queens' College, Cambridge and to Royal Holloway College, London.) He had been awarded an honorary degree by Keele in 1981. The recordings also included Tomlinson's reading of T. S. Eliot's *The Waste Land*, a dialogue with Octavio Paz, the Nobel Prize laureate, and Tomlinson's translations of other poets, to produce a bilingual recording of Bertolucci's poems. The Keele project developed further to produce recordings made by William Carlos Williams, Hugh MacDiarmid and Basil Bunting. Sales found a world-wide market, resulting from successful collaboration and a lot of co-operation.

A number of academic developments included in particular Keele's growing commitment to medically-related research. The Development Trust's very successful fundraising reflected a lot of local support and culminated in building five new laboratories at Keele and ten at the hospital. The names of some of them reflect generous financial support – Charles and Maureen Strasser, Whitfield, William Ridley and Margit Hayek at Keele; and Josiah Wedgwood, Hermann Simon, William George Barratt, Winifred Mary Barratt, the Potteries Marathon, and the National Fund for Research into Crippling Diseases at the hospital.

Research work at the W. E. Dunn Unit continued to attract attention, even if not the financial support it deserved. Dr. Wright and Dr. Furness were awarded first prize in a prestigious science competition by VG Instruments, for designing a suction control for use in open heart surgery; and GEC awarded a gold medal to Paul Morton, a mechanical engineer, for his part in the development of the Morton-Keele pulsatile pump. The rapid increase in the number of open-heart operations to about 20,000 a year in the United Kingdom demonstrated the importance of the pioneering research undertaken since the Unit was established in 1964. The North Staffordshire Heart

Committee was founded in 1979 as a local charity to support cardiac patients and the research work of the Dunn Unit. Under its chairman, Mr. Tony Berry of Newcastle, the Committee has raised over £2M, and given about £250,000 to the Unit.

Another development was the academic study of old age, with an inaugural meeting of the Association for Educational Gerontology at Keele in November 1985. This followed a series of seminars over the previous ten years in association with the Beth Johnson Foundation. The new Association attracted international speakers and went from strength to strength. Credit belongs to Dr. C. R. Phillipson (who was appointed to the Chair of Applied Social Studies and Social Gerontology in 1987) and in particular to Dr. F. J. Glendenning, the Secretary of the Department of Adult Education. He retired as an administrator in 1987, but so highly was he regarded in his field of study that during his retirement, in 1997, a two-day international invitation seminar was held in his honour by the Association for Educational Gerontology and the Department of Geriatric Medicine, with speakers from eight universities. Other developments under the aegis of the Department of Adult Education included the transfer of the District Nurse programme to the Department from the North Staffordshire Health Authority, with a similar development in the Health Visitors programme; and the development of a Centre for Health Planning and Management with the appointment of Professor Kenneth Lee as its director. A further development in the general area of health and medicine was the opening of a new Department of Pharmacy Policy and Practice in 1993.

Not all academic initiatives reached fruition: Irish Studies was proposed – a department, a principal course and a centre, with encouragement not only from the Secretary of State but from ministers on both sides of the Irish Sea. Had the UGC agreed, Keele would have launched the first degree course in Irish Studies in 1986. But at a time of level or reduced funding, the UGC refused a request for the extra number of students which would have made it viable – despite the fact that the UGC had requested universities generally to increase the number of options available in Irish Studies.

When the new Vice-Chancellor came, despite what others might have seen as gloom he showed a bullish outlook. He was an entrepreneur and saw that Keele had real strengths in its teaching programme and in many areas of research. In particular he believed that Keele would succeed or fall by its research. He was also ready to embrace change and to effect changes in organisational structure in line with the new thinking. He focused his attention on the Chemistry Department, recognising that small departments would come under increasing scrutiny. He said he intended to give priority to collaborative work and to link theoretical computing studies with studies at Daresbury, the Rutherford Laboratory, and ILL Grenoble; and industrially motivated research at ICI and with CERAM Research. This led to the appointment of a number of new professors, including Derek Birchall, OBE, FRS, and Kevin Kendall, who was elected an FRS in 1993, two of the country's most innovative and successful materials scientists. Birchall attracted widespread press comment with his advice to drink more beer! His reasons were explained in medical journals. There was a possible link between aluminium and Alzheimer's disease: aluminium had been found in amyloid protein in the brain, but when silicon was added there was a marked reduction in aluminium absorption, and silicon in beer might mop up the aluminium. Volunteers were glad to help! He was good company discussing his work over lunch. He was tragically run over in London in 1995. Similarly the other science departments were boosted with new appointments at professorial level and their collaboration with other institutions was encouraged.

With a large foothold in Keele Village comprising the Hawthorns and the Villa, the University was tempted to expand there. Proposals for housing development off Quarry Bank were turned down by Newcastle Borough Council. Then, as part of the drive to secure more income from conferences, a planning application was made for a Conference Centre. Phase I was for a three-storey centre with eighteen bedrooms; phase II for a further forty bedrooms and conference facilities for a hundred delegates, plus thirty-four parking places. In the village it was felt that there was lack of proper consultation. Plans were rejected by Newcastle Planning Committee, but the University resubmitted phase I, and the Vice-Chancellor said: 'We want to do everything we can to meet the wishes of the village.' The borough council rejected the plans again (against the advice of its planning officers), but had no objection to siting the Conference Centre on the campus. The outcome depended on an appeal to the Ministry of the Environment following the original rejection. The University said that 'the site we have proposed is the only real option available to us', though the chairman of the Parish Council, Dr. J. R. Studd, suggested there were at least four alternative sites on the campus. Plans were finally approved in June 1987 – 'a relatively small development' in the view of the Vice-Chancellor. In the event, by lying back from the road it has fitted into the village better than some expected. It was originally called the 'Study Centre' but the 'y' of 'Study' kept disappearing.

Good news for both the University and the village was the announcement of a bypass for the village, making crossing the main road for a growing population that much less hazardous. On the campus there were developments both old and new: a Victorian garden party was held in June in aid of the restoration of the fountain in the formal garden outside Keele Hall, and plans were underway for the Science Park development on the Observatory Hill, with grants from both the County Council and Newcastle Borough Council. The first block was opened by Princess Margaret in November 1987.

A bizarre footnote in Keele's history is the case of a 'Water Fuel Fraud Case'. The 'inventor' of a scheme to turn water into car fuel was indicted by an American federal grand jury on charges of large-scale fraud. Dr. D. Cohen, the Registrar, gave evidence in the federal court in Dallas to deny that the defendant had attended Keele or been awarded a doctorate in the philosophy of metrology from the 'University of Staffordshire, Keele'.

Chapter 27

WALKING THE TIGHTROPE

W hen wondering which way to go, tempting as it might have been, it was not possible to say: 'If I were you, I wouldn't start from here.' With universities facing further cuts in 1985-86 the UGC was in a logical cleft stick. It could hardly go back on its assessments of successful universities, nor could it further weaken those which had suffered most before. One lesson the UGC had learnt was to provide a 'safety net' for those it chose to disadvantage – so that no institution would be more than 1.5% worse off than the average for 1986-87. Now grants were to be based partly on teaching and research criteria and partly on selective judgements on research. How the money was then to be spent rested with the institutions – but, of course, in the light of any guidance which the UGC might provide. This would include planning numbers in each subject group. The net result was: 'No-one is quite sure how decisions have been reached' (*THES*, 6 June 1986). The Secretary of State explained how three months later: future funding would depend significantly on the implementation of plans for selectivity in research support, the rationalisation of small departments, better financial management and improved standards of teaching. In the Cabinet reshuffle of May 1986 Sir Keith Joseph had been succeeded as Secretary of State for Education and Science by Kenneth Baker who, Mrs. Thatcher wrote, 'would make up in presentational flair whatever he lacked in attention to detail' (*The Downing Street Years*). The grants announced in February 1987 – which for 34 out of 53 institutions were less than the rate of inflation – were described by the Prime Minister as 'a very generous increase'. This put the University of Aberdeen at risk shortly before its 500th anniversary, and Oxford considered cuts in all subjects. *The Times* said it was time that universities earned their entitlement to research funding, rather than insisting on some mystical necessary connection between research and teaching. Others thought that the 1986 research evaluation exercise was 'now beyond question... completely worthless in scientific terms', and Professor Dwyer, Professor of Geography and Deputy Vice-Chancellor, went on to ask in a letter to *The Independent* why no member of the UGC had yet resigned over a major issue in terms of accountability for the wise use of public funds, of academic standards and of personal responsibility.

Another key to efficiency was 'restructuring' – paying people to retire, and there was mention of another £200M for that in June 1986. Even the DES, which was used to special pleading by universities, warned the Treasury that it expected universities to be in deficit by between £100M and £200M by 1989-90 unless drastic action were taken. Staff were urged to leave, yet again, and urgency was added to their decisions by the government funding the costs by 100% in 1986-87, by 75% in 1988-89, and by 50% in 1989-90 – at a cost expected to be in the region of £90M.

In a speech to the CVCP on 30th October 1987 Mr. Baker showed some of his presentational flair: a soft approach followed by a hard line. 'We have both moved well beyond the rather sterile exchanges between government and universities in the aftermath of the 1985 Green Paper... Stumbling on in the old ways would in the long run do far more harm than radical change, uncomfortable though radical change is.' He then detailed the new approach in the new White Paper: contracts, with a stronger link between performance and funding. This meant more research selectivity, more subject rationalisation, improved standards of teaching, staff appraisal, development and training, and with satisfactory progress a precondition for any pay settlement.

Having been charged with producing a financial strategy, Professor Fender in an ebullient mood made the most of the honeymoon accorded to all new vice-chancellors. Above all, savings were to be made on salaries and wages – i.e. on people. A squeeze on expenditure was tightened by delegating responsibilities to a large number of cost centres. These savings were to be coupled with new staff appointments – which could only be funded from further staff losses. There was to be expansion in research and postgraduate students, and especially a major emphasis on more income from conferences and catering. Until everything came right, however, it was going to be a balancing act of losing enough staff quickly enough, keeping a lid on deficits, and spending our way into a brighter future. We were, as Mr. Hayek said in his last report before retiring as Honorary Treasurer, 'walking a tightrope'.

Projected balances – those blends of optimism and pessimism – looked bad and went to worse: a less than expected grant from the UGC for 1986-87 increased the projected deficit for the year from £338,000 to £643,000, and meant more cuts: £50,000 from central administration, £100,000 from maintenance, and £300,000 from academic items. The Vice-Chancellor was prepared to accept a deficit of £300,000 *if* it was clear there would be adequate staff savings in 1987-88 and beyond. Where various items of expenditure at Keele were greater than at other universities (because Keele was different from other universities), they were a target for being brought into line. A reduction of fifteen academic-related staff was going to be the main financial saving, and this was accompanied by a reduction in medical and welfare provision on the grounds that students should take much more responsibility for themselves. The supporting structure of Halls Offices and resident staff in each Hall of Residence was almost dismantled, with a projected saving on student facilities of over £150,000, or 40%. The Library staff had already suffered heavily – reduced from 55 to 37 in five years. The theme was always to seek further savings from a more efficient operation. The Vice-Chancellor interviewed staff over the age of fifty to ascertain their plans for the future – whether they could be persuaded to leave.

Some of the spending for rejuvenation needed to happen before the savings had been made. Within two years, sixteen professors were appointed and 20% of the academic staff had joined the University. This meant that the deficit for 1987-88 was likely to be over £500,000, rising to £750,000 in 1990-91 unless targets on staff losses were reached. The Vice-Chancellor was confident they would be, but with accumulated deficits up to 1990-91 forecast at over £2.2M the urgency could not be overstated. A 'Task Force' – a name reminiscent of the Falklands War in 1990 – was set up, comprising the Vice-Chancellor, the Registrar, Finance Officer, Deputy Finance Officer, Director of Academic Affairs and the Executive Treasurer (Mr. J. Moffat, who had succeeded Mr. Hayek). They believed the University needed to 'tunnel through' a bad period. They identified savings which would have reached £500,000 a year from 1989-90, had they not been offset by a smaller than expected UGC grant, a reduction in funding by the Computer Board and a drop in interest on reduced reserves. They therefore decided to take a more global, five-year view. Cost centres were required to make savings of 5% in 1988-89, 2% the following year and 1% in each of the three years after that. The Task Force achieved the loss of thirty academic and academic-related posts, so permitting five new appointments; fifteen technical posts, so permitting six new appointments; twelve clerical and secretarial posts, so permitting three new appointments, and the loss of eighteen manual staff.

In a paper entitled '1988-89 – A Year of Opportunity', the Vice-Chancellor claimed that we should look forward with more expectations and confidence than at any time since the founding of the University College. He supported his optimism by pointing to a record number of applications and admissions; a major restructuring of the academic programme assisted by the creation of ten schools (later reduced to six) to promote interdisciplinary teaching and research (– a structure which did not survive his departure in 1995); the appointment of new professors; the increase in external research grants; the restructured administration; and the growth of 'Keele Hospitality' – the conference and catering business of the University. The new Science Park building was oversubscribed, and the Study Centre in Keele Village was completed. 'The University is meeting all its current financial targets', he said, and he concluded: 'I am convinced that Keele is beginning to be seen as a thoroughly forward-looking University with an exciting programme. There are no UK universities with more potential for growth in the 1990s. To confirm that statement is the challenge and the opportunity for the coming year.'

Mr. Micawber would have been puzzled: 'Annual income twenty pounds, annual expenditure twenty pounds ought and six, result misery' (*David Copperfield*). His calculations were 'in case anything turned up'. Brian Fender's calculations were to make sure that something would turn up. In 1989 financial projections for 1990-91 looked for a surplus of over £125,000 in order to start making inroads into a projected accumulated deficit of almost £1.5M. Within months the hoped-for projected surplus shrank to £30,000. At Council there had been caution at making any replacement staff appointments, but the Vice-Chancellor's response had been to stress flexibility and opportunity, and the importance of maintaining the vitality of the institution.

What about the reserves kept for a rainy day? It had already been raining for a very long time: the waters had not abated, and the dove had not returned with an olive leaf. Reserves of nearly £3M in July 1988 were largely already committed to fund capital expenditure and deficits. Endowment Funds and Research Fund balances could not be used to finance deficits, but they could be used to offset deficits in cash-flow terms.

Council was seriously concerned that the longer-term targets for surpluses looked like being ravaged by further deficits; the nightmare was that the target of accumulated surpluses of £650,000 in 1992-93 was turning into a deficit of £775,000 – i.e. a shortfall of over £1.4M. What was Brian Fender's response to the Council? That the national financial problem affecting universities affected Keele no more than other universities; and that while he could 'balance' the books by not making appointments and by 'taxing' conference income, such action would jeopardise the longer-term academic programme. His concern was the academic well-being of Keele. His 'longer term' was longer than the Council's.

The University therefore needed to produce income. That would come from having more students and more conferences. That meant spending money on major developments and especially on residences and restaurants. Horwood Refectory, for example, was refurbished, having been described in the *Keele Gazette* as a barn of a place. Pevsner had written in *Staffordshire* that it was 'a sensible room, faced with engineering bricks and roofed by a light-metal space-frame construction. It is the trees which contribute the visual pleasure while you eat' – as he had found out. The 'softer' look, with fixed curtains, fabric hiding the roof, and a bar in the corner, brought it into line for conference use, but lost the brightness, the interesting ceiling and the view of the trees. Above all, capital was needed now to produce income later. The Vice-Chancellor believed in self help. He cut the Gordian Knot: he started the policy of selling the University's houses. Those falling vacant in the summer of 1989 were offered for sale, and that meant that by the end of the year, all capital expenditure was funded. There remained the problem of accumulated deficits of over £1.5M with no reserves to cover them, but a source of capital had been released, and in the years up to 1994-95 he raised over £2.5M from the sale of houses (though with a contingent liability for repurchase). That was how he could outface caution and concentrate on his longer term: but it was going to be a stony journey. Accumulated deficits at the end of 1989-90 of over £1.75M were described as planned restructuring.

Morale in universities generally was low. This was borne out by a survey funded jointly by the AUT and the CVCP. Goodwill was under stress and enthusiasm was crumbling. At Keele, even worse, a number of tragic deaths of members of staff raised concerns about a deterioration in what had previously been a strong sense of community. One of the chaplains expressed the unease he witnessed as follows: 'We hear that the changes are 'all about people'... I begin to worry when they are expected to work around the clock, endlessly producing something; or when time to socialise is seen as time wasted; or when the need to be financially self-supporting is perceived to be more important than the passing on of knowledge; or when subtle discrimination of various kinds is tolerated as somehow 'inevitable'. There seems to be an element omitted from the equation, one ingredient missing from the recipe for success. So I offer you this one word. Generosity.'

Brian Fender's next exhortation at the end of 1990-91 was entitled 'Thinking Big', looking beyond the year 2000 in order to identify the objectives for the next few years. Growth was what he wanted, especially as Kenneth Clarke (who was appointed Secretary of State for Education and Science in 1990) had signalled the start of a dramatic expansion in higher education. Growth was going to be the answer. To remain at 6,000 after the year 2000 would leave Keele small in European and American terms. With attractive courses, a large rural campus for students and staff and an innovative and expansionist outlook, it was time to revive the University's development plans with a target of 7,500 students, and suggestions of 12-13,000 thereafter.

A CVCP booklet in 1991 on *The State of the Universities* also saw growth as the vital ingredient – doubling in the next twenty-five years, and maintaining and improving quality with a CVCP audit unit visiting each university about every three years. But shortage of money, they pointed out, was hampering expansion and threatening quality. When, in February 1991 the Secretary of State said on television that he was 'flatly against charging students', it was not clear where extra money would come from. The government's White Paper praised higher education as 'already amongst the most efficient and effective in the world. The Government applauds what the academic community has achieved in teaching, scholarship and research.' As for money, fine words buttered no parsnips, but a new formula was found to make the same amount of money go further. This was called 'efficiency gains'. The rate of inflation minus an 'efficiency gain' was how universities were to be funded.

There is no need for the reader to attempt to reconcile conflicting views: they do not reconcile. While the government was applauding what the universities had achieved, the House of Commons Public Accounts Committee ws berating the Funding Council (the successor to the UGC) for failing to monitor or control a deteriorating situation. So were those universities which were 'amongst the most efficient and effective in the world' overspending? or were they underfunded? *The Guardian* published what it said were edited extracts from the minutes of a secret session of the Public Accounts Committee. MPs criticised the Funding Council. The Funding Council said its effectiveness depended on the adequacy of government funds and blamed mismanagement in the institutions. It suggested that the universities most at risk could reduce staff, close uneconomic departments, eliminate expensive options, increase student numbers or look for commercial sponsors. Keele's deficit had been incurred to pay staff to go, with the full knowledge of the Funding Council. *The Guardian* further reported that Brian Fender 'was in a relaxed mood yesterday carefully explaining his case to Radio 4... He had, he said, ended a financial system in which spare cash was stacked away in a metaphorical old sock'.

If the government, the Public Accounts Committee, the Funding Council, the CVCP and the universities were all dancing to the same tune, they seemed to be dancing different steps. Perhaps the crisis in higher education was not being given high priority by the government, for in the space of a few months in late 1990 Iraq invaded Kuwait, Mrs Thatcher visited Czechoslovakia and Hungary, Germany was reunited, and Geoffrey Howe resigned from the Government, provoking a conservative leadership ballot and the resignation of Mrs. Thatcher.

Goodwill towards Keele could be seen in the endowment of prizes, some of them as memorials to students and staff. A memorial prize commemorates Clare Colman who died in 1987 just before taking finals; and a memorial fund to help students with disabilities commemorates Donna Lovett who died in 1990; the Robert Walikongo Memorial Fund to help students from overseas is named after a student from Zaire, though technically stateless, who died at Keele. The Shalimar Ward Memorial Trust provides prizes in memory of an American student who died following a cycling accident in 1988. The Michael Akehurst Memorial Prize is a memorial to a distinguished Professor of International Law who died in tragic circumstances soon after he was awarded a personal chair. Molly Badcock endowed a bursary after she retired from Biological Sciences, and Mary Campion endowed a book prize in biology when she retired, shortly before her death in 1992. Relatives, colleagues and friends of Margaret Hawksworth, who had been a lecturer in Physical Education, endowed a prize in her memory after she died in 1987. The Exley Prize was established to honour Colin Exley in Geology, and a memorial bursary was established to commemorate John Lees in American Studies, following his tragic death in 1986. Marion Bailey donated trees at the heart of the campus, next to the Chapel – close to where her office in the Registry had been for many years. The avenue of thirty-one beech trees between the Chapel and the Chancellor's Building was given by Mary Campion on her retirement in 1990. The Vice-Chancellor promised her that the University would put a path between the trees, but so far a start has still not been made. Three hornbeam trees were planted close to the Walter Moberly Hall in memory of Mr. J. G. Hall, the former Chief Education Officer for Newcastle and a long-serving member of the University Council. A garden was planted behind Chemistry (and later moved to the front of the building) in memory of Frank Entwistle, storeman in the department from the start, and a familiar figure going up and down to the lodge at the end of Clock House Drive. Colin Bell, who had graduated in history and geography, and became a professor of sociology at Aston and at Edinburgh, made a generous gift of his books to the Library in 1987, and Mr. E. J. D. Warrillow made a further gift of books and an oil painting. When Ron

Maddison left Keele for Cape Canaveral his pioneering work in the teaching of astronomy was recognised by instituting a lecture, and he attended the first which was given by Patrick Moore. This was followed by Helen Sharman, and Ron Maddison came to lecture himself later, to reassure his audience that it was not a memorial lecture. A series of distinguished lectures has been instituted by the 'Friends of Keele' – lectures given by honorary graduates, the first being by Sir Roy Strong in 1990.

The memory of a number of staff has been perpetuated by memorial lectures. The Michael Akehurst lecture is on a topic of international law. John Vincent was in International Relations for ten years before going to Nuffield College, Oxford, and from there he was invited to the Montagu Burton Chair of International Relations at the London School of Economics. A year later he died, age 47, and the John Vincent Memorial Lectures at Keele are one of the tributes to him. Professor Finer was not only a most distinguished political scientist but he was also the life and soul of Keele as one of the founding professors (1950-1966). The first two annual Finer Memorial Lectures were given by former members of his Department – Professor Jack Hayward of St. Anthony's College, Oxford, and Professor Jean Blondel of the European University Institute, Florence. Alan Hall of the Classics Department, who died in 1986, is commemorated by a biennial lecture series held in Oxford, London, Cambridge and Durham, organised by the British Institute of Archaeology at Ankara of which he was the Honorary Secretary of fifteen years.

Medically-related research was pursued in several departments, ranging from the pure to the applied. Ruth Duncan's work in Biological Sciences was yielding exciting long-term results. Research had developed two drug 'cocktails' which released an anti-cancer drug once it had reached a tumour, so enabling patients to tolerate larger doses – a development described as two 'magic bullets'. A monoclonal antibody laboratory was built on the Biological Sciences building, with generous funding from the Strasser Foundation and the Friends of the North Staffordshire Medical Institute, the Grand Order of Masons and the Keele Development Trust. It was opened in January 1988. Local support continued to be invaluable, especially a very substantial donation from Kidsgrove in memory of Mr. Jack Sutton, a local butcher, and his wife Phoebe. Applied research of note was the development by Mike Topping of a bionic arm to help handicapped people feed themselves. It developed from his undergraduate project to build equipment to help a neighbour suffering from cerebral palsy. By 1995 there were over a hundred in use in schools, community and training centres and homes. Another development was a joint programme with the Peto Institute for Conductive Education in Budapest, to provide Peto-based students with training in primary education, and with a view to developing training in the U.K. Conductive education is an intensive teaching system which has had remarkable results with children suffering from cerebral palsy.

The safeguarding of academic standards by external evaluation generally showed that departments were flourishing. In Music, for example, even though its trend was against the mainstream, the department's concentration on composition and on 20th century English and American music was seen to be far-sighted as those areas became more significant. Russian's standing was recognised as out of proportion to its size. Professor Ted Williams was seen to be leading Electronics by example. The University's continued support for Communication and Neuroscience was specially commended. Reports highlighted the needs for more secretarial support and other resources – but these shortcomings were already well known. A UGC review in 1987 thought that Classics, like Russian earlier, should be run down at Keele (part of a proposal to close 13 out of 37 classics departments): Keele chose to retain Classics, and with strong and active support from the Vice-Chancellor, it continued to flourish with new appointments. A UGC review of Philosophy in British universities in 1989, on the other hand, concluded that cuts had been too severe, but offered nothing in terms of financial help.

The problems of shortage of money were compounded by academic uncertainties: Alan Ryan, formerly at Keele, now Professor of Politics at Princeton, and later Warden of New College, Oxford, wrote in *The Times* that 'foreseeable austerity would have been relatively easy to plan for; continuously threatened disasters that never quite materialised were another matter'. Major reviews in the sciences nationally brought suggestions of tiers or categories of departments. *New Scientist* wrote in March 1988 that the picture emerging from a review of Geology courses was 'one of confusion and skullduggery'. Later in the year it looked from a UGC report as though nearly twenty universities would be left without a physics or a chemistry department, following proposals that departments with fewer than 200 students and 20 staff should be closed or amalgamated. The demise of the UGC allowed any urgent decisions to be shelved until the new Universities Funding Council (UFC) could take research ratings into account. Similar views on the size of departments were to re-emerge at Keele ten years later.

New courses met new needs – e.g. subsidiary courses in Spanish, Chinese, Japanese and Polish. Criminology, which had been offered at postgraduate level for many years, was one of the new courses offered to undergraduates at principal level. The establishment of the Keele China Business Centre in 1989 under the direction of Dr. Robin Porter was a different kind of venture. It was funded by the Leslie and Dorothy Blond Trust to promote trade and technology transfer, and this has resulted in academic research into trade and management in China, training programmes, conferences and publications (including *The China Business Guide*). International projects, some jointly with the Universities of Lancaster, Manchester, British Columbia and South Carolina, have been funded by the United Nations, the World Bank and the government. A change of name to the China Business and Policy Unit in 1996 reflects its continued development as a catalyst for research and project work in China, and the collaboration at Keele of staff from several departments.

To help finance growth the new UFC wanted to see a shift in funding from grants to fees, plus a greater degree of competition between institutions. Funding of teaching was therefore going to be based on competitive bidding for numbers of students against a 'guide price' set by the UFC. Universities were to be encouraged to bid at lower prices, though the UFC would guard against the risk of any loss of quality. John MacGregor had succeeded Kenneth Baker as Secretary of State for Education and Science in July 1989, and when he spoke to vice-chancellors in September 1990 he said he was disappointed that most bids were at the guide price. 'Can universities really have so little marginal capacity that all additional students need to be supported at the average cost? I find that difficult to believe. And I have to tell you that, unless universities can achieve further economies of scale in responding to the increasing demand for places, I shall need to consider carefully the balance between the resources available to the two sectors [i.e. universities and polytechnics]... I do not believe that there is any necessary conflict between efficiency, quality and responsiveness to client needs.' The White Paper *Higher Education: a New Framework* sought to increase competition across the whole of higher education by means of the new Funding Council, and there were rumours again of a league system for universities. In 1992 it became clear that universities which did not receive high research rankings (and hence high research money) would have to rely on expanding teaching in order to attract extra funding. Keele saw the opportunity to make bids for 'fees only' students, and almost half the students who began at Keele in October 1991 were funded by fees only. The following year the UFC responded by providing money for an extra 800 students. Applications for undergraduate places had topped 10,000 in 1990: 'Keele for Choice', as it said on our recruiting literature, was bearing fruit.

The consequences of more and more students at a time of financial squeeze were pressures on the students themselves and how they should be paid for; pressures on teaching and on staff; pressures on accommodation and the need to finance growth; and pressures on the University's neighbours. They were all interconnected.

Not surprisingly, the pressures on staff were being compounded for those who stayed by those who left. It had been frustrating, too, to read in the *Daily Telegraph* in 1988 that the government had earmarked £155M over the next three years to encourage universities to pension off academics who were felt to be too old, inefficient, or surplus to requirements. And Brian Fender was quoted in an article by Francis Beckett – a Keele graduate – in the *TES* in February 1990 as saying: 'We had a lot of people who had been there too long in too uncompetitive a situation.' Loyalty seemed to receive little encouragement. There was little to offer those who stayed, and a long-running pay claim by academic staff reached the proportions of a severe industrial dispute, with boycotts of the examinations and the new appraisal procedures. The DES was still withholding the final payment associated with an earlier pay deal. The release of funding for part of the *1987* pay settlement, the UGC wrote in February *1989*, depended on the Secretary of State being satisfied with progress on arrangements for staff appraisal, probation and promotion. An offer of c. 3% was raised to c. 6.5% (at a time when inflation was running at 8%), and was rejected by the AUT, at which Mrs. Thatcher said that universities had a duty to take 'appropriate action' to ensure that staff complied with contracts. After the brinkmanship came the minor adjustments and the settlement – and a strengthening of the chief executive role of the vice-chancellors.

It was in this charged atmosphere that an open letter was sent to the Vice-Chancellor by Dr. C. J. Harrison in the History department. To some he was a radical: to some a conscience. He urged the Vice-Chancellor to change his policies and his style of government, or go. Others replied that the University's improved reputation had been inspired by a Vice-Chancellor who had revitalised a moribund institution; and that his leadership had been charismatic. The Vice-Chancellor agreed to an open debate on his plans, and Dr. Harrison wrote that 'to be fair... he does have a majority of support on the University Senate'.

In the wake of growth came the new structure of two semesters, displacing the ancient calendar of three terms in a year. And with the semesters came a new structure of modules and credits. At the beginning of 1991-92 it was agreed to adopt the widespread semester system with twelve teaching weeks in each semester; and with it, modularisation of courses was approved in principle. It stemmed from a paper in June 1991 by the CVCP. Their motives included the 'opportunity to reassess course objectives, learning strategies and assessment methods', and to facilitate transfer between institutions at home and abroad. Little common ground emerged from the debate. It was more a matter of management than a question of scholarship.

The government met the need to keep public expenditure down while increasing student numbers partly by introducing the bidding process and partly by making students pay more. Student grants were frozen, and the Secretary of State explained that the introduction of student loans was to increase the resources available to fund expansion, and so make higher education more attractive to all. The next step was likely to be the introduction of payment of tuition fees by students. In December 1990 Joan Walley, the MP for Stoke-on-Trent North, assured students that the Labour Party was totally opposed to the policy of charging students for any of the costs of their tuition, and that if Labour were returned to power they would also end the student loans scheme. A year later, by which time it was estimated that the average debt for Keele students was £1,100, Jack Straw, MP, the shadow education minister, was also reported as saying to Keele students during a protest outside Parliament that a future Labour Government would scrap student loans and bring back a grants system. By the end of 1993-94 the average student debt was in the region of £2,500 and from 1994 grants which had been frozen at £2265 since 1990 were reduced. Substantial debt has become the expected norm as the price students must pay for higher education. As the cash crises facing the institutions continued, speculation guessed that they would, collectively, run up a deficit of £3 billion by the end of the century. Sir Ron Dearing was appointed chairman of a National Committee of Inquiry into Higher Education and was asked to find a solution. Like Sir Alex Jarratt he had been a successful civil servant, with long experience in trade and industry, followed by a business career. He had been the chairman of the Council for National Academic Awards and chairman of the Polytechnics and Colleges Funding Council. In a report entitled *Higher Education in the learning society,* published in 1997, a new 'compact' between the government, students, employers and institutions was the guiding principle behind the Committee's funding proposals: as well as meeting other costs, students should pay £1,000 a year towards tuition fees. The CVCP believed this to be 'the only realistic way to solve the funding shortage and to give students the quality of education they deserve'. To reduce the impact this would have on those less able to pay, the new Labour government introduced a sliding-scale means test; but then (against Dearing's advice) abolished the maintenance grant and introduce a revised system of student loans. An annual survey by ChildWise Monitor found that 20% of boys age 15-16 said they would not go to university if they had to pay, and a Keele student was quoted as saying: 'If I thought I'd be facing over £10,000 debt when I graduated, I would never come to university'. In March 1998, Kenneth Clarke, MP, was asked about fees and grants on Radio 4. From the vantage point of having been Secretary of State for Education and then Chancellor of the Exchequer in the conservative government and able to speak with the freedom of being in opposition, he said that the policy of charging fees and replacing grants with loans was 'not New Labour but Old Treasury'.

If numbers were going to increase, students had to live somewhere. The earlier development plan had proposed developing the Home Farm site, but that was seen as a longer term development, and accommodation was needed more quickly. Firstly, the paddock site opposite the staff flats on the drive to the village. This was one of the prettiest pieces of nineteenth century landscaped parkland in the parish, which contributed much to the gracious impression a visitor received going on to the campus from the village. The villagers had long regarded that open space and that view as part of their purlieu – village folk memory went back to the days before the land along Keele Drive had been incorporated into the Sneyd parkland. Initially there were plans for houses for students, with the possibility of conversion to family accommodation, but the scheme ran into planning permission difficulties and the plans were changed. The Borough Council rejected the revised application (against the advice of its planning officials) because it would create extra traffic problems in the village, and on the grounds that there were more suitable sites on the campus. The University protested strongly: 'The University represents a considerable financial public investment. Therefore, it is important that it is not unreasonably prevented from making the most effective use of the resources and expertise that this represents.' A decision on planning permission was deferred in October 1991. In December the University Council resolved that work should proceed on a slightly modified scheme on the assumption that planning permission might be imminent, and the courtyard development at Lindsay was also put in hand. Any ruffled feelings were hardly smoothed when the President of the Students' Union was reported in the *Sentinel* as saying: 'The parish council is made up of people who only represent the 300 villagers. Yet there are over 3,000 students. It is ridiculous the parish council and

Newcastle Borough Council can actually stop the University from expanding.' Yet in fact the Parish Council was committed to helping the University to grow, as it had made clear in its response to the Draft Local Plan. The plans for 'The Oaks' were revised, resubmitted and approved. In July 1992 a decision on proposals for the next three-storey development at Holly Cross was deferred for further discussions... and so on.

However, 'the 300 villagers' lived here all the year, not just in term time, and they lived here for years and generations, not just the three or four years of a student's career. There were some who still remembered the old Keele Estate, and many who remembered the 1960s. For them it was not just three years here and then away, as for students, nor even the five to ten years here and then away, as for most Vice-Chancellors. Brian Fender wrote a paper on 'Keele University and the Community' in which he suggested education, research, information services, and cultural and social areas as capable of expansion, and he proposed increased involvement with Cheshire, Derbyshire and Shropshire. He did not mention 'the 300 villagers'. A letter from Mr. Jervis made the point: 'In addition to the apparent need for Professor Fender to discuss matters with the University staff and students there is also a need for him to discuss matters with those people living in the village of Keele and to take account of their views. As a villager myself, I feel that the University is taking all the advantages of being the latter day squire without recognising any of the obligations and responsibilities which that status used to carry with it.'

The University's development plans in the 1980s and 1990s often seemed a threat to the way villagers would like to see their surroundings used, and relations with the University were strained from time to time. *The Yew Tree* parish magazine hoped that the arrival of Janet Finch as Vice-Chancellor in 1995 would herald better understanding and collaboration, and she gave welcome reassurances at a Parish Council meeting that there were no plans to enlarge the Conference Centre in the middle of Keele. The assurances were given a setback, however, when in 1997 the University opened a shop at the Hawthorns, to sell the same range of goods as Keele's village shop. This was seen as a threat to the continued existence of the shop, and with it the village post office. It quickly led to a demonstration by villagers and students alike against the University's shop, which was then withdrawn. Nevertheless overall the conjunction of University and village works well (though car parking, litter and disturbances prove irritating). Students at the Hawthorns have made commendable efforts to keep good relations, and the village has proved resilient against being swamped by the University. It should be remembered that without the University it must be in doubt whether the village could have continued to flourish.

Chapter 28

THRUSTING FORWARDS

Whilst waiting for the waters of the flood to abate, and before the dove returned with an olive leaf, legend has it that Noah was commanded to hang up the true philosophers' stone in the ark, to give light to every living creature therein. Finding the stone became the quest of the medieval alchemists, for they believed it would convert all baser metals into gold. Of the twelve stages necessary in this process, the eleventh was multiplication, and the twelfth was projection.

The Business Expansion Scheme seemed to offer something similar. A new company buys existing accommodation from the University. The University buys it back after five years for an amount which provides investors with a high return, and in the meantime invests the money in fixed interest deposits to yield a surplus over what is needed for the repayment. Tax relief reduces the net cost to the investors, to provide them with a high annual return over five years (10.4% for basic rate taxpayers and 14.9% for higher rate taxpayers). Here was another source of money which would have confounded Mr. Micawber. In addition, 'capital refinancing' was another mechanism for releasing capital tied up in properties – the equivalent to a householder remortgaging his own house – to provide an injection of capital and exchanging a large overdraft for a long-term liability, with payment servicing a loan rather than an overdraft. In July 1992 the Council considered the Business Expansion Scheme. For every £1M raised, £864,000 would be needed to be invested to cover the cost of buying back, leaving £136,000 as 'free money' for the University, together with an appropriately named 'letter of comfort' from a clearing bank. Further capital was also raised from the continuing sale of University houses, with a view to retaining only a quarter of them.

There was now, therefore, opportunity for more rapid development. On the campus the Walter Moberly Hall was transformed into a Modern Languages building and was opened by the Chancellor in October 1992. The Oaks residences were opened by Sir John Harvey-Jones in November 1992, and the second stage of the Science Park (the Darwin Building) by Sir Roy Griffiths in December 1992. Lindsay Court was nearing completion, and work had begun on Holly Cross next to the Oaks. Science Park III was named the MacKay Building after Professor Donald MacKay who had died in 1987. The Departments of Psychology, Physiotherapy and Mathematics moved into the building in 1995, allowing other departments to expand in the Chancellor's Building.

After that the next major undertaking would be the longer term development of 76 acres of the Home Farm site, bringing to realisation the foresight of Harry Taylor when he urged its purchase nearly forty years earlier. It was to change the face of the campus more than anything since the building of the ring road. In the meantime, in May 1993, the Vice-Chancellor initiated an Estate Plan for Keele, to review assets and to identify opportunities. For example, there would need to be about twenty more academic staff rooms per year until the end of the century. Storage space could be converted for staff use in the first instance, but there must soon be some new buildings. But, of course, everything else must grow too – more restaurants, more administrative staff, more library facilities, updated information systems, more gas, electricity and water, more shops, more car parks. And with more students, more courses could be introduced. The four-year course in Applied Social Studies had ceased as a result of changes in government policy, but the development of three-year programmes targeted at mature students created an opportunity to develop an undergraduate course. The Vice-Chancellor saw the Research Department of Communication and Neuroscience as a vehicle for increasing undergraduate teaching to the general benefit of the sciences though, as a consequence, that would detract from the department's research time. At last an appointment was made to a chair of Visual Arts in January 1994, with an undergraduate degree programme from 1995-96 which, combined with other subjects, was expected to produce radical and stimulating opportunities to cross discipline boundaries. There was a long list of new courses, with Electronic Music, Environmental Management, Human Resource Management, International History, International Politics, and Radiography starting in 1992-93; plans for Business Administration, Medicinal and Biological Chemistry, Ancient History, Astrophysics, and Educational Studies; and Nursing, Marketing, and Pacific Studies under consideration for later. The University's Corporate Plan, with the general aim 'to strive at all times to improve the quality of all the University's activities' looked to expanding to 10,000 or more students early in the next century; to introduce part-time undergraduate degrees; and to give an international aspect to the studies of all undergraduates, with an international course for half, and a period of study abroad for a quarter of them. Student : staff ratios should not exceed 15:1. There was a policy of accommodation in University property, mostly on the campus, for at least 70% of all full-time students up to 1999. Thereafter the proportion was likely to fall sharply.

From the mid-1980s what Professor Michael Power, Professor of Accounting at the London School of Economics has described as a new theology of quality, efficiency and enterprise had emerged in higher education. It was really an extension of the 'Total Quality Management' which had embraced parts of industry in the early 1980s. A CVCP paper in October 1991 looked at criteria and evaluation techniques for the assessment and reward of effective teaching and 'the need to introduce particular incentives to reward teaching excellence in exactly the same way as has been done for research'. The process was accelerated by the changes which replaced the UGC first with the Universities Funding Council, and then with Higher Education

Funding Councils in April 1993. As well as external peer reviews of research activity there was the Higher Education Quality Council, HEFC Quality Assessments and internal quality audits. Part of the University's Planning Statement was: 'To make sure that Quality criteria are incorporated, appropriately defined and measured, within strategic and operational standards about all our activities.' The use of the word 'audit' for all manner of investigations, inquiries and routine checks, is not included in the 1987 Supplement to the Oxford English Dictionary. However, there is a British Standards Institution definition of both 'quality' and 'quality audit', the latter being 'a systematic and independent examination to determine whether quality activities and related results comply with planned arrangements and whether these arrangements are implemented effectively and are suitable to achieve objectives' (BS4778). The enthusiasm for this new theology needed tempering with a corrective view from time to time. Professor Power highlighted the pitfalls in *The Audit Society – Rituals of Verification*: 'The risk of audit is not simply that it does not work and leads to fatal remedies, although one can assemble evidence for this. Rather, it is that, in the process of continuous movement and reform which it generates, it is also impossible to know when it is justified and effective.'

Professor A. N. Porter, the Rhodes Professor of History at the University of London, conducted an External Peer Review of Research Activity in the History Department, and made a penetrating report on the new trends: 'I was struck by the fact that the first among the stated Research Aims of the School of History and American Studies is 'To raise the external esteem in which the School's research is held'... In so far as it suggests an intention to do what is likely to be popular and fashionable, an inhibiting concern with what others may think regardless of their ability to judge, it is actually subversive of the researcher's obligation to pursue independent and original lines of enquiry... My visit left me with the strong impression that in order to be appreciated outside the School, the Department has to engage in a great deal of obvious if not frenetic activity, and that it will be particularly appreciated the more it secures external funding... it must be stressed that there is absolutely no automatic correlation between these things and the excellence, or originality or worthwhile nature of the research or publication involved... Most historical research is essentially the work of individuals, stimulated by contact with others (not necessarily in the same specialism) but ultimately working alone... They appear to need reassurance on two particular issues: (a) that it is worth their while to engage with big and important questions, and to embark on long-term (5 years or more) projects, which may not sit easily with the short-term mechanisms of appraisal and Research Assessment Exercises; (b) that there will be time available to complete these undertakings. They should be given the fullest support on these issues. Major works alone will in the end build up a department's reputation; time alone will make possible the research and writing they require... Creating conditions where staff have enough time to research and write is often regarded as an indulgence: it is not. Without those conditions excellent and loyal staff will leave or lose interest; consequently there will be no lasting or influential research, and no esteem.'

HEFCE next set up a Value For Money (VFM) steering group to produce packages for self-assessment and diagnosis; and also a Performance Indicators (PI) working group to produce performance indicators covering teaching, research, financial health and estate management. Part of the remit of the National Audit Office is to report on whether value for public money has been obtained. The gentle world of the UGC acting as a buffer between the government and the universities has become but a distant memory.

With 'the ever whirling wheel of change' came some casualties. With the transformation of the Walter Moberly Hall into the Modern Languages Building was lost the concert hall and stage (and, regrettably, the name of Sir Walter Moberly). Drama suffered. The performance of music could manage in the chapel and in the refurbished Foundation Year Lecture Theatre – renamed the Westminster Theatre after a donation of £110,000 from the Westminster Trust. Nearby lecture theatres were given a £100,000 face-lift with state-of-the-art equipment thanks to the generosity of Mr. Charles Strasser, a local businessman who was a member of the Council for twelve years. The Estate Strategy later identified a need for a 350 seat concert hall, plus lecture theatre and exhibition area and a restaurant, linked to the Chancellor's Building. The loss of less tangible facilities, hinted at in Professor Porter's report, also needed rectification. Keele's own Staff Development Unit noted that not enough was done to integrate new staff; review of research in Classics highlighted the loss of common room facilities used by members of different departments that would encourage informal contacts, and with it the feeling that staff had no public forum to air their concerns and views. In addition, the HEQC hoped the University would not lose sight of the needs of staff and students to retain a real sense of participation. It was feared that the squeeze on office space, when almost every other professional advantage was being severely eroded, might reduce the presence of staff and damage the quality of service they gave. What was pinpointed was not just a lack of integration, of facilities, of contacts, but their loss within a few years. Partly it was simply the unfortunate consequence of all the changes already discussed; but at the same time, a more hectic life-style was actively encouraged. The 'Human Resource Plan' in February 1995 acknowledged as a new need the necessity to ensure 'everyone knows what the University and their own departmental aims and objectives are'. They were no longer self-evident. The 'Human Resource Mission' set out 'to ensure the University achieves its academic and business aims and objectives by investing in its people and through the imaginative, flexible and effective management and deployment of them'. Another indication of the drift towards more centralised management and the loss, through expansion, of wider involvement, was the Senate resolution in 1994 that there should be no formal meeting of the 'Examination Senate' in June, but that the Vice-Chancellor, the Registrar and the Director of Academic Affairs should be given delegated powers to act as necessary. On the other hand, as the workload of one major Standing Committee (namely, Academic Review Committee) became too heavy, so responsibility was spread, back to the Boards of Studies, to make recommendations; and the Planning and

Resources Committee was asked to consider its future role, with the suggestion that resource considerations should go back to the originating bodies. The route for constitutional matters, however, was to become more centralised in the Vice-Chancellor's Committee.

Nothing has been said about the Foundation Year for a long time. The structure introduced in 1977 proved to be enduring and flexible enough to meet changing requirements. In the new streamlined committee structure introduced in 1985 in response to the Jarratt Report, the Foundation Year Committee became a subcommittee of the new Academic Standards Committee instead of being one of the principal committees of the Senate; and this signalled a lower profile for the Foundation Year in the University's academic business than hitherto. The University's Planning Statement in June 1990 was for a Foundation Year for about one-third of all entrants, noting that as well as its traditional role it also met particularly well, as it always had done, the needs of mature students, and provided 'access' and 'conversion' courses for the sciences and modern languages. 'The Foundation Year', the Vice-Chancellor told *The Guardian* in February 1990, 'has adapted with time. It now serves the need of mature students without formal qualifications, of students taking education as a concurrent certificate, and of sixth-formers who feel they took the wrong 'A' levels.' But when it came to his paper 'Thinking Big' a year later, it received no special mention. There were some revisions made to the course so that students could take different blocks of lectures, to give more choice and flexibility and make possible a closer association between the lecture course and the Topic tutorial programme. It was no longer thought essential to preserve the same common lecture course for all. It next needed to be made to fit the new module and credits system: Topics needed to be longer to meet the requirement of half-modules, because less than that would not fit in the national scheme of credit ratings for courses. In November 1993 the updated Corporate Plan focused on the proposed international aspect to studies for all undergraduates. This might have been a way of revising the Foundation Year in keeping with contemporary needs, and to produce a new programme in accordance with the original philosophy which had given rise to Lindsay's Foundation Year. Instead, the Foundation Year was now to be provided for only a quarter of all entrants. In 1994 the priorities for Keele were listed as a focus on research, excellence in teaching, the recruitment of alternatively-funded students, the mainstreaming of adult education, a review of support departments and the development of profitable campus activities. When the Foundation Year Subcommittee conducted a review it found that mature students in particular still derived considerable benefit from the course, and that those who wanted to change their mind over which subjects to study were able to make informed choices. Many found the Sessional courses involving a sustained period of study of a less familiar subject were the most useful element. Most were satisfied with Topics, and those taking the Certificate in Education said how well organised and presented it was. However, a lack of enthusiasm by some staff was a matter for comment: perhaps that puts the finger on the pulse. HEFCE's own 'mission statement' in 1992 had said it would encourage diversity in higher education, a wide access for all individuals who wished to benefit from it and who had the necessary qualities (rather than qualifications) to do so – things which the Foundation Year had achieved ever since 1950.

Overall, though, the difficulties of sustaining the Foundation Year were growing greater. The escalating costs for students now made such an extra year a much more significant factor, and recruitment had been growing progressively more difficult. Its role had been changed, to give an emphasis on providing 'access'. The three Principal years had been separated from the Foundation Year when the three-year degrees were introduced. Within the University the Foundation Year occupied a lesser place because it played a lesser role. It was also many years since its philosophy had occupied any place in the appointment of new staff. It was no longer an academic showpiece. The long process of relegation – by no means wholly the University's fault – meant it was no longer a main plank in Keele's educational philosophy. By the mid-1990s, the Foundation Year Handbook simply said: 'The course outlines for students the broad context of knowledge in which their later specialised studies will be set, and introduces them to the scope, methods and inter-connections of many of the main branches of University studies.' It had not been *what* it was that had been so important when it was conceived, but *why* it was. That 'why' had been lost sight of. It was no longer special.

An undoubted success story was the growth in research in the sciences, propelled in part by key appointments, to give research income in excess of £3M in 1989-90 growing to over £8M in 1993-94. Amongst Professor Ted Williams's areas of research were developments in compact discs, electronic bar codes and fire sensors. Professor Richard Challis was awarded the Roy Sharpe Prize by the British Institute of Non-Destructive Testing for his work on the adhesive bonding of metals in the car industry. Dr. Maria Heckl was part of an international team working to reduce the noise caused by trains, and found that the noise could be contained better by spacing sleepers at unequal distances. Professor Deen, with financial backing from the Royal Society, collaborated with Tokyo Denki University to develop co-operating intelligent computer systems, with possible applications for air-traffic control, telephone networks and industry. Professor Bill Stirling was involved in one of the most expensive undertakings, a £2.3M project to build an X-ray facility at the European Synchroton Radiation Facility in Grenoble. There was a lot of research outside the hospital departments which was medically related. Cancer research, in particular, attracted local support: Mrs. Jean Henshall raised £10,000 before her death, and another £10,000 was raised by and as a tribute to Paul Yorke. Professor Duncan's work has been mentioned already, and initial studies had been encouraging. A collaborative agreement between the Cancer Research Campaign and the drug company Pharmacia, where Professor Duncan had become Head of New Technologies, took this exciting new possibility one step further. There were still years of research ahead, but the Cancer Research Campaign described 'magic bullet' research in 1998 as possibly the beginning of the end for cancer. There was other work on cancer in other departments, too: Professor Truscott in Chemistry studied the use of light to stimulate treatment, which would cause less damage than conventional radiotherapy. He achieved more widespread publicity in the popular press with his advice to eat more tomatoes: lycopene was found to work against cancer-producing substances in experimental conditions – though a side effect might be to colour one's face red. Dr. Hegarty in Psychology provided counselling for patients suffering from cancer.

Research into inner ear deafness in Communication and Neuroscience produced a startling result. 'The first time we saw it happen', Professor Hackney said, 'we thought there was something wrong with our computers or something else... we did not quite believe it.' It showed that the loss of hearing as a result of damage by anti-biotics was not necessarily permanent, as had been thought. The team at Keele not only made a vital first step towards a long awaited cure, but Keele was probably the only place in the world with an interdisciplinary team in place which combined the necessary skills. Professor Ted Evans, Professor of Auditory Physiology, who had succeeded Professor MacKay as head of department, was awarded the Rayleigh Medal by the Institute of Acoustics, the James Yearsley Medal by the Royal Society of Medicine, and the J. S. Macrae Medal by the Royal Victoria Hospital, Belfast. Professor Hackney, the next head of department, was awarded the Thomas Simm Littler Prize for 1997 by the British Society of Audiology; and Professor Ainsworth, Professor of Speech Communication in the same department, was also awarded the Rayleigh Medal. Professors in the hospital departments were also accorded national recognition – Professor Cox was elected Dean of the Royal College of Psychiatrists and Professor Heron was elected President of the Association of British Neuro-logists. Dr. Tony Redmond was awarded the OBE for his humanitarian work in Bosnia. At the hospital Professor Templeton set up the Trauma Centre, Britain's first medical centre dealing with victims of major disasters to offer consultant care twenty-four hours a day.

In the Science Park Keele had Britain's only company specialising in gene therapy. Therexsys, formed in 1992 (later Cobra Therapeutics), was developing ways of getting therapeutic genes to the right place in the body – research looking a long way ahead into the next century.

Not all successful research bears fruit. Professor David Morgan's work in Chemistry in isolating azadirachtin from the neem tree to control insect pests by inhibiting their growth was further developed not in Britain but in Germany, and commercially in the U.S.A. He was, however, awarded the Chromatographic Society's Jubilee Medal in 1989 and the Neem Award from the Neem Foundation in Bombay in 1996

In 1993 the British Association for the Advancement of Science held its annual meeting at Keele on the theme 'Science for Life'. It brought well over 10,000 visitors to the campus, and a lot of welcome publicity. There were honorary degrees and dire warnings about the decline of science in Britain. Looking at the past started with Dr. Torrens (Geology Department), a world expert on dinosaurs and recently President of the British Society for the History of Science.

In national affairs, the 1992 General Election had seen three Keele graduates re-turned to the House of Commons: Don Foster, Liberal-Democrat for Bath; Alun Michael, Labour, for Cardiff South; and Ian Taylor, Conservative, for Esher. There were at least six other graduates who were candidates, including John Taylor at Cheltenham. He was later elevated to the House of Lords, where Lord Melchett (who had been a postgraduate at Keele) had taken leave of absence to make it clear that Greenpeace, of which he was Executive Director, was a non-political organisa-tion. Martin Dent (Politics Department) stood as a Liberal-Democrat candidate for Stoke-on-Trent Central without success. In the European Parliamentary elections, Michael Tappin (American Studies Department) was elected MEP for West Staffordshire and Congleton.

Lord Stafford succeeded the Duke of Westminster as Pro-Chancellor in 1993. He gives strong support to the development of Keele's regional role, as evidenced by his own local interests. He has initiated the Lord Stafford Awards to encourage Stafford-shire companies to improve their business performance and profitability by using the wide range of expertise available in West Midlands universities.

Keele had changed. The whole university world had changed, and during the ten years Brian Fender was Vice-Chancellor it changed more than in any other ten years in its history. It had grown and was still growing. Over 25% of our students were now postgraduates. With the Oaks and Holly Cross residences on Keele Drive, development on the campus was spreading outwards, and the University had become a major conference centre. He left behind 75 professors in undergraduate subjects, compared with only 18 in 1985; 325 other lecturing staff compared with 213. There had been an infusion of new-sounding courses. The Department of Geo-logy changed into Earth Sciences; Psychology left the Social Sciences to become part of the School of Computational, Mathematical and Neuro-Sciences. The Library turned into Information Services, and the Sports Centre became a Leisure Centre.

In 1995, Keele knew where it was going.

Chapter 29

DILEMMAS AND OPPORTUNITIES

Nearly thirty years earlier, in 1968, Professor Campbell Stewart had given two lectures during his first year as Vice-Chancellor with the title *British Universities: Dilemmas and Opportunities*. As Keele reached its fiftieth anniversary it faces, along with other universities, dilemmas which, if resolved, will open up a range of opportunities.

The new Vice-Chancellor, Professor Janet Finch, came to Keele in 1995 from the University of Lancaster where she was Professor of Social Relations and a Pro-Vice-Chancellor. Her research interests include the sociology of family policy, and she has written on domestic relationships and the case for single sex higher education for women disadvantaged by class and gender. She has also published on themes of power and legitimacy in the assessment of academic standards. She has chaired the Research Grants Board of the Economic and Social Research Council, and in 1997 was appointed to the newly-created Quality Assurance Agency for Higher Education. In 1999 she was awarded the CBE for her services to social science, and was also appointed a member of the new Academy of Learned Societies for the Social Sciences. (Professor Frankenberg, who had retired from Keele in 1984, and Professor Margaret Maden in Education were also appointed members.) Professor Finch is a self-confessed feminist. When interviewed she said in answer to a question about her management style that she thought she had developed a style of leadership rather than management; and that it was at the top of her agenda to find the ways in which to work more closely with the community over the next few years. At a time of rapid change in universities she wished to emphasize the importance of Keele finding a distinctive role.

The University's finances had broken even in 1994-95, and it was time for consolidation. Keele had spent heavily in building its academic base with an increase of 17% in academic staff in 1993-94 to 1994-95; but growth in the support staff and infrastructure had been much less. This academic growth had been optimistic and had assumed that student numbers would increase to match: but in fact the government decided to halt growth, and between 1993 and 1996 the number of HEFCE supported full-time students remained more or less constant. This was going to leave income from student-related sources trailing behind expenditure. We had sown good seed, improved our research ratings and gone up in league tables; and yet we had to harvest some tares. It had been assumed that growth might resume in 1998-99, but in the face of that being unlikely, *and* in a financial climate which sought further 'efficiency gains' (i.e. reductions in grants) of 3% in 1997-98, 2% in 1998-99, and 2% in 1999-2000, financial projections predicted a funding gap of £3M by 1998-99.

At least this was not the sudden blow of 1981. It was possible to plan to close the gap over a two-year period by increasing income and reducing expenditure. The savings were to be made largely through staff reductions, and the means of achieving them was to be a 'staffing targets exercise'. The academic salary bill was to be cut by £2.4M, and this time the required savings were specified for each department. A formula was devised so that different departments' circumstances – and especially different sources of income – could be taken into account. The options were to lose staff or raise income. The calculation sharpened perceptions of which departments might be said to be subsidising others, and the more so as individual departments which met their targets were still unable to expand until the overall equation balanced. In such a predicament the University was in any case averse to making permanent appointments. No-one would pretend the outcome was popular. Departments with relatively low research income felt disadvantaged. Only three departments, Education, International Relations and Management, were not confronted with the need to shed staff. All the rest were deemed to be overstaffed – perhaps by only one-third or one-half of a post (e.g. Criminology and Psychology), but there were some drastic demands being made. The new staff targets showed that Chemistry, Communication and Neuroscience, and Mathematics had over 40% too many staff; Modern Languages and Electronics more than twice too many. Electronics courses were later withdrawn, with consequent staff losses. Despite all the earlier efforts made to retain Russian and Classics, they now became (as did French to a lesser extent) casualties of the cuts and reconfiguration into multi-disciplinary activities imposed to find savings in the Humanities. The decision to close Russian led to a clash between Senate and Council on an academic matter. Following a recommendation by the Vice-Chancellor's Committee to discontinue undergraduate courses in Russian, the Senate voted to retain them. The Council, however, had the constitutional authority to take a different decision (with appropriate constitutional procedures of referring back for further consultation), and voted for their closure. The Senate then debated a postponement of the closure. The vote was a tie, decided by the Vice-Chancellor's casting vote in favour of the then status quo – namely the Council's decision to close Russian. French was left with considerably reduced staff and a University decision not to replace those staff who had left. Classics has been transferred from Keele to Manchester University. Clearly, the loss of any subject necessarily reduces the number of combinations of subjects available to undergraduates.

The continuing dilemmas facing the new Vice-Chancellor when she took office in 1995 presented an exciting if formidable challenge. At the same time she was able to point to a number of different and interlocking opportunities which Keele would be able to grasp – the prize for resolving the dilemmas. Brian Fender had unlocked one asset, the University's houses, many of which were sold to produce the money to keep the University going. But it seemed that the worsening financial situation would never improve. Janet Finch unlocked another asset: Keele sought to raise further very large sums of money from its student accommodation (as had happened elsewhere). Firstly the University had raised a series of large loans, and then, early in 2000, a 30-year lease was sold to produce over £55M (i.e. the University sold a large proportion of its rental income for the next thirty years: a new company, Owengate Keele plc, has gone into the international financial bond market). This has made it possible to repay existing loans of £20M and to effect a major financial restructuring. It means that there is no debt to service, and there is a large balance in hand. Of this, £25M has been ring-fenced to fund refurbishments, leaving £10M, of which £3M is specifically for academic expenditure.

An asset offering longer-term value is the campus itself – not to be sold, but to be developed once expansion on a large scale became a distinct possibility. The Keele campus is unrivalled among British universities: more than six hundred acres of parkland and landscaped grounds, with half of it untouched. It provides an enormous potential. If nothing else, Keele has the space for growth all on one site. But more than that, thanks to the earlier history of the Sneyd estate, the University has a stately house and grounds which rival many National Trust properties – a fine Victorian country house designed by Salvin, with gardens, parkland, woodlands and lakes to match. There is the potential, therefore, to maintain a high percentage of residence for students, depending of course on demand in the light of students' worsening financial plight. The future rate of students' applications may well prove to be more resilient than sometimes suggested, but there has been a fairly rapid change from a more financially carefree outlook to an era of student debts, overdrafts and loans, with newspaper headlines proclaiming 'It's a question of affording a degree'.

From the time when Professor Stewart had forborne to press on with an Administration Building to ensure instead the extension to the Chancellor's Building for teaching rooms, the envisaged development of an Administration Building and later an Assembly Hall was lost. Instead, buildings were adapted: the Tawney Building to house administration instead of economics, mathematics and modern languages, and the Walter Moberly Hall to house modern languages. Growth was sustained by infilling to make better use of space within the ring road and in the halls of residence, and by the development of the Holly Cross and the Oaks residences along Keele Drive. The Home Farm site offers the long-term answer – a development in the 21st century on a grander scale and with greater freedom of design and layout than at any time in the first fifty years, because the scale will be much bigger than anything which was possible earlier. Readers will recall that the College was envisaged as having 800 students, reduced to only 600 in the 1950s. It had reached 800 undergraduates when it became a University, rising to 1,000 and with a leap forward from 1,100 to 1,400 in the 1960s, with a development plan for 3,000 thought to be a pipe-dream. Moreover, there will not be the same restraints as earlier when there were scarcely enough building materials for the first buildings, whose location was determined by the realities of a war-time army site, the position of existing mains services, and the need to retain existing temporary buildings because they were in use.

Development of the Home Farm site was envisaged by Peter Shepheard many years earlier in his Development Plan. It will also take pressure off any further ribbon development along Keele Drive and further expansion in the village. The bigger scale makes possible larger concepts which could not be accommodated in piece-meal development. One of the requirements on the University was to make a new entrance. That has been built, and there is a new roundabout as one approaches Keele from Newcastle. (The University has also 'sponsored' the planting on the roundabout further down the hill.) The avenue of trees which led to Home Farm from the road has been preserved on one side of the new drive. Some of the less attractive views of residences in Barnes Hall have been exposed, but new planting will hide them again in a few years' time. The new approach makes a different impact on the visitor compared with the drive from Newcastle Lodge between the sports fields and Barnes Hall, by giving an early view of departments and new buildings. The white 'Innovation Centre' provides short-term lets for start-up businesses; a new Health Sciences building is planned, and there is considerable potential for significant development. At some future time, proposals for a concert hall complex would add not only to the cultural provision of Keele but would complement the recent development of a cultural quarter in Hanley. The new entrance and the Innovation Centre were formally opened by H.M. The Queen on 28th October 1999 with the inauguration of the 50th anniversary celebrations. The old entrance by Newcastle Lodge has been closed and the traffic lights there, installed at last in 1996, have been removed.

With each development, tarmac for carparks has spread its unlovely form across the campus. It has been suggested that, to further the 'greening' of the campus and to halt the encroachment of tarmac in the centre of the campus, there should be a traffic-free zone in working areas with peripheral parking. There also needs to be some sort of focus on the area from the Students' Union and the Library to the Chancellor's Building, to take advantage of the avenue of beech trees. The development of the campus in the 21st century will have to include new provision for the Students' Union, which has long fulfilled a role far greater than ever envisaged when it was built and extended. Charges for car-parking were introduced in 1996-97, followed by proposals for large increases in 1998-99, resulting in a widespread exchange of views on e-mail, a failure to gauge how staff would react and a lengthy dispute.

Growth coupled with space makes it possible to look again at some of the proposals which were current before the cuts of July 1981 brought in the new Ice Age. Dr. Borrell, as Postgraduate Warden, had pleaded for a postgraduate hall, but without success. With the growth nationally of postgraduate courses in the 1990s, Keele is well placed to develop the facilities it has to offer, with the possibility of a post-graduate village sometime in the future. Masters' degrees are no longer an add-on qualification for a few, but a mass qualification for 20% of graduates.

Health-related developments not only build on existing success but prompt more integration with other departments. The incorporation of the North Staffordshire College of Nursing and Midwifery as an academic department in 1995 made an important new addition to the University's academic profile and consolidated Keele's position as a major provider of university education in health and medical fields. The postgraduate Medical School has become the largest in the country outside the teaching hospitals. With the government saying once again that more trainee doctors are needed each year, the prospects for a medical school were once again 'set fair'. Dr. Susan Dilly joined the University as Dean of the Faculty of Health, to co-ordinate the Health Faculty departments, and to lead the collaborative bid with Manchester Medical School to have an undergraduate medical school at Keele. In June 1999, at last, this long-term quest was successful. Keele was one of three successful bids, with Warwick and Durham, and they are to share a £25M investment in medical education. The first medical students start their courses in 2000, spending the first two years in Manchester, and then moving to Keele in 2002 for the final three years of their degree course. (The North Staffordshire Hospital and centres run by Combined Healthcare NHS Trust will be the teaching hospitals.) Benefits should accrue not only to the University and the hospitals but also to the local community as Keele takes on a more regional role. It is expected that an independent Keele Medical School will develop from this beginning.

Changing conditions have finally brought an end to the Foundation Year. The final blow to it, coming on top of the rising costs of being a student, was the loss of the *concurrent* course for the Certificate in Education. As a result of a change in government policy on teacher training it was no longer possible to include training for the Certificate within a four-year undergraduate course. The sheer diversity of undergraduate courses at universities in the 1990s can be seen as an answer to some of the fears expressed by Lindsay about specialisation and departmentalism in the 1940s. At Keele, the retention of the cross-disciplinary requirement for most students continues to address some of the shortcomings Lindsay sought to address. But diversity and cross-disciplinary study were only part of the means to the end for which he had founded Keele. The end purpose was a common understanding, necessary to heal the rifts in society, and an understanding of society's values: this meant an appreciation of the 'common culture' of Western civilisation – what should be a shared heritage. The way to achieve this, Lindsay believed, was to get the right balance between specialisation and a general understanding, in order to 'see things together'; and to serve the wider community by closing the gap between the natural leader and the specialist. Broadly, the programme devised to do this in 1950 was firstly an examination of the heritage of Western civilisation, the development of modern society, and the nature, methods and influences of the experimental sciences. In the 1990s the attempt to inculcate a sense of the 'common culture' by means of the Foundation Year was already in decline. Exactly what that 'common culture' might be changes in detail for those born in the Space Age compared with the first undergraduates, all of whom were born before the Second World War. Clearly the topics and the lecture titles continue to change. But the need remains the same. Lindsay believed it was the convergence of the democratic revolution and the technological revolution which had caused the dangerous rifts he sought to bridge. The quickening pace of technological change has only reinforced that clash. Added to that, most of the world is now on one's own doorstep. When Lindsay stood for Parliament in 1938 it was over the Munich agreement and what Chamberlain described as 'a quarrel in a faraway country between people of whom we know nothing'. Now, from Manchester one can get to Prague by plane in the same time it takes to get to London by train. Much of the Western world is in instant touch by e-mail, and a crisis in any continent can be shown on our television screens the same day. A massive politico-economic system which was imposed on a large part of Europe and Asia when Keele was founded – Communism – has collapsed. Countries of Europe have become a Community. And yet after all the bloodshed and slaughter of two World Wars this century, parts of Europe are still being torn apart by deep-rooted differences, and a European capital city has recently been bombed by NATO forces. At a time of an ever-increasing rate of change in a shrinking world, the intellectual case for a Foundation Year is as strong as it ever was.

The Foundation Year had its last intake of students in 1998. Within months of their finishing the year, David Blunkett, the Secretary of State for Education and Employment, urged universities to embrace their diversity to become more competitive and responsive to learner and employer needs. 'The system must now evolve greater diversity', he said; and the *THES* wrote of the universities' 'biggest challenge in 35 years as the government this week opened the door to institutional diversity, vocational foundation degrees, e-universities and differentiated tuition fees' (18 February 2000). Meanwhile, economics had brought an end to Keele's Foundation Year. Nonetheless, even allowing for different circumstances, it is a paradox that as Keele plans to grow to 10,000 students, and with world-wide recruitment, there is now no room for the Foundation Year, the one thing which made Keele so special when it was launched in 1950 with 159 students, and for which the philosophical and educational justification has never been refuted.

Another casualty of the very difficult financial circumstances of the late-1990s – and one which caused a much greater outcry than the demise of the Foundation Year – was the Turner Collection of books on the history and development of mathematics, science and technology. This was the collection given to the University by Mr. Charles Turner in 1968. In July 1998 the collection 'was sold secretly by the University of Keele to a second-hand book dealer' (British Society for the History of Mathematics *Newsletter*). The price was rumoured to be £1M. Other public institutions had been approached with a view to buying the collection: but which they were was not made public. The sale had been debated by the Senate and the Council: the Senate voted (narrowly) against, and the Council voted in favour of the sale. The whole matter was kept 'commercial in confidence' within the University. Just before Christmas, 1998, news of the sale was the main front page headline in the *Daily Telegraph*: 'Fury at £1M sale of Keele mathematics collection', producing widespread angry criticism from scholars. Staff were shocked and embarrassed. The sale of this most generous gift was seen as a betrayal of trust. The collection disappeared from open access for scholars into the book trade, and thence into private ownership. It was broken up and some items were exported. There had been no direct consultation with the copyright libraries; nor was there consultation with Trinity College, Cambridge, which has the largest collection of Newton's surviving books. The question of the financial value of the collection remains a matter of controversy. Not only 'Turner', but a further 200 books which had been bought to supplement the collection, were included in the sale. Other universities saw with dismay their chances of receiving such gifts or legacies in the future greatly diminished as a consequence of Keele's action.

The reason for the sale was that, given the impossibility of providing sufficient funding to remedy defects in the Library service, there was an urgent need for substantial investment in library materials to support current and future teaching and research programmes. The sale was described in the professional journals as a scandal and as 'The Keele Affair'. More widely, it provoked questions over universities' moral right to sell valuable collections abroad, and calls for tighter legislation to protect such collections. The Secretary of State for Culture, Media and Sport felt unable to intervene, but it was reported that he wrote to university vice-chancellors asking them to consider implications of the sale.

Although it was too late to do anything about it, pressure from the 'Turner Action Group' led to the Audit Committee of the University Council conducting an enquiry into the circumstances of the sale. The committee reported in October 1999. When the report was made public the outside parties involved were referred to as 'A', 'B', and 'C'. The committee found that the University was legally entitled to sell the collection, but that there clearly should have been consultation with the British Library before exercising that right. The committee was satisfied that 'best price' was obtained, and emphasized that the total proceeds from the sale had been ring fenced. As for keeping the collection intact, the committee was not able to ascertain whether or not deception occurred on the part of the purchaser or his or her agent. It said in its report that books and other Library materials which should not lose value quickly had been obtained and much needed improvements to the Library's catalogue were being made. The Library also undertook to purchase readily available copies of some of the works sold. The report expressed concerns over the consultation process and the subsequent publicity. The actual identity of the private collector represented as the purchaser remains unknown. The Turner Collection can never be reassembled.

There were various changes in welfare provision and in administration, to modernise services and/or to save money. It was felt that the system of Wardens in the halls of residence harked back to a style of yesteryear, and that what would be more appropriate was a quality of service more in line with modern-day expectations, with a balance between the University's and students' own responsibilities. The increase in the number of students not living on the campus also prompted a review to ensure equal access to welfare services. The University Registry was re-organised in the wake of its changing role over the previous few years, to become a University Secretary's Office.

The development of the Department of Visual Arts, with teaching starting in 1994, was made possible following a bequest which included the Raven Mason collection of pottery now housed in Keele Hall. Funding from Royal Doulton made possible the appointment of a Sculpture Fellow. Visual arts provides an impetus for the development of a much larger integrated arts programme, with more exhibitions and permanent displays. But within a few years teaching was discontinued, with a view to establishing a different and cheaper course in the future within the School of Languages, Literature and Creative Arts.

The Science Park is another asset ripe for exploitation. The successful development of Cobra Therapeutics, in particular, can be seen to justify David Harrison's plans to build a Science Park at Keele. Which developments might take off, and whether the Science Park will play a role, can only be guessed at, but at least the chances are better with increased co-operation and collaboration.

Adding to the beauty of the grounds now has an economic motive as well as being in keeping with the wider movement towards a 'greener' environment. As universities have to become more and more financially self-sufficient, so the need for Keele to generate more money from its own resources becomes more urgent. Keele Hospitality, which generates about 20% of the University's total annual income, must in turn become more competitive. Keele was the first university to be granted a licence for civil marriages under the Marriage Act 1994. Greater exploitation of Keele Hall for weddings and the banqueting market, short conferences and training courses, and the restoration of the grounds would capitalise on an asset which only a few other universities have – a large and beautiful estate. Hence, the new restaurant and exhibition complex attached to the Chancellor's Building will release Keele Hall for more extensive commercial marketing. Keele has recently been voted the best academic conference venue by the Meetings and Incentive Travel Industry Awards.

With growth it is easier to develop and maintain more and more links with other institutions across the world. Scholarship knows no boundaries – especially now that the revolution in information technology provides a springboard across continents at one's fingertips. The sciences are more noticeable for their international collaborations, partly because there is often more money involved, and more people, and partly because, paradoxically, language is less of an obstacle. But arts subjects, too, have embraced the new opportunities, and Music, History, and Classics, for example, have made extensive use of computers. In some ways, making use of I.T. has done something to restore aspects of small group teaching in undergraduate classes, such as where e-mail news groups were set up for specific courses in Classics. In common with all universities, world wide web pages have been extensively developed, with those of Politics and American Studies being recognised as international resources. The Politics pages were inundated with enquiries during the General Election of 1997, while American Studies is accessed more than twice as often from the U.S. as it is from the U.K. This is not to lose sight of earlier achievements. Peter Plesch's links through his work on polymers, for example, continued from when he was first appointed in 1951 and organised the second symposium on cationic polymerisation, held at Keele in 1952, to long after he retired in 1985 as Professor of Physical Chemistry, with about fifty members of his polymer group in twenty countries worldwide, and with new developments in electro-chemistry underway. Physics and chemistry have maintained strong European research connections; earth sciences ranged across and under continents and oceans, while astronomy maintained links with the Apollo missions to the moon in the 1960s. But the accelerating rate of research in the 1990s and the growth of international co-operation – both encouraged by the pressures of successive Research Assessment Exercises – brings a dimension to university affairs almost inconceivable within recent memory outside a few world-class institutions. In the space of a few weeks in 1995, for example, Professor Arme, Professor of Zoology, was awarded an honorary degree by the Slovak Academy of Sciences, and Professor Kelling, Professor of Geology, was a keynote speaker at an international conference in Prague. Professor Kelling was shortly afterwards awarded the OBE for his services to environmental protection (work which included the disposal of nuclear waste and the restoration of water supplies in Kuwait after the Gulf War). Links with China have been growing, and Professor Fairchild, Professor of Earth Surfaces Processes, was elected an Honorary Research Fellow by the Chinese Academy of Geological Sciences. Collaborative programmes have been developed with Japanese institutions in a wide range of areas by the Departments of English, Computer Science and Physics, and there is international collaboration by a number of research groups on medically related programmes.

The structure of departments at Keele had been basically unchanged since it was put in place in 1950. New opportunities have prompted an examination of maintaining 31 separate departments at a time when research activity tends to benefit from having larger rather than smaller groups and when economic pressures as well as academic developments encourage the sharing of the infrastructure and support staff. The academic structure has therefore been restructured to include multi-disciplinary schools. (Details are given at the end of the chapter.) The appointment in 1997 of Michael Redclift as Professor of International Environmental Policy, to head a new Department of Environmental Social Sciences gave the opportunity to merge elements of geography, economics and politics, and to become closely involved in discussions over the European Union's environmental initiatives. Within two years, however, the constituent parts were re-aligned in a different configuration. In keeping with Keele's interdisciplinary tradition, Dr. John Proops was appointed Professor of Environmental Economics in the same department – the third Keele professor to have been an undergraduate here. (Edward Derbyshire had been appointed Professor of Geomorphology in 1984, and Roger Dyson Professor and Director of Adult Education in 1976. A fourth, Miriam Bernard, was appointed Professor of Social Relations in 1999.) Further changes and reconfiguration are underway, such as an alliance between Biological Sciences and Communication and Neuroscience to become the School of Life Sciences. A paper by the Vice-Chancellor in 1999 on the reconfiguration of academic departments recommends the development of 'a template for the minimum size of an academic budget centre' and the reduction in the number of departments to 20, each with at least 20 staff and 250 students (full-time equivalents: students taking two principal subjects therefore count as half a student in each department).

The European Union has led to a lot more European-funded research and collaboration. The Birchall Centre for Inorganic Chemistry and Materials Science, for example, has several partners in Germany, Belgium, France and Greece. Earth Sciences finds common interest in other countries, whether investigating the sources of earthquakes or a project investigating the palaeozoic amalgamation of Central Europe, which involves thirteen institutions in seven countries. Several research teams on the campus and at the hospital are pursuing research into cancer with links worldwide, and there is also research into another major killer, malaria. Another team is working on understanding diabetes. Work on the honey bee resulted in the award to Dr. Kirk of a gold medal by Apimondia, the worldwide union of bee-keeping organisations. Perhaps the most fundamental of all research is to be found in astrophysics, where Professor Naylor, the Director of the Keele Observatory, has done a lot of work on weighing black holes, and Dr. Totten was a member of an international team which discovered a quasar now called APM 08279 + 5255. It shines with the brightness of 100 billion suns, and is the brightest continuously emitting object yet known. It is difficult to see because it is 11,000 million light years away.

Research in the sciences may attract most of the glamour, but the main business of universities is undergraduates, and hence there is a vested interest in particular in what is happening in schools. Keele's long-term commitment to the study of teaching has continued with the appointment of a succession of high-profile professors of education. Tim Brighouse, and then Michael Barber, were succeeded by Kate Myers, who had worked closely with both of them, as Professor of Professional Development in Education, and Margaret Maden as Director of the Centre for Successful Schools. Together with Jenny Ozga, the Professor of Education Policy and Director of Research, they demonstrate Keele's serious commitment to the study of educational policy. Amongst those advising the government on education matters are Professor Brighouse (who was appointed an Honorary Professor when he left

Keele) and Chris Woodhead, the Chief Inspector of Schools, who had taken a research MA at Keele in English.

Student exchanges are perhaps the most noticeable outward sign of the international nature of universities – a return to the scholarship without frontiers of Medieval Europe. We can see how our students compare: they compare very well. Harvard University holds a 'model United Nations', organised jointly with the UN. Keele was the first British university to send a team in 1995, and came third out of 215 universities from around the world. The following year Keele came joint second, with six members receiving individual awards for outstanding performances. Prem Chandram, Keele's head delegate, was commended for his outstanding leadership. We have broken into a monopoly held by the Ivy League universities of America, and Keele students have continued to distinguish themselves in that forum. It is that, and the gaining of two prestigious Marie Curie Fellowships (by Olaf Boettger of the Centre for Social Theory and Technology, and by Francesca Dain, Research Fellow in Chemistry) which serve as a yardstick for what Keele stands for. In turn, too, students coming here, from more than sixty countries, take back with them, we hope, some of the values we cultivate at Keele.

Robbins in 1963, Jarratt in 1985 and Dearing in 1997 are the names which have shaped the environment in which universities operate. Robbins set the seal on changes brought about by the post-war growth in population plus the trend for a higher proportion of the age group to seek university education, and the Robbins Report called for an 88% increase in student numbers over ten years. Jarratt was a response to the harsher financial realities of the late 1970s and the major cuts of 1981, with the need to extract the maximum value for money by examining the whole way universities were run. Dearing proposed a new 'compact' between the main stakeholders in higher education – the government, students and their families, employers and institutions. The government's priorities are to widen access to higher education and to encourage life-long learning, as well as to prepare graduates for employment – but that is within the context that, according to a survey by Barclays Bank, the cost for students of going to university has more than doubled in four years (*The Sunday Telegraph*, 30th January 2000). The need, therefore, is to spread the unavoidable additional costs and not let the opportunity for higher education on a comprehensive scale be thwarted by ever-increasing costs which can no longer be met by central government. Dearing further sought to safeguard the quality of courses by extending the role of the new Quality Assurance Agency, and to reinforce efficient management by revising the universities' business structures and the role of their Councils. He proposed a further major review in five years' time.

The financial position for the country's universities remains difficult: many would say serious; some would say grave. Over a period of about twenty years, public funding of the universities in real terms has diminished by 35% and continues to decline: there is a menace of underfunding. The academic profession has been under growing pressure since the cuts of 1981. At Keele, with its staffing targets not met, and the need to meet the targets re-iterated – the loss of eighteen posts (or the financial equivalent) – the AUT asked how was it that the cuts so far were still not yet enough. Nationally, the Committee of Vice-Chancellors and Principals has reported that academics are so badly paid that some universities are having to hire lecturers with no experience in teaching or research, or were leaving posts vacant rather than appoint poor teachers. The amount of the annual grant from HEFCE is a major concern, and league tables are closely scrutinised. Professor Finch explained when the grant for 2000/2001 was announced, that the publication of league tables paints a misleading picture, and that the settlement for each university moves up and down each year.

Keele has a lot of opportunities: whether or not the University grasps them – or is permitted to grasp them at a time when the whole of higher education remains under such financial pressure – will be a matter for my successor to narrate later, while I can only gaze into a crystal ball.

For the immediate future, Keele's plans are set out in its Strategic Plan 1998/99 – 2001/2002, the first part of which is given in the Appendix. For comparison, the 'Aims of the College' fifty years earlier may be found in chapter 10, and a list of the founding Departments is given in chapter 9. The Schools and Departments of the University are as follows.

HEADS OF DEPARTMENTS, SEPTEMBER 2000

Faculty of Humanities

School of American Studies	Professor Christopher Bailey
School of English and Philosophy	Professor David McNaughton
School of History and Classics	Professor Ann Hughes
School of Languages, Culture and Creative Arts	Dr. Michael Vaughan

Faculty of Social Sciences

Department of Criminology	Professor Tim Hope
Department of Economics	Professor Robin Bladen-Hovell
Department of Education	Mr. Kenneth Jones
Department of Human Resource Management and Industrial Relations	Professor Roger Seifert
Department of Law	Professor Didi Herman
Department of Management	Professor Rolland Munro
School of Politics, International Relations and the Environment	Mr. John Horton
School of Social Relations	Professor Miriam Bernard
Centre for Health Planning and Management	Director: Professor Ken Lee

Faculty of Natural Sciences

School of Chemistry and Physics	Professor Brigid Heywood
Department of Computer Science	Professor Michael Worboys
School of Earth Sciences and Geography	Professor Ian Fairchild
School of Life Sciences	Professor Carole Hackney
Department of Mathematics	Professor Graham Wilks
Department of Psychology	Professor John Sloboda

Faculty of Health

Department of Medicines Management	Professor David Millson
Department of Nursing and Midwifery	Mr. David Latham
Department of Physiotherapy Studies	Ms Marilyn Andrews
School of Postgraduate Medicine	Professor Richard Clayton

'What will the world expect from you?
Courage, Perseverance, Judgement, Integrity,
Intellectual honesty, Friendliness, Humanity, Tolerance,
and an educated Mind'
(Professor Vick, *Degree Day*, 1954).

'Without fully realising it, Keele had endowed
me with precisely what was needed –
intellectual curiosity,
a desire to question established order,
pursuit of logic
and a commitment to equality of opportunity'
(Michael Mansfield, QC,
Keele Society Newsletter, Autumn 1991).

Chapter 30

RETROSPECT AND POSTSCRIPT

W hat sort of mark have Keele people made on the world? Some of their achievements, especially in the early years, have already been noted. What follows is an attempt to give a flavour, not a catalogue.

The beginnings of Keele need no further comment, except to ponder once again what it was that Lord Lindsay did, right at the end of his distinguished academic life: he recognised the impact of the democratic and technological revolutions and, almost single-handed, he altered the course of university education in England. Of the founding professors, Arthur Vick had already achieved much before he came as the first Professor of Physics (1950-59). During the Second World War he had shared an office with (the then) Professor Cockcroft who was director of air defence research. Vick was involved with Ack Ack Command in London, mechanical and proximity fuses, and infra-red applications. From Keele he went on to be Deputy Director and then Director of the Atomic Energy Research Establishment, Harwell. He returned to university life as President and Vice-Chancellor of Queen's University, Belfast for ten years (described in the *THES* as 'Sir Arthur's civilised oasis in a land of terror'), and then became Pro-Chancellor of the University of Warwick for fifteen years. He was knighted in 1973. He died in September 1998, a few days after the death of another founding professor, Professor Gallie. Keele's other founding professor to receive a knighthood was Bruce Williams, Professor of Economics (1950-59). From Keele he went to the University of Manchester and then returned to his native Australia as Vice-Chancellor and Principal of the University of Sydney. He was knighted in 1980. There was a knighthood, too, for Roy Shaw, the first Director of Adult Education (1962-75) who went from Keele to be Secretary-General of the Arts Council of Great Britain. Sir John Lennard-Jones and Sir George Barnes, Lindsay's successors as Principal, had been knighted before they came to Keele; David Harrison, Vice-Chancellor 1979-1984, and Brian Fender, Vice-Chancellor 1985-95, were knighted after they left.

Another mark of distinction, Fellowship of the Royal Society, was conferred on Sir John Lennard-Jones in 1933, long before Keele was founded. The first two Professors of Mathematics, Ian Sneddon (1950-56) and Douglas Jones (1957-64) were both made Fellows after they had left Keele, in 1983 and 1968 respectively. Professor David Smith, Professor of Chemical Physics at the University of Birmingham, was the first Keele graduate to become an FRS. In 1992 Professor Derek Birchall came to Keele as head of a new Centre for Inorganic Chemistry and

Materials Science. He had left school at fourteen, and had been made an FRS in 1982 while he was at ICI. He was joined at Keele by Professor Kevin Kendall in 1993, who was made an FRS that year. In the arts, Christopher Taylor was Keele's first graduate to be made a Fellow of the British Academy in 1995, having been the Head of the Archaeological Survey of the Royal Commission on Historical Monuments. Professor Rivet, the Professor of Roman Provincial Studies, was made an FBA when he retired in 1981, and Professor Finer, the founding Professor of Political Institutions (1950-66), was made an FBA when he retired from the Gladstone Chair of Government and Public Administration at Oxford in 1982. Alan Ryan was made an FBA in 1986, shortly before he went from Oxford to Princeton as Professor of Philosophy.

In Parliament, John Golding was the first graduate to be elected to the House of Commons, as MP for Newcastle-under-Lyme, 1969-86. Clare Short (who had moved from Keele to take her degree at Leeds) has been MP for Birmingham Ladywood since 1983. The 1997 General Election returned a representative group of Keele MPs: Paul Clark, Labour, for Gillingham; Don Foster, Liberal Democrat for Bath (which he had taken in 1992 from Chris Patten, the Conservative Party chairman who became Governor of Hong Kong); Alun Michael, Labour Co-operative, for Cardiff South and Penarth (previously Lord Callaghan's seat), Secretary of State for Wales, and the first First Secretary of the National Assembly of Wales; and Ian Taylor, Conservative, for Esher and Walton since 1987, who had been Under-Secretary of State for Trade and Industry in the previous government. In the House of Lords, Lord Melchett – previously Peter Mond, who had taken his MA at Keele – has been Minister of State in the Northern Ireland Office, and is Executive Director of Greenpeace. Lord Lindsay, the grandson of Keele's founder, graduated from the University in 1966, and has followed a career in the Australian Diplomatic Service. Lord Taylor, who as John Taylor had contested Cheltenham in 1992, is Keele's first life peer. Michael Tappin of the Department of American Studies, was the Member of the European Parliament for Staffordshire West and Congleton, 1994-99. In Whitehall there have been 'the Keele three' top civil servants referred to earlier, and a civil service commissioner. In the prison service 'Toj' Brandon was successively Governor of several prisons, and Ian Dunbar became Director of Inmate Administration and an Under Secretary of State at the Home Office.

Not surprisingly for any university, graduates have gone into academic life and have been appointed to chairs – including in English, history, experimental physics, physical geography, chemical physics, sociology, management studies, applied community studies, political theory, politics, international politics, pure mathematics, education, geology, law, and the economics of education. Sam Nolutshungu, the first South African scholar, was invited to be Vice-Chancellor of the prestigious University of the Witwatersrand, shortly before he died in 1997 aged 52. Keele's first graduate to become a University Vice-Chancellor was Colin Bell, who was appointed Vice-Chancellor of Bradford in 1998. Earlier than that, Harry Law, who came to Keele in 1950, was President of Portsmouth Polytechnic, and died in office in 1990. In 1995 Cambridge University appointed Sandra Dawson the Peat Marwick Professor of Management Studies and Director of the Judge Institute of Management Studies, and in 1999 she was elected Master of Sidney Sussex College.

Some Keele graduates have also been awarded Keele honorary degrees: Harry Law, Professor David Smith, FRS, Margaret Spurr, OBE, Michael Mansfield, QC, Sir Moray Stewart, KCB, Sir Richard Mottram, KCB, Sir John Vereker, KCB, and Owen Powell; and in 2000 Jack Emery, Professor Sandra Dawson, David Pownall and Russell Seal. Another graduate, David Edmonds, Director General of Telecommunications, returns to Keele regularly in his role as the University's Honorary Treasurer.

A well-known figure at Keele, Donald Nicholl in the History Department (1951-1974) became regarded, by the time he died in 1997, as one of the most widely influential of modern Christian thinkers. A notable achievement in the academic world was Donald MacKay's creation of the interdisciplinary Research Department of Communication, which blazed a trail with its unique blend of skills and its work across a wide range of neurological research. Professor John Sloboda has been awarded the British Psychological Society's President's award for distinguished contributions to psychology, including founding the world's most significant research group in the psychology of music. In the Department of Postgraduate Medicine, Professor Redmond and Professor Southall have both been awarded the OBE for humanitarian work. Awards to graduates have included the CBE to Anne Parker, the Director of Social Services for Berkshire; the OBE to David Collett, the Director of VSO and of Wateraid; the OBE to John Duncan at the Foreign Office and the OBE to David Heard for services in Abu Dhabi. Brian Munday already had the MBE when he came up as an undergraduate after service in the Fleet Air Arm.

Keele's first judge is Sir Maurice Kay, the second Professor of Law (1973-82), appointed a QC in 1988 and a Judge of the High Court of Justice Queen's Bench Division in 1995. The first Keele graduate to become a judge was Alistair McCreath; and Michael Mansfield, Michael Todd and Anestafere Weekes are QCs. Keele's first bishop is Jonathan Gledhill, Bishop of Southampton.

Theatre, radio and television have been mentioned already, and flowered early amongst Keele graduates. In classical music the very name of the Lindsays (as the Lindsay String Quartet has become known) evokes the name of the founder. The University's place in electronic music owes much to Tim Souster, who designed and set up the electronic music studio when he was a Leverhulme Research Fellow from 1975 to 1979. He was a prolific and imaginative musician, composing and promoting electronic music of all types. He died in 1994, and the studio at Keele has been developed further and re-named in his honour. Prominent in industry can be found Geoffrey Richards at Shell, Russell Seal at BP, and Bill Bardo at GEC.

Keele people do not score often in the old nursery rhyme *Tinker, Tailor, Soldier, Sailor*, but if one modernises the rhyme to read 'Banker, Bishop, Actor, Lawyer, Governor, Publisher, Policeman, Chief', then Keele is well represented. Kevin Newman became chief executive of the First Direct Bank, and Peter Geer the Chief Manager in Singapore for Barclays Bank. There are governors, not only of prisons but of the BBC, Margaret Spurr, OBE. Tony Elliott is founder and chairman of the Time Out Group, which publishes *Time Out*; and in New York, Marion Boyars (Marion Lobbenberg, one of the first graduates) was described in the *New York Times* as the last of a dying breed of eccentric, entrepreneurial, idiosyncratic publishers who published her passions – and these included four Nobel laureates. Keele policemen have included Charles McLachlan, CBE, Chief Constable of Nottinghamshire and then H.M. Inspector of Constabulary, who took an MA in Criminology while a Chief Inspector; and Ian McDonald, Assistant Chief Constable of Leicestershire. And Keele has given Nigeria a Chief: Martin Dent who was in the Politics Department from 1963 to 1990. Earlier he had been a District Officer in Nigeria and built up a relationship of trust with the three million Tiv people – which stood him in good stead when he quelled a riot. Over thirty years later in 1994 he was invited by the Paramount Chief and the Traditional Tiv Council to become a Chief of the tribe with the title 'The one who heals the land of Tiv'. Only a few months afterwards he was called upon to put this honorary role into serious practice and to settle a three-year old dispute which had already claimed a hundred lives. A marble memorial commemorates the healing of the land by Chief M. J. Dent. His crowning achievement is that he is co-founder of Jubilee 2000, the worldwide campaign to have much of the Third World debt of $2.17 million million written off at the end of the millennium. From a solitary petition sent to the UN, there grew an international campaign at government level. The Chancellor of the Exchequer has announced that Britain will be cancelling debts of £1,600M. Martin Dent has been awarded an OBE in the Queen's Birthday Honours, and Keele awarded him an honorary degree in 2000.

The list of achievements could go on in a wide range of occupations spread across the world. It might be that the next person you bump into is a Keele graduate, as Carol Moore (Alford) and Philip Braithwaite found in the Dallas Museum of Art, thirty-five years after leaving Keele. Rob Collins and Gill Pearce might have met in space: they were both among the shortlisted aspiring British astronauts hoping to join the Juno mission to the Russian space station Mir in 1991.

Whilst concentrating on the healthy mind, students have not neglected the healthy body. Tom Ashibende was an Olympic runner for Kenya. Keele won the universities' netball championship two years running while still a small College. Individuals have excelled in a wide range of athletics and sports, including high diving, judo, fencing, hurdling, canoeing, indoor archery, the modern pentathlon, and flying in the University of Birmingham Air Squadron.

Chief Martin Dent, OBE, ASORTAR-U-TIV

As far as students are concerned, they have been shielded from the worst excesses of vacillating policies. Of course, there are the perennial grumbles of succeeding generations – rent, food and hours rules (until lowering the age of majority swept away outmoded notions of the University acting *in loco parentis*). 'In vain we groan, and grudge the money given to our long-gowned tutors' (La Fontaine). Gradually the academic worsening of affairs becomes noticeable – successive freezes on buying books eventually impinges seriously on reading lists, and tutorial and seminar classes grow larger and time with tutors grows less – but in any one undergraduate's tenure the changes are not generally immediately too drastic. Most of them have been unaware of the political and economic changes which are shaping their, and certainly their successors' careers – until the more recent changes in funding. Fortunately students come to University when they are at their most resilient, and when they can think of themselves as almost immortal.

Although UCNS when small – really small – was no larger than some of the Oxbridge colleges, the tendency towards introspection was more acute because there were no other colleges alongside. Indeed, there was even an estate wall around the perimeter. Moreover, the label 'Keele Experiment' added an air of self-conscious-ness. But for most it was a very agreeable and self-contained existence. The University, ten times larger, however, – and that is larger than a lot of nearby villages and is comparable with Newcastle-under-Lyme in the mid-19th century – is a much more bustling community with its own shops, cafes, its own radio station from time to time, buses going through the campus frequently, suburban car parks, even. It is much more like other British universities. It is confident, too, in its plan for continuing expansion. The democratic revolution which led to Lord Lindsay's vision for Keele brought in its train mass expansion and more egalitarianism in higher education. That is what demands a new vision for the next fifty years.

Some things have remained constant: residence on the campus and the beauty of the grounds, classes, lectures, academic and social contacts, essays, two Principal subjects, cross-disciplinary study, finals examinations, and degree day. Whether in the Walter Moberly Hall, the Students' Union Ballroom, the King's Hall, Stoke-on-Trent, Trentham Gardens, or back at Keele in the Chapel, the *buzz* on that day, the end of being undergraduates, with parents and friends and farewells, but with life-long friendships and a warm attachment to Keele has, I suspect, changed hardly at all.

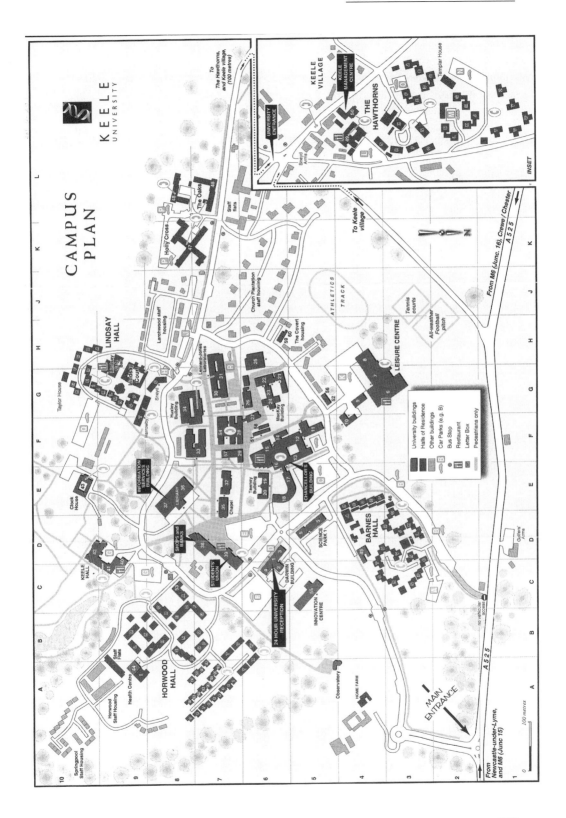

CAMPUS PLAN

KEELE UNIVERSITY

APPENDIX

Keele's Strategic Plan 1998/1999 – 2001/2002

'1. MISSION

Keele University's aim on its foundation was to deliver a high quality broadly-based education – this continues to be a principal part of Keele's mission.

In addition, Keele aims to pursue research in focused areas within all academic fields, with particular emphasis on multidisciplinary and interdisciplinary approaches, which is of at least national significance in all areas, and international significance in key fields.

The University aims to develop the estate as a leading exemplar of a learning and working campus community of students, staff and business.

This mission will be achieved through

Partnership and collaboration

promoting networking, partnership and collaboration between disciplines and organisations at regional, national and international level;

Research

promoting research and scholarship which is of a quality and scale to achieve a national reputation in all fields and an international reputation in focused research areas; encouraging and facilitating the development of multidisciplinary research groups which are of sufficient size and quality to attract major external funding support and recognition;

Education

providing a broad-based education which requires study across discipline boundaries so that all undergraduates study some science and some humanities or social science, and which incorporates a strong international dimension; equipping students with core skills and knowledge which are transferable into post University experience; developing courses and modes of study which facilitate a lifelong learning culture and enable individuals to participate in higher education in accordance with their own needs;

Campus community

developing the campus in an optimum manner compatible with sensitive environmental management; encouraging initiatives leading to the establishment on campus of business enterprises, closely linked with the work of the University;

Quality culture

promoting innovative and flexible policies in the employment and development of staff; conducting effective monitoring and feedback procedures.

2. A STRATEGIC OVERVIEW OF KEELE UNIVERSITY

2.1 Size, shape and nature of Keele University

Keele University was founded as a University College in 1949, and established by Charter as a University in 1962, building on a tradition of adult education which had been developed in the region since the First World War. The establishment of the University was sponsored by the Universities of Birmingham, Manchester and Oxford, and championed by Lord Lindsay, in the recognition that a large region including Staffordshire, Shropshire, and parts of Cheshire and Derbyshire, did not have its own university.

Located on a green field site near Newcastle-under-Lyme in Staffordshire, Keele is a campus-based university with a very high degree of campus-based student and staff residence, which generates a collegiate community. The aim is to grow this community, both in terms of student and staff numbers, and in terms of the individuals, businesses and other organisations which use the campus and are located on the campus.

The academic departments are grouped within four faculties: humanities, social sciences, natural sciences, and health. Traditionally, Keele departments within those faculties have been relatively small, and steps are being taken to develop larger groupings to facilitate greater academic collaboration and more efficient management.

The most significant academic development in the last few years has been the increase in the health-related activity, with the addition of Nursing and Midwifery, Medicines Management and Physiotherapy Studies complementing the long-standing School of Postgraduate Medicine, and leading to the development of a new Faculty of Health. Both educational and research activities in this field involve close partnership arrangements with health authorities and trust hospitals.

Keele has traditionally been a small university within the UK system, though it has grown substantially over the past 10 years. During 1997/98 there were nearly 5,600 full time equivalent students, including 1,400 (25%) at postgraduate level. Keele needs to grow further, to about 10,000 students, in order to maintain a broad range of academic provision and to play a full regional role.

Though these figures include part-time postgraduate students, they do not include the very substantial number of students taking part in Continuing and Professional Education courses, an activity which has long been part of the Keele programme. Over 3,500 students have participated in this programme during 1997/98, and as Keele works with local partners to develop lifelong learning opportunities this is likely to increase significantly.

Keele is a research-based university, which builds on its multidisciplinary ethos to develop collaborative partnerships within and beyond the university. Location on a single campus facilitates networking and collaboration between disciplines and departments.

2.2 Education

Since its foundation, the ethos of Keele University has been to provide a broad educational experience at undergraduate level. This has been most clearly seen in the Foundation Year, compulsory until October 1973, and the dual honours degree programme which offers a wide range of subject combinations and requires all undergraduates to experience both arts and science cultures. The University is still firmly of the view that a broad educational experience is essential if graduates are to be equipped to cope with the needs of varied and changing employment and personal situations. However, the late 1990s has been a period in which the nature of that broad experience has had to be reviewed, taking into account the growing emphasis on key and transferable skills, the requirements of professional accreditation, the expansion of health-related training, student demand, needs for access to lifelong learning, necessity for more efficient teaching methods, and the greater focusing of research activity.

Consequently, there is now a greater diversity in the nature of the undergraduate provision, with the dual honours programme still strong but with emphasis on offering the most popular combinations, the increasing availability of single subject degrees as required by accrediting bodies, and a large number of students on health-related courses such as Nursing and Midwifery and Physiotherapy. With regret, it has been decided to discontinue the Foundation Year after the 1998 intake. There has been a reducing demand over the past few years, and the introduction of tuition fees will make 4-year courses less attractive. Nevertheless, plans are in hand to preserve some of the best aspects of the FY within the 3-year programme.

The nature of the learning experience at undergraduate level has been articulated and agreed, and focuses on academic achievement, breadth of approach, and capability in the development of personal skills. Many course leaders are exploring ways in which key and transferable skills can be developed within their programmes, and some departments are including periods of work experience, either within the modular structure or as an additional year following year two.

Keele welcomes the government's challenge to extend learning opportunities to those groups which have not traditionally benefited from higher education, both through improving the participation rate on undergraduate courses from lower socio-economic groups, and through identifying opportunities for more flexible modes of study to encourage lifelong learning. The University already has strengths in relation to both areas, building on the success of the Keele Access Scheme, projects to improve aspiration and achievement in pupils in Stoke-on-Trent, and the strong tradition of continuing adult education. The North Staffordshire Education Concordat brings together the FE colleges, universities, TEC and education authorities, as a means of identifying and progressing further initiatives.

Keele is already involved with local partners in developing strategies for the University for Industry, and in auditing the University's current provision to identify potential areas of expertise which could be made available on a more flexible basis to encourage lifelong learning. This is likely to be a growth area for Keele, possibly focused on the increasing needs for professional staff to receive regular accredited updating. Nevertheless, it is a process which needs to be managed carefully in order to ensure that all aspects of the academic programme are delivered to a high quality.

Keele also has a high proportion of students studying at postgraduate level within all disciplines. Measures have been taken over the past few years to develop a graduate culture, with the interests of graduate students being overseen by a Dean of Postgraduate Affairs. This has drawn strength from, and contributed to, the increasing research strengths of the University.

2.3 Research
The last 20 years has seen a dramatic growth in the research capabilities of the University. Each Research Assessment Exercise has seen a significant improvement in the ratings and funding given to Keele, such that research funding from HEFCE and external research sponsors is now about £13M each year.

Increasingly, departments are developing research strategies which ensure that academic effort and other resources are concentrated on focused areas of activity, so that research continues to be of at least national standing and significance, and in many areas of international standing. While there is a need to ensure that a proportion of research activity is genuinely blue skies and innovative, funded largely from HEFCE resources, it is also important to address key issues of social and cultural importance, often identified by research sponsors who will fund appropriate projects and programmes. A large and diverse portfolio of research funding remains crucial to the dynamic development of research activity.

In most disciplines, there is a tradition of establishing collaborative research partnerships, not only with researchers in other academic disciplines, but also with potential users and beneficiaries of research, whether in industry, commerce, public agencies or elsewhere. Underpinning the Keele approach is the fundamental belief that a range of perspectives is needed in order to achieve the most profound insights about the physical, social and cultural world in which we live.

2.4 National and international partnerships
A broad-based education requires that students have the opportunity to understand different perspectives, including that of different cultures. This requires an international dimension to the educational programme, which is provided in a number of ways – through the curriculum, by encouraging the development on campus of a multicultural community, and through facilitating student exchanges. Formal agreements are in place with institutions worldwide, supported by such schemes as Socrates.

Research is judged by international standards of excellence, and many Keele staff are judged to be among the best in their field worldwide, as evidenced by the range of international research collaborations, many of which give access to expertise and facilities which it would not be possible for a relatively small university such as Keele to support alone. Programmes of visiting international scholars are being supported by the University in areas of particular strength, and some very eminent scholars are choosing to spend time at Keele.

2.5 Regional partnerships
The University also recognises its particular responsibility to the community within which it is located. Keele is situated in the north of the Government Office West Midlands region, and is working very closely with other universities and various business support organisations within the region to develop initiatives which will assist the economic development of the region. In particular, attempts are being made to improve access to university capabilities and resources by companies not accustomed to working with universities. The ceramics industry, based in Staffordshire, is a particular target for support. The Keele Careers Service is participating in a West Midlands project, Graduate Link, which uses graduate skills in SMEs. The aim for Keele is to consider the development of a graduate placing service in Staffordshire.

North Staffordshire is recognised as being a region of traditionally low educational aspiration and achievement, and Keele is part of the North Staffordshire Education Concordat which brings together the FE colleges, universities, TEC education authorities and careers service, to address this issue. The health-based activities are firmly grounded in the North Staffordshire Health Partnership of NHS Trusts and Health Authority, and within the developing primary care networks, with much support from the NHS Executive (West

Midlands). Research strategies and the development of courses are closely aligned between NHS and university, and significant investment has been made by all parties in the development of a research culture within the NHS.

Although Keele is constrained to a degree by the regional organisational structures which exist and from which it receives significant funding, being in the north of the region enables the University to look to the North West region for collaborative partnerships where appropriate. The bid for an undergraduate medical school is in partnership with Manchester University, and Keele has joined the Network North West for its IT networking development.

The University has made significant advances in recent years in forging closer links with a wide range of organisations and individuals within the locality, not only through educational activities, but through arts and cultural events and activities, leisure and sporting activities, environmental initiatives and many other areas where Keele can contribute to the enhanced quality of life of individuals in the community.

2.6 Campus development

The campus with 617 acres, one of the largest in England, provides students with a distinctive experience of University life. It is capable of a much greater development. The local authority plans, adopted in May 1995, allow for expansion well beyond 10,000 students. The plans take the existing built-up area out of green belt regulations and add a further 86 acres for academic developments, including science park and other activities related to the University as a higher education institution. The immediate priority is to develop a new entrance to the University which will be required before the Home Farm Estate can be opened to development. Plans are in hand to complete the new entrance during 1999.

2.7 Summary

In summary, as a pioneer of broadly based education, Keele intends to take forward this agenda into the 21st century delivering broadly based education more effectively than others, in a campus setting providing a high quality living and working environment. As a leading example of an academic community, in its fullest sense, Keele aims additionally to be a significant provider of postgraduate education with strong research in clearly defined areas, and a significant contributor to the intellectual, cultural and economic life of the region.

3. STRATEGIC PRIORITIES FOR 1998/99

During 1998/99, Keele will advance its mission and aims through the following specific initiatives:

3.1 Student numbers

Taking every appropriate opportunity to increase the number of students, and assessing market demand as a basis for recruitment strategies.

3.2 Research excellence

Continuing to develop support for collaborative and interdisciplinary research.

Starting planning for the 2001 RAE, in response to the publication of units of assessment, panels and chairs, and assessment criteria.

3.3 Budget surplus

Taking every opportunity to increase income generation to continue to achieve a budget surplus.

3.4 Financial transparency

Completing discussions about new financial models as a basis for assessing resource allocation, including staffing, and with implementation from 1999/2000.

3.5 Academic reorganisation

Completing discussions about academic reorganisation, and making specific plans for changes to the organisation of academic departments and the enhanced role of faculties.

3.6 Strategic planning

Identifying and implementing an effective process for strategic planning, including the development of more effective management information.

3.7 Governance

Completing the review of the committee structure, with introduction of outcomes from 1999/2000, at the same time as the introduction of the new composition and operation of Council. Transitional arrangements for Council will be introduced, together with more effective training for Council members.

3.8 Campus development

Finalising agreements for the development of the new entrance to the University, and completion of the entrance, road, roundabout and Innovation Centre during 1999.

Through bidding for external funds, acquiring the means to upgrade campus academic facilities for enhanced teaching and research.

4. IMPACT FACTORS

This section sets out the principal external and internal factors which will have the greatest impact over the next five years, influencing the University's priorities for strategic development.

EXTERNAL

4.1 Student funding arrangements

It is still not certain what impact the imposition of £1,000 tuition fee and the shift from maintenance grants to loans will have on student demand, either at undergraduate level or, more likely, at postgraduate level for students who have accumulated a significant debt. These arrangements may deter some groups from participating in higher education, as has already been seen for 1998 entry for mature students. Additionally, it is not clear to what extent the funds generated in this way will feed back into the University. Nevertheless, it is inevitable that students paying such fees will demand high standards, and will question more the nature of the educational and welfare provision, perhaps most significantly in terms of employability.

4.2 Student demand

The principal income stream for the University is for teaching students, primarily undergraduate but also postgraduate. The University will continue to keep attuned to factors underpinning student choices, and in particular why students want to come to Keele, and will develop ways of responding more quickly to student demand in terms of the principal and master's courses which it offers. This may require more innovation and flexibility in offering multidisciplinary courses as well as single discipline courses.

4.3 Government policy on expansion

In recent years the number of funded students which any university could take has been limited by the institution's maximum aggregate student numbers (MASN) and contract student numbers (CSN). The Government has plans for expansion of HE, on the basis of specified criteria still to be announced, but there will be a significant emphasis on wider participation, and support for current courses with established demand. Keele's ambition is to grow, at a pace which can be supported by the necessary growth in infrastructure and resources, and the University will therefore seize all appropriate opportunities for additional student numbers. Plans are already in hand to submit bids this year when invited.

4.4 NHS workforce policies

The NHS has been developing policies in relation to workforce planning, including the need to expand numbers in nursing and possibly elsewhere. Alongside the move towards nursing becoming a graduate profession is new thinking in relation to continuing professional development and the development of a research culture throughout the NHS. These will give rise to new opportunities for universities in general, and Keele is well-placed to take advantage of them.

4.5 Quality Assurance

Following the Dearing report the Quality Assurance Agency has been established with a remit to develop a qualifications framework and benchmark standards, together with a process of quality assurance. Additionally, the Institute for Teaching and Learning has been established to set and maintain professional standards. Keele will need to participate in the development of these initiatives, and ensure that the University complies with standards and procedures set.

4.6 Medical education

Following the report of the Medical Workforce Standing Advisory Committee, which recommended an annual increase of about 1,000 students to medical schools in the UK, the Government announced in July 1998 that the increase would be phased, such that the current (1997) intake of 5,050 would be increased to 5,450 by 2001, and to about 6,000 by 2005. Discussions are now taking place to determine bidding processes and the criteria for the allocation of these places. Keele is working in partnership with Manchester University to develop an undergraduate medical presence at Keele, using a problem-based learning method already established at Manchester and seen as a leading exemplar of good practice.

4.7 Lifelong learning and University for Industry

The Green Paper on Lifelong Learning and the publication of the prospectus for the University for Industry set a firm agenda for higher education which requires universities to build on their strengths to develop more flexible modes of study and short courses to encourage lifelong learning. Keele has a strong tradition of adult education, and also has many students on part-time professional courses at postgraduate diploma and master's level. To date there has been less activity in the field of short courses for industry and the professions, and Keele will be auditing its capabilities and the possible markets to identify where there is likely to be a demand which the University could meet. The Ufl is likely to provide market analysis to support such audits, and widespread promotional activity for provision which falls within its remit.

4.8 Research Assessment Exercise

The next RAE will be in early 2001, with a census date for publications of 31 December 2000. This will greatly influence the timing of research-based initiatives and support over the next year or so, to ensure that Keele optimises its performance.

4.9 Regional and economic development

There is a growing political requirement for universities to be seen to be contributing much more than hitherto to the economic development of the regions in which they are located. The value of universities is recognised, but the difficulties of ensuring that such value is used to benefit the region are only gradually being overcome. The development of Regional Development Agencies and Regional Chambers will drive this forward, and the University for Industry will provide one mechanism for implementation. Keele has developed many productive partnerships within the West Midlands region in particular, concentrating on making the University's students, expertise and facilities more accessible to industry and employers who can benefit from them. The further development of the Science Park forms an important part of the University's overall strategy in this area. Contributions to regional and economic development will be a growing area of activity.

INTERNAL

4.10 Financial pressures

Keele, like many other universities, continues to face severe financial pressures, managing to break even each year, but finding difficulty in generating surpluses. While there is some additional funding for universities following the Government's Comprehensive Spending Review, it is largely tied to additional student numbers and specific infrastructure initiatives, all of which need to be bid for. The annual level of funding still continues to be eroded, with currently a 1% efficiency gain for 1998/99. The University will ensure that it remains financially viable while allowing scope for further development. There will therefore be a continuing imperative to reduce costs and increase income.

4.11 Many small departments

For historic reasons, related to the provision of a dual honours programme, Keele has a wide range of relatively small departments. While encouraging collegiality, and giving a more personal educational experience to students, it has disadvantages in terms of efficiency of administration and the development of multidisciplinary initiatives, both educational and research. Academic structures will be kept under review to evaluate whether beneficial changes could be made, and in particular, the merging of cognate departments will be encouraged.

4.12 Internal communications

Keele has taken many steps to become more open and transparent in its internal communications, both in terms of finance and more generally. This trend will continue.

4.13 Campus development

The Home Farm Estate is available for academic and business development, and forms an important part of Keele's long term plans. Business development will provide an important income stream to the University as well as providing collaborative opportunities, and if the University is to grow to 7,500 students and beyond the residential and academic provision will need to be increased using the site. None of this can take place until a new entrance and road have been built, and plans are in hand to complete this during 1999.

5. THEMES DRIVING SPECIFIC PLANS

This section identifies six themes which will drive forward the way Keele approaches its development and which underpin nearly all activities. They take account of Keele's mission and the impact factors identified in section 4.

5.1 Market driven

Most university funding now responds principally to market forces, whether in terms of student demand, needs of employers, or external research sponsors. Universities are required to steer a difficult path between responding to market forces, and maintaining the health and vitality of certain (possibly unpopular) areas of academic activity. In general, unless there are clearly defined reasons to do otherwise, Keele will respond increasingly to the demands of the market, and plan its academic programme accordingly. The University has already started looking systematically at market research on its students, and this type of activity will increase.

5.2 Finance and efficiency

There is a growing trend to become more transparent about income and expenditure related to each primary activity, to ensure that each activity does generate sufficient income to cover its costs, including a proportion of central service costs and to help all staff understand more clearly the overall financial position. Where for strategic reasons it is considered appropriate to cross-subsidise an activity, the rationale will be clear and the source of cross-subsidy identified.

5.3 Faculty co-operation

For intellectual and financial reasons, there are advantages to moving towards a position where the faculty has a more important role and identity within the University. Without necessarily moving to a position where the faculty is the budget centre and departments are abolished, departments individually and faculties collectively will be encouraged to identify areas where collective action brings benefits. This includes looking at the way departments within faculties are organised.

5.4 Openness and transparency

The University understands that where there is a culture of openness and transparency, staff morale is higher and there is a greater sense of community and corporate identity. The norm is that information is made generally available as early as sensibly feasible, in a format which is easy to access and assimilate, to enable all staff to participate meaningfully in the development of policy and initiatives. It is anticipated that staff will receive information in the spirit in which it is offered, and engage in constructive discussions to address key challenges which the University faces.

5.5 Quality

Every aspect of the University's activity will be undertaken to the highest standards possible within the resources available. The University will develop benchmarks to provide a framework for evaluating performance, and ensure that there are sufficient monitoring and evaluation procedures in place to inform developments without becoming over burdensome and bureaucratic. The aim will nevertheless be to identify and deal with any low standards. Processes of staff development and performance management will be essential ingredients of developing high quality provision.

5.6 Partnership and collaboration

There are very few areas in which Keele can sensibly operate completely independently. Academic vitality depends on multiple perspectives, collaborative partnerships, exchange of good practice and intellectual ideas. Shared use of facilities, between institutions and departments, makes the best use of resources available. Major initiatives in health and within regional economic development require partnerships with other organisations within the region. Development of access schemes builds on partnerships with schools and FE colleges. Partnership and collaboration underpin nearly all our activities, and this is a source of strength for Keele.'

FURTHER READING

KOLBERT, J.M. *Keele Hall: A Victorian Country House*, 1986

SCOTT, Drusilla. *A. D. Lindsay*,1971

MOBERLY, W. *The Crisis in the University*, 1949

GALLIE, W.B. *A New University: A. D. Lindsay and the Keele Experiment*, 1960

MOUNTFORD, J. *Keele: An Historical Critique*, 1972

'DUNDONALD, J' (LAWLOR, J.J.). *Letters to a Vice-Chancellor*, 1962

ILIFFE, A.H. *The Foundation Year in the University of Keele*, Sociological Review, Monograph 12, Keele, 1968

STEWART, W.A.C. *British Universities: Dilemmas and Opportunities* 1968

FULTON, MOUNTFORD and STEWART. *Twenty-first Anniversary.* Three Addresses, 1972

STEWART, W.A.C. *Roots and Branches: the first twenty-nine years.*1979

HARRISON, C.J. (ed.). *Essays on the History of Keele*, 1986

PAFFARD, M. *Keele: an Introduction to the Parish and the University*, 1998

DRAKAKIS-SMITH, Angela. *Off the Record: a People's History of Keele*,1998

INDEX